VENETIAN SHIPS A

OF THE RENAISSANCE

Venetian Ships and Shipbuilders of the Renaissance

FREDERIC CHAPIN LANE

THE JOHNS HOPKINS UNIVERSITY PRESS

BALTIMORE AND LONDON

Johns Hopkins Paperbacks edition, 1992

The Johns Hopkins University Press
701 West 40th Street
Baltimore, Maryland 21211-2190
The Johns Hopkins Press Ltd., London

Library of Congress Cataloging-in-Publication Data

Lane, Frederic Chapin, 1900–
   Venetian ships and shipbuilders of the Renaissance/by Frederic Chapin
Lane. —Johns Hopkins pbks. ed.
      p.   cm.
   Includes bibliographical references and index.
   ISBN 0-8018-4514-9 (pbk. : acid-free paper)
   1. Shipbuilding—Italy—Venice—History.   2. Venice—Industries—History.
   3. Renaissance—Italy—Venice.   4. Armories—Italy—Venice—History.
   I. Title.
VM80.V4L3   1992
623.8'0945'31—DC20
                                                                    92-11280

PREFACE

The Renaissance was for Venice the period of splendor; her ostentation of wealth and power then attained the acme of pageantry. It was also the pivotal epoch in which her prosperity and political eminence were undermined by the disintegration of her maritime dominion. An investigation of one aspect of that naval crisis, an attempt to figure forth the ships and to reconstruct the achievements and difficulties of the men who built them—such a study must renounce much of the glamour associated with the ornate magnificence of the times, but it may help to reveal the character of the turning point. At least it will minister to that enlarged inquisitiveness which aspires to be acquainted not only with the great men of the past but also with the ordinary men, and to know them not only in their moments of martial violence or religious excitation but even in their everyday work. Moreover, ships and all the story of the sea have a flavor of their own. I have not attempted to present fully the maze of naval archaeology which has been uncovered by technical studies of ancient shipping. A nautical reader may take exception to my deliberate attempt to avoid terminology which would be confusing to other historians who are landsmen like myself. My aim has been by omitting details to bring into relief the main changes, and to relate the types of ships to the purposes for which they were designed. On the other hand, the history of war and commerce enters my theme only so far as necessary to characterize the ships themselves and the industry which produced them, or to suggest the economic importance of improvements in maritime transportation.

I received from Professor Abbott Payson Usher the initial impulse to study Venetian shipping in the fifteenth and sixteenth centuries with the hope of finding clues to changes in the economic life of the city. This investigation was begun under his direction and the results first presented as a dissertation for the degree of Doctor of Philosophy in Harvard

University. Throughout the collection and interpretation of the material his aid and encouragement have been invaluable. For the courtesy of the staffs of the libraries and archives at Venice, and especially for the kindly help of Professor Gino Luzzato, I wish to express my sincere appreciation. To Mr. R. C. Anderson, F. S. A., I am extremely grateful for the generous fashion in which he has given the assistance of his extraordinary competence in all matters of naval archaeology. To the many associates at The Johns Hopkins University, who have given time to reviewing the manuscript, especially to Professor Kent Roberts Greenfield, I owe the constant stimulus of friendly criticism.

F. C. L.

THE JOHNS HOPKINS UNIVERSITY
          JANUARY 1934

TABLE OF CONTENTS

CHAPTER   PAGE

I. THE GALLEYS   1

II. THE ROUND SHIPS   35

III. SOME FAMOUS SHIPWRIGHTS   54

IV. THE CRAFT GUILDS   72

V. THE PROCESS OF CONSTRUCTION   88

VI. THE ACTIVITY OF THE PRIVATE SHIPYARDS . . .   100

VII. INDUSTRIAL ORGANIZATION IN THE PRIVATE SHIPYARDS   112

VIII. THE GROWTH OF THE ARSENAL   129

IX. THE MANAGEMENT OF THE ARSENAL   146

X. THE ARSENALOTTI   176

XI. INDUSTRIAL DISCIPLINE IN THE ARSENAL . . .   189

XII. THE TIMBER SUPPLIES   217

TABLES   235

A. Primary proportions of ships. B. Proportions and measures
of Venetian long ships. C. Measures of Venetian round ships.
D. Number and capacity of large round ships, 1405-1465.
E. Number and capacity of round ships, 1499. F. Number and
capacity of large round ships, 1558-1559. G. Great galleys
made in the Arsenal, 1496-1505. H. Number of great and
light galleys in the Arsenal, 1504-1602. I. Number of ship
craftsmen. J. Rates of wages of ship carpenters at the Arsenal.

APPENDICES   245

I. Weights, measures and moneys. II. Doge Mocenigo's oration and the Venetian fleet of 1420-1450. III. The ship lists
of 1499. IV. Freight rates. V. The age of ships. VI. The cost
of ships. VII. Round ships built by the government.

BIBLIOGRAPHICAL NOTE   268

INDEX   269

ILLUSTRATIONS

PAGE

I. Measures of Venetian Merchantman and Light Galley
of the Sixteenth Century 3

II. Deck of a Trireme 11

III. One-Masted Galley Pictured in the " Fabrica di
Galere " 12

IV. Great Galley Equipped for Pilgrim Voyage about 1485 18

V. A Page from the " Fabrica di Galere ", the Storm Sails
of a Merchant Galley about 1400 20

VI. Three-Masted Galley about 1445 23

VII. Compartments in the Hull of a Merchant Galley . 25

VIII. Thirteenth Century Round Ship 36

IX. One-Masted Cog 38

X. Carack 41

XI. Two-Masted Ship of Fourteenth Century . . . 43

XII. Ship of 600 Tons about 1445 45

XIII. Galleon 51

XIV. Shipbuilders' Tools 87

XV. Diagram in the " Fabrica " 90

XVI. Diagram in the " Instructione " 91

XVII. The Meza-Luna 94

XVIII. The Arsenal about 1560 173

CHAPTER I

THE GALLEYS

Progress in shipbuilding has been achieved through the simultaneous development of a great variety of types of ships. On the one hand there has been regional variation in type, variation caused by the existence of independent shipbuilding traditions. In the European seas there were two main regional traditions, that of the northern seas or the Baltic, and that of the Mediterranean. The northern tradition may be traced back to the long ships of the Vikings, the southern to the war craft and merchantmen of the Romans and their predecessors. Notable borrowing by these two European traditions one from the other occurred after the time of the Crusades, but it was only in the late fifteenth century that they produced a common progeny greater than themselves, the Atlantic tradition.[1]

Besides regional differences, there were variations in type within the same locality because of the diversity of purposes for which ships were used. The warship and the merchantman, the fishing vessel and the carrier for long voyages—to name but some of the most obvious contrasts—presented separate problems to any group of shipwrights who might be called on to meet the needs of a maritime people. In the Mediterranean, where the shipbuilding tradition was older, it was also more complex, and the creation of specialized types was there carried further during the Middle Ages than it was in the north. Moreover, the great serviceability of oarships as well as

[1] My main guides to the technical history of ship types have been: Romola and R. C. Anderson, *The Sailing-ship* (London, 1926); Enrico Alberto d'Albertis, *Le costruzioni navali e l'arte della navigazione al tempo di Cristoforo Colombo* (*Raccolta di doc. e. studi pub. dalla R. Com. Colombiana*, parte IV, vol. I, Rome, Ministero della Pubblica Instruzione, 1893); A. Jal, *Archéologie navale* (Paris, 1840); A. Anthiaume, *Le navire; sa construction en France et principalement chez les Normands* (Paris, 1922); *Idem, Le navire; sa propulsion en France et principalement chez les Normands* (Paris, 1924, lettered on binding: tome 2); Bernhard Hagedorn, *Die Entwicklung der wichtigsten Schiffstypen bis in 19 Jahrhundert* (Berlin, 1914); John Forsyth Meigs, *The Story of the Seamen* (Philadelphia and London, 1924).

1

sailing vessels in Mediterranean waters presented an opportunity for greater variety.

This very diversity in the types of ships may contain a valuable message for the historian of commerce if he be but able to decode it successfully. The ships themselves pictured the trade. The use of a certain type of merchantman was indicative of certain commercial conditions since the peculiarities of each type of ship were largely determined by the requirements of a particular type of navigation, perhaps of a particular voyage—by the nautical difficulties, commercial opportunities, and political dangers involved in that branch of trade for which the ship was designed.

The interpretation of records of the number and voyages of ships requires knowledge of the specialized purposes of the different types, and of the changes, either in ships, in the art of war, or in commercial conditions, which altered their usefulness. Where such an appreciation of the variety of ship types is lacking, there is grave danger of observing with a false perspective only certain types of ships, and accordingly, only restricted parts of the trade.

Conversely, the technical study of the shaping and rigging of ships is alone insufficient to make understandable the development and disappearance of the different types. The commercial or military purposes for which they were designed must be constantly kept in mind. Indeed, a history of merchant shipping which attempted a complete explanation of the creation and abandonment of the varied types would become a history of maritime commerce, and a similar study of warships would include the history of naval warfare. Although these chapters do not attempt tasks quite so ambitious, even for Venetian shipping, yet a brief explanation of the main distinctions in the types of ships in use is a basic preliminary to the study of the industry which produced them.

From the time of the Phoenicians, Mediterranean ships had been divided into long ships and round ships. Long ships were equipped with oars, round ships were dependent entirely on sails, so that in general this distinction was the same as that between oarships and sailing vessels, and that between war-ships and merchantmen. But even when these distinctions in the use and propulsion of the two classes occasionally disappeared and a long ship loaded with merchandise proceeded under sail, the contrast between the two divisions remained because of their different dimensions and deck arrangements. Long ships were low and narrow, round ships were high and wide. Figure I. The mediaeval long ship, the galley, had

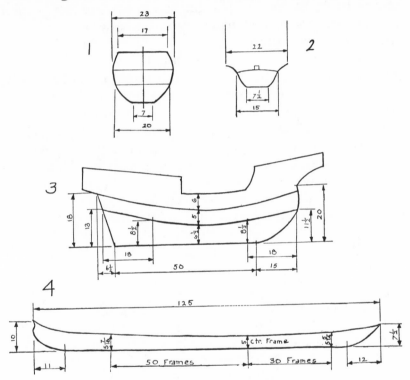

FIGURE I. MEASURES OF VENETIAN MERCHANTMAN AND LIGHT GALLEY OF THE SIXTEENTH CENTURY.

1. Midship section of a merchantman, a typical round ship. 2. Midship section of a light galley, a typical long ship. 3. Longitudinal section of a merchantman. 4. Longitudinal section of a light galley with castles, outrigger, and parapets omitted for clarity.

The height of the round ship made it desirable to narrow the top deck so as to curve the sides inboard as in 1; the use of oars on the long ship made it desirable to build outriggers so that the rowers' deck was wider than the hull as in 2.

The measures are given in Venetian feet according to the *Instructione* of Theodoro for the merchantman and the *Visione del Drachio* for the galley.

but a single flat deck almost wholly occupied by the oarsmen, the contemporary round ship might have two or three decks surmounted by forecastle and stern castle.

In the thirteenth century the representatives of these two types of ships which were most used by the Venetians were the galley, a long ship, and two forms of round ship, the great ship—here later called the " buss "—and the smaller, the " tarette ". Their qualities are revealed by an incident which occurred near Saseno in 1264 during the war between Venice and Genoa. The Venetians had previously despatched a war fleet of fifty-five galleys. Trusting to this force to dispose of the Genoese war fleet the Doge sent out a caravan of merchant ships without special escort. But the war fleet failed to find the Genoese Admiral, Simone Grillo, who had delayed at Sicily. I give a Venetian account of what followed.[2]

When Simone Grillo, the Admiral of Genoa, knew the truth, that the galleys of the Venetians had gone off towards Syria, and learned that the caravan from Venice was coming without the protection of galleys, he made no delay in leaving the port where he had been posted with all the sixteen galleys of the Genoese and went to meet the ships of the Venetians which had just left Venice. The Genoese made such speed with oars and sail that they met the caravan of the Venetians as it was coming on the open sea. And when they caught sight of each other the Genoese began to cry, " [Up and] at them, at them," and the Venetians who were in the ships put on their arms. There was with them one great ship (*nef*) easily defensible. The small vessels clustered about it, and then the Genoese came and attacked the small tarettes and the Venetians defended themselves well so that the Genoese gained nothing so that they withdrew a half league away. And those in the small ships of the Venetians removed the precious goods and put them in the great ship which was called " Roccaforte " (" Roqueforte ") and then betook themselves forthwith therein, and let the small tarettes go adrift in the sea without any men in them, and three of them were scuttled and let go to the bottom of the sea.

When the Genoese saw the tarettes going scattered hither and yon they thought it was a trick and that the Venetians were posted

---

[2] Martino da Canale, *Cronaca veneta* (ed. Filippo Luigi Polidori, Giovanni Galvani, *Archivio storico italiano*, VIII, 1845), pp. 507-508.

within to attack them. And then when they perceived that they were without men, they went and seized them and found within the oil and honey and other bulky merchandise. And know that there were by count ten, and no man was captured on them nor any killed save one. . . . When Messer Simone Grillo was in possession of the tarettes he sent a boat to the ship which told them that if they would surrender he would put them safe on dry land without bodily injury. And Messer Michele Daru, who commanded . . . , replied to them that if they were stout fellows, let them come on, and that the ship was all loaded both with gold and the richest merchandise in the world. And afterwards the boat went back and the Admiral and the other galleys circled about. And then they went off and carried victory from this fight and took the tarettes to Genoa, and the " Roccaforte " turned back to Ragusa.

The Genoese chronicler naturally told a somewhat different story but his account likewise distinguished the different fortunes of the galleys, the great " Roccaforte ", and the small tarettes, each representative of main types of thirteenth century ships.[3] Galleys using both sail and oar composed the war fleet and should have been sent with the merchantmen if it had been expected that they would run into a hostile fleet.[4] The small round ships were quite unable to hold out long against war galleys. They were low, relatively unprotected sailing vessels carrying mostly the bulkier and less precious merchandise. The great ship, on the other hand, with its high towering sides and castles filled with armed men was able to defend itself. A round ship of that type had this definite military value, and many of them were built for military purposes as were the galleys. But, even so, their functions were distinct. In war

---

[3] *Annali genovesi di Caffaro e di suoi continuatori* (ed. Tommaso Luigi Belgrano, Cesare Imperiale, *Fonti per la storia d'Italia,* pub. by Instituto Storico Italiano, Genoa and Rome, 1890-1929), IV, 55-56. The Genoese chronicler attributes a larger fleet to the Venetians: thirteen *taride,* three *naves*—one especially large, two galleys, presumably partly manned galleys acting as merchantmen, one *panzonus,* and one *sagittea.* On the *panzonus* and *sagittea* see A. Jal, *Glossaire nautique* (Paris, 1848). On the encounter cf. Camillo Manfroni, *Storia della marina italiana dal trattato di Ninfeo alla caduta di Costantinopoli,* part 1 (Livorno, 1902), pp. 12-16.

[4] For the use of galleys as convoys see Manfroni, *op. cit.,* p. 199, Andrea Dandolo, *Chronicon* (ed. Ludovico Antonio Muratori, *Rerum italicarum scriptores* 1st ed., Milan, 1723-1751, vol. XII), pp. 371, 373-374, 378, 392, 405; Da Canale, pp. 535, 628.

there was almost as much difference between a round ship and a long ship as there was between a castle and a troop of knights. The round ship could defend herself well against galleys, but in the centuries before the development of heavy guns was useless in attacking them. In this incident the " Roccaforte " could not even manoeuvre against the galleys so as to protect the small tarettes.

As long as hand-to-hand fighting remained decisive in naval warfare the oarships were the favorite warships of the Mediterranean. Fitted for either ramming or boarding, and capable of being marshalled like an army, such ships gave their possessor the advantage over a slower opponent of being able to accept or decline battle at will. The long ships not only dominated Mediterranean naval warfare from its inception to the seventeenth century, they were also important during a great part of that time in the transport of merchandise and passengers. They carried the most precious wares of mediaeval commerce and left to the round ships the bulkier cheaper commodities.

To the romanticist, navies have indeed known but one age of gold bounded by two ages of iron.[5] The golden age, that in which the skillfully captured wind was made to do all the work, fills but a few centuries between the iron ages of the oarsman and the stoker. The military ascendency of the oarship lasted ten times as long as that of the sailing ship. But the toiling oarsmen on the Venetian galleys were not, before the sixteenth century, slaves chained to their benches, but free citizens ready to exchange their oars for their weapons when battle was joined.[6] They were enrolled from the ablest of the

[5] Jurien de la Gravière, La marin des anciens (Paris, 1886), I, 169.

[6] The only suggestion I have found of the use of slaves on private galleys is the statement of a pilgrim that the oarsmen were mainly slaves—" servi emptitii "—of the captain. Fratris Felicis Fabri evagatorium in Terrae Sanctae, Arabiae et Egypti peregrinationem (ed. Cunradus Dietericus Hasseler in Bibl. des Literarischen Vereins in Stuttgart, Stuttgart, 1843), 1, 125. But this hardly seems compatible with the practice of letting them go ashore to trade, nor with the state regulations concerning the payment of the oarsmen. See M. Margaret Newett, Canon Pietro Casola's Pilgrimage to Jerusalem in the Year 1494 (Historical Series, Publications of the University of Manchester, Manchester, 1907), pp. 64-65, 191, 369. Convicts began to be

applicants at the recruiting stations set up in the Piazza San Marco.[7] When the crews of a merchant galley were not paid their wages on the return of the galley to Venice, as was their due, the oarsmen crowded the great staircase of the Ducal Palace and shouted forth their demands until the Senators were moved to put an end to such scandal by compelling the galley commanders to satisfy the complaints of the seamen.[8]

The thirteenth century Venetian galleys, although they might be used to carry cargo, all belonged to the type primarily designed for battle, and it was generally as protecting warships that they accompanied the merchant caravans sailing to Syria or Constantinople. The omission of such a guard had proved disastrous at Saseno even though the " Roccaforte " had been able somewhat to mitigate the losses. In the next century the Venetians used an entirely different arrangement of trading fleets made possible by the introduction at the close of the thirteenth century of a new type, the great galley designed for trade.[9] Thereafter the Venetians built two types of galleys, light galleys for war and the great galleys to carry merchandise on trading voyages. Though the structures of the two types were basically the same they diverged more and more both in proportions and rigging during the following centuries.

The light galleys displayed most clearly the distinctive fea-

used on war galleys about 1530. Alathea Weil, *The Navy of Venice* (London, 1910), pp. 63-64.

[7] Camillo Manfroni, " Cenni sugli ordinamenti delle marine italiane nel medio evo ", *Rivista marittima* (1898), fasc. xii, p. 479.

[8] Marino Sanuto, *I diarii* (eds. Rinaldo Fulin, Federico Stefani, Nicolò Barozzi, Guglielmo Berchet, Marco Allegri, under auspices of the R. Dep. Veneta di Storia Patria, Venice, 1879-1903), vol. II, col. 51; Archivio di Stato di Venezia—cited hereafter as A. S. V.— Senato Mar, reg. 14, f. 165.

[9] Contrast the merchant caravans mentioned by Dandolo and Da Canale, *loc. cit.* above note 4, with those indicated in G. Giomo, " Le rubriche dei Libri Misti del Senato perduti ", *Archivio veneto*, VII-XIX (1874-1880). See also Camillo Manfroni, *Storia della marina italiana dalle invasioni barbariche al trattato di Ninfeo* (Livorno, 1899), p. 455. The " invention " of the great galley is described by Giovanni Casoni " Forze Militari ", *Venezia e le sue lagune* (Venice, 1847), I, 208, on the authority of Galicciolli, but apparently the source is the *Chronica supposta Barbara* (MS.), see notes of Doge Foscarini in Biblioteca Nazionale Marciana, Venice, MSS. Ital. cl. X, cod. 140; cl. XI, cod. 123.

tures of the long ship. Their design was dominated by the desire to give them the speed needed to outmanoeuvre an opponent, and this purpose determined both the proportions of the hull and the arrangement of the superstructure. The length of their hulls, about one hundred and twenty feet on deck, was about eight times their breadth amidships, the deck was only five or six feet above the keel. (Table B.)

Whereas the long ships of the Vikings and others built in the early northern tradition were shaped by the fastening together of heavy, overlapping planking, which was then reinforced by ribs, the strength of the Venetian galleys lay in the framework of ribs and clamps which was built first and then covered with flush planking.[10] The ribs were fastened to the keel at the rate of seventy-two to eighty-eight for every hundred feet,[11] and were tied together by heavy timbers acting as clamps running from stem to sternpost. The deck beams rested upon the highest and heaviest of these clamps. This essential body of the ship, with its planking, was known as the " live work." The superstructures such as the stern castle and the outriggers were in contrast called the " dead work ".

On the shaping of the live work of the hull depended the strength of the galley, and the ease with which it could slip through the water. The arrangement of the dead work of the deck was equally important in determining the speed of the

[10] Anderson, *op. cit.*, chap. IV; Hagedorn, p. 56; Walther Vogel, *Geschichte der deutschen Seeschiffahrt* (Berlin, 1915), I, 59 and 473, esp. note 5. Anthiaume, *La navire . . . sa construction*, p. 44. The distinction is that between overlapping planking and flush planking but the chief importance of the distinction seems to lie in the difference in the strength of the ship.

[11] The number of frames or ribs per 100 feet is given in shipbuilders' notes as follows:

> 73-74 ribs, galleys of Flanders and Romania about 1410.
> 72 ribs, light galley of the guard about 1410.
> 86 ribs, Baxon's war galley about 1410.
> 82 ribs, light galley about 1450.
> 88 ribs, great galley about 1550.

Bibl. Naz. Florence, MSS., Coll. Magliabecchiana, cl. XIX, cod. 7, entitled *Fabrica di galere* and so cited hereafter, ff. 73-82; R. C. Anderson, " Italian Naval Architecture about 1450 ", *The Mariner's Mirror* (The Society for Nautical Research, London, 1925), XI, 138-139; Bibl. Naz. Venice, MSS. Ital. cl. IV, cod. 26 entitled *Instructione sul modo di fabricare galere*, cited hereafter as *Instructione*.

galley since it was through these structures that solution was found for the complicated problem of enabling many men closely packed together to pull enormous oars effectively. Though there has been much question concerning the way in which this problem was solved by the Greeks and Romans, the solutions adopted on the mediaeval oarships have been definitely established,[12] and there are cogent reasons for thinking that the arrangements on the ancient tiremes and quinqueremes were essentially the same as those on the corresponding Venetian ships.[13]

Between 1290 and 1540 the standard Venetian galleys were triremes [14] with twenty-five or thirty benches on each side,[15] and three oarsmen to a bench, each man pulling a separate oar. The galleys had but one deck. That was divided into three parts, a fighting platform in the bow, a larger and higher stern castle, and in between, running almost the whole length of the galley, the rowing space divided into two parts by a gangway down the center. Figure II. The deck space available for oars and rowers extended out beyond the sides of the live work of the hull, for the timbers on which the oars rested, the outrigger frames, were placed out over the water supported by brackets which rose from the beam ends. From the point of view of one on deck, the side of the galley was not the top clamp of the hull frame, but the parapet built on the outrigger frame for the protection of the oarsmen. So a galley with a beam of fifteen feet, a common width, might be said to have an effective deck space twenty-two feet wide and one hundred and six feet long on which to arrange the oarsmen.

The oarsmen were ranged on level benches on each side of the central gangway. These benches or thwarts were not at

[12] Luigi Fincati, *Le triremi* (first pub. in *Rivista marittima*, 1881, quarto tremestre, pp. 55 *et seq.*, 347 *et seq.*; 2nd. ed. Rome, 1884).

[13] W. W. Tarn, "The Oarage of Greek Warships", *The Mariner's Mirror*, XIX (1933), 53 *et seq.*

[14] Marino Sanuto (the Elder) called Torsello, *Liber Secretorum Fidelium Crucis super Terrae Sanctae recuperatione et conservatione* (*Gesta Dei per Francos*, Hanover, 1611), p. 57, gives 1290 as the date of the change from biremes to triremes.

[15] Jal, *Gloss. naut.*, pp. 749, 752; Fincati, *Triremi* (2nd ed.), p. 22; *Fabrica di galere*, f. 79.

right angles to the gunwales, but slanted obliquely towards the
poop so that their inboard ends were further aft than their out-
board ends. This slanting of the benches made it possible to
have all the oars parallel without interfering with one another.
The oars used in the sixteenth century were twenty-nine to
thirty-two feet long weighing about one hundred and twenty
pounds, so that the placing of the outriggers beyond the sides
was necessary to give the rowers sufficient leverage. Even so
only about a third of the oar was inboard, but the deck end
was weighted with lead so that the oar would balance and the
rower be relieved of its weight. In front of the thwarts were
low sets of steps on which the rowers mounted to put their
oars in the water and on which they could brace as they fell
back and threw their weight on the oar.

On the deck of the galley were also posted marines who
were commonly called bowmen even after they had in fact
exchanged the bow for the arquebus. These soldiers could be
placed on the fighting platform at the bow, in the sterncastle
with the commander and his immediate following, and along
the gangway, but their usual station when the galley was cruis-
ing was along the sides at the edge of the benches next to the
parapet. As the oars passed over the outrigger frame in groups
of three, there was a space of about three feet between each
group of oars, and these spaces were the normal stations of the
bowmen. Thus the central gangway was left free for the
manoeuvres of the sailors.[16]

At least eight sailors were necessary to tend the rudder and
the sails.[17] The light galleys usually carried only one mast.[18]
This was placed forward in the ship and lateen-rigged. Two

[16] Fincati, *op. cit.*, gives the most complete descriptions of the deck arrangements.
He testifies that on the occasion of the international geographical congress he built a
trireme in the Venetian Arsenal and rowed it about there for exhibition.

[17] A. S. V., Senato Mar, reg. 17, f. 89, and Museo Civico Correr, Venice, Archivio
Donà della Rosa, busta 153, report of Nicolò Surian.

[18] This was certainly the case in the sixteenth century and is so stated in the *Fabrica
de galere* (c. 1410), f. 78 of the " galley of the guard," but in the first part of the
same manuscript ff. 30-31 is another description of a light galley in which an " arboro
de mezo " and its sail, the " mezana ", are mentioned and it is very likely that many
earlier galleys carried two masts.

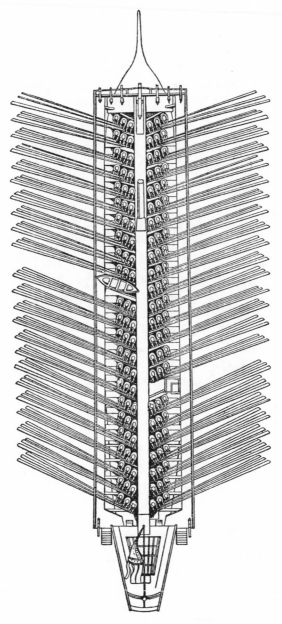

FIGURE II. DECK OF A TRIREME.

The oarsmen all sat at the same level on diagonal benches. The straight line of the outrigger frame contrasts with the curved line of the hull which may be discerned beneath the oars and thwarts. Reconstruction by Admiral Fincati.

sails were carried to be used in turn according to the weather.[19]
Three rudders were carried by each galley, two designed to be
projected from the sides of the stern when the ship was turned,
and one built to fit the curved sternpost. Figure III. Side rudders were the traditional Mediterranean type. The attachment of the rudder to the sternpost was an invention of the

FIGURE III. ONE-MASTED GALLEY PICTURED IN THE " FABRICA DI
GALERE ", ABOUT 1400.

The curved rudder affixed to the sternpost is, elsewhere in the *Fabrica,*
called *timon bavonescho,* recalling its introduction in the Mediterranean
by sailors from Bayonne. Below chap. II, n. 8.

northern tradition which had been introduced in the Mediterranean about 1300, and which gradually displaced the side
rudders.

While the Venetian light galleys were thus like all others
equipped for sailing, they were not particularly good sailers,
for the shipwrights tended to sacrifice seaworthiness to speed
under oar by making their galleys narrower and lower. By the
sixteenth century this tendency had gone so far that the galley
commanders complained that the decks were too easily swept
by waves and the fighters were at a disadvantage when engaging a higher galley. When tacking to windward it was impos-

[19] Jal, *Arch. nav.,* II, 121.

sible to prevent the leeward oars and outrigger frame from dragging in the sea, thus both cutting down by half the speed of the galley and breaking many oars. At the same time, with the increased importance of cannon, the bow of the galley was so heavily loaded with artillery that when the ship was sailing before the wind her forecastle was buried in the waves. But swiftness was still desired, and between the conflicting tendencies to make the galleys more seaworthy and to give them more speed under oar the latter on the whole predominated. Although the Venetian galleys were slower under sail and suffered more damage in storms than the Turkish galleys, yet at the end of the sixteenth century the Venetians still had the reputation of building the finest galleys made.[20]

In the light galley all the peculiarities of the long ship propelled by oars were carried to extremes. Smaller long ships, *fuste, galeotte, bregantini,* and *fregate,* were simplifications of the light galley rowed by one or two men and oars to a bench and used to carry despatches or to patrol the coast.[21] But the great galleys constituted almost a separate type designed as they were to combine some of the advantages of a round ship with those of the galley. At Venice the great galley attained a special importance first as merchantman and later as warship and may be considered more than almost any other a distinctly Venetian ship, a product molded equally by her shipbuilding craft and her commercial system.

The great galleys came into very general commercial use within a decade after the years 1294 or 1298, when they were said to have been invented. To be sure, smaller long ships were occasionally used a long time thereafter in emergencies to carry the wares of Venetian merchants out of danger, or to

---

[20] Jurien de la Gravière, *La guerre de Chypre et la bataille de Lepanto* (Paris, 1888), I, 37-43; report of Nicolò Surian cited in note 17 above; Bartolomeo Crescentio, *Nautica mediterranea* (Rome, 1602), p. 5. In 1570, on report that the galleys were too low it was ordered to make them higher and wider—A. S. V., Arsenale, busta 11, f. 85—but at the end of the century, as shown in Figure 1, they were made as low as formerly.

[21] Casoni, "Forze militare", lists of ship names; Camillo Manfroni, *Storia della marina italiana dalla caduta di Costantinopoli alla battaglia di Lepanto* (Rome, 1897), pp. 182-3.

move quickly especially valuable merchandise such as a cargo of gold from Tunis,[22] but the light galley could carry but little while its large crew made it extremely expensive, and the great galley combined almost equal security with greater seaworthiness and a more capacious hold.

Thanks to the commercial policy of the state, the new type of merchant galley not only displaced lighter galleys but also, and more extensively, displaced round ships. Such losses as that at Saseno—and it was but one among many which occurred during the first two wars against Genoa—led to the inauguration by Venice just after the close of the second war in 1299, of a new system of merchant caravans. A very large class of merchandise was thereafter to be brought to Venice only by armed ships, which meant in practice galleys carrying a crew of well over one hundred men. The merchandise which was reserved for such ships included spices and silks, indeed all the light goods of Venetian commerce save for certain specified exceptions. The great galleys were at the same time made subject to close regulation by the state which elected the commanding officer of the galley fleets and determined the crew, the equipment, and the measures of the galleys, the number to be sent on any particular voyage, the time of sailing and returning, the freight rates to be charged, and innumerable other details. In the second half of the fourteenth century even the galleys themselves were furnished by the state and rented to merchants who undertook the risk and profit of arming and freighting them for their voyage. These state galley fleets were protected against the competition of either round ships or privately owned Venetian galleys which might go on the same voyage, and so gradually the state concentrated all galley building in its own hands.[23]

---

[22] A. S. V., Senato Mar, reg. 19, ff. 82, 101.

[23] Manfroni, *Ninfeo . . . Costantinopoli,* pp. 216, 222, 253-5; Carlo Antonio Marin, *Storia civile e politica del commercio di Veneziani* (Venice, 1798-1808), vol. V, lib. II, cap. III; Weil, pp. 314 *et seq.* This reorganization of the Venetian merchant marine has not yet been carefully studied but "Le rubriche . . . del Senato", ed. Giomo, are full of traces of the change. See also A. S. V., Ufficiali al Cattaver, file 1, cap. 1, f. 65-72. After the system of state galley voyages was established, details of their routes, freight rates, etc., were determined for each voyage by the terms of the

The great galleys which thus came to replace all other ships as the regular carriers of precious cargoes were sometimes said to resemble galleys in the center and round ships at both ends, but such a characterization exaggerates their similarity to the round ship. Although they had higher, blunter prows and wider sterns than the light galleys they had but one deck and entirely lacked the high forecastle and stern castle of the large round ship. They were essentially galleys, in every way bigger than the light galleys, of wider and deeper proportions, and able to carry more sail, but both their superstructures and the primary proportions of their hulls were those of long ships.

Indeed when they first came into use, in the early fourteenth century, they were not very different from the light galleys of the time. The measures which the state approved for use in their construction varied slightly according to the voyage for which they were intended. There were galleys of the measures of Flanders, of the measures of Trebizond, of the measures of Alexandria. The largest, those of Flanders, were then supposed to freight but about 140 tons below deck.[24]

A century later—that is, in the fifteenth century—the Flemish galleys, the type most used, had been enlarged so that they carried about 200 tons below deck.[25] A slightly narrower and lower galley which carried about 150 tons was especially designed for the voyage to Constantinople.[26] The climax of the growth of the great galleys of Venice was reached about the middle of the fifteenth century. Thereafter the merchant galleys for the great trading voyages were practically all of the one large design, able to load about 250 tons below deck.[27]

resolution under which the galleys were auctioned. For the years before 1440 these resolutions are in A. S. V., series Senato Misti, for 1440-1469 in Senato Mar, and after 1469 in a special series called " Senato, Deliberazioni, Incanti Galere ", which comes down to 1569, but in which the years 1499-1519 are missing. The *Diarii* of Marino Sanuto does much to fill this gap.

[24] Giomo, " Le Rubriche " . . . , *Arch. veneto*, XVII (1879), 264, 266, 262, 259; XIX (1880), 98, 100; Marin, V, 202.

[25] A. S. V., Senato Misti, reg. 60, f. 249.

[26] Senato Mar, reg. 1, f. 13, ordered in 1440 as a return to old standards.

[27] Senato Misti, reg. 60, f. 249. This decree of 1440 complained that they were being built of a capacity of five or six hundred milliaria (1 mill. = .47 tons), and fixed the future limits as between 400 and 440 milliaria. Already in 1356 the Senate

Whereas the light galleys were then more than eight times as long on deck as they were wide, the great galleys were only six times as long as their beam. (Table B.) Sinking low in the water when heavily laden, they could be rowed only with great difficulty. They still carried oarsmen arranged as on the light galleys, but the outrigger frames on which the oars rested were comparatively close to the sides so that the oarsmen had less leverage, and the rowers were not even expected to use their oars except in emergencies and in entering and leaving port.[28] Indeed their commanders were known to leave two-thirds of the oars at home so that they would not be broken.[29] Although their superstructures and, more faintly, their proportions preserved the memory of their origin as oarships, the great galleys had become in practice sailing ships. Their sailing qualities are revealed by the return voyage of the Flemish galleys in 1509. Because of the general European league against Venice they were ordered directly home and made what was considered a record voyage. They came from Southampton to Otranto, about 2500 miles, in thirty-one days.[30]

The best descriptions of these hybrid ships are in the

had settled on 400 milliaria as the official size of the Flemish galleys, Roberto Cessi, " Le relazioni commerciali tra Venezia e le Fiandre nel secolo xiv ", *Nuovo archivio veneto, nuova serie*, XXVII (1914), 92. A computation on the bottom of the page, Senato Terra, reg. 3, f. 75, shows that in 1452 the " patron " or merchant who rented the galley for the voyage was expected to collect freight on 430 milliaria. But again in 1480 it was complained that the galleys were of 500 to 600 milliaria, and 450 milliaria was established as the maximum. Senato Terra, reg. 8, f. 114. In 1520 there was another protest against their great size and a limitation placed on their length. Senato Mar, reg. 19, f. 126. Jal quotes a description of them in 1501—*Arch. nav.*, I, 384-387—which said they carried a weight of 500 milliaria below deck and as much on deck, presumably including in the weight on deck the crew of two hundred, the oars, chests, etc. In the later fifteenth century the galleys of the measures of Romania are no longer mentioned in the resolutions for auctioning the galleys.

[28] The regulation of 1480 cited above reads in part: ". . . Chome le prime galie erano manevele, et podevasse andar chon remi a passar ponte, entrar e insir de porti et de altri luogi, cussi queste sono senestrissime e desutele, se per non haver le suo raxon per respecto de la porta e del rio del Arsena, che non lassa insir, si per haver men homeni del uxado, siando siminui la vuoga, come per esser ogni cossa piu greve. Lequal galie se po piu tosto apellar nave che galie."

[29] Senato Mar, reg. 20, f. 176, about 1525. About 1418, the galleys of Alexandria being forced to take refuge on a barren island in extremely cold weather, the oars were used for fuel. A. S. V., Arsenal, busta 5, f. 90.

[30] Sanuto, *Diarii*, VIII, 474.

accounts of pilgrims who sailed from Venice to the Holy Land in essentially similar galleys. The following account by Felix Fabri of the ship on which he made his second voyage in 1483 is especially vivid and detailed, although the reference to the oarsmen as " galley slaves " appears a misunderstanding.[81]

A galley is one of the middle-sized kind of seagoing ships, and is not of the greatest, nor yet of the smallest sort. . . . Now a bireme is one which is rowed by pairs and pairs of oars; but a trireme is one which is rowed by threes and threes of oars, because on each bench it has three oars, and as many rowers. Now the galley on board of which I crossed the second time had sixty cross benches, and upon each bench three rowers with their oars; and to be equipped as a war-galley it has an archer with his bow on every bench together with the rowers.

Now all galleys of the same size are so much alike in all respects that a man who passes from his own galley on board of another would hardly find out that he was on another, except from the officers and crews of the vessels being different, for Venetian galleys are as like one to another as swallows' nests. They are built of the stoutest timbers, and fastened together with many bolts, chains, and irons. The first and foremost part of the galley, which is called the prow, is sharp where it meets the sea, and has a strong beak, made somewhat like a dragon's head, with open mouth, all of which is made of iron, wherewith to strike any ship which it may meet. On either side of the beak are two holes, through which a man can put his head, through which are passed the cables of the anchors, and through which the anchors are pulled up; nor can the sea run in through these holes except in great storms. The beak of the prow reaches high up, and from it the belly of the ship begins to swell round against the sea. The prow likewise has a sail of its own, named *dalum*, which is commonly called *trinketum*, and it has beneath it a small chamber, wherein ropes and sails are stored, and therein sleeps the captain of the prow, who has a crew of his own, who dwell there, and nowhere else, and do the work of that part of the ship; and it is also the place of the poor wretches whom the slaves of the prow pick up. Also on either side of the prow hang great iron anchors which at fitting seasons are let down into the sea.

[81] *The Book of the Wanderings of Brother Felix Fabri in Palestine and Arabia* (trans. Aubrey Stewart in publications of Palgrave Pilgrims Text Society, London, 1892), I, 126-131. The words translated " galley slaves " are in two cases *galeotae* in one case *servi—Fratris Felicis Fabri Evagatorium*, I, 119-121. Cf. note 6, above.

The stern, which is the other and hindermost end of the galley, is not sharp where it meets the sea, like the prow, nor has it a beak; but it is wide and curves from above downwards to the water, and is much higher than the prow, having upon it a building which they call the castle. From it there hangs down into the sea the rudder, or rudderpost, above which, in a latticed chamber, is the steersman,

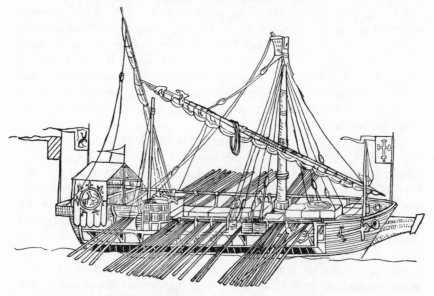

FIGURE IV.   GREAT GALLEY EQUIPPED FOR PILGRIM VOYAGE ABOUT 1485.

The illustrations in Breydenbach's *Peregrinatio in Terram Sanctam* confirm the descriptions given by Fabri and Casola, showing the deck even more encumbered with boxes and cordage than it has been possible to portray in this sketch. The supply of fresh meat appears above the cooking galley. Barrels project from the sides so as to hamper the movement of the oars. The mainmast is amidships, the forward mast very small and its yard foreshortened almost beyond recognition.

holding the tiller in his hands. The castle has three stories: the first, wherein is the steersman and the compass, and he who tells the steersman how the compass points, and those who watch the stars and winds, and point out the way across the sea; the middle one wherein is the chamber of the Lord and captain of the ship, and of his noble comrades and messmates; and the lowest one wherein noble ladies are housed at night, and where the captain's treasure is stored. This chamber receives no light save from the hatchway in the floor above it. On either side of the poop hang the boats, one large and one small, which in harbours are lowered into the sea and used for landing people. On the right-hand side are the steps down which one goes to the boats at sea, or up which one comes from them. The poop also has its own sail, which is bigger than the sail at the prow and which they call *mesavala,* that is 'the middle sail'; its Latin name is *epidromus.* Upon the poop also the flag is always hoisted to show which way the wind is blowing.[32]

Two benches beyond the house on the poop, on the right hand side, is the kitchen, which is not covered in: beneath the kitchen is the cellar, and beside the kitchen is the stable for animals for slaughter, wherein sheep, goats, calves, oxen, cows, and pigs stand all together. Further on, on the same side are cross benches with oars all the way to the prow. On the left-hand side are rowers' benches all the way from the poop to the prow, and on every bench three rowers and an archer. Between two benches on the edge of the ship on either side there hangs a *bombarda* in a movable iron swivel, and on either side there is a *bombardana,* from which, in case of necessity, stones are shot forth. In the midst of the ship stands the mast, a tall, thick, and strong tree made of many beams fastened together, which supports the yard with the *accaton,* or mainsail.

---

[32] Casola's description of the poop—Newett, pp. 156-7—is more detailed: "The fourth part of the galley—that is, from the mizzen mast backwards—was divided, first, into a place called the poop which has three divisions. The lower is called the *pizolo*—a place conceded to distinguished men for sleeping, and also reserved for the storage of munition and of merchandise belonging to the captain and others at the discretion of the captain. In the middle region, which is called the poop proper, the tables are spread for meals, and there is also a small altar where Dry Mass was said for the captain; and at night many mattresses were spread here for sleeping, according to the distribution of places amongst the pilgrims or other passengers. Many weapons, too, were attached to the roof of the said place—crossbows, bows, swords, and other kinds of weapons—for the defense of the galley in case of need; and in that place all the tackle of the galley is made. Above the said poop proper there is a place called the castle, where, for the most part, the captain lived, and also any great persons, if such there happened to be aboard. It is floored with tarred planks so that however much it rains, no water can enter the poop. The navigating compass was kept in the castle, and on the voyage this castle was covered, first with canvas and then with a curtain of red cloth on which the ensign of the Sepulchre and also the arms of the Contarini family were embroidered.

"Behind the aforesaid castle a place is arranged for managing the rudder of the galley, which is moved by the force of men's arms alone. Several times, when there was a great storm at sea, more than two men were necessary to manage it, and it is moved by means of a piece of thick rope. Further behind, there was a place where two terra-cotta vessels full of water were kept, and also a place necessary for purging the body; and these all projected outside the body of the galley on timbers well tarred and well joined together."

On the top of the mast is the chamber which the Germans call the 'basket,' the Italians the 'keba,' the Latins 'carceria.' On deck beside the mast there is an open space wherein men assemble to talk, as in a market place; and it is called the market place of the galley.

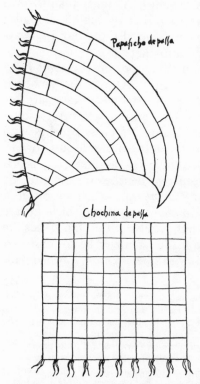

Papaficho de paſſa

Chochina de paſſa

FIGURE V. A PAGE FROM THE "FABRICA DI GALERE", THE STORM SAILS OF A MERCHANT GALLEY ABOUT 1400.

The mainsail has in its width fifty-three cloths, each of which measures more than an ell, but to meet different kinds of weather different sails are hoisted, not so large as the *accaton*. In storms they set a square sail (*sic,* contrast Figure V) of stout canvas which they call *papafigo*. Now on this upper deck of the galley dwell the officers of the galley, and the galley-slaves, each man upon his own bench, and there they sleep, eat, and work. Between the benches along either side is a pretty wide space, wherein stand great chests full of merchandise, and above those chests there is a walk from the stern to the prow, on which the officers run up and down when the oars are being worked.[33]

Close to the mast is the main hatchway, through which one descends by seven steps into the cabin which is the place where the pilgrims live, or where the cargo is put in galleys of burthen. Now in length this cabin reaches from the cellar in the stern to the small chamber in the prow, and in width

[33] The excessive number and size of the chests carried on the decks of the merchant galleys were frequently subjects of regulations designed to prevent the overloading of the galley. Some of the chests were the same width as the *corsia* or gangway and placed on it so that the sailors must have run fore and aft on top of the chests. Senato Misti, reg. 52, f. 72; Senato Mar, reg. 1, f. 17; reg. 13, f. 45; reg. 18, ff. 146-7. On a great galley there were three or four more feet of room between the gangway and the parapet on the outrigger frame than on a light galley. Some of this additional space may have come between the inboard end of the rowers' benches and the gangway, so that chests might be piled there as well as on top of the gangway.

from one side of the ship to the other, and it is like a great and spacious chamber. It receives no light save what comes from the four hatchways by which it is entered. In this cabin every pilgrim has his own berth or sleeping-place. The berths of the pilgrims are so arranged all along the ship, or rather the cabin, one berth joins the next one without any space left between them, and one pilgrim lies by the side of another, along both sides of the ship, having their heads towards the side of the ship and their feet stretching out towards one another. As the cabin is wide, there stands along the middle of it, between the berths, chests and pilgrims' trunks, reaching from the cellar to the chamber in the prow, in which the pilgrims keep their own private property, and the feet of the sleepers on either side stretch out as far as these trunks. Beneath the pilgrims is a large space reaching deep down to the bottom of the galley, which space is called the belly of the galley, for a galley is not flat bottomed like other ships, but is sharp from bows to the stern, so that a galley ends in a sharp foot below, so sharp that when it is not in the water it can not stand upright on the land, but must lie on its side. This sharp hold is filled with sand right up to the deck beams, whereon the pilgrims lie; and the pilgrims lift up the deck to bury in the sand the bottles wherein they keep their wine, and eggs and other things which need to be kept cool. Down below, in the place where the pilgrims live, is the well for bilge water, just by the middle of the mast, and this well does not contain human filth, but all the water which visibly and invisibly enters the galley filters through and collects in that well, and a most loathsome smell arises from it, a worse smell than that from any closet of human ordure. This well has to be pumped out once in every day, but in rough weather the water has to be drawn out of it without cessation. Along the outer side of the galley are places for necessary purposes.

The whole galley, within and without, is covered with the blackest pitch, as are even the ropes, planks, and everything else, that they may not easily be rotted by the water. The ropes for working the sails and anchors take up a large part of the galley, because they are many, and are long, thick, and of manifold kinds. It is wondrous to see the multitude of ropes and their joinings and twinings about the vessel.

A galley is like a monastery for the place of prayer is on the upper deck beside the mast, where also is the market place; the middle part of the poop answers to the refectory; the benches of the galley-slaves and the berths of the pilgrims are the dormitory; the chapter

house is over against the kitchen; the prisons are beneath the deck
of the prow and poop; the cellar, kitchen, and stable are all open
to the sky on the upper deck. Thus, in brief, passing over many
things, you have the portraiture of a galley.

The sails mentioned by Fabri show that at the same time
that the great galley became larger and more dependent upon
sails, its rigging developed in sharp contrast with that of the
light galley. At the opening of the fifteenth century the great
galley had had only two masts, of which the foremast was
much the larger.[34] The first three-masted merchant galley was
probably of the type shown in Figure VI, so that in the middle
of the fifteenth century the merchant galley was rigged much
like the caravel. Quite different was the rig of the ship in
which Fabri sailed, for at an indeterminate date before 1480
the merchant galley adopted an arrangement analogous to that
which, in the same general period, was adopted by the large
round ship, namely, a mainmast in the center with smaller
masts fore and aft. Figure IV. The use of the sails in this
latter arrangement is described in detail by the pilgrims. The
galley depended for its speed almost entirely upon the sails
hung on the mainmast in the center. Those fore and aft were
used mainly for manoeuvring the galley.

Four sails were carried for use on the mainmast. The triangular *artimon,* which Fabri calls the *accaton,* was the fair
weather sail used with light winds, but was too large for use
with a strong wind astern. If such a wind arose, the yard was
lowered, the *artimon* taken off and a smaller sail of the same
type, the *terzarolo,* attached and hoisted in its place. If the
wind increased and the galley was unable to make port and
must needs ride out of the storm, then the sailors again lowered
the yard and hoisted either the small square *cochina* or the
triangular *papafico.* Figure V. If on the contrary the breeze
was favorable but very light, the expedient might be adopted
of hoisting the sail of the forward mast, the *trinketum,* from
the masthead above the mainsail to serve as a topsail. More-

---

[34] *Fabrica di galere,* ff. 8, 73.

over the awning with which the whole galley was sometimes covered from forecastle to stern castle to protect the crew from sun or rain, might be brought out and spread athwart the galley at the mainmast under the sheet of the mainsail so as to catch all the wind possible.

FIGURE VI. THREE-MASTED GALLEY ABOUT 1445.

On the two-masted galleys—and on the two-masted, lateen-rigged round ships—the forward mast was the tallest and carried the largest sail. The earliest three-masters merely added another, smaller, lateen-rigged mast aft as shown in this sketch from Timbotta's notes. Anderson, "Ital. Nav. Arch.," *Mariner's Mirror*, XI, 144.

If the ship was entirely becalmed she would ordinarily have to wait, like any other sailing ship, for a wind to come up, but not if she was just off port. In such a case the oars could be worked to bring her in safely.[35] This was no mean advantage.

[35] Newett, *Casola's Pilgrimage*, pp. 157-159, 169, 197-198, 203, 219-220, 294-295, 319, 323, 325-326, 328; Fabri, I (tr. Stewart), 38, 179 (*trinketum* as topsail), 184 (use of oars). These accounts are from 1480, 1483, and 1494, but all the four sails used on the mainmast had been in use as early as 1365. Luigi Fincati, *Ordini e segnali della flotta veneziana da Messer Giacomo Dolfin* (Rome, 1879) reprint from *Rivista marittima*.

Though the great galley depended on the wind to carry it from one port to another, the ship asserted its independence as soon as it was off port. The oars were idle during most of the voyage, but the few minutes when they were used were vital both for the safety and speed of the voyage. The great galley did not have to wait for days off a dangerous shore, and then perhaps be blown on the rocks or far off to sea again. Not the constant use of the oars, but the possibility of working them for a short time in critical situations made the voyages of the great galleys quicker and more dependable than those of the round ships.

Second in importance only to their seaworthiness was the defensibility of the great galleys, for they were designed to combine not only some of the advantages of oarship and sailing vessel, but also those of warship and merchantman. When naval encounters were but land battles transferred to ships, the essential armament of a vessel was her crew. The large number of men needed on a galley to man the oars furnished the basis of a fighting force far larger than any which could be employed on a round ship. Altogether the crew of a merchant galley was over two hundred men,[36] any of whom might be called on to take part in the defense of the galley. Arms for their use were supplied by the Arsenal and carried in a part of the hold reserved for that purpose.[37] Out of a crew of two hundred, twenty were bowmen—or after 1486 gunners—selected by public contest from among the best shots in Venice.[38] If the voyage was believed to be subject to special danger, ten or twenty extra bowmen were taken aboard by order of the Senate.[39] A fleet of three or four galleys therefore

[36] The crew specified by law in 1412 amounted to 210 from captain to cook but not counting any possible merchant travelers. Of this number 171 were oarsmen. Senato Misti, reg. 49, f. 114-5. At the end of the century the number of oarsmen actually carried was often less—A. S. V., Senato Mar, reg. 15, f. 16-17; Sanuto, *Diarii*, III, 1446, 1226—but Sanuto estimated 500 men lost by the wreck of two galleys—*La spedizione di Carlo VIII in Italia* (ed. R. Fulin as supplement to *Arch. ven.*, 1873), pp. 274-5.

[37] Senato Misti, reg. 47, f. 103; Senato Mar, reg. 27, f. 109.

[38] Senato Misti, reg. 53 copy, f. 488; Arsenale, busta 6, f. 21; Senato, Deliberazioni, Incanti Galere, reg. 1, f. 97.

[39] Senato Misti, reg. 47, ff. 30, 47, 163; reg. 49, f. 86.

represented a military force which might be expected to take care of itself if attacked by any except the most formidable pirate fleets.[40]

For two centuries the great galleys were the safest means of maritime transport available.[41] They offered the best security against either hostile ships or unfavorable weather. There was,

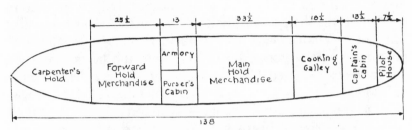

FIGURE VII. COMPARTMENTS IN THE HULL OF A MERCHANT GALLEY.

In theory no merchandise could be carried below deck in the cabins set aside for other purposes, but the galleys of Flanders, on their return voyages, carried in the *scandolar*—the cooking galley and storeroom— some merchandise as well as food and drink. Extra sails and cordage was put in the carpenter's hold. Merchants and their personal baggage might be accommodated either in the cabin of the *scrivan*, purser, or in that of the captain, the *pizuol*. Senato Misti, reg. 47, f. 30; reg. 50, f. 120; reg. 52, f. 21; reg. 53 copy, f. 499; Jal. *Glossaire nautique, s. v. scandolaro.* The distances between partitions are in Venetian feet as given in sixteenth century papers in Arsenale, busta 1, but the divisions are mentioned a century earlier.

therefore, an economic justification for their use as carriers of the costliest wares of commerce. They charged higher freights than the round ships,[42] but the insurance rates were cheaper and the service the quickest and most reliable available.[43]

[40] Domenico Malipiero, *Annali veneti dell'anno 1457 al 1500* (ed. Tommaso Gar and Augustino Sagredo in *Archivio storico italiano,* ser. i, vol. VII, Florence, 1843), pp. 620, 625, 641 on their victories and defeats.

[41] Sanuto, *Spedizione di Carlo VIII,* pp. 274-5, recounting the wreck of two of the Flemish galleys in 1495 considered it marvelous that one of the Venetian round ships rode out of the storm while the galleys were lost. He placed the last such loss of galleys on that voyage in 1437. Malpiero, p. 628, blamed the wreck of 1495 on over-loading.

[42] The freight rates are given in the auction contracts.

[43] Aloys Schulte, *Geschichte der grossen Ravensburger Handelsgesellschaft* (Stutt-gart and Berlin, 1923), III, 412, on differences in insurance rates and freights and II, 65-72; III, 228-9 on the use of the galleys in the west in competition with round ships.

Some merchants considered it waste of money to insure goods sent by these vessels.[44]

Their rather modest capacity below deck, less than that of many of the round ships of the time, fails to represent their true commercial importance. They were required to give preference in loading to precious merchandise and only if none of that was offered might they load cheaper, bulkier commodities.[45] At the height of their fame, about 1500, one fleet brought to Venice every winter about two and a half million pounds of spices from Alexandria,[46] and the fleets that went out to the east carried 300,000 ducats of cash besides the bales of merchandise.[47] Moreover, every member of the crew— mariner, bowman, and oarsman—each carried somewhere on deck a few wares of his own.[48] At each port they went ashore to hold a miniature fair.[49] When this deck load is taken into account it becomes evident that the capacity of the hold is but a partial measure of the amount of merchandise on each galley.

But while in the fifteenth century these great galleys were the most famous of all merchantmen, during the first thirty-five years of the sixteenth century they practically disappeared. Between 1535 and 1569 none sailed from Venice except an occasional two to Beyrut and two to Alexandria.[50] In the seventeenth century the state rented galleys for a voyage to the Dalmatian city of Spalato, then the terminus of an overland route by which silks, spices, and dyes came from the

[44] Enrico Bensa, *Francesco di Marco da Prato* (Milan, 1928), p. 184, note 1, quotes letter of 1398 from Francesco declaring all goods sent should be insured. He has been speaking of *nave*. Therewith is contrasted the following in a letter from Piaciti from Venice 1401: " Non è nostro pensiero pigliare sicurtà d'un grosso su queste V galee; parebbeci gittare via quelli danari vi si spendessono, perocchè troppo sicuro passaggio abbiamo, e niuno pensiero faremo di farvici assicurare.

[45] Senato Misti, reg. 47, f. 106; reg. 49, ff. 81-84, 86, 91; reg. 54, ff. 68-9.

[46] In 1498 the galleys of Alexandria brought 2155 *colli*—Sanuto, *Diarii*, II, 165, 172—or 2,413,600 English pounds. (Appendix I.) In 1501 the galleys of Alexandria brought 2570 *colli*—ibid., IV, 38-39—or 2,878,400 English pounds.

[47] *Ibid.*, I, 270, 734; III, 1187; and Gerolamo Priuli, *I diarii* (ed. A. Segre, *Rerum italicarum scriptores,* 2nd. ed., vol. 24, Part III, Citta di Castello, 1911), I, 94.

[48] The resolutions for auctioning the galleys are full of the difficulties of overloading which resulted.

[49] Newett, *Casola's Pilgrimage,* p. 191; Sanuto, *Diarii,* II, 457.

[50] A. S. V., Senato, Incanti de galere, reg. 2.

east.[51] But this new Adriatic voyage called forth a new type of ship lower and shorter than the merchant galleys which had made the voyage to Southampton. (Table B.)

The passing of the merchant galley was due partly to the contemporary improvement of the round ship, but was precipitated by changes in trade routes and in political conditions at the opening of the sixteenth century. The large crews of the galleys made them excessively expensive. That expense had been justified only by their greater security and only the shippers of valuable wares could afford to pay for that security. In the sixteenth century the Mediterranean lost the monopoly which it had previously enjoyed in the trans-shipment to Europe of the precious wares of the East and the return of cargoes of gold and silver. Shipment by galley, always a luxury, could no longer be so well afforded.

Moreover, there was no longer any good reason for using such expensive vessels. The development of the " full-rigged " ship and of naval artillery had deprived the merchant galleys of much of their special advantage. As gunfire became a more important factor in naval fights the exposed state of the rowers' deck of the low galley placed the long ship under an increasing disadvantage in combat with the round ship which was well manned and armed. The demoralizing effect upon galleys of a well directed broadside was demonstrated with convincing conclusiveness by Drake in his raid at Cadiz and Corunna in 1587.[52] But during the century before Drake brought into operation his conception of the warship as a floating gun carriage, round ships carrying batteries less efficient than those of Drake had given brilliant exhibitions of their capacity to withstand galley attacks. At Zonchio in 1499 and at Prevesa in 1538 great round ships of Venice had been exposed to the attack of the whole Ottoman fleet and in both cases had given good account of themselves.[53] Light galleys maintained for

[51] A. S. V., Cinque Savii, first series, buste 137-139, 145.

[52] Julian S. Corbett, *Drake and the Tudor Navy* (London, 1917), II, 81.

[53] Manfroni, *Costantinopoli . . . Lepanto*, pp. 219, 341-2; Paolo Paruta, *Dell'historia venetiana* (*Degli istorici delle cose veneziane i qualli hanno scritto per decreto publico*, vols. III and part I of vol. IV, Venice, 1718); vol. IV, part 1, p. 68; Malipiero, p. 178.

some time thereafter their supremacy in Mediterranean war fleets only because galleys were needed to take the offensive and drive other galley fleets from the sea. While the round ships stood off attacks stubbornly, they were difficult to manoeuvre in an attacking fleet. But merchantmen required not offensive but defensive strength. The round ships had always possessed this quality in certain measure by reason of their high sides and castles. The development of the use of gunpowder made them even more difficult to capture provided they were defended by an adequate number of men.

The large crew necessary for the defense of either round ship or long ship involved a certain increase in the cost of transportation. The large size of the crews of the great galleys had been the chief reason for the high freight rates which they charged. But on the merchant galleys the large crews had served a double purpose. They manned the oars and gave the vessel a certain independence of the wind in those crucial and hazardous manoeuvres, the entering and leaving of harbors. Though the oars on the merchant galleys were infrequently used, those few occasions when they were brought into play might save many days of battling adverse winds to regain a port already sighted.

In the middle of the fifteenth century there began a revolutionary improvement in the rigging of round ships. The adding of topsail, foresail, and mizzen made the round ship much more manageable. Though the oars of the galley were still an advantage in a calm, the round ship was no longer under so great a handicap. By 1500, and more clearly by 1550, the improved rig of the round ships made them as safe for most long voyages as the galleys.[54]

These technical changes in the art of war, in seamanship, and in rigging ultimately brought about the supremacy of the round ship in all branches of navigation. The abandonment of the voyages of the merchant galleys was but one of their con-

---

[54] In Sanuto's description of the storm which wrecked two Flemish galleys in 1495, the capacity of the round ship "Zorzi" to ride out the storm is as significant as Sanuto's surprise that it should have survived when the galleys were wrecked.

sequences, a consequence the character of which is complicated by the commercial and political changes of the sixteenth century. The privileged position which Venice had held through her geographic location and her political power was slipping from her. The galley fleets were unfitted not only for the new economic conditions of the sixteenth century, but also for the political and naval situation created by the growth of powerful rival states. No convoy of merchantmen could hope to resist the war fleet of one of the great monarchs with whom Venice was then so frequently at war. To concentrate the most precious wares of her merchants in a few fleets was no longer prudent. The Venetian Senate abolished the monopolies which had protected the various galley fleets against the competition of round ships [55] and the full-rigged ships carried on the voyages which the galleys abandoned.[56]

Round ships also completely replaced galleys as passenger ships for pilgrims during the first part of the sixteenth century. Ever since the Crusades Venice had been the leading port of embarcation for pilgrims going to the Holy Land, and it continued for centuries after to be the main center of this lucrative tourist trade. In the fourteenth century galleys were considered definitely preferable as passenger ships because they voyaged along the coasts putting into port each night so

[55] In 1514 round ships were permitted to load spices in Alexandria and Beyrut for Venice—Senato Mar, reg. 18, f. 29; Sanuto, *Diarii,* XVIII, 178—and when in 1524 the galleys brought back no spices it was because a round ship had taken them all— *ibid.,* XXXV, 254, 332, 337. The monopoly of the galleys was then restored for a decade, but after 1534 round ships again brought spices to Venice. Senato, Incanti Galere, reg. 2, libri 4 and 5; Arsenal, busta 8, ff. 2-3. The obligation to ship certain goods from Greece and England in the galleys was similarly removed. Senato Mar, reg. 18, f. 30; reg. 26, ff. 26-27; reg. 21, f. 62; reg. 19, f. 155. Half of the galley freight was retained as a customs duty, for the goods obligated to come on the galleys had been exempt from tolls so that in effect the earlier galley freight had included customs duties. Allan Evans, *Francesco Balducci Pegolotti, La Practica della Mercatura,* a dissertation deposited in the Harvard College Library, vol. 2, pp. 138, 140, 146.

[56] Except the voyages along northern Africa east to Alexandria and west to Spain which had prospered partly by transporting Moorish merchants with safety against pirates, Christian and Mohammedan, a protection which Venice could no longer furnish. Round ships were allowed to go on these voyages but not to take Moorish merchants on board as passengers. Senato Mar, reg. 16, f. 37; reg. 21, f. 44; reg. 22, f. 48; reg. 23, f. 51, and, on Spanish competition, Paruta, III, 290-292.

that the traveler could always eat fresh provisions and incidently see all the sights. If the pilgrim chose to go on a round ship he would not have fresh food and he would see many famous cities only from afar, for the ship went straight across the sea to its destination, putting into port only in case of necessity.[57] So most of the pilgrims then went by galley, even though passage by galley was more expensive.[58] In 1384 six galleys and one round ship embarked six hundred pilgrims, but usually only three or four galleys went each year at that time and two or three in the next century. The pilgrim galleys were not, like the merchant galleys, state ships rented for the voyage, but the Venetian nobles who built and commanded them were required to prove themselves satisfactory to the Signoria and their dealings with the pilgrims were closely regulated. The galleys used on the voyage were almost exactly like the great galleys of trade except that they customarily carried but two oars and men to each bench. They were the only great galleys in private hands which I have seen mentioned during the fifteenth century.

It was considered necessary that at least one galley be ready each Corpus Christi to take care of the pilgrims who assembled in Venice during the spring. Great noblemen, relatives of foreign princes, had to be taken care of, and while they were free to buy their passage on any round ship, they might not find one available or might insist upon having passage on a galley, and in that case the Signoria was practically forced to allow them to travel on one of the merchant galleys going to Beyrut, a disturbance of the trading voyage which the government preferred to avoid. Private enterprise produced the needed pilgrim galleys readily enough until 1500, when the only one intended for the voyage was hardly ready in time. In 1518 none was available. The Senate proposed to provide for the future by auctioning the right to build a galley which should be the only one allowed to go on the voyage. There is no evi-

[57] Leopold von Suchem, *Description of the Holy Land and of the Way Thither* (London, 1895, in publications of the Palestine Pilgrims Text Society), p. 19.
[58] *Viaggio di Leonardo di Niccolò Frescobaldi Fiorintino in Egitto e in Terra Santa* (ed. G. Manzi, Rome, 1818), pp. 67-74; Newett, *Casola's Pilgrimage*, pp. 11, 75.

dence that anyone accepted this privilege. But two round
ships had carried pilgrims in 1517 and in 1520 three round
ships contracted to do so. Apparently the pilgrims had come
to prefer the cheaper transport offered by round ships to the
more expensive voyage by galley. In 1546 all hope of reviving
the use of the galley on the voyage was abandoned and provision made for giving special licenses to round ships of over
240 tons.[59] But the pilgrims were then so much less numerous
than they had been that the voyage to Jaffa occupied only one
such ship a year.[60]

Discarded as passenger ships and as merchantmen, the great
galleys suddenly gained importance as warships. Curiously
enough the same development of artillery which rendered
them less impregnable as carriers of precious merchandise also
made it possible for them to become more formidable additions to the Mediterranean war fleets which were mainly composed of even more exposed light galleys. The deck equipment of the great galley was made over by Gian Andrea
Badoer about 1550 so as to make it better fitted for battle, and
under the new arrangement it carried a load of artillery fear-
some to other galleys.[61] In 1571 great galleys played an important part in the battle of Lepanto, where they were stationed in
front of the Christian battle line and by their fire greatly dis-
organized the Turkish fleet.[62]

At the same time that the great galleys were being transformed from merchantmen to warships by being laden with
guns instead of merchandise, a change in the system of rowing
made it easier to build heavy galleys which could manoeuvre
with the light galleys. Under the new system all the oarsmen
on the same bench pulled the same oar [63] and it was therefore
comparatively easy to increase the number of men on each

[59] Newett, the Introduction, which is a well-documented history of this tourist trade, especially pp. 37, 85, 106-113.

[60] Museo Civico, Venice, Arch. Donà della Rosa, busta 217.

[61] Francesco Sansovino, *Venetia, città nobilissima et singolare* (Venice, 1581), p. 195.

[62] Jurien de la Gravière, *Guerre de Chypre*, II, 162-3.

[63] Meigs, II, 77-78. In 1534 large oars for three men to an oar were sent to the Captain General of the Sea to be tried out—A. S. V., Arsenale, busta 8, f. 37. The new system was introduced on the merchant galleys in 1551—*ibid.*, busta 10, ff. 5-6.

bench. Many efforts had been made before to increase the speed of heavy galleys by placing more men to each bench. Marino Sanuto the Elder writing between 1306 and 1321 to urge the Pope to a new crusade declared that galleys with four oars and four men to each bench had been successfully built by the Venetians before that time, and recommended their adoption in a new crusading fleet.[64] Two such " four-oared " galleys are again mentioned in a Venetian fleet in 1432,[65] and many of them were to be found in the Venetian Arsenal during the first half of the sixteenth century.[66] In 1530 Vettor Fausto, humanist shipbuilder, constructed a galley which was rowed with five oars to each bench; [67] in 1553 Francesco da Fiandra, Admiral of the Arsenal, was sure he had found a way to build a ship which would be faster than any other by placing two men to an oar and two oars to a bench; [68] and a suggestion was even made, though not by a shipwright, for a double-decked galley with oarsmen ranged on each deck.[69] But none of these systems was sufficiently successful to be copied, the idea of two decks was not even tried.

The introduction of one large oar pulled by many men placed the whole problem of propulsion on a new basis, for as many additional men might be placed on the same bench to pull at the single oar as the width of the galley permitted. Even if the extra men helped but little in pulling the oar, they might be useful in battle. In the late seventeenth century the galley of a commander sometimes had as many as eight men to a bench.[70]

The new system of rowing made it possible to increase the speed of the great galleys. The War of Cyprus, in 1571, had revealed not only their strength, but also their weakness. At

[64] *Liber Secretorum Fidelium,* p. 57.

[65] Bibl. Marciana, Venice, MSS. Ital. cl. VII, cod. 134, Chronicle of Gerolamo Savina, f. 224: cf. Senato Misti, reg. 58, f. 111.

[66] Sanuto, *Diarii,* V, 926, XXV, 538: A. S. V., Arsenale, busta 1.

[67] Below, chap. iii.

[68] Senato Mar, reg. 32, f. 114 and files, Nov. 17, 1553; reg. 33, ff. 142-144.

[69] Jal, *Arch. nav.,* I, 374-377.

[70] Marco Vincenzo Coronelli, *Navi e barche usate da varie nazione ne mari e ne fiumi* (Venice, no date), no paging.

Lepanto they had been towed into position, and in the manoeuvres of the next year the Christian armada frequently lost the
chance to force the issue with the enemy because of the time
they took trying to place the great galleys in front of the main
line so that they might repeat their performance at Lepanto in
disorganizing the enemy line.[71] The manoeuvre which succeeded at Lepanto had long been tried with round ships, but
with little success, since if the wind failed the sailing ships
could not take part in the combat.[72] The great galleys served
better since they could make some progress with their own
oars, but still they were too slow to operate easily with the
light galleys.

The slowness of the great galleys was seen to be due to the
shortness of the oars and the closeness of the outrigger frame
to the hull. This fault in their design had developed during
the period when they had been used as merchantmen and
their oars considered merely an auxiliary means of propulsion.
To give them the speed which they needed as battleships the
oars were lengthened and five men placed to each oar.[73] Such
a correction in the length of oar would hardly have been possible when each oar was managed by only one man. But with
the new arrangement the great galleys became warships
reputed to be, at the beginning of the seventeenth century, as
fast as the light galleys. They carried a load of seventy cannon. Eight were in the prow, ten in the poop, and the rest,
small pieces throwing a ball weighing three to five pounds,
were placed along the sides between the oars pointing through
ports in the parapets which rose from the outrigger frames.
Thus they were designed to fire a miniature broadside.[74] In
the military field as previously in the commercial, the great
galley attained a successful compromise between the long ship
and the round ship.

[71] Paolo Paruta, *Della guerra di Cipro* (*Degli istorici delle cose veneziane i quali
hanno scritto per pubblico decreto* vol. IV, part 2), pp. 247-248, 258, 309-325.

[72] Manfroni, *Costantinopoli . . . Lepanto,* pp. 72, 192-3, 225.

[73] A. S. V., Arsenale, busta 1.

[74] Meigs, II, 475; Pantero Pantera, *L'armate navale* (Rome, 1614), pp. 23-24,
45-50.

But the round ship finally achieved its ascendency over the long ship in war as well as in peace. Even as the full-rigged ship developed during the fifteenth century had displaced the merchant galley on the main routes of trade and travel, so finally the ship of the line displaced the war galley in the battle array, and the long ships at last yielded command of the high seas to the towering topsails and heavier broadsides of their sturdier rivals. But that change was not completed in the Mediterranean until later—when the Venetians had fought the last of their sea fights with the Turk.[75]

[75] The construction of "ships of the line" in the Arsenal of Venice was begun in 1660. Mario Nani Mocenigo, *L'arsenale di Venezia* (Venice, 1927, also in *Rivista marittima*), pp. 70, 77; C. A. Levi, *Le navi da guerre costruite nell'arsenale di Venezia dal 1664 al 1896* (Venice, 1896).

CHAPTER II

THE ROUND SHIPS

The sixteenth century round ships which displaced the galleys were so far superior to those which had been employed in the thirteenth century, when the great merchant galley had been introduced, that their rig would have appeared utterly strange to a navigator of that earlier age. On the other hand, it seems no exaggeration to say that the ship captains of the age of the great geographical discoveries, or even those of a generation before, would have had but little to learn before taking charge of a ship of Nelson's day.[1] During the two centuries in which the great galleys played an important part in merchant shipping, the fourteenth and fifteenth, these long ships had been enlarged and improved. But far greater had been the contemporary changes in the round ship. As Venetian shipbuilding and rigging reflected the influence of the Mediterranean tradition of which they formed a part, the history of these improvements in Venetian sailing vessels is interwoven with the still obscure story of the creation of the ships which achieved the conquest of the open oceans.

The " Roccaforte ", on which the crews of the Venetian merchantmen of the caravan of 1264 had taken refuge and defied the Genoese to come and take them, affords an example of the very large ships of the time of the Crusades. This type is here called a " buss ".[2] The " Roccaforte " was the largest

---

[1] Anderson, *Sailing-ship,* p. 115.

[2] Not to be confused with the vessels of that name used much later in the Dutch herring-fishery. For convenience I have adopted the old general terms " buss " and " cog " for use in the special senses explained in the text. The " Roccaforte ", described by Jal, *Arch. nav.,* mem. 7, was called a *nave.* But *nave* is too generic a term to designate the early large round ships, for it was applied also to later types. E. H. Byrne—*Genoese Shipping* (Cambridge, 1930), p. 5—gives *navis* and *bucius* as the two names for the purely sailing vessels of the twelfth and thirteenth centuries. The early Venetian maritime statutes lump together *navis, banzonus, buzus navis, buzo, buzonavis. Gli statuti marittimi veneziani* (eds. Sacerdoti and Predelli, *Nuovo archivio veneto, n. s.,* vols. IV, V, and separately, Venice, 1903), statuto di Zeno, chaps. viii-xi. *Tarrete* have a different statute. Cf. Vogel, I, 503.

of the ships offered by the Venetians to Louis IX of France in 1268 for use on his prospective crusade to Tunis. Her measures are given on that occasion, and show that she was a rather dish-shaped vessel, her keel being less than twice the beam of the ship, and the floor measure less than one-fourth of the beam.[3] These proportions were not characteristic of the smaller ships offered St. Louis—their keels were more than two and one-half times the beam. This contrast between the proportions of the large and small ships suggests that the only

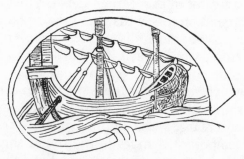

FIGURE VIII.   THIRTEENTH CENTURY ROUND SHIP.

Reproduced in Levi, *Navi veneti,* from *Capitolarium nauticum pro navis a. 1255,* MS. in Bibl. Querini-Stampalia, Venice.

method then known of shaping a ship as big as the " Roccaforte ", that is, of about 500 tons, was to increase its width at the top deck. The military effectiveness of the ship was enhanced by castles at the bow and stern which raised the fighting platforms thirty-nine and a half feet above the keel.[4]

The rig of the buss was much like that of the contemporary galley. She carried two or possibly three masts, lateen-rigged, of which the foremast was the taller. Its height was about the same as the length of the ship on deck, and its yard was even longer than the ship so that it must have stuck out over bow and stern when lowered. Four different sails were carried for use on the foremast and three for the second or middle mast.

[3] Cf. correction of Jal's cross section, R. C. Anderson, " Jal's Memoire no. 7 ". *Mariner's Mirror,* VI (1920), pp. 18-20.
[4] Jal, *Arch. nav.,* II, 355, 376.

They were changed according to the weather in much the same fashion as the sails of the mainmast of the galley. The rudders as well as the sails were of the lateen type. There was no rudder attached to the sternpost, but instead one projecting from each side of the poop. Figure VIII. The smaller vessels which figure most prominently in the thirteenth century merchant caravans, the tarettes, were differently shaped but similarly rigged and steered.[5]

While the Mediterranean tradition was increasing the size and elaborating the superstructures of these two-masted lateeners to meet the transport demands of the crusading armies,[6] the northern tradition developed an entirely different sailing ship, a one-masted square-rigged vessel. On the northern ships the one square sail served for all kinds of weather, the expanse of canvas being enlarged or decreased at need by the use of bonnets and reef-points. In tacking, the one square sail was managed quite differently from the lateen sails of the Mediterranean. With the lateen rig the same end of the yard was always pointed to windward. With the square rig either end of the yard, and accordingly either edge of the sail, might be pointed into the wind. A bowline was then used to prevent the " luff " or forward edge of the sail from curling away from the wind. Another and very important achievement of the northern tradition was the replacement of the side rudders by a rudder fastened on the sternpost.[7]

In 1303 Basque pirates from Bayonne brought such northern ships into the Mediterranean and opened the eyes of the Italians to the possibilities of this type.[8] The larger Mediterranean merchantmen adopted the square rig on the mainmast, and the attachment of the rudder to the sternpost. At about the same time, both in north and south, the castles at prow and

---

[5] *Ibid.*, II, 401, 431-436; *Gli statuti mar. ven.*, pp. 87-88, 168-170. Tarettes carried only three sails for the forward mast.

[6] Anthiaume, *Le navire; sa construction*, p. 46; Jal, *Arch. nav.*, II, 144-150.

[7] Anderson, *Sailing-ship*, pp. 85-100, summarizing many special studies by various authors in *The Mariner's Mirror*.

[8] Giovanni Villani, *Cronica* (ed. Francesco Gherardi Dragomanni, Florence, 1844-1845), II, 101.

stern were absorbed into the lines of the ship so as to appear an integral part of the hull. The resultant " cog ", Figure IX, was the type of large merchant-man used both in the Baltic and the Mediterranean during most of the fourteenth and fifteenth centuries.[9]

FIGURE IX.   ONE-MASTED COG.
From the *Fabrica di galere*.

This revolution in the rigging of Mediterranean ships produced an increase in the security and efficiency of transportation, for the cog was considered both safer and cheaper than the buss, or two-masted lateener.[10] The wide lateen sails of the buss, placed forward in the ship, were dangerous in case of a strong wind astern. It was for this reason that the later merchant galleys, although relying mainly upon lateen sails, carried a square sail to use under such conditions. The lateeners, especially the smaller and longer ships, were better able to sail to windward and handier for coasting voyages. But the big merchantmen stood out to sea and frequently had to run before the wind to ride out a storm. For example, the cog "Querina" of 420 tons bearing wine from Crete to England in 1431 ran into a storm at the entrance of the Channel which blew it way off to westward, " towards Iceland ", said the passenger who told the story. The sailors tried to ride out the storm but their sails were torn to pieces one after the other. For a time they cast anchor by throwing out their three longest cables fastened one on the end of the other, but the storm again grew so fierce that they were forced to cut their cables and run before the wind with a makeshift sail.[11] The square-rigged ship was more

[9] Anthiaume, *Le navire; sa construction*, pp. 46-52.
[10] Villani, *loc. cit.*
[11] Bibl. Naz. Marciana, Venice, MSS. It. cl. VII, cod. 368.

likely than the lateener to weather a storm under these conditions.[12]

Moreover, on a ship like the " Roccaforte " and on the galleys, it was necessary every time the ship went about to swing the yard around the mast in order to keep the head of the sail to windward. Aside from the danger involved, this had the disadvantage of requiring a large crew. So did the frequent lowering of the yard to substitute a storm sail for the fair weather sail. The cog, on which either end of the yard might be pointed into the wind, could be managed by fewer men. Though she must have been slow and clumsy, the cog was seaworthy and economical.

The remoter economic effects of the introduction of the new type would be difficult to estimate, but appropriate changes may be discerned in Venetian shipping. The labor saving is reflected in the maritime statutes of Venice. In the thirteenth century a 240 ton ship was required to carry fifty sailors. No soldier, pilgrim, or person under eighteen might be counted among the sailors.[13] In the fourteenth and fifteenth centuries, by contrast, the prescribed crew of a 240 ton ship was only twenty able-bodied seamen over twenty years of age, eight younger apprentice seamen, and four to eight bowmen.[14] The cog was supposed to have but about half as many men available to manage the rudder and sails as had been required on the buss.

A change in the size of the ships used for the transport of bulky commodities over long distances may also be associated with the introduction of the cog. At the beginning of the fifteenth century the ships generally used for the Syrian voyage had a capacity of about 300 tons and ships hired by the state for military purposes, usually the largest of the time, were a little over 400 tons.[15] The " Roccaforte " had been larger,

[12] Meigs, I, 310-312.

[13] *Gli statuti mar. ven.*, Statuto di Zeno, chap. 20.

[14] A. S. V., *Capitolare dei Consoli dei Mercanti*, chapters 200, 247, 250, 251. In 1426 ships going beyond Gibraltar were required to carry 8 men instead of 6 per 60 tons, but for the purpose of strengthening the defense of the ship. Senato Misti, reg. 56, f. 27.   [15] Table D.

about 500 tons, but the events at Saseno showed how much larger she was than the others in the Venetian merchant caravans of the thirteenth century. The " Roccaforte " was not a private merchantman, but a ship built by the state for fighting as well as for transport. A comparable ship built between 1422 and 1425 was of about 720 tons.[16] Moreover the " Roccaforte " was quite exceptional in her time. Only two others among the fifteen ships which the Venetians in 1268 offered to supply St. Louis approached her in size. The others, five built and seven to be built, were of about 190 tons.[17] This is in accord with the picture of the Venetian merchant caravans of that century suggested by the chronicles—many relatively small ships with galleys or a few very large ships for protection.[18] In the early fifteenth century, by contrast, there were the two types of caravans, those of merchant galleys, and those of round ships of about 300 tons.[19] The former arrangement was that of the age of the buss and tarette, the latter that adopted when cogs and great galleys had become the main carriers of international commerce.

Despite the superiorities of the cog on long voyages, it would be strange if the Italians, with their tradition of two or three masts and the continued example of their use on the galleys, had gone over unreservedly, in their building of big merchantmen, to the one-masted ship. A champion of the superiority of the northern tradition claimed that they did so, and that the next great change in the rigging of large round ships—the transition from the one-masted, one-sail cog to the " full-rigged ship " of three or four masts and five or eight sails—was altogether the achievement of sailors accustomed to the stormy Atlantic.[20] He argued that the Mediterranean peo-

[16] Senato Misti, reg. 54, f. 63. Notatorio di Collegio, Dec. 8, 1422.

[17] Jal, II, 355, comparing the measures of the others either with those of the " Roccaforte " or with those in Table C.

[18] Dandolo, loc. cit. On the sizes of thirteenth century Genoese ships see Byrne, pp. 9-11.

[19] Presumably likewise in the fourteenth century. Frescobaldi sailed to Egypt on a Venetian ship of 420 tons in 1384 which he considered large, but he gives no indication that it was exceptional. Viaggio, pp. 67-74.

[20] Hagedorn, p. 62.

ples, just because they lived about an inland sea, were quite incapable of developing types of ships of more than merely local importance.[21] Other historians of sailing ships are inclined to give the southern tradition the credit for the second

FIGURE X. CARACK.

From a painting by Carpaccio in the Accademia, Venice.

revolution in the rigging of large merchantmen, that which occurred about the middle of the fifteenth century.[22]

The new arrangement, the origin of which is in question, was that shown in Figure X. The type is that which is perhaps most frequently called a carack and was in very general use at the time of the discovery of America. The prominence of the mainmast, which was far larger than any other and car-

[21] *Ibid.*, pp. 1-3, 36.

[22] Anderson, *Sailing-ship*, pp. 116-124; Anthiaume, *Le navire; sa construction*, p. 64.

ried a very large square sail, showed the descent of the new
type from the cog. But there were now added a variety of
sails, all small when first used and probably adding but little
to the speed, but certainly contributing to the sailing qualities
of the ship by making it easier to tack and sail into the wind.
The small mast in the forecastle was square-rigged, the one
or two masts on the stern castle each carried a lateen sail. The
forward square sail made it easier to tack the ship, for it could
be raised for a moment as the ship came into the wind in such
fashion as to catch the wind on the side and swing the bow
over to the new tack.[23] The small lateen sails aft were especially helpful in enabling the ship to beat to windward.[24]
Above the crow's-nest on the mainmast there had been added
a small square sail, prophetic of the coming displacement of
the single deep-bellied mainsail by many smaller square sails
hung on as many yards on the same mast, a change that would
make the canvas stand flatter, the mast look higher, and the
ship stand nearer the wind.[25]

Such were the essentials of the rig which was revealed to
the Baltic ship captains by the voyage of the " Peter of La
Rochelle " to Dantzig in 1462,[26] and which had become almost
universal both in north and south by 1485. It was the decisive
step towards the full-rigged ship of many topsails and many
masts. [27] It may have been invented by the sailors of the Bay
of Biscay who had once before acted as intermediaries between
the tradition of the North and that of the Mediterranean.[28]
The earliest picture I have seen of the new rig is from a dish
which is considered Hispano-Moresque pottery work of the

[23] Anthiaume, Le navire; sa propulsion, pp. 57, 67, 94. He suggests that the forward sail was added before the mizzen sail.

[24] Hagedorn, p. 63.

[25] Meigs, I, 313-4, II, 523, 619, emphasizes the importance of this breaking up of
the sail area.

[26] Vogel, I, 475. The " Peter of La Rochelle " had flush planking which the Dant-
zigers found also a great revelation.

[27] Anderson, Sailing-ship, p. 115. Similarly M. Oppenheim says that sailing ships
of 1485 differed less from sailing ships of 1785 than they did from those of 1425—
A History of the Administration of the Royal Navy and of Merchant Shipping in
Relation to the Navy (London and New York, 1896), p. 40.

[28] Hagedorn, pp. 54-62.

second quarter of the fifteenth century.[29] A small square sail in front of the mainsail and a lateen sail aft are also shown on a Genoese drawing of 1465.[30] Wherever this three-masted arrangement may have been first employed, one element therein seems certainly to have come from the Mediterranean, the lateen sail aft, the mizzen.

Some of the Venetian merchantmen of the fourteenth and fifteenth century, even some of those called cogs, were two-

FIGURE XI. TWO-MASTED ROUND SHIP OF FOURTEENTH CENTURY.
Reproduced in Levi, *Navi veneti*, from Zanetti.

masters using the square rig on the mainmast and a lateen sail on a shorter mast aft. Such an arrangement is shown in Figure XI, which is based on a picture dated 1366.[31] Similar arrangements of masts and sails are indicated by the two shipbuilding treatises of Venetian origin dating from the first half of the fifteenth century. In the earlier of these manuscripts a " chocha " or " nave quadre " is described with an " arboro de mezo " only slightly more than half as tall as the mainmast or " arboro de proda ". The yard of this aft or " middle " mast

[29] R. Morton Nance, " Some Old-time Ship Pictures, vii, *The Mariner's Mirror,* IV (1914), 279-280.

[30] Francesco Podestà, *Il porto di Genova* (Genoa, 1913), p. 500.

[31] Cesare Auguste Levi, *Navi veneti da codici, marini, e dipinti* (Venice, 1892), dis. 98, cf. dis. 96. Most of Levi's pictures from this period are of one-masted cogs. In *Mariner's Mirror* are many " Notes " concerning the rig of two-masted cogs. See especially vol. X (1924), pp. 94-95, 214-216, 309.

is longer than the mast as would be expected with a mast having a lateen rig. Directions for a " mezana " are included among the details of sail cutting.[32] Such instructions for rigging suggest the common use of two-masted cogs at Venice before the introduction of the carack.

The rigging of early fifteenth century Venetian ships was but faintly prophetic of that which came into use at the end of the century. The hulls, on the other hand, already approximated the proportions and general form of those of sixteenth century merchant ships. The shipwrights had learned to build ships as big as the " Roccaforte " without making them inordinately wide. The proportion Keel = 2.5 × Beam now generally applied was that which remained characteristic for a century and a half thereafter.[33] The hulls of the round ships, like those of the galleys, consisted of a strong framework of ribs and clamps covered with flush planking. In a cog the hull curved up at both ends, more pronouncedly in the bow, so as to merge into the high forecastle and stern castle. The sides were curved inboard at the top so as to give the ship tumble home.[34] (Figure XII.) All these improvements, particularly that in proportions, show that the form adopted for the oceanic merchantmen of the sixteenth century had been attained before the middle of the fifteenth century. Thereafter there was no great change until the acceptance of Dutch improvements in the seventeenth century.

After this progress in construction came the yet more important fifteenth century revolution in rigging, the origins of which have already been discussed. Once the new system of three or four masts and more than one sail to a mast had been introduced there was rapid progress in increasing the number of sails. By the end of the sixteenth century Venetian merchantmen carried as many as ten sails, two square sails suspended from the bowsprit, three square sails on both the fore-

---

[32] *Fabrica di galere*, ff. 37-55, 88-90. In the second description the measures are in Venetian feet: Arboro de proda — 94½; yard 81. Arboro de mezo — 52½; yard 60. Cf. Anderson, " It. Nav. Arch.", pp. 155-6.

[33] Tables A and C.

[34] Anderson, " Ital. Nav. Arch.", pp. 149, 155.

mast and the mainmast, and a lateen sail on each of the two mizzenmasts.[35] But the crucial steps towards the new system of rigging had been taken in the fifteenth century. The period of most rapid progress had been before the exploration of the oceans.

The contrast in sailing qualities and seaworthiness between the thirteenth century buss and the sixteenth century carack—

FIGURE XII. SHIP OF 600 TONS ABOUT 1445.
From Anderson, "Ital. Nav. Arch.", *Mariner's Mirror,* XI, 149.

considered in connection with the contemporary progress in the art of navigation and the advantages which the development of heavy ordnance gave to the round ship—make it natural to expect that the commercial usefulness of such large round ships should have developed to correspond with so many technical advances. An increase in the tempo of voyages to Syria, a fall of freight rates charged on the main items of the return cargoes on such voyages, and an increase in the size of ships used, any or all of these changes may have been due to other economic factors, such as the increase in the quantity of

[35] Pantera, pp. 40 *et seq.*

goods to be moved or the better organization of markets, but they are at least in keeping with the improvement in ships.

In the twelfth and thirteenth centuries the merchant fleets left for Alexandria, Cyprus, and Syria twice a year, but the times of sailing of these convoys were so arranged that any one ship, although it took but about six months for the round trip, could make but one voyage to Syria and back each year. They could leave in March and return in September, or leave in August, winter in the East, and return next spring in time for the fair of the Ascension. Thus navigation in the winter months between November and March, traditional period of *mare clausum,* was avoided.[36] But in the fifteenth and sixteenth centuries the same ship usually made two voyages a year. Ships went out in January or February, not necessarily in convoy, loaded in the East in March, and arrived back in Venice in May or June. They left again in July, loaded in the East in September, and reached Venice in time for the Christmas fairs.[37]

With safer ships and more frequent voyages, lower freight rates might be expected. The most important items of bulk in the return cargoes of the Syrian voyage were cotton and alum. Stated in ducats, the freight on these two articles from Syria to Venice was 25% less at the end of the fifteenth century than it had been in the first quarter. There are other signs that freight rates on bulky commodities were declining generally in the fifteenth century. The competitors of Venice reduced by about half the charge for carrying wine from Crete to England.[38]

[36] W. Ashburner, Νόμος 'Ροδίων Ναυτικός. *The Rhodian Sea Law* (Oxford, 1909), p. cxlviii; Adolf Schaube, *Handelsgeschichte der romanischen Völker des Mittelmeergebiets bis zum Ende der Kreuzzüge* (Munich and Berlin, 1906), pp. 152-154.

[37] On the ship lists used for Tables D and F there are many cases of two voyages to Syria or Cyprus in the same year by the same ship. The danger of winter navigation was recognized by a law of 1569 which forbade ships to leave Venice or to leave Alexandria, Constantinople, or Syria to return to Venice between the middle of November and the twentieth of January. But that would not prevent the two voyages a year as described above. *Parti prese nell' Eccellentiss. Conseglio di Pregadi, con diverse leggi cavate dal Statuto in materia de navi e sua navigatione* (stampate per Gio. Pietro Pinelli, Stampator Ducale (no date), pp. 17-18.

[38] Appendix IV.

The fifteenth century increase in the size of merchantmen was such that by the middle of that century the Venetian Levanters were of about the same tonnage as the British East Indiamen of the seventeenth century. About 1400 the biggest Venetian merchantmen had been but little over 400 tons, but in 1450 there were six merchantmen of 600 tons or more in the Venetian fleet,[39] and at the end of the century there was one of over 1000 tons.[40] The size of the round ships built by the Signoria for military purposes underwent an even greater development. Such a ship of 2400 tons is reported in 1486, and while observers may not be trusted when describing ships so large as to be outside of the ordinary range, there are many reports of ships of 1800 tons in the Mediterranean about 1500. The Venetian round ships for war of that time were officially rated at 1200 to 1500 tons.[41] It was not found profitable to build merchantmen of such enormous tonnage, but 600 ton ships became more and more common. Introduced in the mid-fifteenth century mainly for use in the wine trade between Crete and England, they were commonly employed in the sixteenth century for the grain trade and the voyage to Cyprus as well as for the longer voyage west.[42] Their size will seem picayune if they are compared to modern liners,

[39] Table D.

[40] The following large ships in private hands are mentioned towards the end of the century (1 botta = .6 tons, see App. 1):

" Daniel Maducio ", building 1488, 1000 botte, Senato Mar, reg. 12, f. 148.

" Augustinus Maripetro ", built 1488, 1000 botte, ibid., reg. 12, f. 149.

" Nicolaus Coresi ", a Cretan ship of 1000 botte, ibid., reg. 13, f. 33.

" Zustignan ", sailing to England, 1491 and 1493, 1642 botte, ibid., reg. 14, f. 10; and Malipiero, p. 625.

" Sebastian Marcello ", built in 1496, 1085 botte, Senato Mar, reg. 14, f. 100; and Sanuto, Diarii, I, 504.

" Pasqualigo ", built in 1496, 1200 botte, Senato Mar, reg. 14, f. 98.

" Foscara ", sailing to England in 1497, 2500 botte, Sanuto, I, 81.

The " Foscara " is also reported as 3500 botte. She was lost on her maiden voyage. Sanuto, Diarii, I, 81, 668, 722, 846, 849; Priuli, I, 70; Senato Mar, reg. 14, f. 154.

[41] Malipiero, p. 623; Albertis, pp. 36-7; Manfroni, Costantinopoli . . . a Lepanto, p. 207; Sanuto, Diarii, I, 803; Priuli, I, 181; Anderson, Sailing-ship, p. 125; below Table E.

[42] Frederic Chapin Lane, " Venetian Shipping during the Commercial Revolution " in The American Historical Review, XXXVIII (1933), 238.

enormous if compared with the 100 ton caravels of the explorers. A fairer comparison is afforded by the East and West Indiamen of the next century, of which but few were over 600 tons. More generally these freighters of the seventeenth century ranged from 300 to 440 tons as did the Venetian ships trading to Syria in the mid-fifteenth century.[43] Granted the ability of the shipwrights to build large ships of sufficient strength—and the size of the warships is evidence that they had that capacity—one would expect the size of ship used on a particular voyage to be that found most profitable to the shipowners. The profitable size would, in turn, be determined in part by the length of the voyage and the assurance of quickly loading a full cargo. It is therefore indicative of the relatively early date of extensive Mediterranean trade in such commodities as salt, grain, wine, oil, and cotton, that Venetian merchantmen had already attained in the fifteenth century the size characteristic of the oceanic carriers of the seventeenth century.

The " ship of the line ", the sailing ship which was to be supreme in war, was developed in the North Atlantic. In 1660 when the construction of such a ship was first begun in the Venetian Arsenal an English ship was used as a model.[44] Possible contributions of Venetian builders to the creation of a type of round ship designed especially for war must therefore be restricted to the early stages in that evolution.

During the long period in which galleys were the backbone of the war fleet, round ships were regarded as valuable auxiliaries to an armada even though their dependence on the wind made it difficult to manoeuvre the whole fleet in such fashion as to give them an effective part in battle. Round ships were also used to patrol the seas and to hunt pirates, for when these enemies employed a large round ship they could be more easily defeated by ships of their own class than by

[43] Bal Krishna, *Commercial Relations between India and England 1601-1757* (London, 1924), pp. 330-360; Clarence Henry Haring, *Trade and Navigation between Spain and the Indies in the Time of the Hapsburgs* (Cambridge, 1918), pp. 261-263; Werner Sombart, *Der moderne Kapitalismus* (Munich and Leipzig, 1924), II, 279.

[44] Anderson, *Sailing-ship*, pp. 157-159; Nani Mocenigo, pp. 71, 77.

galleys. The defense of the " Roccaforte " showed that the high sides and castles of the round ship presented an obstacle even at that time to attacking galleys. These same features likewise figured in a combat of quite different issue between merchant galleys and a round ship in 1497. In that year the three galleys of Barbary were lying in the Bay of Tunis when there entered a notorious Biscayan pirate ship of about 660 tons, temporarily occupied on the peaceful errand of bringing a cargo of lances to the ruler of the land, but under the command of a corsair well known for his capture of Venetian merchantmen. At first only insults were exchanged. The pirates taunted the Venetians that they were poltroons, that even if they had five galleys instead of three they would not be dangerous. But on the arrival of a Venetian round ship, the " Lesignana," a new vessel of 300 tons, the noble commanding the Venetian galleys decided to turn his merchantmen into warships and have a try at the insolent corsair. He sent thirty men from each galley on board the " Lesignana," fortified it with extra parapets, and gave orders to hoist sails. When the pirates saw the Venetians making sail towards them they cut their cables and forced sail to get out to sea. A momentary lull of the wind enabled the oared galleys to catch their quarry and grapple. But even after the " Lesignana " joined the attack, the Venetians were unable in five hours fierce fighting to take the larger pirate ship by boarding. But meanwhile the caulkers who formed part of the crews of the Venetian ships had succeeded, by using the bottom boards of their ships' boats as a raft, in uncaulking three seams in the stern of the pirate ship. Then the commander of the corsairs, seeing many of his men killed and his ship sinking beneath him, offered to surrender if his life was spared.[45]

The great round ships which the state built for the express purpose of capturing such freebooters were desired as fast and as large as possible, and even when undistinguished by name from ordinary merchantmen they may have been extra

[45] Malipiero, pp. 641-643.

long in proportion to the beam as well as unusually large.[46] But the first great Venetian round ships designed for military purposes and differentiated by their name from the merchantmen were the *barze* of 1200 tons built at the end of the fifteenth century by Leonardo Bressan. Instead of the rotund bow of the merchantman, the *barza* had a prow which was lower, narrower, and straighter like that of a Spanish caravel.[47] In the narrowing of the bow it approached the form of the sixteenth century galleon, and the *barza* may have been one step in the development of this latter type.

Ships called *galeoni* had been built at Venice in the early fifteenth century, but they were designed not for the high seas but for service on the rivers in the Italian wars.[48] They were oarships, a hybird type which defies classification under the categories long ship and round ship. The first precise descriptions of rowed galleons are in a shipbuilder's notes of about 1550. In proportion to their breadth, their length was then slightly greater than that of the " great galleons " built for the high seas, and considerably less than that of the great galleys. Table B. Above their main deck was a " castle " or upper deck which ran almost the whole length of the ship. The oarsmen were within the castle entirely protected by its walls. The oars passed over an outrigger frame which projected from the sides a few feet above the main deck at about the point of the maximum width of the ship. Above, the sides of the ship curved inboard and rose above the castle or top deck to furnish protection to the soldiers who might be placed there. The upper works of the poop were narrowed and heightened so as to give to the stern something of the appearance generally associated with the Spanish galleons.[49] One is tempted to assign the characteristics of this rowed galleon to the ships of the same name built a century earlier, and to see in these river ships of the fifteenth century the precursors of the sailing warship typical of the sixteenth century.

[46] Senato Misti, reg. 54, f. 63; reg. 55, f. 65; Senato Mar, reg. 18, f. 71.

[47] Senato Mar, reg. 13, f. 83; Malipiero, p. 645. The first mentioned is in 1492.

[48] Jal, *Glossaire, s. v. galion*; Senato Misti, reg. 57, f. 182; reg. 60, f. 240.

[49] *Instructione sul modo di fabricare galere.*

The first galleon built by the Venetian state for service on the high seas was constructed between 1526 and 1530. While the name of the type suggests the influence of the river craft, the name of the shipwright, Matteo Bressan, suggests the influence of Leonardo Bressan, the builder of the *barze*.[50] The galleon of Matteo Bressan gave good service for many years, but the next two great galleons built for the state were fail-

FIGURE XIII. GALLEON.

Reproduced in Albertis from a Venetian portolan of about 1560. The sail plan corresponds to that of a model of a sixteenth century galleon in the museum of the Arsenal at Venice.

ures. Although their narrowness in beam and floor gave these ships straighter lines and greater speed than the merchantmen, these same qualities combined with the great height of the poop and the heavy load of artillery carried on the upper decks made them top-heavy and liable to capsize.[51]

Only among the larger vessels, merchantmen or warships, do types of general importance stand out with such clearness

[50] Sanuto, *Diarii*, XL, 672, 714; Senato Mar, reg. 20, f. 192.

[51] Senato Mar, reg. 25, f. 122, reg. 29, f. 125; Albertis, pp. 35-6; John Charnock, *An History of Marine Architecture* (London, 1881), II, 21-23; Crescenzio, pp. 63-73; Pantera, chap. iv. The war galleons must be distinguished from the commercial galleons built in Crete in the sixteenth century which used a lateen rig on the forward mast. A. S. V., Cinque Savii, first series, busta 25, f. 113.

and prominence as to make it possible to trace with any degree of assurance their historical development. The much more numerous types of smaller ships were largely of merely local significance, each type showing some peculiar features of build or rig which adapted it to local conditions. The pecularities of cog and carack were such as to fit them for the main routes of maritime trade. The greater profit which could be secured by using large ships on long, well established voyages made them the main carriers of that part of the trade of Venice which went beyond Crete and Sicily.[52] Moreover, these bigger ships offered better security against pirates, for they possessed fore-castle, stern castle, and crow's-nest, and the smaller types lacked at least one of these features. Accordingly the buss, cog, and carack had an international character and importance attained by none of the smaller types except, possibly, the caravel.

While the square rig had in the fourteenth century made the cog a superior carrier for long voyages, it had also made the cog definitely less fitted for coastwise voyages, for explora-tion, fishing, and cabotage trades. For such purposes a ship with lateen rig was preferable since it could be more easily tacked into the wind and brought into port. In ships designed for such purposes the bulging hulls of large cargo capacity could be discarded and the ship built lower and narrower so as to make it more easily handled. Because of their part in the great oceanic voyages of discovery, the Portuguese caravels are the best known of the small lateeners of this type.[53]

A large class of Venetian ships were also called caravels in the late fifteenth century and may have been of much the same rig as the Portuguese ships of the same name.[54]   About

[52] Ships of 240 tons and more were given by the Venetian government special rights to import grain from the East—Cessi, " Le relazione ", p. 105—and to freight salt in Cyprus—Senato Mar, reg. 13, f. 24; reg. 15, f. 145. The less defensible types of ships, *marani* and *marciliane*, were forbidden to sail beyond Zante. *Ibid.,* reg. 9, f. 19; *Parte Prese*, Aug. 13, 1602.

[53] Albertis, chap. ii.

[54] In the thirteenth century some of the tarettes possessed the characteristics and served the purposes of the later coasting types, but they had relatively wide floors so as to increase their cargo capacity. Sanuto (the elder), p. 58. But tarettes varied greatly in proportions so that some were called " nave-tarete " and some " galera-tarete ".

1500 these lateeners were the favorite ships of the Dalmatians, carried a large part of the Adriatic trade, and made voyages along the coast of Greece to Constantinople. They were mostly of about 120 tons burden. A smaller type similarly employed was the one-masted *gripo* which could use oars as well as sails.,[55] It raced the first of the Cretan wine crop to the Venetian market and made the trip in twenty-two days.[56] In contrast to these lateeners more manageable than the great merchantmen, there were other vessels used in the Adriatic trade which were clumsier, but which, being smaller and without the elaborate forecastles and stern castles, could more cheaply supply the city with oil, grain, wine, wood, and stone from nearby ports.[57] And besides the seagoing craft, the Venetian shipbuilding industry produced a great variety of pleasure boats and transports for the traffic of the lagoon itself and the inland waterways. Even a slight acquaintance with modern Venice suffices to reveal the large number of small craft which must have been needed by a city seemingly built upon water, where gondolas were used instead of carriages and barges instead of farm wagons.[58]

Heyck, *Genua und seine Marine im Zeitalter der Kreuzzüge* (Innsbruck, 1886), pp. 81-83; Jal, *Arch. nav.,* II, 221-223; Albertis, pp. 16-18; Byrne, chap. ii.

The *Fabrica di galere* of about 1410 gives instruction for only two types of round ships—" nave quadra " or " cocha " and " nave latina ".

Ships were classified for harbor dues at Corfu in 1503 as follows: " nave con balladori et cheba [castles and crow's-nest], 1 ducat; charavelle grossi, 16 grossi; schiraci et fuste con meza cheba [these types used both sail and oar], 12 grossi; gripi de mercandantie, 8 grossi ". Senato Mar, reg. 16, f. 19.

[55] Casoni, " Forze ", p. 223; Sanuto, *Diarii,* XV, 14; XVII, 69; XVIII, 413; LII, 14. Sizes from ship lists, see App. III. Mention of a *gripo* going to Constantinople with a cargo worth 12,000 ducats—Senato Mar, reg. 14, f. 54.

[56] Sanuto, *Diarii,* LIII, 522.

[57] Some of the tarettes, the " nave tarete ", may have been ships of this sort. Such also were the *marani* of the fifteenth century, ships originally used to bring firewood and building stone from Istria to Venice—Senato Misti, reg. 47, ff. 152-154—but adopted for more extended voyages. They were lateen-rigged, wider than *nave,* and without forecastles. Senato Mar, reg. 13, ff. 3-5, reg. 18, f. 71. In the late sixteenth century the *marciliane* carried most of the Adriatic trade. Some were as large as 240 tons. Before they were forbidden to sail beyond Zante, in 1602, there were 78 of them, in 1619 only 38. A. S. V., Cinque Savii, ser. i, busta 138, f. 56; busta 140, f. 154; busta 145, f. 33, 156. They were wider and rounder than the *nave,* similarly rigged. Pantera, p. 41 *et seq.*; Casoni, " Forze ", p. 195.

[58] For further discussions of ships peculiar to Venice see Casoni, " Forze ", pp. 189-209, and Pompeo Molmenti, *La storia di Venezia nella vita privata* (7th ed., Bergamo, 1925-1927), I, 230, and on the *bucentoro,* p. 202.

CHAPTER III

SOME FAMOUS SHIPWRIGHTS

The shipbuilders and sea captains of mediaeval times whose nautical inventions prepared the means for the circumnavigation of the globe will probably remain anonymous, buried in the same glorious obscurity with the inventors of the wheel and the compass and the devisers of alphabets. Even were it possible to trace the successive steps of a change such as that from the one-masted cog to the " full-rigged ship " the successive variations would probably appear so gradual that one would find difficulty in saying which was the crucial modification worthy of the name invention, and when even the exact time and place of these technical improvements are in doubt there can be little hope of discovering the inventive personalities responsible. So in Venice great achievements may have been made by craftsmen or seamen of whom no record survives. But a chronicler recorded the name, at least, of the constructor of the first great galley, Demetrio Nadal.[1]

Until the eighteenth century the shaping of a ship was the " mystery " of the craft of ship carpenters.[2] Except for one brilliant sixteenth century attempt to link science to this mechanical art, all the technical details of Venetian shipbuilding were under the domain of craft tradition. A small group among the shipwrights known as foremen, *proti,* designed the ships. Their craft was symbolized by the hatchet or adze, but it was not in skill with tools that the foreman ship carpenter showed his distinction so much as in his capacity to give the ship being built under his direction the proper lines and proportions. His wisdom was purely empirical, dependent on a keen eye and a knowledge of rough rules for determining the ship's proportions, formulas which had been tested by

[1] Casoni, " Forze ", p. 208.
[2] Bibl. Naz. Marciana, Venice, MSS. It. cl. VII, no. 1902, eighteenth century papers concerning the first influence in Venice of the theoretical studies made in France.

experience and handed down from father to son. So tradition created dynasties of celebrated foremen shipwrights. They did not form a closed group, for any ship carpenter was free to be chosen by a group of merchants to build them a ship, and so he might rise, at least temporarily, to the position of foreman. But, naturally, there was at any given time a group of masters abler than the rest who had a reputation among shipowners and were sought out when a new ship was to be built. The sons of these foremen, profiting by their fathers' reputation and instruction, were likely to succeed them. The members of such families were presumably better supplied with this world's goods than their fellow craftsmen, but their superior position depended not upon wealth but upon fame and skill. In the sixteenth century these foremen formed a comparatively educated group, well able to read and write. Some sent their sons to school to study Latin and mathematics.[3] But their knowledge of their art continued to be learned from craft tradition and experience. This experience was gained not only in the shipyards but in the forests whither they went to select the timbers needed for the vessels they had in mind, and on the sea where they served in a variety of capacities and occasionally rose to high positions as navigation officers.

Technical progress before the age of science and machinery was largely due to craftsmen such as these. Generally they can be known only as members of a group, but many foremen ship carpenters of Venice are personally revealed through their relations with the Arsenal. The affairs of the ablest builders of war galleys become affairs of the state, and some slight records of their careers survive while equally skilled framers of stout merchantmen had no such connection through which unconsciously to record their rivalries and triumphs.

The position of Foreman of the Ship Carpenters of the Arsenal carried with it the general direction of all the ship carpenters there employed.[4] While that responsibility implied

---

[3] A. S. V., Arsenale, busta 1, *Visione di Drachio.*

[4] The following list of Foremen is compiled from the *Quaderno dei salariadi*, A. S. V., Arsenale, busta 566, and the "Terminazioni", buste 133 et seq.: Mafio Lero, ?-1380; Jachomelo Jambon, 1380-1406; Jachobeli Bernardo, 1406-1424; Bernardo di Bernardo,

that the Lords of the Arsenal would select as Foreman the man
in whose technical judgment they placed the greatest faith, it
also necessitated their choosing, as head of their largest department, a person of proved managerial ability and probity. This
concern with the administrative duties of the Foreman may
have led them occasionally to pass over the most famous galley
builder in favor of someone more surely able to command the
respect and obedience of his fellow craftsmen. Whether for
that reason or some other, it happened that in the fifteenth
century most of the Foremen faced a rival whose galleys
enjoyed a greater reputation than theirs.

It would seem as though the finest galley builders of the first
half of the fifteenth century were still those masters who were
heirs to an eastern, Greek tradition, for during that period the
native Foremen were confronted by the rivalry of a dynasty of
Greek masters, Theodoro Baxon, or Bassanus, his nephew
Nicolò Palopano, and the latter's son Giorgio. Baxon was
already aged at the opening of the century. At that time the
Senate was moved by anxiety lest he die without having taught
Venetian craftsmen the secrets which made his ships superior
to all others of their class to vote him for life a salary even
higher than that paid the Foreman. Baxon's specialty was the
light galley. His innovation lay in making such warships
stouter vessels without an equivalent sacrifice of speed. Light
galleys of one type attributed to him were a trifle shorter than
the standard light galleys of the time—110 feet on deck
instead of $111\frac{1}{2}$ feet—but were equally high and wide and
of much heavier construction, having 95 frames or ribs in the
hull where the ordinary light galley of the time had but 84.
Other of Baxon's galleys were of the usual length but were
wider in the beam. These were so highly esteemed by the
governing nobility that in 1407 the Senate ordered that eight
of them be kept for emergencies and meanwhile serve as
models to other craftsmen. Some of them remained in the

1424-1437; Marcho Brando, 1437-1442; Giorgio il Greco, 1442-1455; Piero Bon,
1455-1466; Giorgio di Giovanni, 1466-?; Nicolò Vituri, ?-1498; Leonardo Bressan,
1498-1540; Francesco Bressan, 1540-1570; Giovanni Maria di Zanetto, called Zulle,
1570-?.

Arsenal until 1431 and the influence of Baxon upon the craft tradition at Venice was thus prolonged after his death.[5]

It is probable that Baxon died in 1407, for in that year the Venetians began their efforts to secure the services of his nephew, Nicolò Palopano, commonly called in Venice Nicolò the Greek. Nicolò was at that time employed in Rhodes and it was not until seventeen years later that he was finally induced to move to Venice. He was then paid 70 ducats on board a Venetian galley in Rhodes, and was promised a salary of 200 ducats a year—his highly paid uncle had received only 130 ducats a year—50 ducats extra to help him move, and a house at the expense of the state.

In 1424, the same year in which the services of Nicolò were secured at such great expense, Bernardo di Bernardo was elected to succeed his father as Foreman of Ship Carpenters in the Arsenal.[6] Rivalry between this new head of the department and the newly arrived foreign favorite was to be expected. Naturally the state encouraged competition between leading masters. In 1425 galleys of several different masters were sent to the fleet simultaneously to see which would prove itself the best. Besides ships by both Nicolò and Bernardo, there was one which had been made twenty-four years before by Baxon, and one which was the handiwork of a certain Leo, formerly foreman in Crete.[7] But that contest did not lead to a decisive judgment between the two rival masters. Each retained partisans among the nobility. For a time Bernardo, aided apparently by a general craft hostility to the foreign intruder, used his superior position to hamper his rival and prevent Nicolò from having the workers he wished to assist him. Nicolò's backers in the Senate interposed in his behalf to secure him such rights within the Arsenal as to make him quite independent of Bernardo. Thus there were two parts to the ship carpenters' department, each under a separate Foreman, one for the light galleys and one for the great galleys, for

---

[5] Arsenale, busta 566, *Quaderno;* Senato Misti, reg. 47, f. 109; reg. 52, f. 72; reg. 55, ff. 20, 81; reg. 58, f. 55; *Fabrica di galere,* ff. 81-82.

[6] Senato Misti, reg. 47, f. 155; Arsenale, busta 566, *Quaderno.*

[7] Senato Misti, reg. 55, f. 81, reg. 56, f. 1.

Nicolò, like his uncle, was more noted for his war galleys than for his merchant galleys.[8]

In 1432 the Senate ordered the construction of twenty galleys of the types *bastarde* and *bastardelle* which were neither as large as the great merchant galleys nor as small as the light galleys. Since they were intermediate types it was not clear whether their manufacture fell within the province of Bernardo or Nicolò, but Bernardo at the time had a greater reputation for building craft of this type so he was placed in charge. Thus for a while he overtopped his rival.[9] But in 1437 occurred the loss of the merchant galleys of the Flemish voyage, a catastrophe for which Bernardo may have been held responsible.[10] Certainly the favor of the Senate turned from him. In June of that year the Senate ordered that all galleys made in the Arsenal, great or light, be according to the designs of Nicolò and that those begun be changed over to his design. The Senate voted down, 72 to 49, an alternate proposal to place the two masters upon an equal footing.[11] The next month Bernardo's humiliation was completed when the Lords of the Arsenal unanimously expelled him. The galleys he had begun stood half-ribbed exposed to the weather for fifteen years before they were given to other masters to finish.[12]

Nicolò the Greek died within the two months after his triumph. His death had been an expensive matter for his son, Giorgio, who had paid heavily for doctors, medicines, and his father's tombstone. But Giorgio inherited the favor of the Senators. They gave him 150 ducats to help him out, and provided him with the same pay and the same independent position in the Arsenal which his father had held.[13]

The last of this dynasty of foremen, though he was known as Giorgio the Greek, had been so far affected by the Venetian tradition that his specialty was that peculiarly Venetian

[8] *Ibid.*, reg. 57, f. 201.
[9] *Ibid.*, reg. 58, ff. 111, 127, 136.
[10] See chap. I, note 41.
[11] Senato Misti, reg. 60, f. 17.
[12] Arsenale, busta 566, *Quaderno*; Senato Mar, reg. 1, f. 101.
[13] Senato Misti, reg. 60, ff. 31, 92.

type of vessel, the great merchant galley. He was engaged in building such a ship at the time of his father's death, and continued thereafter to be employed in building galleys for the Flemish voyage. He may well have been the ambitious master responsible for increasing the size of the merchant galleys from four to five or six hundred thousandweights, for it was precisely during the years that he was most active in building them that the Senate complained of their inordinate size.[14] But the greater size can not then have interfered very much with their general usefulness since merchant galleys of the larger measures, or " of Flanders ", were at this time replacing those of the smaller measures, or " of Romania ", on purely Mediterranean voyages. And when in 1442 it was decided again to build galleys especially designed for the coastwise voyage to Constantinople, master Giorgio was selected to build them.[15] His election by the direct intervention of the Senate in 1442 as sole Foreman of the Ship Carpenters was a fitting close to the distinguished services which these Levantine shipwrights had rendered to the Queen of the Adriatic.[16] After his death in 1455 both the Foremen and their rivals were alike of Venetian origin, perhaps because the Venetians had nothing more to learn from the East, perhaps because the appearance of a new naval power, that of the Ottomans, prevented the continuance of such migrations.

While these galley builders were winning fame and favor in the Arsenal, the masters specializing in purely sailing vessels were giving evidence of technical progress also by framing the larger round ships which came into use during the fifteenth century. Giovanni Bressan was one of the shipwrights who won a wide reputation by building such big merchantmen in the private shipyards. In 1470 the state gave him employment to prevent his being enticed away from the city.[17] Thus was attached to the Arsenal the family which

[14] *Ibid.*, reg. 60, ff. 41, 60, 87, 127, 130, 170, 202, 249.
[15] Senato Mar, reg. 1, f. 13.
[16] *Ibid.*, reg. 1, f. 101.
[17] Arsenale, busta 6, f. 3; Senato Terra, reg. 6, f. 118.

dominated its shipbuilding department during most of the sixteenth century.

Leonardo Bressan was Foreman of the Ship Carpenters for
the extraordinarily long term of forty-two years, from 1498 to
1540. It is indicative of the strength of family traditions of
craftsmanship that the ship which gained him the favor of the
nobility was a round ship, the *barza* built and armed by the
state in 1492 for use against pirates. Its commander praised
it so highly that Leonardo was immediately set to work on
another.[18] The second *barza,* ready in 1497, was reported to
be of 1200 tons, carrying four hundred and fifty men and over
four hundred guns. When the ship set out on its maiden voyage in April 1497 all the ambassadors assembled at Venice
for the forming of the league against Charles VIII of France
went to see it. The chronicler and diarist Marino Sanuto, who
serves as journalist of the time and to whom we owe much of
our knowledge of the everyday affairs of Venice between 1496
and 1533, described the new ship as " a castle . . . one of the
most beautiful things which has now for many a year been on
the sea ". When ordering the ship, the state had warned the
ambitious master against building a vessel larger than 720
tons, but Leonardo's ship was a success despite its great size.
The captain reported after two months on voyage that Leonardo Bressan might be content, it was a miraculous ship, that
of all the various vessels on which he had had experience
none was a better sailer, and that it was the best equipped to
carry heavy ordnance.[19] Accordingly, Leonardo was set to
work on another *barza* of the same size.[20]

But Leonardo was not only a very successful builder of
armed round ships, he was also, as was to be expected of a
Foreman of the Arsenal, a builder of great and light galleys.
He was superintending the building of eight great galleys and
some light galleys in the Arsenal at the same time that he was
in charge of the third round ship,[21] and it is to be presumed

---

[18] Senato Mar, reg. 13, f. 90.
[19] Sanuto, *Diarii,* I, 607, 767-773.
[20] Senato Mar, reg. 14, ff. 141, 196; reg. 15, f. 48.
[21] Senato Terra, reg. 13, f. 55. Of six of them, only the keels and half the stern-
posts had been laid down.

from his selection as Foreman that he had all along been building galleys as well as round ships. But his galleys were not equally successful. Although he had been chosen Foreman, it was another master, Marco Francesco Rosso, whose galleys were the most highly esteemed. In 1497 the Senate voted that Rosso's galleys were the best then made or which had ever been made, and that he be assigned docks, wood, and masters so as to have constantly building ten light galleys and two great galleys.[22]

The deservedly higher reputation of the galleys made by Rosso and the way in which the skill of a foreman in the Arsenal was judged and his fame attained are shown by Marino Sanuto's summary of a letter from the " Captain " of the Flemish galleys, written November 4th, 1498. " They left Cadiz October 21, were off Cape Saint Vincent October 22, at Lisbon October 23, off Cape Finisterre the 24th, and sailing towards Southampton with high sea and great wind, arrived off Southampton the 30th . . . and in two months and a half after they left Pola they arrived in Southampton and with only forty-two days of sailing which is a wonderful thing. . . ."[23] And the two other galleys suffered some damage in the storm but not his [the Captain's] which was made by Francesco Rosso, so he praised his galley and said that all should be made on its design because the other two were of the hand of Leonardo Bressan, present Foreman, who does not know how to make galleys."[24]

But the career of Francesco Rosso was cut short prematurely by a falling wall during the explosion in the Arsenal in 1509. Sanuto's account of that event gives so lively a picture that it is here paraphrased at length.[25]

After dinner I was in the Senate to hear a letter from Cremona about events at Milan. Suddenly the palace and houses shook and there were two great explosions of cannon and powder. Everyone

[22] Senato Mar, reg. 14, f. 101.
[23] Pola, Istria to Southampton is about 3000 nautical miles.
[24] *Diarii*, II, 187. I have translated " con gran fortuna e vento " " with high sea and great wind " although *fortuna* ought literally to be translated storm.
[25] *Ibid.*, VIII, 17-18.

ran towards the Arsenal. The Senators suspected a conspiracy and came down. Then they all went back up except a few including the newly elected Lord of the Arsenal whose possessions had just been unloaded there that day. I met the captains with four men accused of firing the Arsenal, some saying they were from Trieste and some that they were French. I saw many corpses drawn from the ruins, some without heads and some in pieces. They were being brought out on boards. Among them was Francesco Rosso, foreman, a most worthy man, and much mourned for the good galleys he made. It was rumored that Alvise Loredan, newly chosen galley commander, was dead, but it was not true. Sixty were reported dead. The stones of the walls fell like rain on the Arsenal and did much damage. But only twelve thousandweights of powder burned, because, by the Grace of God, but two days before four thousand barrels had been loaded on barges for Cremona. If it had been there the whole Arsenal would have gone. The explosion ruined many old houses around Castello but the greatest loss was the death of valiant men. There was a high wind. All the stevedores were called from the Rialto and San Marco. The Council of Ten examined the accused men till late into the night but found no reason to use torture. The Archbishop of Crete went with the others to look on. Being dressed in French fashion he was accused and almost put into prison before he was recognized. The Lords of the Arsenal were on foot all night directing workers who were kept in the Arsenal and supplied with bread and wine. Next day the true cause was learned from a half-dead worker. A spark from a hammer set off the powder. The storehouses of the Tana and the wall on that side were destroyed. In 1476, Dec. 9, there had been an explosion of the powder set off by a spark from a horse's hoof. Since then unshod horses have been used to work in the Arsenal. The damage was not as great as thought except the death of Francesco Rosso, wept by all. Next day he was carried to be buried at San Giovanni e Paolo and all the masters of the Arsenal were there to do him honor.

Even after the death of Francesco Rosso, Leonardo Bressan did not lack rivals. Either he was ill, or too old, or not sufficiently able for the task. For a while he was practically replaced by Matteo Bressan, apparently not his son, but possibly a younger brother. Matteo Bressan's ability had first been rewarded by the important position of Appraiser. When Leonardo was ill in 1503, Matteo was made assistant foreman to take his place, and he continued in that position until he became Foreman Mast-maker in 1525. Until his death in 1528 he was one of the foremost builders of galleys and round ships, and one of the technical experts whose advice was most valued and whose services were most in demand. His devotion to the interests of the state antagonized some of the other workers in the Arsenal. One night his house was broken into by some men with whom he had had high words in the course of duty. They did not injure Matteo as they intended, but they did break up all the things on which they were able to lay their hands.[26] His technical skill was so far recognized by the Lords of the Arsenal that in 1522 they ordered that twelve out of twenty-one new galleys be made under his direction, although none of the other expert masters then chosen to build was assigned more than one or two galleys.[27]

Matteo Bressan also took the lead in 1526 when the Signoria again desired to build some form of round ship to use against pirates. In the hearings before the College and Senate he figured equally prominently with Leonardo, and had ready a fine model of a galleon. The Senate decided that one galleon of 480 tons be made by Matteo and that two *barze* be built, one by Leonardo who, now that it was a question of round ships, was again in a field where he excelled.[28]

All three of these ships proved very successful, but the galleon of Matteo Bressan won the highest praise. In 1540 two more like it were authorized though not built, and when Matteo's galleon was finally declared unseaworthy and was torn down in 1547, the Senate ordered that its measures and design be carefully taken by experts to guide future makers of galleons.[29]

[26] Arsenale, busta 133, ff. 3-4, 16, 68, 82, 92. Sanuto, *Diarii*, XLVII, 227, records his death—. . . " homo ne l'arte soa excellente, et assa operato per la Signoria nostra. Fu sepolto honorifice a San Francesco di la Vigna." *Ibid.*, XL, 803, records that in 1526 a new galley made by Matteo Bressan on a new design was granted to a galley commander at his request despite the law against sending out new galleys.

[27] Arsenale, busta 133, f. 68.

[28] Sanuto, *Diarii*, XL, 672, 714; Senato Mar, reg. 20, f. 192.

[29] Senato Mar, reg. 25, f. 122; reg. 29, f. 125. Casoni, " Forze ", p. 230, gives some of the history of this galleon but credits the invention of the galleon to Fausto!

It was during this time, when Matteo and Leonardo Bressan were busy with their galleon and *barza,* that their position as the highest technical authorities on shipbuilding was suddenly threatened by a new and alarming competitor, a man who was not a member of one of the famous families of the Arsenal, who was not even a ship carpenter, but a humanist, a professor of Greek, who had lectured on Hesiod and Pindar.

Vettor Fausto, though of poor and obscure parentage, set himself while still young to the study of the humanities and became the pupil and inseparable companion of Gerolamo Maserio, public teacher at Venice. When older he traveled in Italy, Spain, France, and Germany seeking everywhere to learn and meet the learned. On his return he served Venice so well in war as to win the praise of the Condottiere Bartolomeo d'Alviano. In 1519 he won in public competition the post of public lecturer on Greek eloquence at Venice, and for the next six years performed the duties of that office amid the applause of his friends and the criticisms of his enemies.[30] The spirit of the new learning, the adoration of the Greeks and the Romans, was then at the height of its power, and literature, philosophy, and the fine arts had felt its exciting influence.

Vettor Fausto thought that naval architecture might similarly be improved. Accordingly he set out to make a quinquereme, and thus restore in shipbuilding the models of the ancients even as they had been restored in terrestrial architecture. Vettor Fausto was as well fitted for the task as a man might be, for he had studied not only literature, but also mathematics, and had published a restored text and translation of the *Mechanica* of Aristotle. But although he claimed to have found the measures for his quinquereme in the most ancient Greek books, he had also talked with the mariners of many nations, Catalans, Provençals, Normans, Basques, and

---

[30] A general account of the life of Fausto which follows the exaggerations of his humanist friends is given by Frate Giovanni degli Agostini, *Notizie istorico-critiche intorno la vita e le opere degli scritore viniziani* (Venice, 1754), II, 448-472. See also Sanuto, *Diarii,* XXVI, 52, 107, 127; XXXVII, 195.

Genoese, and with the leading commanders and builders of his time.[81]

Consequently in 1525-1526 when the College and Senate were considering what ships to use against pirates, and Matteo Bressan presented his model of a galleon, Vettor Fausto presented likewise his model of a quinquereme.[82] The round ships were the first ordered, but Fausto was assisted by the nobles in the Senate sympathetic to the humanists and continued to urge the quinquereme. Leonardo Bressan was uncompromisingly opposed, but Matteo Bressan praised Fausto's model, and in general the experts of the Arsenal were inclined to admit that the ship Fausto proposed would indeed be as strong, seaworthy, and fast as he claimed, provided he could arrange the rowers five to a bench, each with a separate oar, as he suggested, but they all agreed in saying that they could not see how that was to be done. Fausto confidently boasted, however, that he could make the fifth oar row better on his galley than did the third oar on the ordinary galleys.[83] Since only the system of rowing remained in doubt, the Senate voted that Fausto should demonstrate that to the College. If the demonstration was convincing, he was to be given a dock in the Arsenal and wood and masters to build his quinquereme; otherwise he was to have

[81] So Fausto stated in his petition to the Senate given by Sanuto, *Diarii*, XLII, 766-768, and in his letter to Ramusio in *Epistolae clarorum virorum, selectae de quam plurimis optimae* (*Coloniae Agrippinae*, 1586), pp. 128-133. As for his study of mathematics and his translation of Aristotle, they are mentioned in *Victoris Fausti Veneti, orationes quinque* (*apud Aldi Filios, Venetiis*, 1551), in the dedication written by Paulus Rhamnusius. The translation of Aristotle I have been unable to find, but it is given by Giovanni degli Agostini as follows: " Aristotelis mechanica Victoris Fausti industris in pristinum habitum restituta ac latinitate donata, Vaenundantur in aedidus Jodoci Badii. Imprimebat Jo. Badius ad nonas Aprilis M. D. XVII, in 4°."

[82] Sanuto, *Diarii*, XXXIX, 322. Jal, *Arch. nav.*, I, 377-384, discusses the quinquereme of Fausto. He also (*loc. cit.* and p. 279) describes galleys proposed by Picheroni which were to be rowed by oarsmen placed one above the other. Jal states that Picheroni also was trying to revive the ancient biremes, triremes, and quadriremes, but in Picheroni's MS. I have found no mention of the ancients. Marciana, MSS. Ital. cl. VII, cod. 379. Another example of the inventiveness of Picheroni is his petition concerning a mill he had invented. A. S. V., Prov. di Com., busta 5, December, 1565. I know no reason to think that Picheroni's galleys were ever built.

The quinquereme of Fausto is also discussed by Casoni, " Forze ", and *Dei navigli poliremi usati nella marina degli antichi Veneziani* (Venice, 1838), and by Fincati, *Triremi*.

[83] Sanuto, *Diarii*, XXXIX, 440; XL, 672, 714; XLII, 766; LVI, 995.

every facility for making over a *galea bastarda* so as to employ thereon his system of rowing.[84] When the College had seen Fausto's demonstration they voted that he build his quinquereme at once.[85]

In April, 1529, the quinquereme was launched. Most people said it would be a failure.[36] It was to be tried out in a race with a light galley, for its success depended on its capacity to keep pace with or pass an ordinary light galley or trireme despite its greater size, armament, and seaworthiness. Fausto himself was confident, and the race was well advertised. When on the twenty-first of May Sanuto saw the quinquereme leave the Arsenal with its full load of artillery he thought it was rowed right well and fast.[37] The race was held the twenty-third off the Lido. Sanuto describes the occasion: [38]

Therefore after vespers His Serenity [the Doge] invited all the ambassadors . . . and with boats and accompanied by many nobles went to the castle . . . where seats had been prepared under cover from the sun. And there were an infinite number of boats outside the two castles and throughout the canal, and today some gondolas have been paid eight or ten lire just to see such a thing. I saw many ladies in boats, and the Procuratori, and finally the Most Reverend Cardinal Pisani with the Archbishop of Nicosia. . . . Now at the hour fixed, when the signal was given, the said galleys came rowing, racing one with the other, and in front rowed the [trireme] " Cornera ", but when they had almost arrived at the castles the quinquereme was on the outside, and the "Cornera" hugged the land so close that the quinquereme passed it in front of His Serenity [the Doge] and so came ahead rowing as far as San Marco, with so many boats in the canal, and sails of large barks and fishing boats that it seemed like an armada. It was most beautiful to see. This quinquereme has [great] power in its oars, but is little ahead of the other

---

[84] *Ibid.,* XLII, 765.   [36] *Ibid.,* L, 227.
[25] *Ibid.,* XLIII, 112.   [37] *Ibid.,* L, 346.
[38] *Ibid.,* L. 363. I give the part of Sanuto's words which are difficult to translate, although I have done my best with them. " . . . et prima vogava la Cornara, ma zonti quasi a li Castelli, la quinqueremes era di sora et pense tanto la Carnera a terra che la passò devanti il Serenissimo et cussi vene avanti vogando fino a San Marco con tante barche per canal et velle de barche grosse state in pielago che pareva una armada. Fo bellissimo veder. Questa galia cinquiremi ha la sua vuoga ma è poco avanti di le altre galie sotil; sichè Vetor Fausto autor di darli il sesto sarà immortal."

light galleys, so that Vettor Fausto the author who gave the design for it will be immortal. And afterwards, when the Doge had returned to San Marco, the said quinquereme galley went rowing up the Grand Canal as far as Cà Foscari where it turned around, but with very great difficulty because it was twenty-eight paces long, and more than three paces longer than the light [galleys]. There were a very great number of boats in the Grand Canal, and I there among them, and the celebration lasted till evening.

Fausto was thus triumphant. His humanist friends, Ramusio and Bembo, exchanged enthusiastic letters celebrating this new conquest of the revival of Greek science, and describing how Fausto had at first restrained his rowers and how, when at the end he urged them on, they had easily passed the trireme.[39] The quinquereme was sent to the war fleet that fall under the command of Gerolamo de Canal, who wrote back an enthusiastic praise of it. Yet he did not claim that it was faster under oar than any other vessel, merely that very few could go faster. Under sail it was excellent. He recommended that ten quinqueremes be built for he claimed that with them at the head of a fleet of light galleys no enemy would be able to stand against it. Yet he added that they were not ships to use in ordinary times both because of their reputation and because of their expense.[40] The next spring Canal must have learned another reason why quinqueremes were not the ships for ordinary use. On the way to Crete he ran into a storm so that for fourteen days he did not dare to raise the awning which was ordinarily put up in the middle of the galley to protect the rowers from sun or rain. It was cold. The feet of the oarsmen were nearly frozen. Many of them died, and the quinquereme gained the reputation of a charnel house.[41] The high mortality

[39] The letter of Bembo is given by Agostini, p. 457, and is as obviously a description by one who was not there, as Sanuto's description is that by a man who was there. As a matter of fact the quinquereme had shown extraordinary speed for a ship of its size, but had not proved that it was faster than a light galley.

[40] His letter is given by Sanuto, LII, 594-595.

[41] Ibid., LIII, 118, and Visione de Drachio. Drachio says it was " un hospital, et un lazaretto, ansi uno spettacolo di morti, ne fu però detta sua galea migliore ne più presta delle altre ordinarie bireme ne trireme de quel tempo." Drachio might be accused of prejudice as a pupil of Francesco Bressan, but he goes on to praise the

was no doubt due primarily to the weather, but the weather is something with which seamen always have to reckon, and the crowding of the rowers which was necessary in placing so many men to a bench must have increased the mortality.

Perhaps for that reason, perhaps because of the expense, nothing came of Fausto's suggestion that he build five more quinqueremes.[42] But Fausto was a practical man and his mind was now absorbed in ships.[43] He was not limited by a pet theory, but was ready to adapt his large knowledge of mathematics and mechanics to practical circumstances. He recognized that his quinquereme was not going to replace the types of ships in use so he set to work to better those types. In 1532 he offered to build over the five *galee bastarde* in the Arsenal so that they could be rowed as fast and as easily with their four men and four oars to a bench as the light galleys were with three—increasing their height by building above the existing structures according to the art which he claimed had been lost since the fall of the Romans but which he had rediscovered. His offer was accepted with the understanding that if he did not succeed he was to restore the galleys to their former condition at his own expense.[44] Apparently he was successful because he worked for the Arsenal continually thereafter, and the ruling nobles gained more and more confidence in him. He proved himself a generally valuable man to have on hand.[45] When in 1536 he announced that he had found a new way to make light galleys using less wood—this time offering to save expense instead of increase it—the Senate ordered that three of his galleys be at once tried out and no more made till it was seen how well they served.[46] In 1543 he was given a galley to

intelligence of Fausto, who, he says, was much superior to the ancients, and adds that he was "buonissimo filosofo et scientifico delle lettere Greche, Hebrèe, et Caldèe." !

[42] Sanuto, *Diarii*, LVI, 623.

[43] In 1530 he had been assigned the building of a great galley of his design. Arsenale, busta 133, f. 107. He was also building *bregantini*; Sanuto, *Diarii*, LIII, 278; LIV, 548.

[44] Arsenale, busta 8, f. 26, and his petition, Sanuto, *Diarii*, LVI, 991-2.

[45] Sanuto, *Diarii*, LVII, 92-3, 141, 160.

[46] Senato Mar, reg. 23, f. 125.

test a new system of arranging the decks of the light galleys to make the rowing easier.[47] Not only did he devise new arrangements for rowing, which seems to have been his original invention and interest, but he also built such good hulls that those of his workmanship were in great demand and he was permanently assigned several docks in the Arsenal in which to build.[48]

Moreover he even tried his hand at a round ship. When in 1540 the Senate ordered that two more galleons be made like that of Matteo Bressan, one was assigned to Vettor Fausto.[49] But he did not live to finish it. That was only done on the eve of the war of Cyprus by a pupil of Fausto amid great controversy over the secure fastening of the sternpost.[50] But Fausto had here again begun too ambitiously, his galleon was so large and high as to be topheavy and unseaworthy.[51]

Did Fausto accept the task of a craftsman and shape with his hands the ships he designed, or did he merely instruct craftsmen who shaped the timbers according to his ideas? The Lords of the Arsenal in assigning him the building of galleys made no distinction between him and the other masters, but the ever helpful diarist Sanuto distinguishes, and when he says that the quinquereme was made by Fausto he is careful to add that Fausto made the design for it. Apparently the advent of Fausto to the Arsenal was the occasion for a temporarily complete separation between the workmen who made the product with their hands and the technical expert who made the plans. If such a sharp distinction had been permanent one of the essential properties of the craftsman would have been lost by the ship carpenters. But it was not. Those who inher-

---

[47] *Ibid.*, reg. 26, f. 160.

[48] Arsenale, busta 135, ff. 1, 70, 73. In 1544 he was first assigned 3 *squeri*, and then all the *squeri* in the second arm of the Newest Arsenal. Earlier in 1533 he had built a *fuste* of his design. *Ibid.*, busta 133, f. 142.

[49] Senato Mar, reg. 25, f. 122.

[50] Arsenale, busta 136, f. 94.

[51] Chronicle of Gerolamo Savina, Marciana, MSS. Ital., cl. VII, cod. 134, p. 328. Giovanni Casoni, *Guida per l'arsenale di Venezia* (Venice, 1829), p. 45, says that the model of a galleon there existent is of the galleon made in 1570. In that case it must be the one begun by Fausto many years before, although how Casoni knew the history of the model I do not know.

ited Fausto's ideas and skill, so far as they were inherited, were the master ship carpenters who had worked under him in the Arsenal.

Judged by his own standard, this humanist shipbuilder must be counted a failure. Fausto dreamed of winning fame as a second Archimedes, and remaking the shipbuilders' art by the study of the lore of the ancient Greeks and Romans, by mathematics and mechanics.[52] Therein he failed. His friends said he had died before his time.[53] Francesco Bressan succeeded his father as Foreman in 1540,[54] and by the middle of the century most of the light galleys were being made of his design.[55] Fausto had, however, won the confidence of the construction chiefs of the Arsenal. To them he was " the great Fausto ",[56] and it is impossible to estimate fully his influence upon the traditions of the craft.[57] But at least one important line of influence can be traced. At the end of the century, when the great galley designed for war, the *galeazza*,[58] had become

[52] So he expresses himself in the letter to Ramusio cited above. He praises the inventive capacities of man and asks what is the use of erudite letters if a man can not do something for his fatherland and friends.

[53] The preface or dedication to the *Orationes*. Giovanni degli Agostini says of the date of his birth merely that it was after 1480, and can place his death no closer than between 1537 and 1551. It has been shown above that he was alive in 1544. On the other hand, in 1549 a carpenter spoke of having worked with him for 18 years, but implied that he was then dead. He had begun work on the quinquereme in 1528 and 18 years would bring his death in 1546 or later. He can not then have been very young when he died.

[54] Arsenale, busta 135, f. 43; Senato Mar, reg. 21, f. 73.

[55] As a rule carpenters built on Bressan's designs. Senato Mar, files, September 29, 1548; December 21, 1553; April 29, 1563. See also Senato Mar, reg. 37, f. 79; Arsenale, busta 10, f. 22, and busta 11, ff. 1, 16. Apparently some of his were too large to be rowed by galley slaves.

[56] Drachio has Francesco Bressan refer to him as " el Gran Fausto."

[57] Surian—MS. Museo Civico, Donà della Rosa, busta 153—refers to him equally with Bressan, as an authority on galley construction. Casoni, " Forze," p. 228, says he gave his name to the *timone alla ponentina*. According to a photostat of a part of a Venetian MS. of 1686 in the British Museum, Add. 38655, furnished me by the courtesy of Mr. R. C. Anderson, the rudder which was curved to fit the curved sternpost of the galley, a rudder essentially similar to that in Figure III of c. 1410 when it was called the *timone bavonesche*, was in 1686 associated with the " pupa alla Faustina". The " pupa alla ponentina ", i. e. western fashion, presented a straight sternpost to which to attach the rudder.

[58] There was no sharp distinction in the use of the two terms *galea grossa* and *galeazza*, but the latter seems generally to be applied to the warship and I so use it here. Cf. Manfroni, *Costantinopoli . . . Lepanto*, p. 183.

quite distinct from the few great galleys still used in trade, there was a great interest in the possibility of making these heavy warships with their valuable load of guns as mobile as the light galleys. The shipwright chiefly consulted was Giovanni di Zaneto who had succeeded Francesco Bressan as Foreman at the latter's death in 1570.[59] Giovanni prided himself on being the pupil of Fausto, and in his report on the question, dated 1593, he recalled the quinquereme and attempted to apply the principles which had been responsible for her speed to the new war galleys, although they were rowed very differently than in Fausto's time. Fausto had arranged five oars to a bank with one man to each oar. In the new *galeazze* many men pulled at the same oar. But in either case the mechanical problem involved in deciding the length of the oars, and the locations of the oarlocks and the rowers' benches was but an application of the principle of the lever. In his knowledge of that principle, at least, Fausto's theoretical training had given him an advantage over the purely empirical craftsmen. So the government again turned to a theorist and sought advice from an authoritative source, from their local professor of mathematics, Galileo Galilei.[60] These tenuous links connect Fausto's dream of a quinquereme and the celebrated Venetian *galeazze* of the seventeenth century.

[59] Senato Mar, reg. 34, f. 114; reg. 36, f. 72; files March 31, 1557, August 28, 1563; Arsenale, busta 136, ff. 93, 94, 102.
[60] Papers in Arsenale, busta 1, and in the Sala Margherita, A. S. V.

CHAPTER IV

THE CRAFT GUILDS

While some of the members of the dynasties of foremen who formed the aristocracy among the shipbuilding craftsmen may be known individually, the lives of the mass of the workers can only be glimpsed through a study of the industry in which they made their living and of the guild organizations which gave expression to their collective interests. At Venice guilds never attained the political importance which they possessed in some other mediaeval cities. The firm rule of the oligarchy of merchant princes deprived them of any influence in affairs of state, and limited their activities to the performance of religious and vocational functions and the furnishing of social insurance to members. Though the records of the guilds may seem, therefore, to afford only a tale of petty professional quarrels, humdrum problems of sick benefits, and trivial devotions, yet they are the expression of the laborer's constant concerns—of his desire for worship, for help in illness and old age, for companionship, and for work.

The Venetian guilds were the result of the amalgamation of two institutions distinct in purpose and origin. The earlier was the *scuola*, a society of devotion. The *scuola* existed for common worship, assistance, and banqueting. The second was the *arte,* an association for maintaining craft discipline, for regulating the professional activity of the workers and settling minor disputes among them, and for insuring the performance of the labor which was owed to the Doge or commune. The institution of the *arti* had been effected by the state in order that the craftsmen might all be supervised by the Justices who were appointed by the state for that purpose. The *scuole* had existed long before as societies of devotion. But when the *arti* were created the two institutions became fused. They had the same elected officers and both were sub-

72

ject to the jurisdiction of the Justices.[1] All the craftsmen in Venice were required to join the appropriate *arte* by swearing to the statute of their craft. But not all who came from other lagoon cities to Venice to work became members of a *scuola*.[2] Moreover, it was still possible for the craftsmen to form a *scuola* for worship or mutual assistance distinct from the *scuola* of their craft. But, as a rule, by the end of the thirteenth century, the *scuola* and the *arte* were but two phases of one and the same organization of the workmen here called the guild. The shipbuilding craftsmen were from an early date organized into three such guilds—that of the ship carpenters, that of the caulkers, and that of the sawyers.

Throughout the organization and activity of the guilds appear traces of their double character. From one point of view they were branches of the state or city administration through which the government, or the ruling oligarchy, enforced its will upon the craftsmen. From another point of view they were associations of craftsmen for the furtherance of their own interests. The " gastaldo," the officer at the head of the guild, acted as representative of the craftsmen in disputes between guilds, in the care of guild property, and in the collection of dues, but he was also the representative of the Signoria responsible for the fulfillment of the obligations of the masters to the state and for the enforcement among them of the regulations which the state officials had made or approved. He was assisted by boards of judges and deacons—the judges to aid him in deciding disputes, the deacons to help in the management of the guild's property. There was also a steward who had more immediate charge of the possessions of the guild. The gastaldo and judges were required to be at their places at the booth of the craft at San Marco every Sunday morning to hear such cases as might be brought before them. The guild officials were not elected by the craftsmen, but

[1] Molmenti, vol. I, chap. v; *I capitolari delle arti veneziane sottoposte alla Giustizia e poi alla Giustizia Vecchia dalle origine al MCCCXXX* (ed. Giov. Monticolo, *Fonti per le storia d'Italia*, Rome, 1896-1914), vol. II, pp. xxi and cviii.

[2] *Ibid.*, pt. I, " Capitulare de marangonis ", chaps. 5, 8, 16, 39, 54, 56, 57; " Capitulare callefatorum ", chaps. 20, 36, 47, 52, 56, 76.

selected indirectly by the retiring officers. Redress against them might be had by bringing suit before the Justices.[3]

The business meetings of the guild were limited by the government to two a year. On these occasions the reports of officials were received, new officers installed, and the guild statute to which all had sworn was read to the masters and additions were suggested.[4] The handsomely written and illustrated volume which contained the statute of the guild was one of its most treasured possessions. That of the caulkers had a silver cover weighing 79 ounces, 1 quarto, 18 carats, and its manufacture had cost 50 ducats.[5]

At only one of the meetings was a banquet permitted and any remains from the banquet had to be sold and the money distributed among the poor of the craft. No food could be taken out from the banquet save one platter to each of the officers. The profusion of public festivals for which Venice was for centuries famous partially compensated for these restrictions on the private festivities of the guilds. The state both cultivated and regulated the love of pageantry and *feste* so as to focus it upon the glory of the Republic and its protector, San Marco. Guilds took a large part in some of the ceremonies. In that called the *convito all'arti* each guild decked out its own booth in the Piazza, and the Dogaressa circled the square going through the forms of partaking of the hospitality of all the guilds.[6] But the most brilliant displays and the most prominent places in the pageants went naturally to the richest guilds, not to those of such day laborers as formed most of the membership of the shipbuilding crafts. Ship carpenters and caulkers did occupy places of honor and prominence on public occasions, but mainly through their connection with the Arsenal. It was as *arsenalotti*, not as guildsmen, that they obtained their full part in the pageantry of the Republic.

[3] *Ibid.*, "Marangonis", chaps. 11-21, 40, 41, 43, 44, 69; "Callefatorum", chaps. 14-15, 17, 22-25, 36.
   [4] *Ibid.*, "Marangonis", chaps 20, 32, 44, 61; "Callefatorum", chaps. 27, 40.
   [5] B. Cecchetti, *Mariegole dei Calafai* (Venice, 1882), p. 16.
   [6] Sansovino, pp. 151-157; Molmenti, I, 159-162. *I capitolari,* "Marangonis", chaps. 5, 62; "Callefatorum", chaps. 46, 74-75.

The religious activities of the guilds were more extensive. Each guild was especially attentive to certain saints before whose shrines its members burned candles. The money collected for this purpose, the *luminaria,* became a regular part of the guild dues, and, in the case of the ship carpenters, was deducted from the pay of the masters by the foremen or employers.[7] About 1600, the caulkers and carpenters, following the example which had been set them by the oarmakers, permitted the wives of members to take part in these devotions as sisters of the guild by paying entrance fees and the *luminaria.* But the women were limited, at least by the carpenters, to one candle and one saint.[8]

The guilds possessed chapels, tombs, and altars with their religious ornaments. The guild of the caulkers by contract with the monastery of San Stefano in 1454 acquired in the refectory of the monastery a place of meeting and in the church the site of an altar and of a tomb.[9] In 1455 a special tax was laid on the members to be used in building the altar and decorating its chapel.[10] For the honor of God, the praise of the guild, and the good reputation of the men of the craft, it was added to the duties of the gastaldo in 1461, that on the day of San Marco he was to call all the men of the guild to Mass, solemnly prepare the altar, and hire trumpeters and two pipers for the celebration of that Mass.[11] Among the religious objects possessed by the guild in 1578 were an image of the Holy Eternal Father figured in gilded silver holding the world in his hand, and a Holy Cross of Christ Crucified with various saints at his feet, among whom was San Marco distinguished as ever by the Book and the Lion, and San Fosca, the patron of the craft, holding a ship in his hand—all done in gilded silver

---

[7] Arsenale, busta 6, ff. 13-15. Caulkers provided that if the *luminaria* of 4 *s.* a year was not paid, the delinquent would be cut off from the *scuola* and receive no earthly aid in this life, nor prayers after death. Bibl. Naz. Marciana, MSS. It. cl. VII, cod. 560, *Mariegola dei calafai,* cited hereafter as Marciana *Mariegola,* chaps. 39, 46.

[8] The carpenters in 1583, A. S. V., Arti, busta 706, *Cap. dei squerarioli,* f. 16; the caulkers in 1604, Marciana *Mariegola,* f. 95.

[9] Cecchetti, *Mariegole dei calafai,* p. 3.

[10] Marciana *Mariegola,* f. 32.

[11] *Ibid.,* f. 35.

and studded with precious stones.[12] The guild of the caulkers also provided in their statute that each member must say twenty-five Ave Marias and twenty-five paternosters for each brother who died.[13] The guild of the sawyers required only five Ave Marias and five paternosters.[14] All guilds required that their members accompany to the church the bodies of those departed and remain in attendance to do them honor until the body had been buried.[15]

Thus a large amount of the money collected by the guild from its members was spent on religious objects and services. The greater part of it, however, was devoted to providing various kinds of social insurance. The provision for old age or unexpected misfortune which may now be sought through savings accounts, insurance policies, or governmental systems of social insurance was furnished to workers in that age by their guild organizations. To the best of its capacity each of the guilds supplied its members with sick benefits, dowries for marriageable daughters, old age pensions, and burial expenses.[16]

For caulkers and carpenters old age pensions were provided at the expense of the employers. At first this took the form of requiring every foreman or shipowner who hired six masters to include among them one master over fifty-five years of age. These old masters were known as veterans. If he who hired the masters failed to take one of the veterans the gastaldo of the craft might assign him one.[17] As long as there was no provision for how much the veterans were to be paid, the shipowners or foremen naturally paid them just what they pleased,

---

[12] Cecchetti, *Mariegole*, p. 16.

[13] Marciana *Mariegola,* cap. 25.

[14] Museo Civico Correr, Venice, MSS. Mariegole, no. 185, larger vol., chap. 17.

[15] *I capitolari,* " Marangonis ", chap. 66; " Callefatorum ", chap. 58.

[16] *Ibid.,* " Marangonis ", chap. 43; Marciana *Mariegola,* ff. 35, 67, 89. The guild of ship carpenters had hundreds of ducats invested in state funds, 500 ducats of which were reserved to provide dowries for daughters. A. S. V., Arti, busta 706, *Cap. dei squerarioli,* ff. 10-15; Giustizia Vecchia, busta 2, reg. 4, ff. 73-4. In 1578 the caulkers had 700 ducats deposited in the mint. Cecchetti, *op. cit.,* p. 16.

[17] *I capitolari,* " Marangonis ", chaps. 77-78; Senato Misti, reg. 47, f. 149; Marciana, MSS. It. cl. VII, cod. 560, chaps. 55, 56. This *mariegola* of the caulkers is generally cited as Marciana *Mariegola.*

and consequently it was necessary to stipulate that the veterans must be paid the wage which was given the best worker.[18] Then the employers of the masters naturally selected the veterans they hired from among the strongest and ablest so that the weakest and neediest lacked employment, and the obligation to hire veterans failed of its intention of providing for the old age of the craftsmen who most needed help. Accordingly the guild ruled that the veterans must be taken by rotation each in his turn.[19]

Special complications were encountered in the effort to make the heads of small shipyards, who needed but few masters to help them, bear their share of the support of the veterans. They would have escaped entirely if they had had to employ them only when hiring as many as six masters. Therefore they were required to employ one veteran whenever they had three masters at work including themselves.[20] Presumably they could pass along the additional expense to their customers. But the veteran they were to employ changed with each new job which came to them, according to the rotation system, so they complained that they were compelled to run every hour to the booth of the gastaldo at San Marco to take a new veteran and thus lost time on their work. To meet that difficulty they were allowed to employ the same veteran or veterans for the whole week.[21] But still the hiring of the veterans was a nuisance, and this obligation was transformed about 1440 into the obligation to pay a tax to the guild for the veterans according to the number of workers employed.[22]

The guild of the sawyers was also in a general way charged

---

[18] *Ibid.*, chap. 60. Since the *mariegola* of the ship carpenters is not to be found, the information concerning provisions for veterans comes almost entirely from the *mariegola* of the caulkers. But the few extracts that can be found from the *mariegola* of the ship carpenters indicate that the evolution was the same in both cases.

[19] *Ibid.*, chap. 62.

[20] *Ibid.*, chap. 58.

[21] *Ibid.*, chap. 66.

[22] *Ibid.*, ff. 23-4; Arti, busta 706, *Cap. dei squerarioli*, f. 11. This provision for veterans in the form of a tax was extended to cover all the caulkers and carpenters in the Dogado so that workers outside Venice might not underbid those of Venice. In 1571 the caulkers provided that no one might receive the pension of a veteran unless he was 60 years of age and had paid 38 *luminarie*. Marciana *Mariegola*, ff. 29, 87.

with the care of the old and sick,[23] but theirs being a rather
precarious craft, and many of the masters continually on the
move, thirty-seven or more of the guild members led by the
gastaldo decided in 1524 to form a " fraternity " within the
craft, consisting of some but not all the masters, for the special
purpose of providing for sickness and accident. Although the
statutes of the fraternity provided that every brother master
who died should have a Mass said for the remission of his
sins in the church of his choice, yet save for that one provision
the fraternity was purely a mutual insurance association, and
is of special interest in presenting in detail the features of such
an association unconfused by mixture with any other functions
of the guilds. Its officers were a steward or *masser,* and six
compagni who collected, kept, and distributed the funds of the
association. To prevent family coalitions from dominating the
election to such offices, the electors were chosen by drawing
red and white balls from a hat. Those who drew red balls
chose the steward, those whe drew white chose his companions.
The *masser* and *compagni* were to be at the booth of the association in San Marco every Sunday morning to receive the
weekly fees of one *soldi* from each member who had been able
to work the past week. Beside the weekly fees there was an
entrance fee of 30 *soldi.* The weekly fees had to be paid in
person and whoever fell so far behind in these payments as to
be in debt to the association for the sum of 16 *soldi* was expelled from the association.

The money was kept in a strong box to which there were
three keys, one kept by the steward, one by the gastaldo of the
craft if he was in the fraternity, and one by a third man
selected for the purpose. During the first year no money was
paid out. Thereafter aid was to be given to the suffering. The
expected causes of suffering were disease, the pest, a fall during work, and injuries from falling timbers or from tools.
The sick sent word to the steward to his booth in San Marco,
and the steward and his companions went to see if the illness
was such as to require alms. If they decided it was, the steward

[23] Museo Civico, Mariegole no. 185, larger of the two volumes, cap. 27.

brought the sick member 40 *soldi* a week—about one-third of a week's wage working by the day at the Arsenal—beginning five or six days after the illness and continuing for eight days after he was up and out of the house. Whenever the funds of the association were reduced to less than 50 lire the steward could levy 20 *soldi* on each of the members. A member who wished to withdraw from the fraternity would not receive back any money. Any one member might prevent any alteration of the statutes of the association.[24] By such a special association some of the sawyers sought to obtain the protection against misfortune which the caulkers and ship carpenters presumably received from their richer craft guilds.

The guilds existed not only to provide for their members against the misfortunes of this world and to better their chances in the next, but also to improve the conditions of employment. The early statutes of the carpenters and the caulkers did not go much further than to lay down certain elementary rules of fair play between the employer and the craftsman. Craftsmen who worked by the day were required to be at their work promptly at the customary hours,[25] and if they only worked a half day Saturday they were to be given but a half day's pay.[26] A master who had agreed to do a certain piece of work and had been paid in advance might not leave his employer before the work was done. If he did, the gastaldo of the guild could compel him to return and finish the job.[27] An employer might not dismiss his workers before the end of the week unless all the work was finished.[28] If an employer failed to pay the workers as he had agreed, the gastaldo might forbid any master of the craft to work for him.[29] If an employer had given work to a carpenter under a contract to do it at a certain price, that carpenter must himself

---

[24] *Ibid.,* the smaller of the two volumes, ff. 1-9.

[25] *I capitolari,* " Marangonis," chap. 83.

[26] *Ibid.,* chap. 9. That is for the carpenters; the caulkers were required to work all day Saturday. " Callefatorum ", chap. 28.

[27] *Ibid.,* " Marangonis ", chaps 3, 33. Callefatorum ", chap. 9.

[28] *Ibid.,* " Callefatorum ", chap. 50; and Marciana *Mariegola,* chap. 22.

[29] *I capitolari,* " Marangonis ", chaps. 2; " Callefatorum ", chap. 9; Marciana *Mariegola,* chap. 34.

do the work, hiring other masters as there was need, but he could not sublet the job to other masters.[30] Every master was obliged to inform the shipowner of any flaws that he might find in the material on which he worked,[31] and the gastaldo of the craft was responsible for informing the employer which masters did inferior work and were accordingly to be paid less.[32] But there were very few provisions for insuring the high quality of the work done, presumably because those for whom these craftsmen worked were sufficiently informed to hold the masters up to a high standard. The reason given for forbidding the caulkers to work by the job was that when they worked by the day the employer could have the work done in the way that he wished.[33]

The early statutes of the sawyers' guild fixed in detail the piecework rates for which sawyers were to work, and it was a rule of the craft that larch and pine should not be sawed otherwise than at so much per piece.[34] The early statutes of the carpenters and caulkers, on the other hand, left the masters free to make their own terms with their employers. If they did the work before agreeing with their employers as to their wages, they were forced to take whatever the latter chose to give them.[35]

In 1460 the amount of freedom thus left the masters for individual bargaining no longer proved advantageous to the caulkers. That was at the beginning of a slackening of activity in the Venetian shipyards. As the caulkers described the situation in that year, the shipowners agreed together, ten or twelve of them, not to pay more than a certain wage. Thus they drove wages so low that the caulkers could not make a liv-

---

[30] I capitolari, " Marangonis ", chap. 33.

[31] Ibid., " Marangonis ", chap. 67, " Callefatorum ", chap. 7.

[32] Ibid., " Callefatorum ", chap. 16. In the Mariegola dei Calafai at the Marciana, f. 24, under date 1444 is a regulation that the caulkers might not leave a job till it was well done and then the Justices were to go to the shipyard and see by the aid of experts that it had been well done, and if not the worker was to be fined 25 l. But no more is heard of such an inspection of their work as would be expected if it had been enforced, and it seems an unreasonably heavy demand upon the time of the Justices.

[33] I capitolari, " Marangonis ", chap. 46; " Callefatorum ", chap. 33.

[34] I capitolari, vol. II, pt. 1, " Seccatorum ", chaps. 4 et seq.

[35] I capitolari, " Marangonis ", chaps. 4, 71, " Callefatorum ", 72.

ing. If the caulkers objected and attempted to force higher wages by mutual agreement on their part, the shipowners accused them of conspiracy. The caulkers met the situation by suggesting that they be hired in rotation and that the state should fix a fair wage, remembering that because of bad weather they had employment only half the year. All the names of the craftsmen were to be put in a sack by the gastaldo and whenever a shipowner or a foreman wished to hire caulkers he was to go to the booth of the craft at San Marco, put his hand in the sack, and take out as many slips as he needed men. Whichever men's names were on the slips he was to be compelled to hire, and they were to be compelled to work for him. The Justices and the Board of Manufactures approved this arrangement and fixed a wage scale.[36] Thus the caulkers arranged to distribute among them whatever work there was to be had, and all those employed on a particular task except the foreman changed every week. The freedom of a shipowner to select at will the foreman caulker whom he wished to supervise the work and to arrange directly with him concerning his wage was left undisturbed by this arrangement for establishing equality between the other masters.[37]

Besides regulating the relations between masters and their employers the guilds provided for fair dealing between masters and apprentices. The essential point was to force all the masters to enroll their apprentices on the guild records and those of the Justices. The Justices then granted a certificate of apprenticeship which on the one hand enabled the

---

[36] Marciana *Mariegola*, ff. 33-4, 67.

[37] Marciana *Mariegola*, ff. 60, 63, 81, 82, 88. The exemption of those caulkers who were chosen to act as foremen from taking their turn at having their names drawn out of the sack is clearly implied in these sections although no special rule was made granting them such exemption. At f. 85 is a provision for collecting dues. The ordinary masters were compelled to pay by the provision that if they did not they would not again be sent to work. The foremen, on the other hand, had to be threatened with expulsion from the *scuola* for two years, and an accounting whenever they might wish to be sent according to the alphabet like the ordinary masters. The exemption of the foremen was probably inferred from their right of exemption from going to work in the Arsenal according to the alphabet. *Ibid.,* f. 25.

master to charge his employers for the services of his apprentices, and on the other assured the apprentice that he would be given credit for his services.[38]

After the apprentice had become a master he was debarred for a time from himself taking apprentices—the carpenters for seven to ten years, the caulkers for two years.[39] This restriction upon the young masters was the only trace of the journeyman's period which in many mediaeval guilds intervened between the worker's completion of his apprenticeship and his setting up shop for himself as a master. Such a period could have no vital significance in these crafts since most of the masters were never heads of shipyards.

The tendency found in most mediaeval guilds to limit the number of apprentices a master might take was present also in Venice, but in the early fourteenth century the ruling class did not favor such restriction and the Justices decreed in 1323 that any master might take and teach as many boys as he pleased despite any guild statutes to the contrary.[40] Nevertheless there remained in the statutes of the caulkers the provision that no master might have more than two apprentices.[41] In 1477 ordinary ship carpenters were limited to one apprentice, only the Foreman of the Arsenal and the *squerarioli* were allowed two.[42]

In 1402 the minimum age at which boys might be taken as apprentices was fixed for both ship carpenters and caulkers at twelve years for those not sons of masters, and ten years for sons.[43] These regulations insured that boys would not be taken when too young to learn or to be of use, but the caulkers found it also wise to provide that they should not

[38] *I capitolari,* " Marangonis ", chaps. 53, 64, 85, 86; " Callefatorum ", chaps. 5, 61.

[39] Carpenters, see Arsenale, busta 6, ff. 13-15. Caulkers, see Marciana *Mariegola,* f. 38.

[40] *I capitolari,* " Marangonis ", chaps. 82, 86.

[41] *Ibid.,* " Callefatorum", chap. 5; and note 4.

[42] Arsenale, busta 6, ff. 13-15.

[43] Arsenale, busta 5, third series of chapters, July 20, 1402. Strictly the law of 1402 merely fixed the minimum age at which they would be paid for, but the law of 1465—Senato Terra, reg. 5, f. 134—which definitely says none shall be registered except on the ages stated, implies these were the customary minimum ages. See also Marciana *Mariegola,* chap. 52; Arsenale, busta 5, second series of chaps., July 28, 1367.

be taken when too old, and in 1480 the maximum age for those beginning their apprenticeship was fixed at fourteen years. The Lords of the Arsenal favored that provision on the ground that grown men accepted as apprentices did not learn the craft well. The guild favored it not only on that ground but also because work was done by grown men pretending to be apprentices in order to avoid the tax for the aid of veterans.[44]

The statutes of the thirteenth and fourteenth centuries did not prescribe any fixed term of apprenticeship nor any tests to be gone through by a candidate for mastership. Apparently the apprentice was made a master on the testimony of his master, accepted by the gastaldo, that he had learned the craft. But during the fifteenth century there was a general tightening of the requirements. The term of apprenticeship for the caulkers was fixed at six years,[45] that for the carpenters at eight years.[46] About the middle of the century an examination by the gastaldo and his assistants of young caulkers applying for mastership was required.[47] At the same time the applicant was called on to pay a fee of one or two ducats on being accepted, and the eagerness of the gastaldo to receive the fees took away all severity from the examination. In 1489 the caulkers laid a penalty of 100 *lire* on the gastaldo in case he accepted apprentices who were incapable or who had not served their time, and the examining committee was increased to twelve.[48] What measures the carpenters may have taken can not be learned because of the loss of their statutes for this period, but with regard to all master carpenters who had the right to work in the Arsenal, the Signoria placed on the Lords of the Arsenal the responsibility of admitting apprentices to the mastership. Indeed, as the activity of the Arsenal increased in importance the regulation of the shipbuilding crafts fell more and more into the hands of the Arsenal officials. Through the Arsenal

[44] Marciana *Mariegola*, ff. 50-52.
[46] Marciana *Mariegola*, f. 38.
[46] Arsenale, busta 6, ff. 13-15.
[47] Marciana *Mariegola*, ff. 23-4.
[48] *Ibid.*, f. 53.

the Signoria governed the recruiting of masters in accordance with the general interests of the state, and there was no chance for a guild oligarchy to adopt a selfish policy of restriction.

By the latter part of the sixteenth century only one group of shipbuilders remained fairly free from the supervision of the Arsenal. This group, known as the *squerarioli,* consisted of the shipwrights who were independent heads of shipyards. Most of them possessed quite modest establishments in which they built small craft. Only in great emergencies were they employed in the Arsenal. Both by their economic position and the character of their work they came to be distinguished from the shipwrights working in the Arsenal. The latter, together with all the other masters regularly employed there, were called *arsenalotti.* That a shipwright was one of the *arsenalotti* did not debar him from employment in the private shipyards. On the contrary, most of them were ready to take whatever work they could get from the private shipowners and were the masters normally employed in the construction of large merchantmen in private yards. But it was their privilege, whenever they failed to find work in the private shipyards, to be accepted in the Arsenal. They were distinguished from *squerarioli* precisely by this right to employment in the Arsenal.

In consequence of this differentiation among the ship carpenters a division of their guild occurred early in the seventeenth century. During the sixteenth century the difficulty experienced by the Venetian state in securing oarsmen for the galleys led to the assignment to each guild of a quota of oarsmen which the guild was required to furnish. In 1568 the ship carpenters accepted at the Arsenal were exempted from this burden because they were required to serve personally as officers when asked.[49] Since the burden of supplying the oarsmen fell entirely upon the *squerarioli* they began petitioning, in 1589, for a right to a separate guild of their own. The rights and obligations of the two groups of ship

---

[49] Arsenale, busta 11, f. 48.

carpenters had become so different that their organization into separate guilds might seem to follow naturally, but the ship carpenters of the Arsenal opposed the petition of the *squerarioli,* no doubt fearing quite correctly that if the latter had a guild of their own they would try to prevent the carpenters of the Arsenal from going to work in private shipyards or would at least try to make those who did so bear part of the burden of supplying oarsmen. Not until 1606 did the *squerarioli* finally obtain, by virtue of a decision of the Chiefs of the Ten, the right to a guild of their own. The Chiefs of the Ten stipulated that the organization of this guild should in no way take away the right of the carpenters of the Arsenal to go and work outside the Arsenal. Yet the *squerarioli* did succeed in requiring any master of the Arsenal who built two ships outside the Arsenal to pay the fees of their guild.[50]

Before the *squerarioli* became involved in this quarrel with their fellow shipwrights over the sharing of their obligations to the state, they had been engaged in a controversy with the caulkers which arose from the very nature of their occupation. In 1425 the field of activity of the *squerarioli* had been at once assured and defined by a law permitting them to build on their own initiative, or for a prearranged sum, vessels under 94 tons. All work on larger ships must be paid for by the day.[51] But the manufacture and sale of gondolas and similar canal boats could be carried on by the *squerarioli* as independent masters. They naturally desired to include the caulking of these boats within their craft. When the caulkers obtained from the Board of Manufactures a decision forbidding the carpenters to do or have done any caulking, or to sell or promise to make, any boats otherwise than uncaulked, the carpenters protested and carried the case to the College which decided in their favor. The *squerarioli* were permitted to caulk any vessel of 94 tons or less in their

[50] A. S. V., Capi di Consiglio di Dieci, Notatorio no. 33, f. 176; Giustizia Vecchia, busta 212, squerarioli, parti; Arti, busta 304, house carpenters vs. ship carpenters, ff. 25-27, 71; busta 706, *Cap. dei squerarioli,* f. 1-10.

[51] Senato Misti, reg. 55, f. 78.

own shipyards; but were required to pay yearly dues to the caulkers' guild. The *squerarioli* did not, however, take the tests of a master caulker nor were they allowed to enjoy any other of his privileges.[52] They had won on the essential point, for they had gained a legal basis for one of those long drawn out quarrels over the division of labor between crafts which appear typical alike of the mediaeval guilds and the modern trade unions. The caulking of small craft became a battle ground over which each guild fought in an effort to win for its membership as much work as possible. The *squerarioli* reached a mutual understanding that when they needed assistance they would hire each other. The caulkers protested successfully. Then the *squerarioli* tried a new dodge, promptly discovered and denounced by the caulkers, by registering themselves as apprentices to other heads of shipyards. After renewed appeals to the highest authorities had produced a decision that such work must be equally divided between the two crafts, the gastaldo of the caulkers had to be ever on the watch to see that the *squerarioli* did not get more than their share of the work.[53] Continual bickering over such matters gave expression to a primary purpose of the guild, the defense of the economic self-interest of a particular group of craftsmen.

Yet, on the whole, a very large part of the guild's activities were not the outgrowth of interests peculiar to its members as masters of one and the same craft. The chapels and altars, saints and candles, banquets and burials, sick benefits and old age pensions met needs distinctive of no special vocational group. The common occupation was the basic tie that determined the membership of the guilds, and so it was their constant concern to render that occupation profitable. They sought a monopoly of as large a field of production as possible. They attempted to improve the conditions

[52] Marciana *Mariegola,* chaps. 65, 86; A. S. V., Arti, busta 304; cf. *I capitolari* " Marangonis ", chaps. 36, 79.

[53] Marciana *Mariegola,* ff. 52, 54, 63, 66, 73, 75, 86, 108, 113, 114; *Cap. dei squerarioli,* ff. 12, 13.

of employment of their members. But, in the case of these guilds at least, it would obviously be quite inappropriate to speak as if the guilds controlled the industry to which their members belonged. The regulations created through the guilds did not touch the technical details of the process of constructing a ship, nor did they determine whether the masters worked as shipyard owners or as hired wage earners. The guilds gave no standardizing formulation to the technique of their crafts, and exercised no decisive influence upon the forms of industrial organization in which their members were employed.

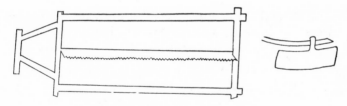

FIGURE XIV. SHIPBUILDERS' TOOLS.

The saw appears in the hand of the patron saint on the statutes of the sawyers' guild. The hatchet is sketched in the records of the Arsenal beside rules concerning shipwrights.

CHAPTER V

THE PROCESS OF CONSTRUCTION

The specialized capacities of the various guildsmen were coordinated by the preëminence of the foremen shipwrights whose position gave unity to the process of production. The woodchoppers who felled the logs, the sawyers, the assisting carpenters, the caulkers, and the entirely unskilled laborers employed to move materials about—all or none of these workers might be in economic dependence upon the foreman shipwright, but they were all more or less dependent upon his technical direction.

He was responsible for the selection of the timbers needed. Sometimes these might be obtained from lumberyards, but often the foreman ship carpenter went to the woods to oversee the cutting of the proper logs for the ship which he had in mind.[1] Generally the logs were brought to Venice before being sawed; only those for the larger ships could be sawed where felled.[2] The sawyers cut the logs as directed by the ship carpenters. They worked with a long saw set in the middle of a wide frame. Figure XIV. The pair of sawyers stood one above on the log, the other below on the ground, and pushed or pulled the saw up and down through the length of the log. Generally they were assisted by laborers who placed the logs in position for them on sawhorses, but even if a log was too heavy to lift, it could still be sawed by the expedient of digging under one end a pit for the lower sawyer.[3]

Once the lumber had been brought to the shipyard, the next step was to lay the keel. The ship carpenter drove a

---

[1] For example, Senato Mar, reg. 4, f. 162.

[2] Senato Misti, reg. 54, f. 5; reg. 59, ff. 19, 153.

[3] Museo Civico, Venice, Mariegole no. 185; A. S. V., Arsenale, busta 6, f. 86; similar saws and descriptions of their use in Henri Louis Duhamel du Monceau, *De l'exploitation des bois* (Paris, 1764), II, 657-660, plate 35. Although there were many applicants for patents for devices which it was claimed would saw wood far cheaper than it could be done by hand (A. S. V., Prov. di Com., busta 5, reg. 1) there is no indication of their use in the records of the guilds or of the Arsenal.

line of piles or stakes spaced about seven feet apart sunk three feet into the ground and projecting two feet above the surface. They were leveled off and formed the base on which the ship rested. A slight sheer was given to the keel. This curve was indicated by taking a long cord and holding both ends at points slightly above the horizontal line at the end stakes, stretching the cord and yet letting it sag in the center so as to touch the leveled line. As the building progressed the hull was supported with props on each side.[4]

It was in this next step in the building, the formation of the framework, that the celebrated shipwright showed his special skill and gave his vessel its individuality. The heart of the shipwright's "mystery" lay in the determination of the main proportions of the ship and the shaping of the curves of the ribbed framework. Some hint of the content of the craft tradition which was transmitted from father to son may be gained from a group of notes or treatises on shipbuilding dating from the fifteenth and sixteenth centuries and written or inspired by the galley builders of the Venetian Arsenal. Though largely written in a cryptic style and obscure vocabulary intended for other masters who had been raised in the shipyards, these documents are a great help in illuminating the secrets possessed by the successful shipwrights.[5]

The dimensions of the ship were determined by starting with one basic measure and working out the rest so far as

[4] *Visione di Drachio*; Fincati, "Le triremi", in *Rivista marittima*, 1881, quatro trimestre, pp. 349-350.

[5] In "Venetian Naval Architecture about 1550," *Mariner's Mirror*, January, 1934, I am publishing extracts from the *Instructione sul modo de fabricare galere* of Pre Todaro or Theodoro, MS. in Bibl. Naz. Marciana, Venice, MSS. Ital. cl. IV, cod. 26. There I discuss the authorship of some of the other treatises to the expositors of which I am much indebted:

The *Fabrica di galere*, MS. in Bibl. Naz., Florence, Coll. Magliabecchiana, cl. XIX, cod. 7, partially published and translated by Jal, *Arch. nav.*, mem. 5, appears from internal evidence to have been composed about 1410 by someone closely associated with the Venetian Arsenal.

The notes of the merchant Giorgio Timbotta of about 1445 are largely published and translated by R. C. Anderson, "Italian Naval Architecture".

The *Visione di Drachio*, 1593, MS. in A. S. V., Arsenale, busta 1, was extensively used by Admiral Fincati for his study "Le triremi".

A Venetian MS. of 1686 on shipbuilding, in the British Museum, Add. 38655, has

possible from that one. The beam of the ship was most frequently taken as the starting point. A certain number times
the beam gave the foreman the
length of his ship, or more
specifically, the distance from
the point where the top clamp
was attached to the stem to the
point where the top clamp was
fastened on the sternpost. This
distance he marked on the leveled line which had been obtained on the piles. Then, by
allowing for the rakes fore and
aft, he marked the length of the
keel.[6] To know the width of
the floor the shipwright went
back to the beam measure and took a certain fraction thereof
as the floor measure.

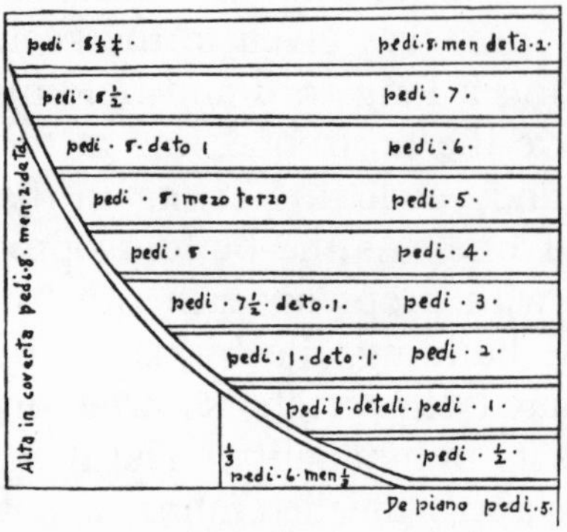

FIGURE XV. DIAGRAM IN THE "FABRICA"
(C. 1410) OF HALF OF MIDSHIP
FRAME: FLEMISH GALLEY.

Not all the needed measures could be obtained by applying traditional rules of proportion. Nor could they always
be stated as simple ratios one of the other. But there was a
strong tendency to try to find standard proportions between
the different measures so that principles of design might be
found which if once adjudged sound by experience with
one ship might be applied to other vessels which were of
the same type though of different measure. It would be superfluous to suspect a Platonic passion for geometric proportions. As a practical means of making experience valuable
it was desirable to simplify the number of different measures used in determining the lines of the ship. The more
simply these determinants could be stated the greater was
the possibility of finding widely applicable ratios between
the various measures.

This search for simplification may be the explanation of

been called to my attention by Mr. R. C. Anderson. It may be that described by
Christoforo Tentori, *Saggio sulla storia civile, politica, ecclesiastica e sulla corografia e
topografia degli stati della Republica di Venezia* (Venice, 1785-1790), I, 346.

[6] So in the *Visione di Drachio*, at least.

the contrasts between the earlier and later treatises in the methods indicated for determining curves. In the two earlier manuscripts, which date from the first half of the fifteenth century, the curve of the midship frame was described by giving " beams " at one or one-half foot intervals above the

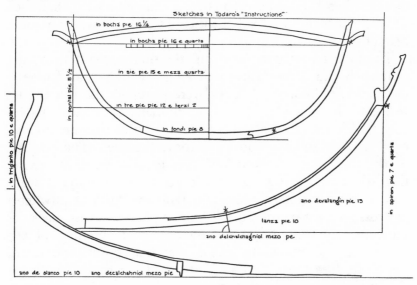

FIGURE XVI. DIAGRAM IN THE "INSTRUCTIONE" (C. 1550) OF MIDSHIP FRAME, STEM, AND STERNPOST: GALLEY OF A CAPTAIN GENERAL.

floor. Figure XV. The two later treatises, dating from the second half of the sixteenth century, used a more sophisticated method. The depth from the first deck was divided into three equal parts. Figure XVI. The two dividing lines between the deck and the floor were called the *trepie* and *siepie*. The length of these two imaginary lines at one-third and two-thirds of the depth determined the curve of the midship frame, and rules were then formulated for deriving their measures from that of the floor. The methods of finding the curvature of the stem and sternposts of the galleys, so far as revealed by the diagrams in the manuscripts, had also undergone a similar though less complete simplification.

The shipwright started with his designs of the stem, the

midship frame, and the sternpost. They were the first timbers to be fastened into place on the keel.[7] He now faced the
problem of shaping the frames fore and aft of the center
frames. In doing so he could take his midship frame as a
basis of design, but he must so alter therefrom the design
of the other frames as gradually to narrow and to heighten
the ship fore and aft. What measures could he find to guide
his cutting?

The first step was to determine the shape of certain frames
near each end of the ship which were called " tail-frames "
or " heads of design." [8] They were probably the last frames
fore and aft that were true floor timbers, the last U-shaped
ribs. Before and abaft the tail-frames the ribs became V-
or Y-shaped, and the floor rose above the keel. The position
of the tail-frames on the keel was usually fixed by giving
their distance from the perpendiculars dropped from the heads
of the stem and stern. The tail-frames were the equivalents
of cross sections of the hull at known points. Their measures
indicated the amount of narrowing or heightening of the
frames which was to be effected at that point, and could
therefore, like the measures of the midship frame, serve the
shipwright as a basis of design for the other ribs.

Perhaps the whole problem of shaping the ribs had at one
time been left to the practiced eye of the shipwright who
hewed the timbers without mathematical guidance. The
Y-shaped frames of the prow and poop were largely so determined even at the beginning of the seventeenth century.[9]
But the very earliest of the treatises gives some measures

---

[7] *Visione.* In a list of large merchantmen in process of construction in 1507 their
state of completion is described in the following ways:
    1) serada del toto, mancha el fondi, i. e., planked completely, lacks floor.
    2) imboscata, i. e., frames in place.
    3) una cavo da prova cum le columbe solamente, i. e., stem and keel only.
    4) imboscata in fili, i. e., frames and clamps in place.
    5) imboscata del primo maier in zoso. i. e., ribbed up to the first clamp.
A. S. V., Notatorio di College, reg. 24, f. 7.

[8] *Chodera chorba* in the *Fabrica di galere,* *qudiera chorba* in Timbotta's notes; *chavo
di sesto* in the *Instructione, capo di sesto* in the *Visione.*

[9] Crescenzio, p. 19, says of these frames " hanno per modello l'occhio del maestro,
tirando due lenze o regole fina alle ruote."

for the tail-frames and also for the frames eighteen feet fore and aft of the midship frame. In the sixteenth century the design of every fifth frame was worked out with the aid of mathematical guides,[10] and these frames were the first placed in position.[11] Perhaps the shaping of the intermediate frames was still left to the eye of the master who cut the frame timbers.

Separate dimensions even for every fifth frame would have involved an enormous number of measures. It would have been extremely difficult to reduce so many separate measures to rules of proportion applicable to ships of different sizes. But in the sixteenth century geometric schemes were found by which this result was attained.

These geometric devices involved taking as starting point the extent to which the shape of one of the tail-frames differed in some respect from the shape of the midship frame. The problem of narrowing the bow of the ship will serve as example. The shipwright has his midship frame in place. He must make the frames forward from this frame each slightly narrower than the preceding so as to effect a very gradual curve inward of the side of the ship. The first measure he determines is the extent to which the lower part of each side of the tail-frame will be narrower than the corresponding part of the midship frame. That measure is tradi-

[10] Drachio, *Visione*, says every fifth frame was a *chorba della onza*, meaning one whose design was calculated. Giuseppe Boerio, *Dizionario del dialetto veneziano* (3d ed., Venice, 1867), *s. v. onza*. *Chorba della onza* occurs in Timbotta's notes, Anderson, " It. Nav. Arch.", pp. 150-1.

[11] In the list of great galleys in the Arsenal in 1503 given by Sanuto, *Diarii*, V, 926, the unfinished galleys are listed as follows:

" 2 galie mancha a serar (i. e., lacks planking)

1 galie mancha serar de fora

2 galie mancha serar gran parte

1 galie in filli, postiza, e bachalari (" filli " were clamps running along the frames below the wale; " bachalari " were the timbers which rose from the ends of the deck beams to support the " posticcia " on which the oars rested.)

3 galie imboschade (ribbed)

8 galie bona parte imboschade

2 galie in corbe dale onze."

Similar phrases are used to describe the different stages in the construction of a ship in the other lists of ships in the Arsenal entered on Table H.

tionally a certain part of the floor measure or some other measure of the ship. The shipwright must next decide how many frames are to be fastened to the keel between the mid-ship frame and the tail-frame, say forty, the number used in the bow of a great galley about 1550. If the narrowing of every fifth frame only is to be determined mathematically, the builder has eight frames—including the tail-frame—for which to figure the amount of narrowing. He must make each of these successive eight frames slightly narrower than the preceding so as to have effected, when he reaches the tail-frame, the total narrowing desired.

Two diagrams which might be employed to determine these measures, and show them all in one drawing, are pic-

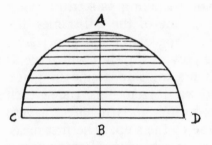

FIGURE XVII. THE MEZA-LUNA.

tured in some notes on Vene-tian shipbuilding written about the middle of the fif-teenth century.[12] The way in which they were to be em-ployed is explained by Cres-centio, a Neapolitan writer, a century and a half later. The diagram whose applica-tion Crescentio explains most fully is that shown in figure XVII, and called at Naples the *meza-luna*, the " half-moon." A half circle was drawn using as radius the extent by which the tail-frame was narrower at the base than the midship frame. This half circle was divided into two quadrants by the radius *AB*. The length of that line accordingly equals the total amount of narrowing to be ef-fected. It is to be divided into eight progressively smaller fractions. The frames set up from midship frame to tail-frame will then each be made narrower than the preceding by the amount of one of these fractions. In order to divide the line *AB* into these unequal fractions the two quadrants *CA* and *DA* were divided into eight equal parts. Lines were drawn connecting these dividing points along the quadrants,

[12] Anderson, " It. Nav. Arch.", p. 154.

and these lines divided the radius *AB* in the desired eight fractions of the total.

The divisions of the line *AB* thus obtained were then marked off on a rule and the rule placed on the model midship frame, the point *A* being put at the middle point of the floor. The marks were transferred from the rule to the base of the midship frame. In designing the first of the frames forward from the midship frame the shipwright narrowed it at the base an amount equal to the smallest of these divisions, namely, that marked on the midship frame nearest to the mid-point of the floor. He narrowed the second frame forward by the amount of the two smallest of the divisions, that is, the distance from the mid-point of the floor to the second mark, and so on until he reached the tail-frame which was narrowed by the whole length of the line *AB*. Thus the ship carpenter was able to find in one pattern or model all the measures to be used in narrowing the frames and did not need to make a separate calculation for each.[13]

The width of the tail-frames was but one respect in which their shape differed from that of the midship frame, for the frames were also heightened and widened at the tops so as to approach the shape of the Y-frames fore and aft. In the sixteenth century the Venetian shipwrights applied four different modifications to the shaping of the ribs.[14] In each case the total amount of modification at the tail-frame was first determined—preferably as a ratio of some other measure— and then the amount of variation for each successive frame was discovered through an application of the *meza-luna* or some other geometric means of dividing a line of given

[13] Crescenzio, pp. 14-18. The measure or system for narrowing here described is by Crescenzio called the *brusca,* by Drachio the *partisone del fondo,* by Theodoro simply *partisone.* Anderson, " It. Nav. Arch.", p. 154, says the radius of the circle was the half-beam, although there is written along it, " questo e el morelo de la parttison ", i. e., " this is the measure of the *partison* ". I presume Anderson thought the length of the *partison* to be the same as the half-beam, but such is not the case in Theodoro or Drachio.

[14] Theodoro and Drachio both mention besides the *partisone del fondo,* the *stella* which heightened the frames—Crescentio, pp. 20-21—the *ramo* or *legno in ramo* which broadened the tops of the frames, and the *scorrer* of unexplained significance.

length into progressively smaller parts. Each of these four measures used in modifying the design of the frames was called a *partison* by the Venetians, but when that term was used alone without a qualifying term it referred to the measures for narrowing the floor of the ship, or to that section of the framework between midship frame and tail-frame. It therefore seems likely that methods like the *meza-luna* for producing a very flat curve were first applied to the problem of narrowing. But the Venetians then applied the same method to secure further refinements in the molding of the hull.

Probably each of the mathematical calculations necessary to determine the proportions and lines of the ship, even a simple process of division such as deriving the floor measure from the beam, was worked out not by arithmetic but by geometry. The beam measure may have been marked out on a board, or by stakes on the ground, and the carpenter have divided by compass, cord, or measuring rod, and put the result in the floor in the literal sense of putting the cord, compass, or rod on the floor timber to guide his signs for cutting. Some figuring may have been done with full sized diagrams in the shipyard. In the sixteenth century the shipwrights of the Arsenal frequently prepared, as proof of their powers and evidence of the excellence of their design, models of the ships they wished to build.[15] These may or may not have been scale models from which they took their lines in building. The first treatise on shipbuilding to show a scale on the diagrams is that of 1686. The drawings in the earlier collections of instructions have more the appearance of illustrations than of working plans.

The shaping of the curved timbers of the ship's hull completed the most complicated and distinctive part of the work of the foreman shipwright. That process was sometimes dragged out over years, at least in cases of galley building when the shipwright was a foreman in the Arsenal who was

---

[15] Arsenale, busta 133, f. 134; Senato Mar, reg. 29, f. 132; reg. 32, f. 114 and files, Nov. 17, 1553.

working on several galleys at once and did not need to hurry them to completion.[16] There is a suggestion that this part of the building was sometimes done with unseasoned wood which was easier to work. The half-built frame was then left to season before it was put in final form to be planked.[17] Slowly building a number of galleys simultaneously gave the shipwrights of the Arsenal a greater chance to choose logs of just the desired curvature from the varied timber which periodically came into the Arsenal's lumber yard.

When the ribs had been hewn into the desired shapes by axe, hatchet, or adze, they were fastened in position on the keel by heavy timbers forming a keelson placed above the frames so as to hold them firmly in place. The framework was completed by tying the ribs together with clamps and strakes.[18] Deck beams—those in the center of a galley of the form shown in figure XVI—were dowelled into the top clamps binding the two sides. At each end of the rowers' deck of a galley was a straight lateral deck beam of extra breadth and thickness called the " yoke." The timbers of the central gangway, the *corsia*, were notched into these yokes and into the intermediate deck beams so that they served to tie together the two ends of the ship.[19] So firmly were all the timbers of the frame joined together that the dangers of breaks in the framework lay less in the joints themselves than in those portions of the timbers which had been weakened by notching.[20]

[16] Such is the implication of records of the activity of Bernardo, Giorgio the Greek, and Leonardo Bressan, chap. III.

[17] Marino Sanuto (the elder), *Liber Secretorum*, lib. II, pt. IV, cap. XII.

[18] These *fili*, clamps or strakes, are referred to in the following regulation ordering the building of experimental galleys in which only every other clamp would be notched into the ribs. " Al presente se debba far doi galee sottil de dentro via solum cum il suo contromaier and contrazento, et sotto la contro zento doi fili amorssadi et poi un fil vacuo et poi metterne un altro amorssado, et cosi andar fin su la soraverzena, un fil vacuo et l'altro pien ". Arsenale, busta 136, ff. 97-8.

[19] Crescentio, pp. 28-31.

[20] Museo Civico Correr, Venice, Archivio Donà della Rosa, busta 153, report of Nicolò Surian; A. S. V., Arsenale, busta 11, ff. 40-41; Senato Mar, files, Dec. 20, 1567.

When the ship carpenters had shaped and fastened the frame of the hull, the work of the caulkers began. According to their double task the caulkers of Venice were divided into two groups. Those who were called " calafadi da fizer " (or " figgier ") and received 2 *soldi* a day more than the others worked with dowels and nails fastening in place those planks and timbers which were exposed to the weather. Those called " calafadi da maggio " drove tow or oakum into the seams of the ship, and covered them with pitch. During part of the construction the carpenters and caulkers worked together on the ship, the carpenters marking timbers to show where they should be fastened by the caulkers.[21] After the frame had been built, the carpenters still had work to do building the superstructures and the cabins, but the double nature of the caulkers' craft caused the amount of labor required from them on a ship to exceed that of the carpenters.[22] Throughout the following descriptions of the work in the private shipyards and in the Arsenal where caulking is mentioned, it must be remembered that the term covers both filling seams and fastening timbers and planking.

Though the most distinctive part of the craft of the shipwrights was embodied in the basic structure of the hull, the live work, much carpentering remained to be done upon the dead work before the ship was complete. The partitions below deck and the upper works of the castles might be built almost

[21] The caulkers did much which would commonly be called carpentering. Cecchetti, *Mariegole*, says: " I calafati si dividevano, come adesso, in due branche: da figger or ficcar, che inchiodano le varie parti di legno del corpo della nave mediante chiodi, perni, suggi, e caviglie; e da maglio che riempiono di stoppa i commenti della nave, la battono, e impeciano ". In the regulations by the Inquisitors, 1785—Arsenale, Inquisitori al Arsenal, unnumbered envelope—the work of the two groups is similarly indicated, and in the tests there prescribed for the carpenters it is frequently required of them that they indicate where the parts are to be fastened by the " calafato da figger ".

In the *Fabrica di galere*, f. 76, the labor of the caulkers is described as " forar (drill), fichar (fasten), chalchar (drive in tow), & impegolar (pitch)." In the Arsenal, nails were given out to both carpenters and caulkers.

The most probable division of labor seems to me to be that the carpenters fastened together the framework of the galley and did all the work on the superstructures, while the caulkers fastened in place parts exposed to the water.

[22] Below chap. VIII, note 33.

equally well by house carpenters.[23] But the construction of the outriggers of the galleys and the correct spacing of the thole pins and rowers' benches were integral parts of the "mystery" of the shipwrights. Upon the correct arrangement of these features of the dead work depended the efficiency with which the galley could be rowed, and the ships' officers frequently thought they knew more about how they should be arranged than the masters of the Arsenal. Vettor Fausto's knowledge of the theoretical science inherited by scholars from the Greeks had been applicable to this small section of the craft tradition. But it is doubtful whether he spread among the masters an appreciation of the mechanical theories applicable to this particular variation of the use of the lever.

In connection with the rigging of the ship, there developed two specialized branches of the craft of ship carpenters, the pulley-makers and the mast-makers. The pulley-makers were frequently independent heads of workshops in which they made for sale such accessories as pulleys and shafts for capstans.[24] The mast-makers might also be independent as heads of lumberyards in which they prepared masts, spars, and rudders.[25] They were experts in selecting the standing trees fitted for their purposes. But it does not appear that they were themselves dealers in lumber; more probably they acted for shipowners in selecting and finishing the necessary logs.

As the ship neared completion work on it came to consist more and more of the assemblage of parts prepared by these and other specialized craftsmen. The services of the unskilled laborers or stevedores, a group of laborers who at Venice possessed their own peculiar system of organization, increased in importance. The building merged into the outfitting of the ship for her maiden voyage and passed gradually from the direction of the foreman shipwright to that of the ship's mate or captain.

[23] Until 1560 house carpenters were allowed to work as ship carpenters and ship carpenters as house carpenters. Then there occurred a complete mutual exclusion which was modified, however, in 1588 in such fashion as to permit house carpenters to work on the cabins of ships provided no ship carpenter would undertake the work at the regular rate of pay. A. S. V. Archivio delle Arti, busta 304, suit of house carpenters against ship carpenters.

[24] *Ibid.*   [25] Arsenale, busta 566, *Quaderno dei salariadi.*

CHAPTER VI

THE ACTIVITY OF THE PRIVATE SHIPYARDS

The most distinctive mark of the craft age of industry was the union in the same person of the manual laborer and the technical expert. As long as that union lasted the possibilities of industrial capitalism were definitely limited. Craft work and capitalism remain, therefore, convenient labels of contrasting systems of production even though the line between them may, in specific cases, be found to be blurred beyond recognition.

But craft work usually implies far more than the technical self-government of the laborer. It suggests a master craftsman independent of any employer, possessor of his own shop, buying his raw materials and selling his finished products in the open market—in short, a man who was the head of a small independent business as well as both technician and laborer. A combination of so many different functions in one person could be expected to prevail only in industries conducted on a small scale. Either an extension of the market or the employment of a large amount of capital in the process of production led to a division of labor. A distinction appeared between the manual laborer and the entrepreneur, between the craftsman and the merchant. This division of labor robbed the craftsman of his individualistic self-reliance by making him dependent upon whoever supplied the capital or controlled the market.

It has been recognized that the shipbuilding of the mediaeval Italian cities was conducted on too large a scale to be entirely organized as a retail handicraft; but the activities of the Venetian Arsenal have been so much more celebrated, and so much better recorded, than those of any private shipyards that it has been thought that handicraft was followed

100

not by a capitalistic but by a communal organization.[1] But even at Venice the development had no such simple unity.[2] The same distinctions in ship types—light galley, great galley, and round ship—which pictured the political and commercial conditions of navigation were also basic in distinguishing the forms of production. The diversity in the output of the shipbuilding industry allowed the simultaneous existence of diversely organized enterprises. The building of rowboats, the construction of large merchantmen, and the maintenance of war fleets involved different economic problems.

The communal shipbuilding organization, the Arsenal, was the great center of galley building. Its primary purpose was the outfitting of the war fleet. Retail handicraft was an utterly inadequate method of building and maintaining a large number of ships expressly designed for military use. For that purpose communal action was adopted and by the fifteenth century had come to exclude private capitalism completely. But the Arsenal entered relatively little into the production of merchant shipping, so that for a long time the larger field of activity was left to private enterprise. To be sure, merchant galleys were built by the government, at least from the middle of the fourteenth century until the discontinuance of their voyages. But very few round ships were built in the Arsenal and those few were warships. And surveys of the Venetian fleet in the fifteenth and sixteenth centuries show that the merchant galleys formed but a small part of the total tonnage of the merchant fleet.

Since the economic form of the shipbuilding enterprise varied with the character of the product, an at least approximate quantitative analysis of the composition of the Venetian marine is necessary to an intelligent appraisal of the economic organization of the industry. The volumes of the various kinds of shipping give indications both of the

---

[1] Sombart, *Moderne Kap.,* vol. II, pt. 2, p. 779.

[2] Though it is true, cf. Sombart, *loc. cit.,* that the Arsenal furnishes an example of a large scale industrial undertaking earlier than any capitalistic shipbuilding enterprise of which the records have been found.

proportion of the Venetian fleet produced by the Arsenal, and also of the relative importance of large merchantmen and canal boats in the varied activity of the private shipyards. In such a quantitative survey, particularly in an analysis of the fleet of round ships, classifications based on size must be used to supplement the distinctions in form and rig hitherto emphasized. But the following groupings based on size, which are used for the round ships, roughly correspond to differences in type and use.

Groups a) 600 tons and over, cogs, caracks, *barze,* and galleons, naval auxiliaries and exceptionally large merchantmen.

   b) 240 to 600 tons, cogs and caracks, carriers on the long and well established routes of inter-regional trade.

   c) 100 to 240 tons, mostly lateeners employed in the Adriatic and cabotage trades.

   d) under 100 tons, mostly canal and river boats.

At a time when the maritime fame and prosperity of Venice was still undimmed, the Doge Mocenigo outlined the extent of the maritime life of the Republic. In the years just before his death in 1423 the Doge repeatedly urged his countrymen to avoid the dangers of an adventuresome Italian policy and emphasized the blessings of peace by extolling the existing prosperity. They had, he said, three thousand vessels of less than 100 tons burden, three hundred larger ships, and forty-five galleys.[3]

The very large figure given by Doge Mocenigo for the number of ships of the smallest class emphasizes the fact that the large round ships so important to students interested either in the historical development of the ship or in international commerce were but a small part of the shipping of such a port as Venice. Both long ships and round ships may be included among these three thousand craft of less than 100 tons burden, but boats under 5 tons were specifically excluded.

[3] The following analysis and the reliability of the figures in the " death-bed oration " of Mocenigo are discussed in Appendix II.

Of the three hundred ships of 100 tons or more, five-sixths were probably vessels of about 120 tons employed in fishing or in carrying about the Adriatic and Ionian Seas such humble cargoes as grain, oil, wood, and stone. But about 1450, at a time when Mocenigo's figure of three hundred was still applicable, some thirty or thirty-five of the three hundred were castellated cogs of 240 tons or over, great merchantmen of that day making the standard voyages to England, Syria, and the Crimea.

About eighteen great merchant galleys made similar voyages at that time, and two or three went each year to the Holy Land with pilgrims. These ships account for twenty of the forty-five galleys. The remainder were probably light galleys designed for war. Twenty-five is too large a number for the galleys in the police fleet sent out from Venice in time of peace but is a moderate figure for a war fleet.

The compilation of this information in numerical form involves a very large element of guesswork, and is here given only for the purpose of showing the predominance of the round ships.

Ships		Capacity
Groups a & b) 35 round ships of 240 tons or over............	15,000 tons	
c) 265 round ships of 100 to 239 tons............	28,000 tons	
d) 3,000 vessels under 100 tons.................	30,000 tons	
e) 2 pilgrim galleys.......	500 tons	
Total: Products of private enterprise.............		73,500 tons
Groups f) 25 light galleys.................	2,500	
g) 18 great galleys.................	4,500	
Total: Products of the Arsenal.................		7,000 tons

Despite a margin of error so great that the mathematical statement is of no absolute value, the tabulation emphasizes more clearly one aspect of Mocenigo's figures. The building of round ships was in his time the bigger part of the ship-building industry; the production of the private shipyards was larger than that of the Arsenal.[4] Even though the relative importance of different types varied from time to time, these estimates give some sense of proportion with which to proceed.

Two surveys of later date—one in 1499, the other at about 1560—supplement Doge Mocenigo's enumeration of the fleet of round ships. These later ship lists are more valuable as aids to further analyses of the activity of the private shipyards than as indications of the expansion of communal shipbuild-ing, since the growth of the Arsenal may be traced by the direct study of that institution as well as by indirect evidence from the size of the war fleets.

An extensive mobilization of Venetian shipping occurred in August, 1499 during a war against the Turks. The lists of ships detained in ports or in the fleet give a picture of the large round ships of Venice which is practically complete, but which reflects abnormal conditions.[5] The enumeration reveals the effects of both a quarter century of severe depres-sion and of urgent special efforts to surmount the crisis. The decline in Venetian shipbuilding had become acute by 1480, and the lowest point had been reached in 1487 when it was asserted that no ships of any kind were being built in the city. The main cause of the slump was believed to be the severity of the competition of the eastern coast of the Adriatic, but the very largest merchantmen (group a), which had been princi-pally employed in the wine trade between Crete and England and in moving salt and grain in the western Mediterranean, had suffered also from the underbidding of Genoese, Basque, Spanish, and Portuguese.[6]

The two largest classes of round ships (groups a and b) were lumped together in the analysis of the figures for 1420-

---

[4] So recognized also by Gino Luzzato, " Per la storia delle costruzioni navali a Venezia nei secoli xv e xvi ", *Scritti storici in onore di Camillo Manfroni* (Padua, 1925), pp. 384-5, by inference from the guild regulations, here discussed below, chap. X.

[5] List summarized in Table E, analyzed in Appendix III.

[6] Lane, " Venetian Shipping ", pp. 223-225.

1450 because ships of more than 600 tons did not come into commercial use until after the death of Doge Mocenigo. But during the middle decades of the fifteenth century a half-dozen such ships were a usual part of the merchant marine.[7] By 1486 they had entirely disappeared. The government had become accustomed to using these large merchantmen to supplement the battle fleet and to clear the seas of pirates. The rise of the Ottoman navy made them all the more necessary to the state. The government tried three different policies for remedying the shortage which existed during the last quarter of the fifteenth century. It offered substantial bounties to all who would undertake to build such large ships.[8] When these offers called forth very slight response, the state decided to build, itself, the large ships needed as auxiliaries. This outburst of governmental building accounts for the very large ships in the fleet in 1499. While the state was meeting its minimum needs by building for itself, it imposed discriminatory duties to exclude foreign vessels from the shipment of wine west from Crete and thus stimulated some private building of large ships between 1490 and 1499.[9]

Altogether, the survey of 1499 indicates about twenty-five private Venetian merchantmen of 240 tons or more having about 10,000 tons capacity. The combined capacity of these ships and the four very large state-built vessels was about the same as that of the corresponding two classes (groups a and b) a half century before. But only an extraordinary, war-time effort kept so much shipping afloat in 1499. In 1502 it was asserted that there were but sixteen Venetian ships large enough to be included in these two groups.[10]

Of the smaller ships which the Venetians built for the Adriatic and for cabotage trade, the ship lists of 1499 give but an incomplete enumeration mentioning seventy-three ships of about 130 tons each. But even that glimpse is enough to

[7] Table D.

[8] Senato Mar, reg. 9, ff. 20, 21, 37, 99, 105, 120-1, 162, 172, 186; reg. 12, ff. 87, 156-7.

[9] Above chap. II, note 40, and Lane, " Venetian Shipping ", p. 225.

[10] Appendix III.

reinforce the impression concerning their importance given by the estimates of Doge Mocenigo. The builders of these medium sized vessels (group c) had also felt the depression which the competition of neighboring regions had caused at Venice, though it is impossible to say to what extent their production or that of the builders of yet smaller craft had already fallen from the high figures given by Mocenigo, or even just how many of the seventy-three mentioned in 1499 were actually built at Venice.

A third opportunity for an analysis of private Venetian shipbuilding is offered about 1560. A report of the Board of Trade of 1561 stated that the building of the ships of about 120 to 140 tons (group c) had practically ceased, that the craft which supplied the city with grain, wine, oil, and cheese from nearby regions were all bought abroad, that there were no Venetian-built ships able to go on these voyages. The use of foreign ships was a violation of the law but a necessity.[11] At the time of Doge Mocenigo the Venetian shipyards must have produced thirty-odd ships of this class each year in order to maintain some two hundred sixty-five ships in use. During the intervening century the Venetian shipbuilding industry had been permanently maimed by the cessation—or at least by the serious diminution—of the construction of these medium sized ships. The making of yet smaller vessels, under 100 tons, had likewise been on the decline, but the continued activity of the *squerarioli* testified to the continuance, at least, of the building of barges and canal boats.

On the other hand, although the private shipyards of Venice were probably never again as active as they had been at the time when they furnished the 3300 craft of which Doge Mocenigo boasted, more very large ships were being built in Venice in the mid-sixteenth century than ever before. It is an often verified theory of economic geography that when an industry has begun to shift from an old center to a new, the old center retains longest its production of those grades of goods which are of the highest quality, which require the most

[11] A. S. V., Cinque Savii alla Mercanzia, ser. i, busta 135, ff. 99-100.

advanced technique. It is in accord with this hypothesis that the Venetians should continue to build great 600 ton ships after competitors had robbed them of the business of supplying the commoner, smaller, less elaborate ships used on shorter voyages. Though wood and iron might be more plentiful elsewhere, Venice still had the advantage of a body of skilled craftsmen. In the years 1558-1559 there were in the merchant fleet almost forty round ships of 240 tons or more (groups a and b) with a total capacity of nearly 18,000 tons.[12]

A synthesis of the three surveys at the approximate dates 1450, 1500, and 1560 is possible only for the private ships of 240 tons or more. While the fleet of such ships about 1560 was twice the size of that in 1502, it was but slightly larger than the fleet estimated for 1450. Accordingly, we may regard the normal merchant fleet of round ships of this size as between thirty and forty. A fleet of that number of ships was " normal " for these two centuries in the sense that it furnished the shipping necessary to import the usual amounts of grain and salt and to handle the other business in Venetian hands. When the number of such ships was seriously diminished, as it was in the last quarter of the fifteenth century, the state felt it necessary itself to build so as to make up the difference.

An estimate of the scale of production based on this estimate of the size of the fleet to be maintained accords closely with scattered examples of the production for specific years. Applications for bounties offered between 1502 and 1507 give an idea of the scale of production in prosperous times. The subsidy, offered only for round ships of 240 tons or more, was claimed for five ships in March, 1504.[13] In 1507, when the law was repealed, there were seven ships under construction not counting those which had been built above the first deck.[14] A similar rate of building is indicated at a somewhat later period, likewise considered one of prosperity for the builders of large merchantmen, though the state was again

[12] Table F.
[13] Sanuto, *Diarii*, V, 1000.
[14] A. S. V., Not. di Coll. reg. 24, f. 7, July 5, 1507.

offering aid to the industry. Between November, 1556 and November, 1557 applications were made for bounties for eight different ships in various stages of completion.[15] Two ships were launched in December, 1557, four in the year 1558, one in 1559, and four between January and June, 1560.[16] These instances suggest a very irregular rate of production; the number launched in one year varied at least from one to five.

Barring accidents the average life of a ship was about ten years. In that case the launching of an average of three or four ships a year would maintain the fleet at its usual strength. Perhaps one ship a year additional would be required because of wrecks. Since two years were frequently spent in building a ship, the number on the stocks in process of construction in normal times should have been eight to ten.[17]

An industry producing so small a number of units was peculiarly subject to temporary crises of overproduction or underproduction. The supply lagged far behind the demand because a year or two might elapse between the cutting of timbers and the launching of the ship. The hazards of wind and wave, pirate and privateer, might at any moment create a great shortage of ships, while the failure of a grain crop occasioning extensive importation or the sudden need of sending soldiers and war supplies to an eastern possession might with equal unexpectedness, and perhaps simultaneously, create a demand for them. If such a need occurred, presumably during the summer, capital might be mobilized and wood cut during the ensuing winter, but the ships would not be ready for service until at least the end of the following year. Meanwhile, more ships would normally have been lost or become unseaworthy with age. In a fleet of some thirty-five large merchantmen each of which was good for but about ten years of service, the possibility that their number would be thus suddenly reduce below what was considered essential for

[15] Cinque Savii, ser. i, busta 135, ff. 73-78.

[16] Museo Civico Correr, Venice, Arch. Donà della Rosa, busta 217.

[17] Luzzato—" Costruzioni navali ", p. 394—figured that the amount of the subsidies of 1533 provided for the building of 12 or 18 ships of 300 tons in three years. On age of ships see Appendix V.

the provisioning of the city and for the maintenance of its trade and its defenses was a constant concern of the state. The offering of subsidies for ships begun at once and finished within a stipulated time need not, therefore, be taken as necessarily signifying any more than the danger of a temporary shortage.

The policy of the government towards so unstable an industry naturally varied: sometimes it tried to protect prospective shipowners by forbidding foreigners to build at Venice and so compete with them for the services of the artisans; more frequently it tried to protect the craftsmen—and the merchants who had already built—by forbidding the purchase of foreign ships or the construction by Venetians of ships elsewhere than at Venice or a few favored places within her dominions.[18] After the middle of the fourteenth century measures for the protection of the native builders by the exclusion of foreign competition were reenacted with increasing frequency—an indication that they were needed if not that they were enforced.[19] As crises of underproduction repeatedly occurred despite this protection, the offers of bounties became more numerous, and culminated, after 1533, in a consistent policy of subsidizing the builders of large ships.[20]

The permanent subsidy program grew out of increases in the freight paid by the Signoria for the transportation of salt from Cyprus and Iviza to Venice. In order to be sure that the additional appropriation made to pay a higher freight for the salt would really be used to aid the building of new ships, it was advanced to the builders and collected by deductions made from the freight due them for the next three years. But the loans were made to all builders, even those who did not use their ships to bring salt, and the limit of repayment was

---

[18] Luzzato, " Costruzioni navali ", pp. 388-391.

[19] *Loc. cit.*; Lane, " Venetian Shipping ", pp. 224-225, 233.

[20] Besides those mentioned by Luzzato, *op. cit.*, pp. 389-393, subsidies were offered in 1433, for 600 ton ships—Senato Misti, reg. 58, f. 173—in 1469—Senato Mar, reg. 9, f. 20—in 1470—*ibid.*, reg. 9, ff. 37, 99—in 1471—*ibid.*, reg. 9, ff. 105, 120-121—in 1494—*ibid.*, reg. 14, f. 27—in 1502—*ibid.*, reg. 15, f. 145—in 1515—*ibid.*, reg 18, f. 71.

later fixed at seven years even if no salt was carried, so that the increases in salt freights—probably balanced by the general rise in prices—sank into the background. The subsidy thus came to consist in advancing capital without interest charge, a form of industrial stimulation still employed. The number of great merchantmen in the Venetian marine in the middle decades of the sixteenth century was considered a highly gratifying response to this policy and a good reason for its continuance.[21]

But the activity of the private shipyards, even their production of big ships, diminished alarmingly at the end of the century. Offers of even larger subsidies met with insufficient response. Although the government still made loans to Venetian builders, it finally abandoned the hope that they could supply the ships needed. The impossibility of enforcing the law against the purchase of foreign ships was confessed by frequent grants of Venetian registry to such ships after 1590. In 1606 about half the large ships in the Venetian merchant marine had been built in such distant regions as Holland, Patmos, and the shores of the Black Sea. As the number of ships still proved insufficient for the demand, the Signoria in 1627 offered large loans to encourage purchases abroad, a revelation of the utter inadequacy of the domestic industry.[22]

This long drawn out decline in the output of the private shipyards, first of small ships and later of larger vessels, brought the activity of the Arsenal into greater prominence. Moreover, the production of war galleys was so increased between 1470 and 1540 as more than to counter-balance the discontinuance of the voyages of the merchant galleys.

By the middle of the sixteenth century the Venetian shipbuilding industry came to be divided into three distinct branches—the construction of large merchantmen, the build-

[21] The development is described by Luzzato, " Costruzioni navali ", pp. 393-398. He emphasizes the fact that the subsidies were not initially conceived as advances of capital without interest charge, but does not give equal emphasis to the rapidity with which that became their most prominent feature. Cf. laws of 1549, 1551, 1559— Senato Mar, reg. 30, f. 45; reg. 31, f. 30; reg. 34, f. 70.

[22] Lane, " Venetian Shipping ", pp. 233-236.

ing of gondolas and other canal boats, and the maintenance of a war fleet. The activities of the early fifteenth century were not so clearly differentiated, for the production of the merchant galleys and of the ships of about 120 tons designed for Adriatic voyages involved intermediate types of industrial organization. But in the sixteenth century there were sharp contrasts between the forms of industrial organization employed in the three types of shipbuilding and corresponding diversities in the economic conditions under which the craftsmen worked.

CHAPTER VII

INDUSTRIAL ORGANIZATION IN THE PRIVATE SHIPYARDS

The simplest form of industrial organization was that under which worked the builders of the smallest craft. Though much of this business had been lost during the fifteenth century to the barge-builders further inland, there was enough production left at Venice to support a class recognized as distinct from the other shipbuilding craftsmen, the *squerarioli*. The type of industrial organization prevailing in the group of enterprises in which they engaged is adequately characterized as retail handicraft.[1] They required but a small shipyard, a few helpers, and a little capital to buy lumber, nails, and other supplies and to support themselves when business was slack. Possessed of these essentials they were in an independent position, able to fill the orders that might come to them. Their establishments might be considered boat shops just as those of other artisans would be considered shoe shops or hat shops.

Guild statutes dating from the thirteenth century insured both caulkers and ship carpenters the right to keep shipyards and to have on hand pitch, tow, nails, and other necessities of their crafts. They could employ other masters to work for them.[2] In 1407 the *squerarioli* were mentioned by that distinguishing name in a new craft rule which forbade launching any ship or barge until all the masters had been paid.[3] In 1477 they were allowed by the shipwrights' guild to have two apprentices each although other masters, even the foremen or *proti*, were forbidden to have more than one.[4] The forest code developed in the sixteenth century made special provision for

---

[1] As the expression is used by N. S. B. Gras, *Industrial Evolution* (Cambridge, 1930), chap. ii.
[2] *I capitolari*, " Capitulare callefatorum ", chaps. 31, 34; " Capitulare de marangonis ", chaps. 23, 24, 73, 74.
[3] A. S. V., Arch. delle Arti, busta 304, house carpenters vs. ship carpenters, ff. 35-36.
[4] Arsenale, busta 6, ff. 13-15.

the cutting of oaks by the *squerarioli* in the reserved woods, but limited them, in 1584, to twelve trees twice a year.[5]

According to the early guild regulations the ship carpenters were permitted to do work by the job, namely, to do a given piece of work for a fixed sum. That was essential to the independent position of the *squerarioli,* who built boats for sale and sold not their labor itself but the product of their labor.[6] But since such a system also made for speedy rather than careful work, the caulkers, on whose care the seaworthiness of the vessel immediately depended, were forbidden to work in that manner on any job costing more than 20 *soldi,* a sum which about 1500 would have been less than their daily summer wage.[7]

In the first part of the fifteenth century some of the ship carpenters began to build big ships under contract, charging so much for the ship or job, and taking upon themselves the organization and supervision of the enterprise. The Senate interfered and forbade work by the job on boats of 47 tons or more, alleging that the ships so built were not well made, and that the practice was ruining the craft of ship carpenters.[8] These may have been the true reasons, but possibly the ruling class of merchants wished to preserve that field of economic activity for themselves and keep the craftsmen dependent on them. At all events, the Senate found it wise in 1425 to modify the law made three years before so as to

[5] A. S. V., Arti, busta 706, *Capitolare dei squerarioli,* f. 16. Also: *I capitolari,* "Marangonis", chap. 42; Senato Mar, files, Dec. 28, 1546.

[6] *I Capitolari,* "Marangonis", chapters 33, 71, 77, and 78. *Supra se, supra de sè, sopra sè* are the expressions used in the sources which have been interpreted as meaning by the job, under contract, or as their own bosses. The exact meaning of the expression is most clearly revealed when it is used in connection with the work in the Arsenal.

Chapter 55 is interpreted by Monticolo as forbidding work *sopra de sè.* It reads: "quod si aliquis magister dicte artis tulerit seu acceperit aliquod laborerium supra se ad faciendum, non audeat ipsum laborerium recipere modo aliquo vel ingenio. . . ." But is it not possible that the subject of "audeat" is understood to be "any other master", so that the purpose of this chapter like that of chapter 33 is on the one hand to prevent the owner from changing his contractor, and to prevent any master from cutting in and underbidding another master. Unless the paragraph is so interpreted it is inconsistent with itself and with chapters 71, 77, 78, which are of later date and which clearly imply work *supra de sè.*

[7] *Ibid.,* "Callefatorum", chaps. 3 and 33.   [8] Senato Misti, reg. 54, f. 6.

raise the size of ship which could be built under contract from 47 tons to 94 tons. The earlier law, it was asserted, had caused the shipwrights to demand such high wages that fewer boats were being made at Venice.[9]

The activity of the shipwrights heading shipyards of their own in which they built for prearranged prices or for sale was thus limited in law to the field of production which was naturally theirs for economic reasons. In contrast with their modest enterprises the building of a large merchantman was an ambitious venture which could not be undertaken save by those well supplied with capital. The larger the ship the more difficult it was to secure the necessary timbers, many of which had to be brought from afar at great expense. It was necessary to have one of the largest shipyards of the city, and employ some score of workmen. Those financing the venture had to lay out money for a couple of years while their product as yet brought no return.[10] Moreover, with the demand calling for only four or five such ships a year even in the best of times, it would have been a bold man indeed who undertook so costly a venture on the chance of finding a customer when the job was done. Normally, therefore, those who wished to own a ship took the lead in having one built.[11]

[9] *Ibid.*, reg. 55, f. 78.

[10] The following examples indicate the time it was expected to take or actually took to build big ships:

State Ships.

1422. Ordered in November of 1422 to be done the next December. One launched July, 1425 and the other later. Senato Misti, reg. 54, f. 63; reg. 55, ff. 65, 134.

1498. Ordered January, 1498, begun before September, 1499, about to be launched May, 1501, launched June, 1501. Senato Mar, reg. 14, ff. 141, 196; Sanuto, *Diarii*, III, 122, 140; IV, 51; Arsenale, busta 133, f. 3.

1554. Wood already cut and building begun, December, 1554. Practically done but boarded over for the winter, October, 1556. Ordered launched February, 1558. Senato Mar, reg. 32, f. 179; reg. 33, f. 96; reg. 34, f. 64.

Private Ships, being built with loans or subsidies.

1486. Must be ready to sail in two years. Senato Mar, reg. 12, f. 87.

1490. Building must be begun three months from the time of the offer, launching one year later, masts up two months later. *Ibid.*, reg. 13, ff. 27-29.

1534. Ship must be launched in two and a half years from the date of the passing of the law authorizing loans. *Ibid.*, reg. 23, f. 25.

1535. Those intending to build with loan from state must register their intention in six months, and have the ship launched two years later. *Ibid.*, reg. 23, f. 88.

[11] That this was actually the case is shown by the fact that before 1570 all those

This they might do in one of two ways: either they could find a wealthy craftsman who would contract to supply them the ship at a fixed price, or they could themselves take full economic control of the enterprise, merely hiring by the day the foreman who was to design the ship and supervise the craftmanship of the other masters. If the former were the case, then, theoretically, the boss carpenter who took the contract might be in a position close to that of a capitalist producer, and have his own shipyard, buy his own supplies, and hire and pay his own workers. He might be a man of considerable means able to wait for his pay till the job was done. Under these conditions he would be in a position to organize the work in his shipyard according to his ideas of efficiency. Since the technical secrets of building were in his possession, it is conceivable that he would come to occupy himself only with the design of the ship and leave the hewing of the timbers and all other manual labor to the masters he employed. He could then thrust himself between the shipowners and his fellow craftsmen who would become no longer his fellows, but his laborers over whom he ruled as employer, designer, and taskmaster. If, on the other hand, the merchant customers took control, they might be the ones who furnished the craftsmen with materials, rented a shipyard for the occasion, engaged the workers and saw to it that they did not loaf, kept all the accounts, and bore the financial burden. As between these two theoretical and contrasting systems, it was something much nearer the latter than the former which prevailed at Venice from about 1425 to about 1570.

Accordingly the first move towards the creation of a ship was an agreement between merchants to finance and direct the building and sailing of a ship, or the decision of some more permanent association, such as a family partnership, to invest their funds in that way.[12] Large ships were usually owned by

anywhere mentioned as having accepted the loans of the state and started building ships were owners thereof, *patroni, parcenevoli,* and not craftsmen.

[12] Shares in ships are mentioned in many agreements creating *fraterne* in A. S. V., Sezione notariale, Cancelleria Inf., busta 149, notary Francesco Bono.

an association of shareholders, not by one individual.[13] Shares in ships had been a recognized form of negotiable wealth in Venice since the eleventh century.[14] By means of such shares the capital needed for building and outfitting a ship might be recruited from a large number of different people and the risks involved widely distributed. The individual shareowner was risking only the value of his shares in the ship. If he did not pay his portion of any expenses which might be incurred on account of the ship he forfeited his shares to the other partners. The shipbuilding association offered an opportunity to invest without incurring unlimited liability.[15]

The following abstract of the terms of a partnership concluded in 1519 illustrates the nature of such an association. Michele Foscarini, Nicolò Semitecolo, Giovanni Francesco Giustinian, and Gerolamo Badoer agreed to build a ship of 300 tons through a partnership (*compagnia*) between all four in which each was to have six shares (*carati*). Any profit or loss resulting from the building was to be to the common profit or loss of all four partners. They each promised to contribute proportionally all the money necessary for the construction of the ship, to cut wood, to pay the labor of masters, and to fit it for sailing. In case any partner failed to do his share, the others could continue building, paying the portion of the defaulting partner who would be excluded thenceforth from the partnership. The ship was to be begun after the next Christmas and labored on continually till finished.

[13] The owners of ships are almost always referred to in the plural in the general regulations and in mention of specific ships both in Sanuto and in the official records; for example, A. S. V., Notatorio, reg. 30, ff. 80-82.

[14] Schaube, p. 21; L. Goldschmidt, *Handbuch des Handelsrechts*, I, *Universalgeschichte des Handelsrechts* (Stuttgart, 1891), pp. 290, 340, 341.

[15] In the *Codice per la veneta mercantile marina* (Venice, 1786), p. 8, the other partners are permitted to borrow on the shares of the defaulting partner. Straccha, *de navibus*, II, 6-8 (in *Clarissimi iuris consulti Beneventi Stracchae paritii Anconitani de mercatura seu mercatore tractatus*, Venice, 1553, pp. 148-9) implies that all the shareholders were to be consulted before repairs were made on a ship, but that, in case the repairs were desirable, one shareowner could make the necessary expense and hold the other owners liable. In case one of the owners failed to pay his share for the refitting or rebuilding of the ship, he lost possession of his shares. They passed to the owner who did fulfill his obligations. Straccha then considers in what cases a ship rebuilt might be considered a new ship.

They agreed in the election of Nicolò Semitecolo as leader
to keep accounts and pay the expenses as they occurred,
but he was to take counsel with his partners before making
any disbursement and to show them his accounts whenever
they requested it.

The partners agreed in the election of Giovanni Francesco
Giustinian captain (*patron*) of the ship. He was to have
charge of engaging and paying the crew, and of furnishing
the ship for sailing. He was required to keep accounts which
would be open to all the partners. He was to have eight
thousandweights of freighting space for his personal profit
and a salary of sixty ducats a month beginning at the time he
was sent to launch the ship. He could accommodate passengers
in his cabin, but the freight of any merchandise carried in his
cabin was to belong to the partnership. He was allowed one
ducat a head (a month ?) for feeding the crew. He could
not be removed from his captaincy without manifest cause,
but could renounce his captaincy whenever he no longer
desired to sail.

Because the ship was to be built outside the city, therefore,
if the partners were not able to make adequate arrangements
with the foreman (*proto*) making the ship, whichever partner
would take the task with least expense should be considered
elected to go to take charge at the place where the ship was
to be built. He was to keep a good account of all goods sent to
him there. If any goods were sold by him, they were to be
to the profit or loss of the partnership.

To avoid lawsuits, Angelo Badoer was elected judge in all
controversies which might arise between the members of the
partnership.[16]

Another contract reveals a different way of dividing the
expense and management of the construction of a ship. One
of the contracting parties, Francesco di Vicenzo, was explicitly
charged with the supervision at the place of building, Curzola.
The other, Antonio di Ambrosio Grattaruol, was to stay at

[16] Museo Civico Correr, Venice, codici Cicogna, 3431/X. Attested before witnesses
by the notary Francesco Brochetto.

Venice and send to Curzola all the wood, iron, and other wares which Francesco might request, and money for other materials for the body of the ship. Francesco was responsible for having the ship constructed as specified and paying the labor. The cost, size, dimensions, equipment, and date of completion of the ship were stipulated in the contract. When the ship was completed Francesco was to receive the rest of the price agreed upon, or might, if he wished, take shares in the ship in payment.[17]

The building of a warship, undertaken in isolation from the general maintenance of a navy, was an enterprise similar to the construction of a large merchantman. Since the Arsenal of Venice was, before 1660, devoted almost exclusively to galley building, and was not suitable for the construction of round ships, special arrangements were usually made when such vessels were to be built by the government. Of course, the project could be turned over to private enterprise by auctioning the undertaking to the lowest bidder. Such a possibility was considered but not used between 1400 and 1570 to obtain large warships. Instead the government set up a special organization similar to that used by a private ship-building partnership. Its essential features were a foreman shipwright, an accountant, and a superintendent who was not a craftsman but on the contrary a member of the nobility paid for his services. The foreman shipwright was responsible for the technical direction, both in selecting timbers and shaping the ship, but did not himself buy the wood, nor hire and pay the masters, nor was he made responsible for speeding up the workers. When it was desired to hasten the building of two ships under construction in 1424, the Lords of the Arsenal were ordered to hire sixty caulkers, and later to employ fifteen or twenty ship carpenters and the same number of caulkers, to finish either one or both of the ships as soon as possible. Moreover, one of the Lords of the Arsenal was to go and stay

---

[17] The ship was to be 168 tons below deck. It seems extremely unlikely that Francesco di Vicenzo was a shipwright for nowhere is he called a foreman, master, or ship carpenter, and he did not promise to make the ship himself but might have it made—" se hobliga fabrichar overo far fabricar." A. S. V., Consoli dei Mercanti, busta 128.

morning and afternoon every day to oversee the masters so
that the work might be finished more quickly.[18] For each of
the two ships ordered in 1451 the College chose a foreman
shipwright, a superintendent, and an accountant. The masters
were paid directly and individually by treasury officials. To
secure the timbers needed for such large ships instructions
were sent to the government officials resident in Friuli ordering them to have the wood cut, sawed and transported.[19] The
foreman and the accountant went to the woods, the foreman
to select the timber and to determine the measures and design
by which it was prepared before being shipped to Venice.[20]
In 1554 when work was begun on a new galleon in the shipyard of Sant' Antonio the Lords of the Arsenal provided the
wood, chose one of the expert shipwrights of the Arsenal,
Giovanni Maria Spuazza, foreman of the ship, and appointed
also a steward to guard the supplies, a foreman for the caulkers, and an accountant to make out the payroll of the masters
and to keep track of the pitch, tow, and iron used.[21]

These organizations were typical in that the initiator of
the building, whether the state or a private association of
shareholders, assumed the economic direction of the enterprise. The shipowners, who, from the craftsmen's point of
view, were the customers or consumers, generally took it upon
themselves to supply the lumber. For example, Gentile Contarini and Brothers asked in 1472 for the privilege of importing sawed timbers for the 600 ton ship they were having
built.[22] The many petitioners who in the sixteenth century

[18] Senato Misti, reg. 55, f. 65.

[19] Senato Mar, reg. 4, ff. 87, 88, 91, 96, 154, 185; Senato Terra, reg. 3, f. 9. Foremen, supervisors, and accountants were also chosen for the ships ordered in 1432
and the workers paid by the *Officiales Rationum Veterum*. The noble elected supervisor was paid 10 ducats a month. Senato Misti, reg. 58, f. 103. Supervisors to be
paid 70 ducats to the completion of the ship had been provided originally, in 1422,
for the two ships which the Lords of the Arsenal were made responsible for complet-
ing in 1424. *Ibid.*, reg. 54, f. 63; Notatorio, no. 7, f. 184.

[20] Senato Mar, reg. 4, ff. 88, 162.

[21] Arsenale, busta 135, ff. 141-147. After 1475 the direction of the building of
government round ships was given to the Lords of the Arsenal. In 1475 and 1487
they were permitted either to let contracts for the ships or have them built by masters
working by the day. They chose to have the work done by the day under foremen
from the Arsenal. Senato Terra, reg. 7, ff. 98-99, 145; above chap. III.

[22] Notatorio di Collegio, no. 13, f. 11, January 11, 1472.

successfully sought licenses to export lumber duty free to Curzola all appear to have been nobles, owners of ships, not craftsmen.[23] The law of 1559 which forbade the cutting of Venetian oak for large ships named the shareholders of the ships as those who could no longer cut. That same law immediately brought forth protests from two such shipowners who boasted of their efforts to find oak for their ships both in Venetian territory and in foreign parts.[24]

The shipyards were usually obtained from a third party and only for the occasion. In a list of all the ships being built in 1507, whenever the owner of the shipyard was mentioned he was not the same either as the foreman ship carpenter or as the owner of the ship. In no case was the shipyard stated to have belonged to either the foreman or owner of the ship being built there.[25]

The foreman of the caulkers employed was required by the statutes of his guild to limit his activity to his technical functions. He was forbidden to take work except by the day.[26]

[23] Senato Mar, reg. 21, f. 61; reg. 22, f. 13, and there are many other examples in the series Mar.

[24] *Ibid.*, reg. 54, ff. 57, 81, 114.

[25] Notatorio di Collegio, no. 24, f. 7, July 5, 1507. The ships were:

" La nave de Nobel homo Ser Philippo Bernardo e fradeli . . . al squero di Saloni driedo la doana da mare . . . Bartholomeo Todeschini proto de dicta nave,

La nave del nobel homo Ser Michele Malipiero . . . al Sancto Spirito al squero de Jacomo Brochta . . . Domenego de Zorzi soprastante de dicta nave. Uno cavo da prova nel dicto squero . . . dicto Domenego proto . . . e . . . Dimitri Greco, manangon de dicta nave. . . .

La nave de i Nicolesi e compagni sopra el squero de Polo da Locha al Spirito Sancto . . .

Una nave nel squero de cave de muola da chà Navaier del nobel homo Ser Luca Donada e fradelli. . . . (The proto mentioned but not named.)

La nave del nobel homo Ser Piero Contarini . . . nel squero de Bartholomio Navaro al Spirito Sancto . . . Maistro Mathio Trevisan, proto de quella. . . .

La nave del nobel homo Francesco Malipiero que Ser Peratio è a presso Quantavale per mezo Castello . . . dicto Maistro Mathio proto."

In this connection it is interesting to note a law of 1467—Senato Terra, reg. 5, f. 79—which stated that the owners of the *squeri* where ships came to be refitted had been forcing the shipowners who wished to use their docks to buy from them at exorbitant prices the materials used for refitting. That makes it clear that the noble merchants who built and owned ships did not have their own *squeri*. There is nowhere in the law any reference to craftsmen, so presumably they also were not the owners of the docks.

[26] Note 7, above; chapter 20 of the " Capitolari " of 1577 also printed by Monticolo, *I Capitolari.*

Not he but the shipowners determined the rate at which the masters who assisted him were to be paid, at least until wage cuts drove the caulkers to persuade the state to fix the standard.[27] Either the owners or the foreman engaged the workmen and gave them their pay.[28] But the craft rules held the foreman responsible for declaring any defects he might find in the wood or in the caulking, for decreasing the pay of any master whom the gastaldo of the guild had declared to be inferior, for sending the workers home to dinner at the proper hour, and for docking the pay of those who came late or went away on their own business during working hours.[29] If he had had a personal economic interest in the amount of energy displayed by his fellow masters, it would hardly have been necessary to require by statute that he decrease the pay of those that did not work full time.

The foreman employed by the day was primarily a salaried technical expert. But the foreman shipwright did not always restrict his functions to that rôle despite the law of 1425 which prohibited work by contract on large ships. The quarrels between the caulkers' guild and the *squerarioli* over the enforcement of that law indicate that for a time it was enforced, but ultimately it was disregarded, and the extent to which the government had work done by the job in the Arsenal raises some doubts as to how strictly the prohibition was ever interpreted. Nor is a system of day labor suggested by a deed of sale of 1442 by which a noble transferred to a ship carpenter, Francesco de Janutiis de Negroponte, a Russian female slave named Christina for the price of sixty gold ducats which the noble acknowledged he had already received in work done by the said shipwright on his ship.[30] Sixty ducats was at that time about half the yearly salary of the Foreman Shipwright of the Arsenal.

[27] Marciana *Mariegola dei Calafai,* ff. 33-4. The *patroni* are held responsible for forcing wages down.
[28] *I Capitolari,* " Callefatorum ", chap. 29. Marciana *Mariegola,* chaps. 55-6, 62, 72.
[29] *I Capitolari,* " Callefatorum ", chaps. 16, 84. Marciana *Mariegola,* chaps. 31, 73.
[30] A. S. V., Sezione notariale, Cancelleria inf., busta 149, notary Vettor Pomino, April 10, 1442. Probably the same Francesco de Negroponte chosen to build the state cog in 1422.

But the careers of the most active foreman shipwrights of the mid-sixteenth century give evidence that few if any were independent heads of shipyards. Typical was Francesco di Antonio Rosso who built one ship launched at Quintavalle in 1557 and another launched at Sant' Antonio in 1560. In petitioning in 1553 that his pay in the Arsenal be raised from 24 *soldi* to 40 *soldi* a day, he based his request on faithful service, proved capacity, and, as was usual in such petitions, his need for a higher wage in order to support his family, three sons and a daughter. The latter plea need not be taken literally, but it shows the homage still paid to the idea long associated with craft work that the artisan should earn only what he needed to support himself. The bulk of his petition was devoted to recounting his services. He built the first ship of Giovanni Dolfin, the "Corneretto" made at Meduna, also the "Marcella" made at Motta. When war galleys were urgently needed he took contracts to build in the Arsenal with the materials there furnished two galleys of the design of Alvise Scatola and two of the design of Francesco Bressan. Then he was vice-captain of the oak reserve of Montello for sixteen months, and for four years was employed by the state cutting wood in Asolo and Cenedese. No sooner had he returned to Venice that the *Magistrato sopra le Acque* sent him to Padua to cut piles. On his return he immediately set to work and built of his own design the large ship "Liona" at Murano.[31]

Piero Zaparin and Giovanni Maria Spuazza also built two ships launched between October, 1557 and July, 1560 and in neither case were the two ships built in the same shipyard. The fathers of both had been construction chiefs in the Arsenal, and the sons worked there also. Before 1548 Spuazza had been selected by shipowners to make ten merchantmen, and counted it a point in his favor that he had constructed them of foreign timbers so as to preserve the Venetian forests.[32] There emerges only the name of one shipwright

[31] Senato Mar, reg. 32, f. 125 and files, Dec. 21, 1553.
[32] *Ibid.*, reg. 28, f. 93 and files, 1545; reg. 33, f. 41 and files, Sept. 26, 1556; reg. 29, f. 182 and files, June 29, 1548.

active at that time, Antonio Pegoloto, who was particularly associated with one shipyard.[33]

The position of the foreman ship carpenter did not, of course, have to be one of the two theoretical extremes previously outlined. The customer merchants might supply him with the shipyard, the lumber, and money enough to keep going, and still he might contract for all the labor, or he might contract to make repairs or additions to a ship already built. The exact relations between those wishing a ship and their boss shipwright were defined by a special agreement in each case. In default of the evidence of many such contracts it is not possible to state positively how the details were arranged.[34]

The construction of the medium sized ships, 100 tons to 240 tons, presented a type of industrial enterprise in which the foreman ship carpenters might very well be able to contract to furnish all the labor necessary and very likely part of the materials as well. The law of 1422 is evidence that they were doing so. Such undertakings must have been very numerous in the days of the Doge Mocenigo, but this type of building had almost ceased at Venice by the middle of the sixteenth century.

[33] Lists of ships launched of 240 tons or more in Museo Civico, Arch. Donà della Rosa, busta 217. Of eight shipwrights whose ships were launched between Oct., 1557 and July, 1560 only Rosso, Zaparin, and Spuazza built two. Marco naso di vin and Antonio Pegoloto, who each built one during the period covered, are mentioned in a petition of Giovanni Morello in 1545. Morello had employed on a *marciliana* in the Po River " Marco Nasavin " and other Venetian shipwrights and caulkers at 5 ducats a month. Then he had brought the ship to Venice and finished it in the shipyards of " Antonio Pegoloto " at Sant' Antonio. The ship built by Giovanni Antonio Pegoloto in 1559 was also made at Sant' Antonio. Senato Mar, reg. 28, f. 92 and files, October, 1545.

Antonio Bordola, who built one ship in 1559, had been given a regular position in the Arsenal in 1547. *Ibid.,* reg. 29, f. 120.

The other two, not otherwise known, were Tommaso Puglieri and Agostino de Martin da Sibinico.

[34] Sampling in the notarial archives at Venice failed to find such contracts. Bryne's study of Genoese contracts of the twelfth and thirteenth centuries reveals much the same situation in regard to the position of the foremen as that I here attempt to establish for Venice from indirect sources, except that he suggests that usually the foreman contracted for the labor and hired the masters. *Genoese Shipping,* pp. 25-26. The *Codice per la veneta mercantile marina* (Venice, 1786), pp. 4-7, provided that there must be a written contract between shareowners and foreman which would stipulate the dimensions of the ship, and that the foreman should choose and pay the masters who assisted him.

Large scale industry and vigorous capitalism were not to be found in the private shipyards between 1425 and 1570. The building of a large merchantman certainly required capital, but that came chiefly from the merchants, not from the industry itself. Such an enterprise was usually an isolated industrial episode incidental to the general commercial activity of those who initiated and financed it. The shipwrights working in private shipyards fell into one of three groups: the great majority were ordinary masters, skilled manual laborers who worked by the day; one minor group was composed of the independent heads of small shipyards; and another and distinct minority were the foremen builders of big merchantmen who were generally salaried technical directors but might also contract for the labor.[35]

At the end of the sixteenth century a new type of craftsman shipbuilder suddenly came into prominence in connection with the state subsidy policy. Many of this new generation of boss carpenters were apparently descendents of those just mentioned. Shipbuilding in Venice was proceeding at an abnormally slow pace, the capital won in commerce was seeking employment elsewhere, and the state, anxious to aid the declining industry, reversed its previous opposition to enterprises directed by craftsmen on their own initiative and gave financial support to their ambitions.

The leading figure in this new group of craftsmen entrepreneurs was Bernardin Sebastiano Rosso. Already in 1565 he had built a sizable ship in his own shipyard.[36] The clearest statement of his position comes in a petition which he presented to the Signoria in 1589.[37] The preamble read:

I, Bernardin Sebastiano Rosso, see that the building of ships is being destroyed and annihilated not only because of the great expense of [building] them, but also because of the scarcity and remoteness of good timbers from foreign lands, and for other reasons which are well known to Your Serenity, so that in a few years there will be no more serviceable ones. And I have up till now

[35] This conclusion is in substantial agreement with that of Luzzato, " Costruzioni navali ", pp. 386-387, except that he does not distinguish between the last two groups.
[36] Senato Mar, files, December 18, 1565.

built twenty or more vessels as is known to everyone, and finally have attempted to sell my last, which I have been obliged to keep three years on the shipyard to my great loss. And it has befallen me to lose off the two castles [of the Lido] in the building of said ships three small ships and finally a large barge loaded with oak. And I wish to build in this city ten ships of 360 tons or more in ten years and as many as I may have occasion to sell. For these reasons, and in order that I may be sure to be able to sell these ships with the chance to have imported a great quantity of timber from El Monte [88] and other foreign places which will serve wonderfully well for building and the profit of the city, and because of the reverence which I owe to the Most Serene Government, therefore, as above said, I petition that there be conceded to me the things here following below. Likewise I petition for some provision for the sustenance of my family in order that I may live and die in this famous city in the service of Your Serenity as I have desired, having refused good offers from other Princes who wished that I should serve them, nor ever wishing [to accept them] because of the particular inclination which I have for the service of the Republic, and especially because of firm hope of being rewarded as the munificence of Your Serenity deigns, and has done to so many others.

The first of the concessions which he asked was that a credit of 7000 ducats be extended for each ship which he built. He did not ask that he himself receive the loan, and in the resolution by which the Senate in the main granted his requests it was specified that the buyers of the ships were the men responsible for the repayment of the loans. Indirectly the state would in part finance his undertaking, but only indirectly through the usual merchant buyer. Moreover, it is hard to believe that Rosso himself was in 1589 in a position to lay out much capital, however much he may, as the earlier portion of his petition indicates, have done so before, since he was at the same time petitioning for a dole from the state to support him and his family and was voted 5 ducats a month for that purpose.

[87] *Ibid.*, May 31, 1589, and Cinque Savii, first series, busta 25, f. 39. The construction of the preamble of his petition has necessarily been changed considerably since in the original it is all one sentence.

[88] Although it may be a long shot, I take this to refer to Monte Sant' Angelo in Apulia named by Crescenzio, pp. 3-5, as famous for the ship timbers obtained there.

The largest part of his requests concerned a stable labor supply. He asked that for every ship which he built he be able to employ the following eighteen workmen who could not be taken from him by anyone: four ship carpenters, two caulkers—one *da figgier* and one *da maggio*—with their four grown apprentices, four stevedores for moving materials, and four grown apprentice ship carpenters, who, when they had worked on three ships continuously till their completion, would be accepted to take the tests and be eligible for employment in the Arsenal at the usual pay given masters. In addition he asked that these men be employed in the Arsenal on any day when, because of rain or other good reason, they could not work in his shipyard His desire for a permanent group of workers is suggestive. He may merely have wished to be free from the interruptions which would come from having his laborers called away to work for the government. Then again, he may have had ideas of his own of how things were to be done, ideas which he hoped to teach his employees. This would be more possible as out of the eighteen men only six were master craftsmen. Finally, he may have thought that by giving to his workers the surety of constant employment, either in his shipyard or in the Arsenal, he could engage them for less than they would have taken if they had had to allow, like most of the craftsmen, for many idle days in each year.

Rosso was also concerned with cutting down the cost of materials. He obviously expected to secure and prepare them himself. He asked that two or three ships which he intended to keep for importing wood be free to sail wherever he wished without interference from any official, and that the wood which he imported from abroad might be sawed and prepared in any way he might find convenient to save expense.

While Rosso appears to have been the trail breaker for the boss carpenters into fields of greater initiative and management, he was not alone. Giacomo Zaparin was also an independent and ambitious director of a shipyard. In 1599 he too presented a petition, offering to build six ships of from 300 to 600 tons in the next six years if he were granted loans and other concessions.[39] The outcome of that offer is uncertain, but in 1608 loans were granted by the state for two ships built in his shipyard,[40] and in that same year he proposed to build ten galleons of 180 tons for commercial use if subsidized. The Board of Trade recommended that if he built galleons of from 240 to 300 tons, their purchasers be granted the loans.[41]

The case of Piero Solto is somewhat different, since it was he and not the purchaser who was to receive the loan from the state. In 1587 when granted a loan he had been for three years building a 720 ton ship. He had arranged the price with a purchaser, but was unable because of lack of funds to finish the ship. In view of the need for large ships and of the services which he and his eight brothers had given in the war—he had been at gunner at Famagosta—the state helped him out with a direct loan of 5500 ducats.[42]

Giorgio da Andrea was likewise granted a loan directly. His petition indicates that he was a boss ship carpenter who had been unable to find employment because of the few ships which were being built. It was the prodding of necessity which induced him to set to work to build a large ship on his own responsibility.[43]

It is probable that the motives professed by Giorgio da Andrea also influenced many of the other boss ship carpenters. In the decline of the Venetian shipbuilding industry which took place at the end of the century these technical experts were the worst sufferers. The merchant princes who were accustomed to finance such projects could readily turn their funds to whatever other uses they found to be more profitable. The skill of the workman was not so mobile. Either they must earn their living by the craft which they had learned from their fathers and practiced from their youth, or else surrender entirely their high position as aristocrats among craft

---

[39] Senato Mar, reg. 55, f. 146; Cinque Savii, first series, busta 140, ff. 64-5.
[40] *Ibid.*, third series, busta 97.
[41] *Ibid.*, first series, busta 142, ff. 51, 58.
[42] A. S. V., Miscellanei codici, no. 665.
[43] Senato Mar, files, August 24, 1591; Cinque Savii, first series, busta 26, f. 47.

workers. It was easy for a merchant to transfer funds to Holland and build his ships there instead of in Venice. It was extremely hard and unnatural for the descendant of a famous family of shipwrights to leave the beloved and renowned Venice which he and his forefathers had served in battle and go to live in foreign lands to practice his craft. To avoid that they took the initiative in building ships and turned to the state for loans and concessions which would enable them to practice their art in the city of their birth.

The state was ready to aid them. To be sure, they were violating the law of 1425, but conditions had changed since then. That law had been made when the industry was flourishing and merchant nobles of the ruling class were ready to invest in and supervise the business. Now, in the late sixteenth century, the state was ready to aid anyone who would help to save from destruction an industry which had once been her glory and her strength.

It would be a mistake, however, to think that a few ambitious boss carpenters were the only men taking the responsibility for the construction of ships. On the contrary, among the petitions for loans made during the last years of the century, those from merchants are far more numerous than those from craftsmen.[44] The four cases cited above were but highly interesting exceptions. It was still the expected thing that associations of merchant princes should take the initiative in building the ships which carried their wares.

[44] Examples: Silvestri and Cabianca began to build a 600 ton ship because the previous January they had lost a large ship bound for Sicily for grain. Senato Mar, files, August 17, 1596.

Balbiani started a 420 ton ship because he had lost one returning from Syria, *ibid.*, November 5, 1596.

Barozzi built anew because he recently lost two ships, *ibid.*, September 4, 1596.

Leoni in asking a loan to build said that he was the foremost at Constantinople in exporting grain, *ibid.*, April 2, 1594.

Giovanni Nani gave as his reason for building the fact that not enough of the shipowners are making provision to build to keep up the supply, *ibid.*, July 13, 1591.

CHAPTER VIII

THE GROWTH OF THE ARSENAL

The equipment of a war fleet and the preparation of the reserves of arms and rigging needed for its maintenance called for a more permanent and elaborate organization than the temporary arrangements which sufficed the merchant builders. But not until the Venetian navy attained its greatest strength, in the sixteenth century, were methods of large scale production needed to build the war fleet. Though both the construction and the arming of warships were always functions of the Arsenal, it was probably at first relatively more important as a depot of munitions and naval stores than as a center of Venetian shipbuilding.

From its foundation in 1104 until the fourteenth century the Arsenal enclosed only about eight acres,[1] an area which in the sixteenth century furnished room for five sizable warehouses and docks fit for storing or building twenty-four light galleys. It was governed directly by three nobles elected by the Great Council to act as its *patroni* and paid for their services.[2] These Lords of the Arsenal were required to live in houses near the Arsenal which acquired the suggestive names of " paradiso ", " purgatorio ", and " inferno ".[3] The early statutes implied that the masters employed were given their meals in the Arsenal.[4] If the number working exceeded six, one of the Lords was supposed to be present in person to supervise them.[5] The Lords were required to go personally around the

---

[1] Casoni, " Forze ", pp. 94-96 and plan; measures in A. S. V., Arsenale, busta 1.

[2] Arsenale, busta 5. It is noteworthy that they were called *patroni* as were the owners or captains of ships built in the private shipyards, but the rendering " Lords " has been chosen as most suggestive of the status of their office.

[3] Casoni, " Forze ", pp. 146-7.

[4] Arsenale, busta 5, chap. 59 of first series (1331).

[5] *Ibid.*, chap. 38; Maggior Consiglio, Liber Magnus, ff. 23-24; *Deliberazioni del Maggior Consiglio di Venezia* (ed. Roberto Cessi, *Atti delle assemblee costituzionali italiane dal medio evo al 1831*, pub. by R. Accademia dei Lincei, ser. iii, sez. i, Bologna, 1931), II, 243-244. This rule was in force before 1273 and was modified thereafter.

Arsenal every three days, to inspect all ships returned by commanders, to report the condition of the vessels in the Arsenal every three months, and to " see and feel " all the rigging and arms twice a year.[6] As a reserve fleet, they were to keep always ready four galleys and two smaller craft.[7]

The fleets of nearly one hundred ships sent out by Venice in her thirteenth century wars with Genoa give no indication of the scale of the building carried on in the Arsenal in that century, for it was then the custom to recruit war fleets by enlisting or conscripting private merchant vessels.[8] Venice was ahead of most contemporary naval powers in maintaining from an early date a small permanent war fleet.[9] But even this nucleus of state ships was not always constructed within the walls of the Arsenal. Galleys as well as round ships were sometimes built for the state elsewhere in the city under the direction of the Lords of the Arsenal,[10] and sometimes galleys were constructed for the government by private contractors.[11]

Ship construction in the Arsenal increased enormously at the time of the introduction of the great galley and the cog. The size of the communal shipyard was quadrupled by two additions, one begun in 1303, the other in 1325. Together they formed the New Arsenal and gave the government shipyard the form it kept for the next one hundred and fifty years.[12] The contemporary change in the character of the trading caravans made this enlargement necessary to meet the regular needs of the state. The voyages of the merchant galleys were so regulated as to limit the commercial opportunities for their

---

[6] A. S. V., Maggior Consiglio, Liber Magnus, ff. 23-24 (1301).

[7] *Deliberazioni del Maggior Consiglio* (ed. Cessi), II, 244 (1276); Arsenale, busta 5, chap. 20 of first series.

[8] Manfroni, *Ninfeo . . . Costantinopoli,* pp. 210, 207; W. Carew Hazlitt, *The Venetian Republic* (London, 1915), II, 534-535.

[9] Manfroni, *Costantinopoli . . . Lepanto,* pp. 29-30.

[10] *Deliberazioni del Maggior Consiglio,* II, 244. In 1301 the Lords were forbidden to have ships prepared outside the Arsenal except by order of the Ducal Council. A. S. V., Maggior Consiglio, Liber Magnus, f. 24.

[11] *I prestiti della Repubblica di Venezia (Documenti finanziarii della Repubblica di Venezia,* editi dalla Commissione per gli Atti delle Assemblee Costituzionali Italiane, R. Accademia dei Lincei, ser. iii, vol. I, pt. 1, Padua, 1929), doc. 72 (1301).

[12] Casoni, " Forze ", pp. 104-115.

use to a few great caravans which navigated under close state supervision. For a time some of these caravans were composed of galleys built by private merchants, but during the next half century the Senate settled on the policy of forming these fleets out of galleys rented by the Signoria to merchants who leased the ships in hopes of paying the rent, the wages of the crews, and a profit for themselves out of the freight collected from the shippers. Thus the state took upon itself almost all the galley building in Venice. The addition of the New Arsenal made it possible, about the middle of the fourteenth century, to concentrate this activity within the walls of the government shipyard.[13]

The relative importance of the Arsenal in Venetian ship-building was correspondingly enhanced. The addition to its original military functions of the maintenance of a part of the merchant marine more than doubled the work thrown upon the Arsenal in time of war. Private merchantmen were still used to increase the war fleet. Even in peace a couple of large cogs were frequently hired by the state to act as warships in pursuit of pirates,[14] and all the Venetian marine was counted a naval reserve which the state might call upon if the need arose.[15] But the change which had taken place in the type of merchantmen in common use by private shipowners made such auxiliaries less and less fitted to form a part of the war fleet. Cogs could not readily be manoeuvred to cooperate with galleys in battle. In the thirteenth century, or in the early fourteenth, there had been a large number of long ships in private hands which could, if needed, be converted into war-ships able to fight side by side with the galleys built in the Arsenal.[16] But after the state had given her own merchant galleys the monopoly in most trades in which galleys were profitable, almost no ships were left in private hands which

[13] Arsenale, busta 5, chap. 84 of first series (c. 1368).

[14] Examples (1406-1417): Senato Misti, reg. 52, f. 1; reg. 47, f. 64; reg. 49, f. 75.

[15] *Lettere di Collegio, 1308-1310* (ed. G. Giomo, *Miscellanea di storia veneta* edita dalla R. Dep. Veneta di Storia Patria, ser. iii, vol. I, Venice, 1910), pp. 289, 329; Christoforo Tentori, *Saggio . . . sulla storia della repubblica di Venezia* (Venice, 1785-1786), VI, 139; Sanuto, *Diarii*, III, 668; Hazlitt, *loc. cit.*

[16] Giomo, " Le rubriche ", *sub rubrica disarmatum navigium.*

could be used in line of battle.[17] The burden of building and outfitting those merchantmen which were most valuable in the war fleet, the great galleys, fell upon the same shipyard which supplied the light war galleys, the Arsenal.

The addition of the New Arsenal rendered the state shipyard capable of furnishing war fleets which apparently were regarded as adequate for the Genoese wars and the other maritime enterprises of the Republic before 1470. The great Venetian armaments of those years hardly ever exceeded thirty galleys unless they included many great galleys diverted from their voyages to the war fleets.[18] A substantial part of the navy was contributed by the Adriatic and Levantine colonies, but frequently the Venetian Arsenal furnished the galleys armed in Dalmatia or in Crete.[19] In normal peaceful years, the government authorized arming, for the police of the gulf, ten war galleys—or more precisely " galleys of the guard "—and a part of the ten were actually sent out.[20] The appearance of a rival armament was the signal for the election of a Captain General of the Sea to be given twenty or thirty galleys, but seldom were many more than twenty light galleys actually outfitted in the first year of hostilities. In 1378, the first year of " the death grapple with Genoa ", the Captain General of the Sea, Vettor Pisani, commanded twenty to twenty-four galleys.[21] Most of this armada was destroyed at Pola in the spring of 1379 and the surviving six were sent to join the thirteen buccaneering galleys which still kept the sea under

[17] Of course there were the pilgrim galleys. Cf. Malipiero, p. 54.

[18] Fleets equipped 1324-1355: Laurentii de Monacis, *Cronicon de rebus venetis ab U. C. ad annum 1354* (ed. Flamininus Cornelius as app. to *R. I. S.,* Venice, 1763), pp. 178, 205, 209, 211-215, 221; Mario Brunetti, *Contributo alla storia delle relazioni veneto-genovesi dal 1348 al 1350* (*Miscellanea di storia veneta,* ser. iii, vol. IX); Vittorio Lazzarini, "La battaglia di Porto Longo nell' isola di Sapienza", *Nuovo arch. veneto,* VIII (1894).

[19] Monacis, p. 219 (1354). The galley hulls regularly sent in the sixteenth century were called *arsili.* Arsenale, busta 11, f. 51.

[20] Monacis, p. 175 (1363); Senato Misti, reg. 47, ff. 24, 90 (1405 and 1407). Cf. Manfroni, *Costantinopoli . . . Lepanto,* pp. 191-192.

[21] Daniele Chinazza, *Cronaca della guerra di Chiozia tra li Veneziani e Genovesi* (ed. Muratori, *R. I. S.,* vol. XV), cols. 713-714; Giorgio Stella, *Annales genuenses* (ed. Muratori, *R. I. S.,* vol. XVII), cols. 1107-1110.

Nicolò Zeno.[22] Then, while the Genoese were besieging
Venice within her lagoon, the straining of every resource in
December of 1379 fitted out nine great galleys and twenty-five
light galleys which went forth to blockade the blockaders at
Chioggia.[23] In not one of the twenty-two years between the
close of that war and 1404 did Venice have as many as ten war
galleys at sea.[24] For the mainland wars which absorbed most
of the military energies of the Venetian state in the first part
of the fifteenth century the Arsenal outfitted flotillas of rowed
galleons,[25] but the fleets provided for the expeditions against
Genoa in 1431 and 1432 were of about the same size as those
of a century before, twenty-four and thirty-two galleys.[26]

Between 1325 and 1470 there was little if any progressive
change in the demands made upon the Arsenal for war fleets.
Less than ten light galleys were maintained in service in ordinary times; ten or twelve more were kept in such condition as
to be provided quickly at threat of war. The number of ships
which the Lords of the Arsenal were commanded to keep as a
reserve ready to be equipped at short notice had been increased from the thirteenth century figure—four galleys and
two smaller craft—to twenty-five galleys, great and light. The
latter figure was repeated in 1417 in a plea that the order
actually be observed.[27]

The trading fleets of state galleys grew steadily during the
same period. In the middle of the fifteenth century, if not
before, their maintenance constituted the greater part of the
activity of the government shipyard. In 1332 three fleets were
sent—eight galleys to the Black Sea, seven to Cyprus and
Lesser Armenia, and eight or more to Flanders. Only the
galleys to the Black Sea were ships which the state rented to

[22] Chinazza, cols. 720, 746-749.
[23] Ibid., cols. 732-744; Stella, col. 1114.
[24] Camillo Manfroni, " Le crisi della marina militare di Venezia dopo la guerra di
Chioggia ", Atti del Reale Istituto Veneto di Scienze, Lettere, ed Arte, tomo LXIX,
parte seconda (1910), pp. 983-991.
[25] Senato Misti, reg. 57, f. 182 (1430); reg. 58, f. 33 (1431); reg. 60, f. 240
(1440).
[26] Marino Sanuto, Vitae ducum Venetorum, italice scriptae (ed. Muratori, R. I. S.,
vol. XXII), cols. 1018-1019, 1029.
[27] Senato Misti, reg. 52, f. 72.

merchants for the voyage.[28] The other voyages were made by private galleys under strict governmental control. Around the middle of that century the number of galleys in each fleet was cut about in half coincidentally with the introduction of the larger merchant galleys permitted to load in the hold about 200 tons—instead of 140 tons—of merchandise,[29] the private galleys were replaced by state built ships, and the two voyages to Alexandria and Beyrut replaced the one to Cyprus and Lajasso.[30] Fourteen great galleys were outfitted for these voy· ages each year at the beginning of the fifteenth century.[31] In the next seventy years, not only did their size continue to increase, but new fleets were added: the galleys of Aigues Mortes to serve the northern shore of the Mediterranean from Sicily to Aragon, the galleys of Barbary to traffic with the Moors from Tunis to Granada, and the galleys *al trafego* which cruised twice between Tunis and Alexandria and returned in the fall from the East to swell the spice caravans. Altogether, twenty merchant galleys freighting about 250 tons each were annually sent to sea in the last third of the century to furnish the most reliable transport then available to all the ports of the Mediterranean and to Cadiz, Lisbon, Southampton, and Flanders.[32]

The refitting and replenishing of this merchant fleet was far greater labor than the maintenance of the war fleets then commonly equipped. The completion of four or five galleys every other year was necessary to keep twenty great galleys afloat, for though many served twelve years, a few were lost at sea. The maintenance of the police fleet may have called for two new galleys a year since these ships probably did not last as

[28] Marin, V, 197; Cessi, "Relazioni . . . tra Venezia e le Fiandre", p. 44.

[29] The figures given are those for the Flemish galleys, Cessi, *op. cit.*, p. 92.

[30] *Ibid.*, pp. 92, 114-116; Sanuto, *Vitae*, col. 618; Sansovino, p. 136; Marin, V, 193; A. S. V., Misc. MSS., no. 10, notes of Cecchetti.

[31] Ex., in 1407: three of the usual measure to Romania, four " ad mensuris Romania " to Beyrut, three " de mensuris grossis " to Alexandria, four of the usual measure to Flanders. Senato Misti, reg. 47, ff. 86, 116-118.

Manfroni, "La crisi", p. 984, says that in the later part of the fourteenth century twenty to twenty-five great galleys went annually to Alexandria, the Tana, Beyrut, Romania, Aigues Mortes, and Flanders!

[32] Senato, Deliberazioni, Incanti Galere, reg. 1.

long. The building of a great galley was counted twice as much work as the construction of a light galley. Accordingly the energies of the Arsenal were mainly devoted to merchant galleys except in the rare years when great armaments were needed.

A hint of what this rate of production meant in terms of human labor can be gained from estimates of the labor time expended on each galley at the beginning of the fifteenth century.[33] Assuming the work on several ships so distributed that masters of the three crafts involved were continually employed 250 days a year, then five sawyers, ten carpenters, and thirteen caulkers, with apprentices and stevedores, could bring five great galleys to completion every other year.[34] To furnish four light galleys required slightly less than two years labor—figured on the same basis—by two sawyers, five carpenters, and five caulkers. Assuming twenty light galleys were, on rare occasion, built in half a year to meet an emergency in war time, that necessitated thirty-two sawyers, ninety-six carpenters, and ninety-six caulkers. Actually great galleys were usually built in groups of four or five;[35] war galleys in yet larger batches with a long time elapsing between the decision to build and

[33] In the last part of the *Fabrica di galere* these figures are given: light galley—200 sawyers, 600 shipwrights, 600 caulkers; galley of measures of Flanders—500 sawyers, 1000 shipwrights, 1300 caulkers; galley of measures of Romania—270 sawyers, 450 (should be 950?) shipwrights, 1100 caulkers. I assume the figures stand for the number of days' labor.

[34] The accountants of the Arsenal reckoned that the masters were paid for 250 days a year or 22 days a month, 270 days a year. Arsenale, busta 533, Taduri's memorandum; Museo Civico, Arch. Gradenigo, busta 193. Cf. Marcello Forsellini, " L'organizzazione economica dell'arsenale di Venezia nella prima metà del seicento " *Arch. ven.*, ser. v, vol. vii (1930), p. 85. I have taken the lower figure to make allowance, probably insufficient allowance, for days lost because of bad weather. Sombart multiplies the number of Genoese war galleys of 1242 by the estimates for the Venetian Flemish galleys at about 1410 and seems to assume 100 working days a year. *Kreig und Kapitalismus* (Munich and Leipzig, 1913), pp. 191-2.

[35] Sample orders: 1407, three galleys of Romania—Senato Misti, reg. 47, f. 48; 1414, three galleys of Flanders for only one being built—*ibid.*, reg. 50, f. 152; 1433, two great galleys to be started besides those already building, and wood to be prepared in the next six months for six " galeis grossis " and three " galeis sextis Romanie "—*ibid.*, reg. 59, f. 3; 1439, four great galleys—*ibid.*, reg. 60, f. 130; 1454, four great galleys—Senato Mar, reg. 5, f. 62; 1487, twelve great galleys—Arsenale, busta 6, f. 21. Cf. Table G.

the completion of any substantial number of ships.[36] Fourteen ship carpenters and three sawyers were considered a reasonable working force for Giorgio the Greek when he was ordered to build four great galleys,[37] but, to prepare a galley needed for the Flemish voyage, the Lords of the Arsenal were instructed in 1441 to put at least thirty carpenters to work on it.[38] Of course, the above estimates are quite imperfect indications of the number of masters employed in the Arsenal, for they do not include either the masters engaged in outfitting and repairing ships nor those manufacturing the furnishings of the galleys.

The great galleys were rented at auction in about the same number at about the same time each year so that this part of the activity of the Arsenal could proceed at a fairly steady pace. New galleys were destined for the voyage to Flanders, the oldest ships sent to Beyrut or the Barbary coast.[39] Punctual delivery of the galleys to their renters a month before the dates fixed for their departure was desired especially for the Levant voyages. Those of Romania were supposed to leave by July 25, those of Beyrut by August 24, those of Alexandria by the end of August. Thus they would all be able to return in time for the Christmas fair.[40] Sometimes all these and the galleys *al trafego* came back together, twelve hulls of dyes, spices, and silks anchoring together at the entrance to the Grand Canal while the bells in the *campanile* sounded the news of their safe return.[41] The officers of the Arsenal at once went aboard to assess the damages incurred to the oars and rigging. The cargoes were taken in charge by the customs officials, one of whom was a deputy from the Arsenal. The customs officers collected from the shippers the freight due the *patroni* who had rented the galleys. From the freight received the Arsenal was paid the rent and the assessments made for damages; the

[36] Baxon worked on nine light galleys at once. Senato Misti, reg. 47, f. 109. See chap. III on Bernardo, Rosso and Bressan.
[37] Senato Misti, reg. 60, f. 202.
[38] Senato Mar, reg. 1, f. 20.
[39] The list described in note to Table G.
[40] Arsenale, busta 5, ff. 94, 99; Senato Mar, reg. 1, ff. 145-146 (1443 and 1457).
[41] Sanuto, *Diarii*, I, 379-380; Museo Civico, Arch. Gradenigo, busta 170.

remainder was turned over to the *patroni* or their other creditors. At least that was the theory, in practice the Arsenal was
often the last to be paid.[42] The galleys were returned to the
Arsenal where within eight days—again in theory—masters
were assigned to clean and repair them so that they would be
in readiness for the next year.[43]

Thanks to the fiscal regulations protecting these voyages,
the Arsenal did an apparently profitable business leasing merchant galleys. The richest rents came from the spice carriers.
The galleys of Beyrut and Alexandria yielded about 12,000
ducats a year between the sample years 1418 to 1427. The
galleys of Flanders and Romania brought in about 6000 ducats
more.[44] These revenues were assigned to the Arsenal and at
times covered all its expenses.[45] A regular appropriation of
9600 ducats a year additional was made in 1418. In 1443 it
was repealed by the Great Council on the ground that the galley rents were sufficient, but was almost immediately reëstab-
lished by the Senate and College.[46] Though the merchant galleys did not yield enough to provide for all expenditures on
war fleets and munitions as well as the costs of their own construction, during the first sixty or seventy years of the fifteenth
century they were the main sources of income, as well as the
main products, of the Arsenal.

A great change in the character of the Arsenal occurred
between 1470 and 1540. The production of merchant galleys
reached its peak about 1504 when, in February, there were
seven out on voyage, and, in the Arsenal, nine ready for use,

[42] Arsenale, busta 5, third series of chaps., Sept. 22, 1418, Jan. 9, 1435, Nov. 15, 1435; busta 133, f. 114; Senato Mar, reg. 4, f. 93; reg. 12, f. 50; reg. 14, f. 50.

[43] *Ibid.*, reg. 1, f. 36 (1441).

[44] The amount received for the galleys is recorded in the registers of the Senate series Misti after the resolutions stating the terms at which they were to be auc-
tioned. These resolutions were offered at about the same time each year, those for the Flemish galleys in January or February, those for the galleys of Beyrut, Alexandria, and Romania late in May or in June. The galleys also went during this period to Aigues Mortes, usually auctioned in January, sometimes in July, and they yielded an average yearly profit of about 1850 ducats, but I am not sure whether or not this went to the Arsenal.

[45] Senato Misti, reg. 47, ff. 22, 18, 70; Arsenale, busta 5, Oct. 19, 1415, in third series of chapters.

[46] Notatorio di Collegio, no. 10, f. 1, April 17, 1444.

twenty in process of construction, and three over fourteen years old—forty-six ships altogether.[47] But in July, 1518, when seven were at sea, there was not one ready built in the Arsenal, only nine were under construction.[48] The oarship's day as a merchantman was over; almost all the trading voyages were discontinued by 1535. The provision of the war fleet became the all absorbing business of the Arsenal.

The creation of a large and permanent war fleet was a result of the advance of the Turk. It was foreshadowed by the decision in 1442 to finish fifty new galleys and make ready twenty-five others, and by another order in 1453 for the preparation of fifty.[49] But not till 1470 did the Venetians realize that the acquisition of Constantinople by the Ottoman Empire meant the creation of a naval power of far different and more formidable character than any which had yet disputed the dominion of the seas. The fleets sent between 1461 and 1466 to assist the campaign in the Morea or to uphold the banner of San Marco in the Ægean were of twenty or thirty galleys like those which had earlier sufficed for the struggles with Italian rivals.[50] Rumors of great preparations at Constantinople were half believed, and the fleet of the Captain General in the east raised to what might well have been considered the extraordinary size of forty galleys.[51] The utter inadequacy of their traditional naval preparations was not fully realized, however, until in 1470 the Turk sent against Negroponte that fleet of three or four hundred sail which was described as a forest on the sea, when heard of incredible, but when seen terrible. Before that armada, which included one hundred light galleys and twice as many auxiliaries, the forty Venetian galleys retired to Crete to await reinforcements, which came too late.[52] The Arsenal sent out that year seventy-three galleys, great and light, so that no ships remained save twenty-four

[47] Sanuto, *Diarii*, V, 926.
[48] *Ibid.*, XXV, 538.
[49] Senato Mar, reg. 1, f. 129; Senato Terra, reg. 3, f. 75.
[50] Malipiero, pp. 11-15, 37.
[51] *Ibid.*, pp. 39, 43-46; Manfroni, *Costantinopoli . . . Lepanto*, p. 67.
[52] Malipiero, pp. 49-58.

unfinished.[53] In their effort to meet the new standard in war fleets set by the Ottoman Empire the Venetians raised the appropriations for their Arsenal to 100,000 ducats,[54] and kept fleets of seventy or even one hundred galleys afloat during the next few years.[55] But when in 1474 they proposed to arm one hundred light galleys besides twenty great galleys, it was not expected that so great a number could be prepared within the Arsenal.[56] Its equipment was not sufficient to supply the fleets needed to meet this new enemy.

If the Arsenal was to maintain a huge war fleet it must be equipped with covered docks and storehouses so that galleys might be built when needed regardless of the weather, and the galleys and their equipment be preserved till needed without damage from sun and rain. In the mid-fifteenth century the docks were all uncovered. The sheds which had once been over them had been torn down because they had been found too small. When there was heavy rain or very hot sun, the masters could not work. In 1449 the Senate ordered that new sheds be built over the docks sufficiently high and long to leave plenty of room for the workers.[57] The walls were made of brick or stone, the roofs of wood. Between 1450 and 1460 some twenty such sheds able to hold two galleys each were built in the Old Arsenal and along the south side of the New Arsenal in the section called the "Campagna", and by 1480 other docks in the New Arsenal were similarly roofed over so that there was altogether covered space for eighty galleys built or building.[58]

[53] *Ibid.*, p. 63.

[54] Earlier extraordinary demands had occasioned extra appropriations. For the completion of 50 galleys, 1452-1453, a total of 52,500 ducats had been provided for the purpose—Senato Terra, reg. 3, f. 75; Senato Mar, reg. 5, f. 34. In 1471 a regular 62,400 ducats a year was added to the galley rents and the 9,600 ducats. In 1472 there was added, but only for five months, 2,000 ducats a month. Arsenale, busta 6, ff. 6-7. A general description of the Arsenal about twenty years later stated that 100,000 ducats was spent a year. Museo Civico, Venice, Arch Cicogna, Coll. 969.

[55] Malipiero, pp. 63, 70, 74, 79, 105.

[56] Arsenale, busta 6, f. 7.

[57] Senato Terra, reg. 2, f. 114.

[58] The dates of the building of the different parts of the Arsenal have been worked out by Casoni, mainly from inscriptions. On the above, "Forze", pp. 102, 109. See also Senato Terra, reg. 4, f. 62; reg. 7, f. 157.

That space was obviously inadequate, however, if one hundred light galleys were to be provided for the war fleet besides the twenty odd merchant galleys for the trading voyages and the smaller craft built for scouting and river work. Accordingly, in 1473 an enlargement was ordered which nearly doubled the size of the Arsenal.[59] This addition, called the Newest Arsenal, was made by dredging out the area north of the New Arsenal so as to leave a basin surrounded on three sides by land and connecting on the east directly with the lagoon. It was promptly surrounded by walls and towers, work on which began in 1476, so that ships could safely be left on land there or kept in the basin, but covered docks were not built there until after 1519.[60] In 1525 there were twelve, and more were gradually added there as in other parts of the Arsenal during the rest of the century.[61]

This enlargement of the Arsenal was essential to meet the Turkish challenge, but it was not in itself sufficient. The Arsenal must be so organized that the war fleet of the Republic could be raised to one hundred galleys at short notice. It was fruitless to suffer in peace the burdens of war through continually arming the fortresses in the east and maintaining fleets which would have been considered great armaments a generation or two before, unless, when the Turkish threat did materialize, the war fleet could be at once made equal to the Infidel armada. The attack in 1499 caught the Venetians absorbed in Italian affairs and ill prepared. In December, 1498, Venice had only thirteen light galleys at sea. The government hoped to arm fifty-three the next year,[62] but in the fleet which met the enemy in August of 1499 there were only forty-eight light galleys. To be sure seventeen great galleys had been diverted from their voyages to serve in the battle fleet. A decisive victory was missed, however, largely because of the untrustworthiness of these converted merchantmen. It was

[59] Casoni, " Forze ", p. 117; Arsenale, busta 6, f. 7.
[60] Casoni, " Forze ", pp. 118, 120; Arsenale, busta 6, ff. 18, 61; busta 7, ff. 22, 49; Senato Terra, reg. 7, f. 157.
[61] Arsenale, busta 7, f. 49; Senato Mar, reg. 37, f. 193.
[62] Sanuto, *Diarii*, II, 105, 224.

less the ships themselves than the men on them who were at fault. The crews engaged for trading voyages and the merchant captains who rented the ships, though they had fought well enough in the earlier wars with commercial rivals, showed, in certain cases, a distinct reluctance to come to grips with the Turks.[63] Even though the lack of discipline might have been overcome and morale restored by vigorous leadership, the great galleys passed out of commercial use shortly thereafter so that merchant galleys were no longer available as warships in emergencies. The need of a specialized homogeneous battle fleet was inescapable.

In most European states the seventeenth century was the age of the creation upon a large scale of both permanent war fleets and standing armies. The " ship of the line " was then first so clearly differentiated from the converted merchantman as to make the latter inadequate for service in the battle fleet. In consequence, the states then aspiring to dominion of the seas, Holland, France, and England, were forced to maintain large fleets of ships of the special design required for combat.[64] For Venice the need of a large permanent navy came earlier, between 1470 and 1540. The vessels needed were not line ships of fifty guns or more, but galleys of maximum speed. Therefore the Venetian Arsenal, unlike the shipyards of the oceanic naval powers, confronted problems peculiar to the building and outfitting of oarships.

In 1525, after the work on the Newest Arsenal was well advanced, the maintenance of the galley reserve was regulated at a higher level. Fifty light galleys were being built. None of them was to be given to a commander without explicit orders from the Senate; all available old galleys were to be used first. The fifty new ships were to be kept on land fully built in readiness to be caulked, launched, rigged, and armed. Their masts, spars, cables, shrouds, sails, anchors, oars, thwarts, foot-braces, and all their deck furnishings and arms were to be

[63] *Ibid.*, II, 1230-1297; Malipiero, pp. 175-179; Manfroni, *Costantinopoli* . . . *Lepanto*, pp. 73, 215-219.

[64] Anderson, *Sailing-ship*, p. 158; George Norman Clark, *The Seventeenth Century* (Oxford, 1929), p. 116.

kept in readiness, each piece in the warehouse assigned it. If any of the new galleys were put into service, others were to be immediately begun to take their place.[65]

But fifty light galleys were soon found to be too few for the reserve fleet, and that standard was submerged by the furious pace at which work was carried on in the Arsenal in preparation for the next Turkish war, that which began in 1537. By August of that year the Arsenal had furnished one hundred galleys, and in addition had ready to be caulked six new light galleys, two old light galleys, four old *galee bastarde,* and nine great galleys.[66] After the war the standard for the reserve fleet was increased to one hundred light galleys, four—then ten— great galleys, eight *fuste,* eight *bregantini,* and eight long-boats. Under order of the Council of Ten, twenty-five of the galleys were to be kept in the basins armed and equipped to sail. The rest were to be kept on land complete in hull and superstructure, ready to be launched as soon as the caulkers should have filled their seams with tow and pitch. Both the docks on which they were stored and the water in front were to be kept cleared so that they could be quickly launched. Each galley was to be numbered, and its rigging and other furnishings were to be marked with the same number, so that they might be assembled as quickly as possible.[67] The maintenance of this hundred galley reserve became the chief goal of the Arsenal's activity, and remained so until the standard was lowered to fifty in 1633.[68]

A hundred finished but unused galleys waiting in reserve

[65] Arsenale, busta 7, ff. 46-7, and repetition of the order in 1532, Senato Mar, reg. 22, f. 130, where it is specified that the galleys be kept ready, " redutte in vuoga, serate et tagliate, si che non mancho loro che il calcarle et impegolarle." They still required caulking according to the usual meaning of that term, but according to the division of labor among the Venetian craftsmen part of the labor of the caulkers had already been done.

[66] Arsenale, busta 8, f. 69.

[67] Arsenale, busta 9, f. 36-7; busta 11, f. 143; Senato Mar, reg. 28, f. 128 ff.; Arsenale, busta 10, f. 70. In the last mentioned reference to keeping the 100 light galleys it is implied that they are all kept on land, no separate mention being made of the 25 kept by orders of the Council of Ten. For increase of great galleys to 10 in 1557, Arsenale, busta 10, f. 46.

[68] Forsellini, p. 54.

constituted an ideal rarely if ever attained. Frequently, even in times of peace, forty or at most sixty galleys were kept at sea as guards against the corsairs or the large fleets which periodically issued from the Dardanelles for unknown destinations.[69] New galleys were constantly being sent to the fleet so that there were always large numbers of galleys being built to fill up the reserve. Everyone elected to command a galley wished a new one despite the restrictions which the Senate placed upon its own generosity in making such grants.[70] An attempt was made to get more service from the used galleys by dividing them into two groups, those fit for long voyages and those fit only for short voyages, and by requiring the captains arming for short voyages to take one of the latter group.[71] Still new galleys disappeared fast. Lists of the galleys actually in the Arsenal show a comparatively small number of completely finished galleys waiting to be launched, and a far larger number in various stages of construction.[72] Although there was a comparative stabilization of the number of light galleys in the Arsenal from 1540 to 1633, the volume of production was highly unstable, fluctuating with the military needs of the moment.

As the work was then organized in the Arsenal there were three stages in the production of a galley. First the frame was built by the ship carpenters. Then the planking was fastened into place and the cabins and superstructures built. Here there was work for both caulkers and ship carpenters. Finally, when the galley was called into service, its seams were filled with tow and pitch, the hull covered with tar or grease, the galley launched, the deck fixings fastened in place, the rigging and moorings provided, the oars and arms given out to the crew. In this final stage of production all the departments of the Arsenal were involved.

The speed attained in the first stage of the process, the building of the frames, is illustrated by the construction of thirty in

---

[69] Paruta, *Dell'historia venetiana*, III, 526, 607, 618, 628-630, IV, Part I, 147-148, 231, 236.   [71] *Ibid.*, busta 10, f. 77.
[70] Arsenale, busta 10, f. 1.   [72] Table H.

six months or less between November, 1534 and May, 1535,[73] and of fifty in ten months or less between June, 1537 and April, 1538.[74] The rapidity of building in those years may have been abnormal, but the production of galley frames frequently proceeded on that scale if not at that pace.[75]

The greatest achievement of the sixteenth century Arsenal, that with which it dazzled the eyes of foreigners, was the despatch with which it could complete the third process in the preparation of a war galley, the launching and outfitting of the waiting galleys when they were needed for the battle fleet. When Henry III, King of France, visited Venice in the summer of 1574, a galley was assembled, launched, and completely armed for his royal entertainment—all inside of one hour.[76] What was expected in a serious crisis is shown by the orders of the Senate on January 28, 1570, when the Turkish design to attack Cyprus became known. They ordered that thirty galleys be put in order by the middle of February, thirty more by the end of that month, and forty more by the middle of March.[77] Assuming the galleys ready on the docks, all the needed oars, cordage, anchors, sails, masts, spars, deck furnishings, and arms

[73] Senato Mar, reg. 23, ff. 85, 44.

[74] Arsenale, busta 8, f. 77.

[75] Other similar orders: Oct., 1529, 20 light galleys and 5 great galleys to be done next February—*ibid.*, busta 7, f. 85; May, 1535, 25 light galleys to be done the next October but were not—Senato Mar, reg. 23, ff. 85, 125; April, 1538, 50 light galleys—Arsenale, busta 8, f. 77; Sept. 1551, 30 light galleys—Senato Mar, reg. 31, f. 127; May, 1558, 41 light galleys—Arsenale, busta 10, f. 53; March, 1565, 2 light galleys—Senato Mar, reg. 37, f. 5; Nov. 1565, 30 light galleys—*ibid.*, reg. 37, f. 113; June, 1570, 40 light galleys for which the cutting of the wood had been ordered in March or April—Arsenale, busta 11, ff. 73-6, 88; August, 1571, 30 light galleys for which the order to cut wood had been given that March—*ibid.*, f. 90.

[76] Pier de Nolhac and Angelo Solerti, *Il viaggio in Italia di Enrico III* (Rome, Turin, Naples, 1890), p. 143. The author quoted in a note on the page cited explicitly states that the galley was pitched and launched. Since the exploit was designed as an entertainment, it seems likely that the galley was launched in the royal presence, but it may well be believed that many preparations, including practically all the caulking, had been performed before his arrival.

[77] Senato Mar, reg. 39, f. 90. Earlier orders of a similar nature may be cited. On February 20, 1557, the Lords of the Arsenal were ordered to have 25 galleys ready by the middle of March, and 25 more by the end of that month. Arsenale, busta 10, f. 40. On January 27, 1565, the Senate ordered that 15 galleys be sent out of the Arsenal by the end of February, and that 50 galleys more be prepared and launched, half to be ready by the middle of February and half by the middle of March, so that in case of need the fleet might be quickly strengthened. Arsenale, busta 11, f. 19.

ready and sorted in the warehouses assigned them, the whole
fleet of one hundred galleys was to be sent out of the Arsenal
fully equipped inside of fifty days! Nor did the Arsenal fall
much behind expectations. The fleet left Venice at the beginning of April. When it had been joined by the galleys already
at sea and those sent from the Venetian Arsenal to be manned
in the colonies, it numbered one hundred and twenty-four light
galleys and twelve *galeazze*. Since that same spring four galleys were left to guard the Adriatic and twelve old galleys were
given to the Pope to arm, the Venetian Arsenal had put in condition to be manned at least one hundred and fifty-two war
galleys, great and light, old and new.[78] The futility of the
naval operations of that year was due to the plague which
decimated the crews, the lack of soldiers, or the lack of daring,
not to the lack of ships.[79] Signs of the decadence of the Venetian marine appeared in the officers and crews, but the Arsenal showed in this crisis an ability to meet the new conditions revealed a hundred years before when the first great
Ottoman fleet put to sea. The Turkish menace had been met,
not by keeping a hundred galley fleet permanently in commission, but by keeping a fleet on land, and putting the
Arsenal in such order that the ships unlaunched might yet
be counted ships in readiness.

[78] Paruta, *Guerra di Cipro*, pp. 24, 61, 64-75, 115. Manfroni, *Costantinopoli* . . .
Lepanto, pp. 459-460, gives yet larger figures.
[79] *Loc. cit.* and *ibid.*, p. 476.

CHAPTER IX

THE MANAGEMENT OF THE ARSENAL

Even after the Arsenal of Venice had become what was perhaps the largest industrial plant of the time—covering sixty acres of ground and water, employing one or two thousand workmen within its walls, and annually spending one or two hundred thousand ducats—its internal organization preserved much of the informal system which had sufficed in the thirteenth century. The transition from a comparatively simple and personal organization to a more complex and impersonal one was a slow process which began in the fourteenth century, but which proceeded fastest between 1470 and 1540.[1] Of the problems created by size—accounting, arrangement of materials, discipline of the workers—some were solved with an efficiency which made contemporaries marvel; others remained throughout the sixteenth century a source of great waste. But between 1540 and 1570 the management of the Arsenal was adjusted to the maintenance of the large reserve fleet, and the demands then made upon it were as large as ever in the history of the Republic.

Both the failures and successes of the management are partly explained by its constitution. The committee which may most properly be considered the board of management, composed originally of the three Lords of the Arsenal, grew both in size and in functions so as to hold in the sixteenth century a position of great authority in the administration of the Venetian navy. Special executive and deliberative commissions with extraordinary powers, including the arming of war fleets, were frequently elected by the Great Coun-

---

[1] A gap in the Arsenal archives between the *Quaderno*, in busta 566, which concludes in 1463, and the *Terminazioni*, busta 133 *et seq.*, which begin in 1500, and the consideration that special officers were probably in existence before being mentioned in regulations make a chronological survey impracticable, so that the organization about 1560 has been made the foreground of this presentation. The dates of regulations, when not mentioned in the text, have been given, within parentheses, in the notes.

cil when emergencies arose in the fourteenth century;[2] but during the fifteenth century the upkeep of the navy, as well as the regulation of commerce and the conduct of diplomacy, became the regular business of the Senate.[3] To prepare resolutions for its acceptance or rejection committees of *savii* were created. These *savii,* or secretaries of state, also acted as the agents of the Senate in carrying out its orders and reporting on their execution. Together with the Doge and his Councilors they formed the College and the Signoria, the supreme executive of the state. Five *Savii agli Ordeni,* or Secretaries of the Marine, were especially charged with considering maritime affairs, but since they were young nobles still serving their apprenticeship in government, their work was subject to revision by the highly responsible *Savii Grandi.*[4]

When the menace of the Ottoman navy made it repeatedly necessary to prepare extensive armaments, administrative officers to assist the *Savii* became permanent elements of the bureaucracy. Most of them were elected by the Senate, some by the Great Council, some by the Ten. They received orders from all these councils according to their respective jurisdictions. Special duties were assigned committees composed of delegates from the College and from magistracies concerned.[5] The most important officials involved in the administration of the navy in the mid-sixteenth century—aside from the *Savii* of the College, the Captain General of the Sea in command of the battle fleet, and the Commissioners of the fleet who kept the Signoria informed of its condition and acted as its seconds in command under the Captain General—were the *Provveditori all' Armar* in charge of enrolling crews, and the *Patroni e Provveditori all' Arsenale,* or

[2] Tentori, *Storia,* VI, 137: [Besta], *Il Senato veneziano (Miscellanea di storia veneta,* ser. ii, vol. V, 1899), pp. 131-134.

[3] *Ibid.,* pp. 120, 131, 136.

[4] *Ibid.,* pp. 64-68, 176-196.   Horatio F. Brown, *Studies in the History of Venice* (London, 1907), I, 300-302.

[5] *Il Senato,* pp. 61, 109, 139, 141, 181.

Lords and Commissioners of the Arsenal, who headed the munitions, maintenance, and construction departments.[6]

The post of Commissioner of the Arsenal was an office supplementary and slightly superior to that of Lord of the Arsenal. During the second half of the fifteenth century the management of the Arsenal became an enormously complicated task not only because of the size of the industrial plant to be supervised, but also because of the innumerable purchases and shipments necessary to supply the fleets. The Lords of the Arsenal could no longer exercise the direct supervision over the work of the masters and the care of ships with which they had been personally charged in the fourteenth century. They became occupied in financial management, the collection of funds, the purchase of supplies, and the sending of munitions. The burden of these duties alone was more than they could manage and at the same time make reports and suggestions to the College, the Senate, or the Council of Ten.[7]

Once the visits of the Doge and the frequent and direct reports of the Lords of the Arsenal to him had been sufficient to insure the necessary close connection between the governors of the state and the chief source of its military strength.[8] These visits of the Doge continued in the sixteenth century as matters of ceremony, and are described by Sanuto with due regard for the details of the Doge's apparel and the number of illustrious men who accompanied him.[9] More business-like reports might be expected from the semi-annual inspection of two *Savii agli Ordeni* and two *Savii di Terra Ferma*.[10] But there was need not only for deputations from the Signoria to the Arsenal, but also, and more particularly, for members of the governing board of the Arsenal who would be free to come before the College

[6] Tentori, *Storia,* VI, 385-387; VIII, 297-315.

[7] Senato Mar, reg. 23, f. 43; reg. 33, f. 144; Senato Terra, reg. 5, f. 57; Arsenale, busta 11, ff. 99-100.

[8] Maggior Consiglio, Liber Magnus, ff. 23-24 (1301).

[9] *Diarii,* XLVI, 379; XLIX, 357. Cf. Senato Mar, reg. 25, f. 107.

[10] Tentori, *Storia,* VIII, 190.

or Senate and move proposals there so that the Lords of the Arsenal might have no excuse for not attending to their duties in the Arsenal.[11] The Commissioners of the Arsenal were created accordingly to strengthen the connection between the Senate and the Arsenal. At first, in 1442, they were elected only when the Arsenal was unusually active, and were charged particularly with assisting in the preparation of a specified group of galleys,[12] but such special elections soon became the general rule, and in the second quarter of the sixteenth century two Commissioners became a regular part of the governing board of the Arsenal.[13] But they did not lose the character of liason officers. They were free to appear before the College and the Council of Ten and to make motions in the Senate. It followed that they were primarily responsible for keeping the rulers of the state informed of the needs of the Arsenal.[14]

As members of the naval administration the Lords and Commissioners also acquired a general administrative power which extended not only beyond the walls of the Arsenal but beyond the field of shipbuilding. They were ex officio members of the *Collegio da Milizia da Mar* which revised

[11] The creation of *Provveditori* was accompanied by limitations of the right of the *Patroni* to come to the Senate and College, Senato Mar, reg. 9, f. 55; Senato Terra, reg. 13, f. 96.

[12] Senato Mar, reg. 1, f. 129 (1442); reg. 7, f. 88 (1462); reg. 9, f. 55 (1470); Senato Terra, reg. 3, f. 73 (1453); reg. 5, f. 57 (1463), f. 102 (1464), f. 125 (1465). In 1487 the older system of cooperation was tried and two *Savii di Terra Ferma* were chosen to go twice a week to the Arsenal to see that it was supplied with funds—Arsenale, busta 6, f. 21—but the next year *Provveditori* were again chosen—Senato Terra, reg. 10, f. 111—and in 1495—*ibid.*, reg. 12, f. 86. Those elected in 1498 were to correct abuses in the administration which had grown up in the last ten years—*ibid.*, reg. 13, f. 55—and a third *Provveditore* was added next year—*ibid.*, reg. 13, f. 66. In 1500 the motion to elect two *Prov. al'Arsenal* was defeated by the alternate motion to give that office to two *Prov. de le cose da mar* already chosen. *Ibid.*, reg. 13, f. 150.

[13] Judging from the way they are referred to in the *Terminazioni* of the governing board itself, Arsenale, busta 133 *et seq.* From 1533 to 1550 they were elected by the Council of Ten, thereafter by the Senate, *ibid.*, busta 8, f. 84; Senato Mar, reg. 31, f. 51.

[14] Duties are indicated in resolutions to elect, especially those of 1488—Senato Terra, reg. 10, f. 111—of 1522—Senato Mar, reg. 20, f. 9—and of 1533—Arsenale, busta 8, f. 84.

the lists of crews and petty officers.[15] They retained a vague preëminence over the Commissioner of Artillery who had been appointed to relieve them of the immediate responsibility for the purchases and output of that department.[16] They exercised greater authority over the Hemp Officials in charge of the state rope factory—a jurisdiction which arose from their demand that that factory give satisfactory service in preparing the ropes and cables needed in the Arsenal. Concern over adequate supplies of hemp and wood led to further extensions of the Arsenal's activity.[17] The native hemp industry was fostered and regulated by officials subject to the Lords and Commissioners, and they were the executive heads of the administration of forests containing trees of any value to shipbuilders.

Private shipowners were aided by many small services which the Arsenal performed for all the shipping of the port. As early as the fourteenth century the Lords of the Arsenal had been ordered to keep ready a longboat well supplied with cables to be sent to aid ships in distress off the port, and both the men who manned this bark and the guardians of the lighthouses were included in the personnel of the Arsenal.[18] If a ship had to be launched or salvaged the Arsenal was called on to loan timbers and cables. Indeed the Arsenal served as a reserve lumberyard whence private builders could borrow or buy timbers which could not readily be obtained elsewhere.[19] On the other hand, no private property could be brought into the Arsenal.[20] The enforce-

[15] Vettor Sandi, *Principi di storia civile della Repubblica di Venezia* (Venice, 1756), part III, vol. II, p. 595.

[16] Created in 1526 or shortly before, Arsenale, busta 7, f. 63.

[17] Frederic Chapin Lane, "The Rope Factory and the Hemp Trade of Venice in the Fifteenth and Sixteenth Centuries", *Journal of Economic and Business History*, vol. IV supplement (1932), pp. 830-847.

[18] Arsenale, busta 5, chaps. 48, 80 of first series; busta 7, f. 31; Senato Mar, reg. 22, f. 30. Museo Civico, Venice, Arch. Morosini, busta 302. Repairs on the port were sometimes assigned to the Arsenal. Arsenale, busta 5, chap. 52 of first series.

[19] Senato Terra, reg. 4, ff. 112, 127, 132, 188; Senato Mar, reg. 20, f. 153; reg. 22, f. 55; files Feb. 21, 1556.

[20] Arsenale, busta 5, chap. 25 of the first series (1289) and chap. 8 of second series (c. 1376).

ment of the navigation laws had at first been the business of the *Consoli dei Mercanti,* but in 1516 the duty of estimating all Venetian ships was transferred to the Admiral of the Arsenal, and a revision of the laws concerning overloading in 1527 made the Admiral of the Arsenal responsible for their enforcement.[21] Thus, in the sixteenth century, the Arsenal, as well as the Board of Trade, was responsible for supervising and encouraging the merchant marine.

The varied activities of the Lords and Commissioners of the Arsenal, both as administrators of the government shipyard and as heads of the service of supply, are reflected in lists of their expenditures from 1535 to 1544. During two of the war-time years, 1537 and 1538, those in which their expenses were greatest, approximately one-fourth of some 200,000 ducats spent went to masters working by the day, one-eighth more to carpenters, caulkers, sawyers, and oarmakers employed on piecework. Almost all the rest went for the purchase of materials. But the expenses for construction of ships and those for the purchase of naval stores and munitions cannot be clearly distinguished, nor can a sharp separation be made between what was spent to buy materials ready made, and what was spent on their manufacture. The gradual shading off of these activities one into the other was characteristic of the Arsenal's functioning. The same articles were sometimes bought as finished products, sometimes

[21] Senato Mar, reg. 18, f. 138; reg. 21, f. 53.

The title " admiral ", " armiraglio ", was applied at Venice to holders of three offices distinct in character. In the fleets the " armiraglio " was not the commanding officer—that was the " capitano ", a noble elected by the Great Council to direct any fighting and diplomatic business necessary. The " armiraglio " of the fleet was selected by its " capitano " to advise him in nautical matters and to execute his sailing orders.   Manfroni, " Cenni sugli ordinamenti "; Bibl. Naz. Marciana, Venice, MSS It., cl. IV, cod. 177, ff. 6 *et seq.*

In the Arsenal the highest paid permanent official was called the " armiraglio " after about 1376. Earlier records do not mention an " armiraglio ", but instead a " soprastante ". *Ibid.,* ff. 35 *et seq.*; Arsenale, busta 5: " soprastante " mentioned in first series of chapters, " armiraglio " in second.

In charge of the pilotage of the port of San Nicolò of Venice was a third " armiraglio " who was not numbered among the personnel of the Arsenal, but who was subjected to an examination at the Arsenal before being installed in office. A. S. V., Arch. di Cattaver, busta 1, cap. 2, f. 63.

manufactured from the raw material, and sometimes bought in a half-finished state and the manufacture completed under the direction of the Lords of the Arsenal. Their manufacture might be undertaken by the Lords employing masters for day work within the Arsenal, or by their giving out the materials to masters who prepared the products in their own shops, or by a combination of the two methods. Certainly ship-building absorbed most of the money, and the expenses for raw materials and for masters employed in the Arsenal exceeded those for finished products or for the labor of masters who worked outside.[22] But in addition to their responsibilities as managers of a large industrial plant, the Lords and Commissioners had substantial duties as purchasers and shippers of naval stores and arms to the fortresses and auxiliary arsenals of the empire.[23]

In their administration of the Arsenal, the Lords and Commissioners were subject to continual supervision and intervention by the deliberative and executive organs of the government. No one man, not even any one group of men, had full power and responsibility for the organization of the government shipyard. The Arsenal was considered the foundation of the power of Venice, the heart of the state.[24] The College, the Senate, and the Council of Ten participated directly in its management even to the extent of determining the number and pay of the masters to be employed, the duties of minor officials, and the work assigned to particular shipwrights. The Lords and Commissioners themselves were a continually changing group of nobles who held their offices only for terms of from one to four years.[25] There was, there-

[22] Lists in Arsenale, busta 1: tabulated in my *Venetian Ships and Shipbuilders of the Fifteenth and Sixteenth Centuries,* a dissertation deposited in the Harvard College Library, Table J.

[23] Arsenals at Corfu—Senato Mar, reg. 36, f. 77—at Lesina—*ibid.,* reg. 36, f. 108—and Crete—*ibid.,* reg. 35, f. 166. In 1458 the Senate boasted that the storeroom for arms contained weapons and munitions for arming fifty galleys. In 1462 it had been depleted by shipments to forts in the East. Senato Terra, reg. 4, f. 61; reg. 5, f. 11.

[24] Bibl. Querini-Stampalia, Venice, MSS. cl. IV, cod. 130, *Cuore veneta legale.*

[25] Lords elected for 4 years—Arsenale, busta 5, f. 94 (1443); Commissioners for one year between 1550 and 1579—*ibid.,* busta 8, f. 84. Senato Mar, reg. 31, f. 51. In the *Terminazioni* one name rarely appears for more than three years.

fore, no permanent executive with the authority so to organize the work of the Arsenal as to secure the greatest produc-
tivity at least expense. On the contrary, there was a group
of political councils and administrative committees laying
down regulations and distributing rewards to the master
craftsmen employed.

The Council of Ten assumed responsibility for the guardianship of the Arsenal. The Ten ordered the doorkeepers
never to leave their posts during the day even if ordered
otherwise by the Lords of the Arsenal. Buckets and shovels
were kept ready for use in case of fire. During the night,
while some watchman made the rounds of the walls, those
posted in the fifteen towers called to one another every hour,
and any one who twice failed to answer the call was dismissed. The Ten forbade the Lords or other officers of the
Arsenal to open the doors during the night, or to bring in
boats to go fishing.[26]

Of the various business problems which resulted from the
growth of the Arsenal the first to be recognized and regulated was that of accounting. In so far as the Arsenal performed the functions of a supply department, strict ordering
of the bookkeeping was the obvious first consideration in
the minds of those regulating its management. Complete
and accurate accounts appeared the chief requirement whether
the Arsenal bought in the open market or contracted for
products with craftsmen whom it supplied with the materials
and paid by the piece. New problems created or made patent
by the removal of these craftsmen from their own shops to
places allotted them in the Arsenal were also met by insist-
ence on strict accountability. Steps towards efficiency proceeded in harmony with the demand for more comprehensive
accounting—first accounting of moneys, then of materials,
and finally of men and their use of their time. Thus the
orderly spirit of bookkeeping ultimately touched, though

[26] Arsenale, busta 6, ff. 68 (1513); busta 7, ff. 58-59 (1515). In 1460 there were
3 doorkeepers, 14 night watchmen on the towers, and 6 who went the rounds. Senato
Terra, reg. 4, f. 145.

slightly, the realms of the craftsmen—the processes of production.

As long as the activity of the Arsenal was small enough, the Lords of the Arsenal were supposed to attend personally to the handling and recording of appropriations, but by the middle of the fourteenth century they had the assistance, in the central office alone, of two bookkeepers and three pages. Out of the custom which the bookkeepers developed during the sixteenth century of using their sons as assistants grew the two posts of assistant-bookkeeper. The pages, five in the sixteenth century, acted as personal messengers and assistants of the Lords of the Arsenal, counting money, collecting debts, and carrying messages or commands from the Lords to other officials or to workers needed in the Arsenal.[27]

By regulations of about 1370 all accounts were consolidated in two journals and one ledger.[28] One journal was kept by the Lord of the Arsenal whose turn it was to tend the cash box and who was consequently called the cashier. The chief accountant entered the items in the ledger from the second journal which was kept by the second accountant. Every few months two Lords of the Arsenal working together checked their journal with the ledger to see that there had been no mistake. Each September the ledger was balanced, each account separately, the balances carried over into a new ledger, and the old books sent to the treasury officials to be audited.[29]

A separate book was kept to record the wages due the masters.[30] After 1530 the pay roll compiled from that book

[27] Arsenale, busta 6, ff. 39-40; busta 133, ff. 17, 83, 114; busta 135, ff. 41, 84, 106, 108; busta 136, f. 71; busta 11, f. 118. The office force could be enlarged by employing there men counted among the *fachini. Ibid.*, busta 135, f. 98.

[28] *Ibid.*, busta 5, second series of chaps., i-iv. The record in the *quaderno grando* was to be kept " cascuno cossa per si e lo conto de la cassa, per lo muodo el qual faxe le hofficiali del formento di realto ".

[29] On contemporary accounting see Heinrich Sieveking, " Aus venetianischen Handlungsbüchern, ein Beitrage zur Geschichte des Grosshandels in 15 Jahrhunderts ", *Jahrbuch für Gesetzgebung, Verwaltung und Volkswirtschaft in deutschen Reich*, XXV, 4 (1901), pp. 299-331.

[30] Arsenale, *loc. cit.*

was presented every Saturday morning by the Lords of the Arsenal to the Commissioners who, when they had approved it, took it to the College to have the payments authorized.[31] It had been provided in the fourteenth century that in case some of the masters did not come for their pay they were to be entered as creditors in the journal and ledger so that no old debts would be carried in the wage book.[32]

In 1546 an attempt was made to divide all the expenses of the Arsenal into three accounts.[33] The first was to cover necessary fixed expenses, namely the pay of the workmen ordinarily employed. This account was to be kept by the Lord whose turn it was to be cashier, and he was to collect the money needed for it from the treasuries of specified mainland cities subject to Venice.[34] The second account, which was kept by the Lord who the month before had taken his turn as custodian of the cash box, was to cover necessary but unlimited expenses such as the purchase of furnishings for the one hundred light galleys of the reserve. A fixed sum from the funds of the Senate was provided for this account,[35] and the contracts of purchases were approved every Saturday morning by a committee of the College.[36] A third account provided for extraordinary expenses.[37] A separate fund had been

[31] Senato Mar, reg. 21, f. 168; *Bilanci generali* (ser. ii published by the R. Commissione per la pubblicazione dei documenti finanziarii della Repubblica di Venezia, Venice, 1912), vol. I, tomo 1, pp. 273-274, 345.

[32] Arsenale, *loc. cit.*

[33] Senato Mar, reg. 28, ff. 128, 196.

[34] The sums assigned in 1546 totaled 3431 ducats a month. Estimates dated 1553— Museo Civico, Venice, Arch. Morosini, busta 302—considered 3400 ducats a month the regular provision, but estimated that 1600 ducats a month was spent in addition. Estimates of 1559—*ibid.*, Arch. Gradenigo, busta 193—show 47,400 ducats a year as the regular expenditure for labor and 4000 ducats as extraordinary expense.

[35] The appropriation in 1546 was 46,000 ducats, but that was probably temporary. The estimates of 1559 cited above indicate that 15,000 ducats was the regular appropriation.

[36] Cf. also Arsenale, busta 6, f. 38; Senato Mar, reg. 21, f. 168. Reports of Lords or of foremen sent to cut wood or buy hemp had to be similarly approved within eight days of their return. *Ibid.*, reg. 22, f. 29.

[37] In the estimates of 1559 these expenses, including the purchase of raw materials, were considered assignable, as was the payroll account, to the " casa corrente ". The appropriation for that " casa " was 5600 ducats a month or 67,200 ducats a year, the total expenses 88,000 ducats.

established earlier for the gun foundry under the Commissioner of Artillery.[38] This division of the income of the Arsenal into separate funds for different purposes and the occasional orders of the Senate that special accounts be kept of this or that led to such a multiplication of the number of books kept that in 1555 it was again felt necessary to stipulate that, while the funds were to be separately accounted for, the one ledger and the two journals should record all transactions.[39]

After the books kept at the central office furnishing a record of the manner in which appropriations had been expended, the next need was a record of the receipt and distribution of the wares bought or manufactured. Under the comparatively informal organization which prevailed before the development of the large reserve fleet, materials received or sent out were recorded by the Admiral, the arms steward, or the foreman concerned, without any very definite assignment of responsibility. In 1494 the Senate thought to put a stop to the abuses which naturally arose by ordering that no goods be accepted at the Arsenal nor sent out from it save in the presence of the Lord who was cashier and of one of the accountants who would record it. The keys to all the warehouses were to be in the hands of the Lords of the Arsenal.[40] But abuses could not be remedied by this attempt to return to the thirteenth century system and increase the duties which the Lords had to perform in person. They were already overburdened. Instead, new officials had to be created or the responsibilities of those of long standing more closely defined.

In regard to materials leaving the Arsenal a careful allocation of responsibility was ordered. The detailed record of what munitions were sent out and where they were sent was kept by the arms steward. He was also charged with preparing wares for shipment. Whether the munitions or

---

[38] The separate account was ordered in 1506. Arsenale, busta 7, ff. 37-40. It was given as 15,000 ducats in 1559 making the total expense estimated for the Arsenal 118,000 ducats. Museo Civico, Venice, Arch. Gradenigo, busta 193.

[39] Arsenale, busta 10, ff. 26-27.

[40] Senato Terra, reg. 12, f. 40.

lumber was sent out by order of the Lords of the Arsenal themselves, the Commissioners of the Fleet, or the Secretaries of the Marine, the arms steward was to write the order in detail in a book and note when such supplies were sent.[41] If it was a question of ropes, cables, or timbers loaned to private shipowners, the Admiral also kept a record.[42] The Lords of the Arsenal had in any case to sign the permit for the wares to leave the Arsenal. The actual physical oversight of all that passed out of the Arsenal was left to the door-keepers. They were to permit nothing to go out without the signed permits of the Lords of the Arsenal and were to keep the permits.[43]

The arms steward also kept records of wares received,[44] but special officials were created to keep track of the wood bought or cut by the Arsenal. These were the Appraisers, master carpenters rewarded for good service by this higher office. They were a great deal more than mere tally-takers, for not only did they record the wood received so that sellers were made creditors of the Arsenal according to their records, but they also were responsible for inspecting timbers offered, seeing that good wood was delivered, and reporting its value to the Lords who formally contracted for it.[45] From being inspectors of raw materials they rose to be appraisers also of finished products and came to have a prominent part in overseeing the work of the ship carpenters and sawyers.[46]

Though adequate provision was made through these officers for recording wares received at the Arsenal, no regular system

[41] Senato Mar, reg. 20, f. 181 (1525), regulations also for freighting and sending bill of lading.

[42] *Ibid.*, reg. 22, f. 62 (1531); and Arsenale, busta 135, f. 82, reference to the records of both the *masser* and the *armiraglio* concerning a cable on which payment was due.

[43] Senato Mar, reg. 28, f. 129 (1546).

[44] Arsenale, busta 133, ff. 102-3; and Senato Mar, files, May 2, 1564, *masser's* receipt for goods delivered.

[45] First mention, 1509: Arsenale, busta 133, f. 33. Duties: *Ibid.*, busta 135, f. 45, 130-1 (1554); Senato Mar, reg. 32, f. 192 (1555) and files Dec. 9, 1560. By 1554 they had presumed to buy wood without consulting the Lords, and were forbidden to do so if more than five ducats were involved—Arsenale, busta 135, f. 139.

[46] See chap. XI below.

was devised before 1564 for the orderly arrangement after delivery of the chief raw material consumed, the lumber. Although enough timbers for the construction of forty or fifty galleys were frequently piled in the Arsenal at once,[47] the tradition of individual shipyards long prevailed and the wood was dumped confusedly in the basins or docks. When a worker wanted a piece he went around looking for it, or fishing for it, till he found one to suit him. Naturally, under these conditions, logs were not always put to the use for which they were best suited, and many rotted in sun and rain. The first step towards a better system was taken in 1554 when six construction chiefs were delegated to see that wood brought into the Arsenal was taken to the docks where it was needed, and that wood which had been sawed was placed where it would not be wasted. But these men were appointed guardians over the parts of the Arsenal assigned them as much to prevent the stealing of equipment from finished galleys as to prevent waste of wood, and they were also to continue their work as builders.[48]

The arrangement of the wood was still bad in 1564 when, as the accountant testified, 500 ducats a year were spent in finding wood and moving it around the Arsenal. Moreover, as long as the wood was kept in the basins in front of the docks, it was necessary to clear the lumber out of the way whenever a ship was launched, and 1200 ducats were spent each year in dredging wood out of the way. Accordingly the Senate had instructed the College in 1553 to decide upon a separate place for a lumberyard,[49] but nothing was done until 1564 when the garden of the monks of Santa Maria della Celestia, which lay just west of the Newest Arsenal, was taken

[47] Arsenale, busta 11, ff. 73-76, 90.
[48] Arsenale, busta 135, ff. 132-133. The six men and their assignments were:
   " Christoforo Rosso, deputato alla guardia in l'arsenal nuovo della (di la) dal ponte.
   Vicenzo Vituri deputato di qua dal ponte.
   Antonio Bordolla, deputato in Campagna.
   Piero Zaparin, deputato in Arsenal Vechio.
   Domenigo del Fausto, deputato in novissima.
   Alvise Scatola, deputato oltra li volti dal aqua."
[49] Senato Mar, reg. 32, f. 86.

over for the purpose. On the north the garden overlooked the houses where the powder was stored, and on the south it abutted the Old Arsenal. Within this area a basin was dug where oak wood could be kept under water, and a space 225 feet by 60 feet was roofed over to keep other wood, especially sawed planks and timbers. It was expected that the wood piled there would be kept in order so that a piece could readily be found when wanted.[50] But in 1583 it was said that while the wood was all kept in one place it was not in order so that it cost three times as much to find a log as the log was worth.[51] Wherever the timbers were put, the essential was that they be kept in order, and that was not done, for any long period of time at least, before the end of the sixteenth century.

The casual treatment of the lumber contrasted sharply with the orderly disposal of the finished products. Intelligent arrangement of materials was a prerequisite of efficiency in both cases, but was first provided in the storage of the furnishings of the reserve. To send out promptly the emergency fleet of light galleys it was necessary to have ready at hand at least 5000 benches, 5000 footbraces, 5000 or 15000 oars,[52] 300 sails, 100 masts, 100 rudders, and 200 spars not to mention the cordage, arms, pitch, ironwork, and similar quantities of smaller but equally essential items. Each great galley called for an even larger number of furnishings. All these had to be kept carefully stacked and counted.

When the replenishing of this reserve had become the main goal towards which the activity of the Arsenal was directed, the assignment among the officers of the Arsenal of the responsibility for these galleys and their equipment was made the basis for a division into departments. One foreman was

[50] *Ibid.*, reg. 36, f. 187 and reports of accountant and foremen in files, Dec. 13, 1564; Arsenale, busta 11, f. 47.

[51] Report on Arsenal by Francesco Contarini in Bibl. Naz. Marciana, MSS. It. cl. VII, cod. 1745. Cf. memorandum by Drachio in Arsenale, busta 533.

[52] According to which system of rowing was in use, one or three oars to a bench. An inventory of 1559 lists: " palamenti integri per galie 73 (triremes by implication), palamenti fati di remi grandi de 3 homeni per uno per galie 6 ", and various special and unfinished oars—Museo Civico, Venice, Arch. Gradenigo, busta 193.

responsible for having the carpentering on the one hundred light galleys completed, another for the pitch, tow, and nails, and for the caulking of the galleys, a third for the masts, spars, and rudders, a fourth for oars, a fifth for pulleys and windlasses. The Admiral was specially charged with keeping the supply of cables, shrouds, ropes, sails, and anchors; the arms steward with that of guns, munitions, and armor.

This division into departments gave a basis on which to appropriate money,[53] figure the cost of a fully equipped galley,[54] and estimate the degree of preparedness of each part of the work.[55] It hardly affected the primary stages of production, but it was the basis for the efficiency displayed in outfitting the galleys. Accurate records of the manufactured equipment on hand required orderly disposal of these goods in definitely assigned warehouses. Only if the spars, sails, benches, anchors, etc. were all neatly stacked and numbered in their appointed places could the equipment of a new galley be so rapidly brought together and put in place that the ship might leave the Arsenal the same afternoon in which the hull was launched. The systematic arrangement of materials was adopted with an appreciation of the saving of time and labor in assemblage which was thus gained, but the regulations assigning definite warehouses to various products expressed also the concern for an accurate inventory, an extension of the traditional concern with bookkeeping.

As an industrial establishment the Arsenal had a threefold task: the manufacture of galleys, arms, and equipment; the storage of these till they were needed; the assemblage and refitting. The Admiral was the official responsible for the

[53] Senato Mar, reg. 37, ff. 3-4.
[54] Statement of cost of light galley given in Appendix VI.
[55] Bibl. Naz. Marciana, MSS. Ital. cl. VII, cod. 1745; and Museo Civico, Arch. Donà della Rosa, busta 181; Gradenigo, busta 193: reports on the Arsenal in which only the pulley-makers do not appear as a separate department. See also A. S. V., Secreta, Relazioni Collegio, busta 57, report of Priuli, 1591. Priuli's report is detailed, covering the Arsenal place by place. A report of 1590—Museo Civico, Arch. Gradenigo, busta 170, f. 220—described the conditions of all seven departments and also the materials which the foreman of the ironsmiths had ready, and the pitch prepared by the " pegolotto ".

storage, assemblage, and refitting. He was generally reputed the supreme head, under the Lords and Commissioners, of the whole Arsenal, but it has already been pointed out that there was no one general manager in quite the sense in which that term would be used today. On the one hand, all the Councils of the Republic interfered more or less to determine how it should be run, and on the other, some foremen enjoyed such prestige as to be practically independent in the control of their craft. The first stage of manufacture was in large part decentralized into the hands of master craftsmen. The following list of the employees working in the Arsenal about 1560 indicates their number, organization, and pay.[56] The yearly salary of 100 ducats was equivalent to about 46 *soldi* a day, but the wages of the ordinary workers and the officials are not comparable without qualification, for the foremen, besides receiving their dwellings rent free, were granted extra pay and privileges for sons registered as apprentices.

The Admiral, paid 150 ducats a year and his house.

  13 warehouse supervisors.
   2 boss stevedores, one paid 20 *s.* a day, the other 30 *s.*, one
        given his house.
  60 to 80 stevedores, paid 10 *s.* a day in winter and 13 *s.* in
        summer.
   2 bosses of unskilled laborers, paid 20 *s.* a day.
   2 bosses of caulkers engaged in unskilled labor, paid as master
        caulkers.

[56] Lists given in MSS. in Museo Civico, Venice, Arch. Gradenigo, busta 193 (1559) and Arch. Morosini, busta 302 (1553) have been supplemented by additional information found in the archives of the Senate and the Arsenal at passages referred to in the appropriate discussions in the text. Earlier lists are: for 1503, in Sanuto, *Diarii,* V, 107, 928-930; for 1518, Arsenale, busta 7, f. 18; for 1546, Senato Mar, reg. 28, ff. 128 and 196. Though less complete they are in substantial agreement.

The numbers of apprentices have been estimated when possible from data given in notes to Tables L and M., and the following notation in Arch. Gradenigo, busta 193:

Oarmakers with apprentices—in 1538, 19; in 1536, 22.
Oarmakers without apprentices—in 1538, 17; in 1536, 18.
Pulley-makers with apprentices—in 1538, 17; in 1536, 10.
Pulley-makers without apprentices—in 1538, 7; in 1536, 10.

A list of the houses furnished by the state, about 1550, is in Arsenale, busta 1. Besides the three for the Lords, there were 35 houses which the state furnished to officers. The more important officials had a garden with the house.

40 unskilled laborers, paid 8 *s.* a day in winter, 10 *s.* in summer,
or caulkers employed at unskilled labor.
1 mistress of the sailmakers, paid 8 *s.* a day.
25 women sailmakers, paid 5 *s.* in winter, 6 *s.* in summer.
1 boss pulley-maker, paid 36 *s.* a day.
30 masters making pulleys, windlasses, etc.
15 apprentices.
1 boss ironsmith, paid 29 *s.* a day.
30 master ironsmiths, paid from 12 *s.* to 23 *s.* a day
(and their apprentices ?).
1 cleaner of the galleys.
1 boss mason, paid 32 *s.* a day and his house.
10 master masons (and apprentices ?).

The Foreman Shipwright, paid 110 ducats a year and his house.
3 Appraisers, paid 40 *s.* to 42 *s.* a day.
17 to 23 construction chiefs, paid from 32 *s.* to 52 *s.* a day, and
a few received houses.
1 supervisor of masters making cabin and deck furnishings,
paid 24 *s.* a day.
580 master shipwrights, paid 6 *s.* to 30 *s.* a day.
290 apprentices, paid 2 *s.* a day.
1 supervisor of the sawyers, paid 27 *s.* a day.
8 sawyers, paid 20 *s.* to 24 *s.* a day.
12 sawyers working by the piece.

The Foreman Caulker, paid 100 ducats and his house.
1 sub-foreman of the *calafati da figgier,* paid 28 *s.* a day.
1 sub-foreman of the *calafati da maggio,* paid 26 *s.* a day.
3 gang bosses, paid as masters.
300 master caulkers, paid 7 *s.* to 26 *s.*
150 apprentices, paid 6 *s.* half of which went to the master.
4 supervisors of the materials used, paid as masters.
1 pitch-maker, paid 40 *s.* and 10 *s.* for his apprentice.
6 unskilled laborers assigned pitch-maker.

The Foreman Mast-maker, paid 90 ducats a year and his house.
30 master mast-makers, paid as carpenters.[57]
10 to 15 apprentices.

[57] The mast-makers are apparently included in the figure 600 given for master ship

The Foreman Oarmaker, paid 96 ducats a year and his house.

   60 master oarmakers, 50% were paid 22 *s.* to 24 *s.* a day, the rest down to 7 *s.*

   30 apprentices, paid 2 *s.*

   7 to 10 unskilled laborers assigned to oarmakers.

The arms steward, paid 144 ducats a year and his house.

   2 unskilled laborers assigned the arms steward.

   1 foreman of the cuirass-makers, paid 30 *s.* a day.

     6 master cuirass-makers (with apprentices?).

   4 masters to make and repair muskets.

   2 master sword-makers.

   2 master lance-makers.

   2 unskilled laborers to clean arms.

   1 powder-maker, paid 54 ducats a year and his house.

   4 gun-founders, paid 60 to 100 ducats each a year and their houses (with apprentices?).

   1 smith to make gun carriages.[58]

Chief bookkeeper, paid 180 ducats a year and his house.
Second bookkeeper, paid 145 ducats a year and his house.

   2 assistant bookkeepers.[59]

   4 or 5 pages.

3 paymasters, paid 33 *s.* to 52 *s.* a day, two received houses.
Captain or policeman(?).[60]
4 doorkeepers, paid 40 ducats a year each and their houses.
42 night watchmen, paid 24 ducats a year each.
Bell ringer.
Keeper of the clock.
Wine steward and 12 assistants, paid 25 ducats a month altogether.

---

carpenters by the lists of 1553 and 1559, only in Sanuto's list of 1503 are they listed separately, namely 318 carpenters, 20 mast-makers. I have estimated the figure for about 1560 on the basis of Sanuto's figure and the increased number of ship carpenters at the later date.

[58] Not named in Sanuto's list. Instead he mentions 11 ship carpenters making gun carriages.

[59] Under this heading or that of the pages may probably be counted the *contador,* mentioned 1559, the 2 *coadjutori* mentioned 1553—cf. Arsenale, busta 135, f. 106—and *cogitori* mentioned in 1546—Senato Mar, reg. 28, f. 196.

[60] Probably the same officer whose functions are explained by Forsellini, p. 63, charged with enforcing such police regulations as those against fires and peddlers, but possibly one of the captains of the woods, therefore not employed in the Arsenal.

In the main the work of making the equipment which the Admiral stored and assembled was carried on by groups of artisans who were only superficially affected by the assignments of responsibility for the outfitting of the reserve fleet. They were grouped in separate shops under foremen members of their own craft who directed their work. In most cases this direction consisted in distributing materials to the workers, in accepting from them only well made products, and in keeping an account of the output of each master. Technical proficiency together with care and honesty in appraising workmanship and in keeping records were the qualities demanded for their duties.

Four craft Foremen were outstanding, those of the carpenters, caulkers, mast-makers, and oarmakers. As one of the Secretaries of the Marine stated in 1591, none of the others deserved the high title Foreman or *Proto*; they were really only gang bosses or *capi d'opera*.[61] The four Foremen were all masters of the craft they supervised elected to their posts by the Lords of the Arsenal or, in case these failed to agree, by members of the College.[62] They were all paid yearly salaries which had been fixed by the Senate or College and which the Lords were unable to change. Like many lesser officials of the Arsenal they lived in neighboring houses provided them by the Signoria. They were each allowed to keep two apprentices for whom they were paid at least double the usual apprentice wage.[63]

The Admiral and the four Foremen were the technical advisers of the Lords and Commissioners and with them constituted a committee for planning the work of the Arsenal.

[61] A. S. V., Secreta, Relazioni Collegio, busta 57. Report on the Arsenal by Giovanni Priuli.

[62] Arsenale, busta 11, ff. 82-3. Not till 1570 were the Commissioners given a part in their election.

[63] *Ibid.*, busta 7, ff. 9-10. The apprentices of the Foremen of the carpenters, caulkers, and mast-makers had to be 12 years of age and were paid 10 *s.* a day for the first three years and 12 *s.* a day for the next four. If they were sons of the Foremen, however, they might begin their apprenticeships at 10 years of age and would be paid 12 *s.* all the time. The Foreman of the oarmakers was allowed two apprentices at 7 *s.* a day each.

In contrast to the office force and the purely disciplinary officials they formed the corps of executive agents on whose directive activity depended the execution in the shipyards of the orders of the Lords of the Arsenal. In view of their importance it is surprising to find how late the Arsenal acquired the sole claim to their services, that only in the sixteenth century they all became full-time employees. The Admiral and the Foreman Shipwright had been forbidden since 1301 to leave the Arsenal to work in private shipyards,[64] but until 1500 the Foremen Mast-makers kept shops outside the Arsenal in which they worked for private shipowners.[65] Whether the Foreman Caulker should give all his time to the Arsenal was still in dispute in 1440 when a newly elected incumbent was forced to resign that position temporarily because he wished to go as " admiral " on the galleys of Aigues Mortes.[66]

The Foremen of the carpenters and of the caulkers headed such big departments that they were permitted, by the sixteenth century, to delegate many of their original duties to subordinates. The Foreman Shipwright shifted responsibility for wood received to the Appraisers; the distribution of wood to the masters remained his problem but one which he can hardly be said to have solved so long as the wood was kept in confusion.[67] The Foreman Caulker selected four members of his craft to be permanently employed as supervisors—one of tow or oakum, one of pitch, one of planks, and one of nails and other ironwork.[68] Paymasters who

[64] A. S. V., Maggior Consiglio, Liber Magnus, f. 24.

[65] Arsenale, busta 566, Quaderno, f. 3; Arsenale, busta 6, f. 48.

[66] Arsenale, busta 566, Quaderno, f. 21-25; Senato Mar, reg. 1, f. 224.   Cf. note 21 above.

[67] According to Forsellini, p. 60, he issued orders for wood to be used by the carpenters. But I fail to find in the sixteenth century any trace of a superintendent of wood to whom such orders might have been issued.

[68] Arsenale, busta 10, f. 5 (1551).   Such a supervisor of materials was demoted in 1525 for allowing good tow to be carried away.   Arsenale, busta 133, f. 76.   The place of the pitch-makers in the Arsenal is obscure.   In 1529 there is recorded the election of a " pegolotto de la Casa ".   Arsenale, busta 133, f. 104.   In 1560 a certain Piero Pegolotto presented himself claiming he had found a new way of cleaning the pitch so that ten per cent. more of it was saved and asking 40 s. a day.   His proposal was referred to the pitch-makers in the Arsenal.   He was voted the salary of 24 s. a

checked the hours of the masters working by the day took over
most of the burden of making out the pay roll of the workers. Gang bosses and construction chiefs helped solve the
problems of industrial discipline created by the large number and peculiar status of the masters of these two crafts.
The Foremen were thus enabled to concentrate on their
duties as technical directors.

Shipwrights and caulkers worked scattered more or less
through the whole Arsenal; the mast-makers and oarmakers,
on the other hand, were assigned to particular shops or
sheds. A new workshop was built for the oarmakers in 1562
so spacious in character that the Great Council held its meetings there after the fire of 1577 in the Ducal Palace.[69] The
Foremen of the mast-makers and of the oarmakers were responsible for the selection and efficient cutting of the wood
they used,[70] as well as for supervision of its manufacture.
Since a large number of oarmakers were paid by the piece,
one of the chief duties of the Foreman was the inspection of
their work, and he also supervised the training of their apprentices. One Foreman even took the initiative in having
a couple of lance-makers employed in the Arsenal to teach
the apprentices so that many of them became expert lance-
makers as well as oarmakers.[71] Curiously enough the concentration of workers in the Arsenal to meet the military
needs of the state in this instance resulted in decreased spe-
cialization since it was desirable to be able to shift readily
from one line of activity to another according to whichever
product, oars or lances, was most needed. One of the lance-
makers hired went himself, in turn, to the woods and showed
the woodcutters how to cut trees for lances, an art of which

day and the first place which might become vacant among those deputed to the pitch.
Senato Mar, reg. 35, f. 57; files, December 12, 1560.

[69] Museo Civico, Venice, Arch. Cicogna, Coll. no. 3281, IV, 63.

[70] Arsenale, busta 136, ff. 68, 80; Senato Mar, files, Dec. 22, 1556. The Fore-
manship of the mast-makers suddenly increased in importance when held by the
expert shipwright Matteo Bressan.

[71] Arsenale, busta 133, f. 20; Senato Mar, reg. 31, f. 142; reg. 29, f. 192, and
especially the petition in the files, Nov. 3, 1551.

they had previously been ignorant—a neat example of how greater efficiency might be made to result from the unity of direction which the Arsenal gave to the whole process of production.[72]

The less important craft foremen or bosses worked themselves with a small group of masters in shops assigned them in the Arsenal. For the manufacture of arms there was a foreman of the cuirass-makers, another of the bowmakers, naturally of more importance in the fifteenth century than the sixteenth,[73] a supervisor of powder-makers, sword-makers, shield-makers,[74] and various gun-founders. These were under the arms steward in the sense that he kept a record of what munitions had been given him by the masters and that they were credited accordingly. In the assignments for the one hundred galleys the arms steward appeared the head of the arms department merely because he received the products of the craftsmen and gave them out to the crews.[75]

Minor groups of artisans more closely concerned with ships fell similarly under the supervision of the Admiral because of his responsibility for the equipment of the reserve fleet. The pulley-makers hardly deserve to be considered an independent department, for as late as 1564 the products of the craft were turned over to the Admiral for safekeeping. In that year a foreman of the pulley-makers was dismissed by the Lords and Commissioners. Whereas a year before he had promised to provide each week the furnishings of his craft for one light galley, yet when called in by them and asked how many he had made, he could merely reply that he had not kept count, and when the Admiral was called he said

[72] Senato Mar, reg. 34, f. 4 and files, March 10, 1558.

[73] A foreman of the bowmakers paid 54 ducats a year appears on Sanuto's list of 1503—*Diarii*, V, 107. For the election of a master bowmaker to do all of his craft necessary for the Arsenal (repairing?) and to make 100 bows a year see Arsenale, busta 566, *Quaderno*, f. 24. Cf. *Ibid.*, ff. 7, 9.

[74] Senato Mar, reg. 35, f. 75 and files, May 24, 1561.

[75] That this was the position of the arms steward is to be inferred from the manner in which he is referred to in the itemized list of the cost of a light galley and in the lists of the supplies of the Arsenal cited above. Moreover in Arsenale, busta 136, f. 97, there is a reference to crediting a gun-founder for guns noted on the books of the *masser*.

none.[76] Thus slowly was the necessity of taking inventory leading the management to check up on the activities of the craftsmen.

Presumably the Admiral supervised much more closely the work of the women employed in sail-making, for he alone was responsible for having the sails ready for the galleys. These women cut and sewed under the immediate supervision of a mistress paid 2 s. a day more than the others, but the Admiral was responsible for choosing the workers, for keeping the sails safe in their warehouses, and for giving them out to the galley commanders.[77]

For a time some sailcloth was made in the Arsenal. Before 1504 the foreman in charge was paid 40 ducats a year, thereafter 4 *soldi* for each piece of cloth. He then occupied one of the government houses adjoining the Arsenal. Since the windows of the thread storehouse opened upon his court, it was thought safer to move him to another house.[78] During the century the manufacture of sailcloth in the Arsenal was discontinued and the product purchased as needed.

A foreman who could claim to be as important as the boss pulley-maker was the one who was at the head of the iron-smiths.[79] Nails, anchors, rudder hinges, grappling irons, and the like were made by masters working in the Arsenal for daily wages, by others employed on piecework, and by iron-smiths also paid by the piece who worked in their own shops with iron supplied them by the Arsenal. In this branch there was an almost insensible gradation of the forms of industrial organization used to supply the Arsenal. The foreman of the ironsmiths was responsible in any case for seeing that the masters were supplied good iron and that they turned in good work.[80] But the distribution of the products was not in

[76] Arsenale, busta 136, f. 60.

[77] Arsenale, busta 135, f. 87; busta 136, f. 64; busta 531; mentioned in the *Edificazioni* of Sanuto, Museo Civico, Arch. Cicogna, busta 969, f. 17, " sono femene che li lavorano le velle, e che in altre salle le cuseno ".

[78] Arsenale, busta 6, f. 56.

[79] First mentioned in 1504 when a " proto di favri " having died a " proto di ancore " was given both positions to save the extra salary—Arsenale, busta 133, f. 22.

[80] Arsenale, busta 133, ff. 3, 9; busta 135, ff. 22-24, 74, 75, 140; busta 8, f. 80; Senato Mar, reg. 28, f. 196.

his hands. The spikes used by the ship carpenters were kept and distributed to them before 1539 by the arms steward; thereafter, since his ignorance of the craft led him to give out too many, by two aged carpenters.[81] Nails were distributed to the caulkers by one of their own craft.[82] The Admiral was responsible for keeping ready the anchors and grappling irons. The orders for ironwork came from three different departments, but the masters were neither divided up nor assigned some to the carpenters, some to the caulkers, and some to the Admiral. Only unskilled laborers and sawyers were placed under another craft. The production of ironwork was united in one department under a craft foreman, the distribution divided between special supervisors and the Admiral.

The extended authority which the Admiral held over these smaller groups of craftsmen was largely due to the importance attached to inventory or reserves, and to distribution or assemblage. The work which he personally directed of launching, beaching, and careening the galleys involved the use of a large number of ropes and cables, and gave, therefore, a double reason for holding him responsible for all cordage made for the Arsenal, used there, stored for the hundred galleys, and loaned or sold to private shipowners. All cables and high grade cordage were manufactured in the Tana, the state rope factory adjoining the Arsenal, under the supervision of the officials of that institution from hemp furnished them by the Lords and Commissioners. But the Admiral was expected to see that all ropes and cables were properly made and of the desired length and thickness.[83] About 1500 a rope-spinner was employed at sixty ducats a year to repair ropes and manufacture those made of the low grade hemp which the Tana was forbidden to use.[84] Soon thereafter, contracts

---

[81] Arsenale, busta 135, f. 37.

[82] *Ibid.*, busta 133, f. 53.

[83] A law of 1525—*ibid.*, busta 7, ff. 46-47—held the foreman of the Tana responsible for the new ropes for the 100 galleys, but in all subsequent laws and inventories the Admiral was considered in charge. See also Drachio's description of his duties, Bibl. Naz. Marciana, Venice, MSS. It. cl. IV, cod. 177, ff. 35 *et seq.* On sale of old ropes see Arsenale, busta 133, ff. 111, 128.

[84] Sanuto, *Diarii*, V, 107; XX, 130; Arsenale, busta 133, ff. 8, 35, 85.

for most of this work were periodically let to the lowest bidders, the contractors being held responsible by the Admiral for the quality of their work.[85]

Thus the Admiral, although he was considered the director of the whole process of manufacture because he was responsible for the final outfitting of the galleys, in fact concerned himself with only some of the primary stages of production. His authority over the storage of the materials produced was made effective by the appointment of aged laborers to guard his warehouses. These irregular employees first received a legal status in 1554 when the Lords instructed the Admiral to choose from among his unskilled laborers thirteen trusty men to be permanently employed to supervise the storerooms.[86] But some of the responsibility for the equipment being kept in readiness fell also on the Foremen and the arms steward.

It was in what may be considered the final stage of production, the assemblage, that the Admiral was indeed supreme. That task, not being a distinct craft in itself but concerning many, escaped the jurisdiction of any one craft foreman. The Admiral was always a man of long maritime experience. In 1552 the Captain General of the Sea requested that Francesco da Fiandra, then Admiral of the Arsenal, be permitted to serve as his " admiral," that is, as the chief navigation officer or chief of staff of his fleet.[87] The same Francesco was a few years later building a galley of his own design.[88] Alvise Biondo, his successor in 1561, had been Foreman of the caulkers.[89] But, whether caulker or shipwright, the Admiral was in any case a man possessing a special competence in providing for all the needs of a ship at sea.[90] Of course the officers of

[85] Arsenale, busta 135, ff. 6-8.

[86] Arsenale, busta 135, f. 136. Earlier mention of warehouse guardians—*ibid.*, busta 133, ff. 78, 128.

[87] Senato Mar, reg. 32, f. 6. The request was granted on the grounds that Francesco had already arranged such rule and order in the Arsenal that he could be spared. I take it that his main job was done when he had outfitted the fleet, and so he was allowed to go along to keep it in trim.

[88] Arsenale, busta 136, f. 16; and above chap. III.

[89] *Ibid.*, busta 136, f. 48.

[90] Those elected in the first half of the fifteenth century were usually away on

each galley were personally concerned in the excellence of their ship and the completeness of its equipment. The four Foremen as well as the Admiral could count on tips of a ducat apiece from each galley commander.[91] That the Admiral was the man in charge where so many important personages were concerned made him appear the head of the Arsenal.

The Admiral was also responsible for inspecting galleys when they were returned by their commanders, for seeing that they were cleaned, refitted, and repaired as need might be, and for launching new galleys and stepping up the masts.[92] In such work he used unskilled laborers, at least forty in winter and sixty in summer, or caulkers assigned to him because there was no work for them in their own craft. He was assisted in directing them by gang bosses who had the power to dock the pay of those who did not attend to their duties, and who saw to it that his orders were executed. Before 1537 there was only one such boss, but the large amount of work that year and the extra number of workers employed caused their number to be raised to two. There it remained until in the great rush of preparation in the spring of 1570 it was raised to three.[93]

Assembling on the launched galleys the equipment which had been waiting ready in the warehouses involved the labor of a great many *fachini,* stevedores or porters. The *fachini* of Venice were organized under chiefs according to the wards or *sestieri* of the city. In time of need they might be conscripted for work in the Arsenal,[94] and accordingly the number employed there ran up very high when many galleys were

voyage or about to leave. The pay was then 200 ducats but many men chosen declined the office. *Ibid.,* busta 566, *Quaderno.*

[91] *Ibid.,* busta 135, ff. 87, 118; busta 136, f. 71; busta 10, f. 71; busta 9, f. 80.

[92] *Ibid.,* busta 11 f. 65; busta 135, f. 26; Senato Mar, reg. 22, f. 62.

[93] Arsenale, busta 135, ff. 26, 105, 136; busta 11, f. 65. In 1570 it was stated that the Admiral was to have three "capi di manuoli" chosen from among the carpenters and caulkers. These men might be counted, in the lists of 1553 and 1559 referred to above, among the caulkers and carpenters, yet the lists mention one *capo.* Sanuto, *Diarii,* LIII, 578, mentions a "proto di manoali". Perhaps there were four *capi* in all, one not chosen from the craftsmen.

[94] Arsenale, busta 136, f. 11 (1555).

being sent out and many wares had to be carried hither and yon to get them ready. Eighty in summer and sixty in winter was the number fixed by the Senate in 1546, but in fact more were customarily used. The Admiral assigned a few to each of the craft foremen, some worked under contract unloading wood at so much a barge-load,[95] but the majority worked directly under his orders supervised by two gang bosses.[96]

An efficient arrangement of the warehouses facilitated the assemblage by making it possible in some cases to bring the galleys to the equipment instead of the equipment to the galleys. As early as the fifteenth century there is a suggestion of a direct-line layout. The Spanish traveler, Pero Tafur, gives the following picture of what he saw at the Arsenal of Venice in 1436.[97]

"And as one enters the gate there is a great street on either hand with the sea in the middle, and on one side are windows opening out of the houses of the arsenal, and the same on the other side, and out came a galley towed by a boat, and from the windows they handed out to them, from one the cordage, from another the bread, from another the arms, and from another the balistas and mortars, and so from all sides everything which was required, and when the galley had reached the end of the street all the men required were on board, together with the complement of oars, and she was equipped from end to end. In this manner there came out ten galleys, fully armed, between the hours of three and nine."

What Pero Tafur described as streets with the sea in the middle must have been the banks of the *rio dell' Arsenale* and the basin of the Old Arsenal. Figure XVIII. Their junction was again in 1560 the sole entrance to the Arsenal, for the opening which had connected the Newest Arsenal with the lagoon when that addition was first built had since been walled up.[98] Perhaps rather as a natural result of the manner

---

[95] *Ibid.*, busta 135, f. 60 (1542).

[96] *Ibid.*, busta 1, lists of assignments of *fachini*. In 1587-1588 the number employed beyond the ordinary 60 or 80 varied from 19 to 114.

[97] *Pero Tafur, Travels and Adventures, 1435-1439* (ed. Malcolm Letts, Broadway Travelers Series, New York: Harper and Brothers, 1926), p. 170. Reprinted by permission of the publishers, George Routledge and Sons, Ltd., London.

[98] Casoni, " Forze ", p. 124. In general the plan and description of the Arsenal are

of its growth than as the conclusion of a well calculated concern with industrial efficiency, the Arsenal was so arranged in 1560 that it is easy to imagine building beginning in the remoter sections and the hull moving through the basins

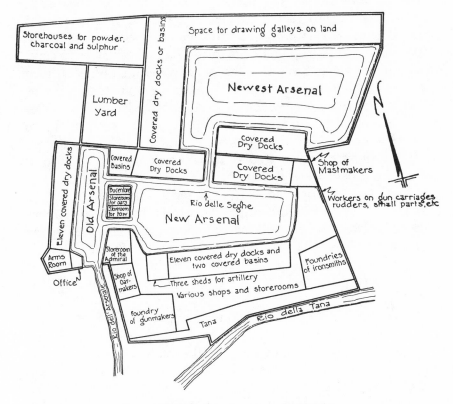

FIGURE XVIII.   THE ARSENAL ABOUT 1560.

acquiring rigging and arms as it neared the outlet. The older parts of the Arsenal, which were nearer the *rio dell' Arsenale,* had been more completely filled with buildings—storerooms,

based upon the articles of Casoni and Nani Mocenigo and the many valuable illustrations given by the latter, but special reliance has been placed on the enumeration of the buildings in the booklet on the Arsenal in busta 193 of the Arch. Gradenigo at the Museo Civico, and that in Arsenale, busta 1. The former enumeration is dated 1560, the latter is with the enumeration of ships in the Arsenal in 1544. The *Relazione* of Priuli, 1591, Collegio Relazioni, Secreta, busta 57, and the seventeenth century plan in the Sala Margherita at the Archivio di Stato have also been found useful.

workshops, and covered docks under which finished galleys might be kept protected from the weather.

The docks used for building new ships were about equally distributed between the New Arsenal and the Newest Arsenal—twenty-six in the former, twenty-seven in the latter. Each dock had room for two galleys. The covered docks in the Old Arsenal were used to keep finished galleys or to store artillery, and some docks in the New Arsenal were similarly used as warehouses—three on the south side for storing artillery, three on the north for preparing and storing masts. Altogether there were enough dry-docks and covered basins for one hundred and sixteen galleys, built or building, to be kept under cover, besides some small craft. Additional galleys might be given a covering of boards on the open land to the north of the Newest Arsenal.

Powder was stored in a separate enclosure of about three and a half acres which connected with the three basins where the ships were built and kept only through one tower in the Newest Arsenal. This section was added in 1539 and leaden roofed powder houses built there shortly before 1566, but after the explosion of 1569 all powder was removed from the Arsenal.

Most of the shops of workers not immediately concerned in building ships were placed on the land called the Campagna which lay to the south of the basin of the New Arsenal. Here, just north of the Tana and between the two foundries which filled the south-east and south-west corners, were the shops for preparing saltpetre and the warehouse for storing it, a storehouse for pitch received and another for heating it and for storing the prepared pitch, a storehouse for ironwork used on the galleys, the shop of the pulley-makers, the shop of the lance-makers, the storeroom of the wine, a storeroom for sailcloth, the shop of the cuirass-makers, and various other storerooms for arms and munitions.

Since the craftsmen making furnishings for the galleys were all located together on this side of the Arsenal, they were near the buildings where their raw materials were kept and their products stored. Galleys built in the Newest Arsenal were probably brought into the New Arsenal to be equipped with masts, rudders, and artillery.

But the busiest center of activity when galleys were sent out was still the same as that Tafur described, the outlet to the south of the Old Arsenal. On one side, behind the office, was the storeroom whence the arms were given out; on the other side were the warehouses in which the Admiral kept the sails and deck furnishings. The cordage was kept in these storerooms or in the Tana. Outside the exit, the wall of the oarmakers' shop was pierced by a small opening through which oars could be passed out to the galleys as they left the Arsenal. Thus the materials which were the last to be distributed were all stored near the exit. Provided the Admiral had been diligent in seeing that the warehouses were full and in order, the Arsenal could easily astound the visitor with the rapidity with which it completed the equipment of the galleys.

The responsibility which was his within the Arsenal, and the authority which the Admiral acquired in the sixteenth century over all the shipping of the city, made him the premier among the whole body of shipbuilding craftsmen. His funeral at San Marco was attended by all the masters. As his body passed through the two doors of the cathedral, the four Foremen who bore it raised it twice in the air—at the first door to show that he had read all the laws respecting his office, at the second to show that he had executed their provisions.[99] But the test of his abilities came on the days when the great reserve fleet of galleys was to be fitted for the sea. More than any other one man the Admiral was responsible for the preparedness and the handy arrangement of the mass of rigging and materials then to be assembled, and he commanded the feverish activity of putting the hundred-odd ships in order. The efficiency with which these tasks were done, on show days and in time of crisis, indicated that the regulations governing the materials had indeed been executed.

[99] Museo Civico, Arch. Gradenigo, busta 193, pt. 2, f. 59.

CHAPTER X

THE ARSENALOTTI

The difficulties created by massing so many materials within the Arsenal were of a kind inevitable in any large industrial enterprise; those resulting from the large number of workers acquired a distinct character because the relation of the masters to the Arsenal was altogether different from that which existed between them and private employers. On the one hand, the masters were obliged to work for the Signoria. On the other hand, they were given rights to employment in the Arsenal in dull times and treated as a select reserve corps of petty ship officers and palace guards.

The overwhelming majority of the employees were master ship carpenters and caulkers. From these two crafts were recruited the technical directors and most of the disciplinary officers. As late as 1565 the Senate thought the employment of any save masters a sign of superfluous expense and ordered that the names, salaries, and duties of all those not master ship carpenters, caulkers, oarmakers, mast-makers, and pulley-makers be submitted to the College to be voted on one by one with a view to eliminating all not approved by a three-fourths vote.[1]

As stipulated in the early guild statutes, the obligations of the craftsmen to the state were of two kinds. There was an obligation to the Doge to build and repair his ships. Whenever a *bucentoro* was built the carpenters were obliged to work three days on it, the sawyers one day. For this they received only their food and drink from the Doge. If that labor did not suffice the gastaldo of the guild must see to having the work finished. Then there was also the obligation to work for the state at the current rate of pay, or that fixed by the Doge and his Council.[2]

[1] Senato Mar, reg. 37, f. 20.
[2] *I Capitolari,* " Marangonis ", chaps. 1, 4, 5, 7; Marciana *Mariegola dei calafai,* f. 52.

This latter obligation of the craftsmen was of primary importance for the management of the Arsenal for it enabled the Lords of the Arsenal, as the need arose, to command craftsmen to come to work in the Arsenal. This obligation extended to all the caulkers in the Dogado, to all branches of carpenters, house carpenters as well as ship carpenters, and to sawyers and oarmakers. At times when great speed in preparing galleys was required this power of the Lords of the Arsenal was extensively used.[3] It was a measure of conscription and properly a war-time measure. But this same power might be used by the Arsenal in times of peace to break up combinations for higher wages and to insure the needed number of workers for the completion of the regular merchant galleys.[4]

Until about 1480 the majority of the craftsmen were normally employed in private industry and the obligation to work in the Arsenal was considered a burden which the craftsmen did their best to avoid. It was necessary to lay fines upon craftsmen who left a shipyard when they saw the gastaldo coming to collect men for the Arsenal, and upon foremen who hired caulkers who had been ordered to go to the Arsenal.[5] In dull times, on the other hand, craftsmen were glad to find work in the Arsenal.

Among several measures taken about 1400 to increase the number of shipbuilding craftsmen was the provision that the ship carpenters should have the right to go and work in the Arsenal.[6] The master who thus came for employment had to come at the beginning of the week, but if he found work outside at a higher wage during the week he was free to leave and take the other work. Mast-makers and pulley-makers, although part of the ship carpenters' guild, were not to have

[3] Senato Mar, reg. 23, f. 21; Arsenale, busta 11, f. 71.

[4] Arsenale, busta 5, first series of chapters, chaps. 63, 76; Senato Mar, reg. 11, f. 81; reg. 24, f. 13.

[5] I Capitolari, "Marangonis", chap. 81; "Callefatorum", chap. 78; Marciana Mariegola, chap. 75, f. 25 (1445), f. 52.

[6] Arsenale, busta 5, f. 93, December 14, 1407, out of chronological order in the third series of chapters. Masters were to be paid 6 GROSSI a day, then equivalent to 24 soldi, apprentices 1½ GROSSI.

in this case the privilege of ship carpenters. For a time forgotten, this provision for securing employment to all Venetian ship carpenters was reënacted in 1422, this time by the authority of the Senate, and in 1447 it was made a more practical measure from the Arsenal's point of view by giving the Lords of the Arsenal the power to cut the pay of inefficient masters.[7]

During the depression in private shipbuilding in the latter part of the fifteenth century the Signoria felt the disadvantages of this form of unemployment insurance which it had given the carpenters. Such large numbers flocked to the Arsenal for work that in the sixteenth century the Arsenal employed a larger number of ship carpenters than did private builders.[8]

The influx of masters to the Arsenal laid such a heavy financial burden on the state that in 1504 the Senate acted to cut down the labor expenses of the Arsenal. Something was saved by ordering the dismissal of practically all employees not master craftsmen and of all carpenters who had been employed beyond the strict legal obligations of the Arsenal, namely, all house carpenters and *squerarioli.* All wage increases which had been granted to ship carpenters within the last three years were annulled. To prevent too rapid increases in wages in the future a special committee was created to determine thereafter the pay of the masters. The committee consisted of the Lords and Commissioners of the Arsenal and delegates from the College and is here referred to hereafter as the College of the Arsenal. It was supposed to meet twice a year, in March and September, to pass in review the

[7] *Ibid.,* ff. 96, 102, March 3, 1422, and May 6, 1447. Lowest wage for masters was then 10 *s.*

[8] The indications of Table I are that a little over half of the total number eligible were actually employed in the Arsenal. It might be argued that after 1504 the number of ineligible *squerarioli* was sufficient to make the number employed in the Arsenal less than half of the total membership of the guild. But even so it is likely that more ship carpenters were employed in the Arsenal than in private shipyards in the middle of the century, since some allowance must be made for those serving on board ship.

merits of each master employed and to raise the pay of those who deserved advancement.[9]

Thus the determination of the wages paid the shipwrights in the Arsenal was given to a committee of high government officials the membership of which was continually changing. These men could have little or no personal knowledge of the skill or energy of the hundreds of craftsmen whose wages they fixed. In part they may have relied upon the recommendation of the Foreman, but in the main they seem to have based raises of pay upon years of service. In theory the College of the Arsenal was to lower the pay of the undeserving as well as raise the pay of the meritorious, but in practice they did no lowering.[10] Whoever had been accepted as a master was raised fairly regularly every few years until he attained the maximum of 24 *soldi*. Above 24 *soldi* advances might be made only by the vote of the Senate itself. Such advances were fairly frequently given, however, so that all those who held offices of high trust and who had shown special skill by building a galley of their own design were customarily granted 32 to 42 *soldi*, and a very few were granted in addition the privilege of having an apprentice who was paid 12 *soldi* a day by the state.[11]

A natural extension of the authority of the College of the Arsenal over wages was their control over the admission of apprentices to mastership, for in the sixteenth century the distinction between master and apprentice had become in the Arsenal little more than a difference in wage. At first the interference of the Arsenal management with the system of apprenticeship had been merely supplementary to the regulation of the guild. A tendency for the less efficient masters—

[9] Senato Terra, reg. 15, f. 23; Arsenale, busta 6, ff. 55-56; busta 133, f. 21. Originally the delegates of the College were 2 *Savii di Terra Ferma* and 2 *Savii agli Ordeni*. In 1565 the membership of this committee, which the Arsenal records frequently refer to simply as the *Collegio* or *Colleggetto*, was changed so that it consisted of one Ducal Councilor, one Chief of the *Quarantia*, one *Savio Grande*, one *Savio di Terra Ferma*, one *Savio agli Ordeni*, and the Lords and Commissioners of the Arsenal. Senato Mar, reg. 37, f. 20.

[10] Senato Mar, reg. 37, f. 198.

[11] For complaints of the Senate over its own generosity see Senato Mar, reg. 31, f. 69; reg. 35, f. 46.

those who failed to find employment in private shipyards—
to come to the Arsenal, and the eagerness of the gastaldo
of the craft for his fee of a ducat from each new master, led
the Senate in 1465 to give the Lords of the Arsenal the
right not to employ any ship carpenter unless he passed an
examination which they attended.[12] It then became the rule
for masters to register their apprentices not only with the
guild officials but also with the Arsenal so that they might
be accepted there as masters when they had served their time.[13]
These measures opened the way for the management of the
Arsenal to step in between master and apprentice. In 1520
the College of the Arsenal was empowered to accept as masters such apprentices as they might find had served full time
even if their masters had failed to record their services correctly.[14] Six years later, on the ground that masters did not pay
their apprentices properly, wages were paid directly into the
hands of the apprentices.[15] The customary line between mastership and apprenticeship was almost completely obliterated
when the College of the Arsenal, in 1541, adopted the practice of granting mastership to boys who had served six of
their seven years, but not granting them the 6 *soldi* which
was then the traditional minimum wage of a master until
their seven years had been completed. For a year they had
the name of master but the 2 *soldi* pay of an apprentice.[16]
No economic difference then remained in the Arsenal between master and apprentice where both alike were paid
directly by the Lords of the Arsenal and were alike deprived
of their pay if found away from their jobs by the paymasters.
Apprenticeship had so far lost its traditional personal char-

---

[12] Senato Terra, reg. 5, f. 134.

[13] Arsenale, busta 6, ff. 13-15.

[14] Senato Terra, reg. 21, f. 138.

[15] Senato Mar, reg. 21, f. 26 (1526). Masters who took apprentices had been paid from 4 *s*. to 8 *s*. a day additional out of which came the 2 *s*. wage for the apprentice. Senato Terra, reg. 5, f. 134 (1465).

[16] *Ibid.*, reg. 26, f. 45, 56; reg. 27, f. 49; reg. 28, f. 139; reg. 29, f. 160; reg. 33, f. 21. The sons of the Foremen of the Arsenal were made masters with pay ranging from 6 *s*. to 10 *s*. a day even if they had served no time with a master. This was considered a legitimate favor to the father. Probably the only effect was to increase the earnings of his family.

acter that in some cases the apprentice did not go with his master when the latter obtained employment in private shipyards nor even work beside him in the Arsenal.[17]

The caulkers were less completely protected and controlled by the Arsenal than the ship carpenters. They did not enjoy the right to steady work, and only in critical times when many galleys had to be made ready immediately was a majority of their craft employed by the state. But they did win the privilege of half-time employment.

The Turkish war which ended in 1540 must have kept a great number of caulkers busy in the Arsenal or in the war fleet. After the conclusion of peace these masters claimed that they had not enough work to support their families. To keep them from emigrating the Senate decided that half of them should be employed each week in the Arsenal.[18] Those engaged for a given week were chosen by the system of rotation which the caulkers' guild had imposed on the private shipbuilders in 1460. Although the government had approved that system readily enough when not directly affected, it had periodically rebelled, when the state was the employer, against the selection of workers by the alphabet or by drawing names from a hat.[19] But the Signoria recognized the desirability of helping to support the caulkers as a group somewhat as they supported the ship carpenters, gave up the right to choose its workers from among the most industrious, and acquiesced in hiring caulkers by rotation so as to relieve the lively discontent of the unemployed.[20] The guild elaborated its rules for spreading the work among the whole group by providing that the master designated one week to work in the Arsenal, even if that week had been a short week because of holidays or if he had found work that week outside the Arsenal and taken it, was not to go again to the Arsenal until his turn came.[21] When all the caulkers had thus become

[17] Forsellini, p. 79.

[18] Senato Mar, reg. 26, f. 15.

[19] At least after the caulkers had become anxious for work in the Arsenal, namely in 1482 and 1501. Senato Terra, reg. 8, f. 160; Arsenale, busta 6, f. 66.

[20] Arsenale, busta 6, f. 66.   [21] Marciana *Mariegola*, ff. 59-61.

regular employees of the Arsenal, the College of the Arsenal developed for them, as it had earlier for the ship carpenters, a control over the registering of apprentices and a wage scale based upon years of service.[22]

Only one other group of craftsmen received right to employment in the Arsenal, the oarmakers. Though their importance in the shipbuilding industry was not comparable to that of either caulkers or carpenters, the oarmakers were even more clearly a group of craftsmen of whom the state might require far greater numbers in time of war than the market could support in peace-time. Quite logically, therefore, they were in 1532 granted the same privilege of working in the Arsenal which had earlier been given to the ship carpenters.[23]

Between 1530 and 1560 the number of master ship carpenters and caulkers in Venice doubled, a rate of increase very must faster than that of the whole population of Venice.[24] The renewal of activity in building large merchantmen may have had an influence, but the greatest single factor in the increase in the number of these craftsmen seems to have been their assurance of employment in the Arsenal. The Lords of the Arsenal had tried to avoid the great expense of engaging half the caulkers by ordering that all caulkers who might be needed by private shipowners were to be taken from the half whose turn it was to work in the Arsenal.[25] Under such an arrangement the caulkers could not have had more than half-time work even in the summer. But it is probable that in the 'fifties more caulkers were needed by shipowners than the Arsenal cared to spare, and that the Lords and Commissioners did not insist that private shipowners pick their workers from among those whose turn it was to work in the Arsenal. Moreover, although laws of 1481 and 1513 had provided for paying some caulkers less than the standard wage of 18 *soldi* or 24 *soldi* a day, even the youngest masters

[22] *Ibid.*, f. 98; Arsenale, busta 135, f. 136; busta 136, ff. 31-35.

[23] Senato Mar, reg. 22, f. 100.

[24] J. Beloch, " La popolazione di Venezia nei secoli xvi e xvii ", *Nuovo archivio veneto, n. s.*, III (1902), 9-12. Below Table I.

[25] Arsenale, busta 9, f. 25 (1541).

were paid the maximum until 1554 when a graduated scale for the younger men was finally introduced.[26]

To be sure, wages in the Arsenal were less than those in private shipyards, and they did not rise in the mid-sixteenth century as did the general level of prices. The rates paid by private shipbuilders rose until they were nearly double the Arsenal wages.[27] Nevertheless the number which came to the Arsenal was so great that they were considered an undue financial burden.

The state had helped to stimulate the rapid multiplication of ship carpenters by the policy it had pursued before 1540 towards the apprentices. The small number of master shipwrights paid in 1531, two hundred and twenty-one, had so alarmed the Senate that the College of the Arsenal had been instructed to speed up the transformation of apprentices into masters, even disregarding when necessary the seven-year rule. Masters were created who had served only twenty-eight months as apprentices.[28] Juggling with the apprentice system offered the most reasonable way of regulating the labor supply. It had been tried long before with the oarmakers. In 1401 an attempt had been made to increase their number by offering 100 lire to each master who would take a green apprentice and train him at his own expense to be an able master. Lest the master lose through the death of a partly trained apprentice the state had offered to pay him 3 *soldi* a day for the expenses of that apprentice.[29]

The control of apprentices was seized on in 1560 and 1561 as a means of cutting down the great numbers of caulkers,

[26] Arsenale, busta 135, f. 136.

[27] The carpenters regularly received 20 *s*. more in private shipyards, at least by 1588—A. S. V., Arti, busta 304, house carpenters vs. ship carpenters. The caulkers' rates outside were raised in 1534 to 40 *s*. a day in summer and 30 *s*. in winter—Senato Mar, reg. 23, f. 31. Earlier, when the Arsenal had had to compete to obtain the desired number of workers the spread was presumably less. In 1425 the pay of sawyers had been raised from 6 GROSSI to 8 GROSSI because they earned 9 GROSSI outside the Arsenal and their numbers were decreasing. Senato Misti, reg. 55, f. 159.

[28] Senato Mar, reg. 22, f. 76. A great many masters were created in disregard of the rules of apprenticeship between 1530 and 1539. *Ibid.,* reg. 22, f. 24; reg. 23, ff. 92-3; reg. 24, f. 50; reg. 25, ff. 40, 69.

[29] Senato Misti, reg. 45, f. 79. Cf. Senato Terra, reg. 5, f. 55.

carpenters, and oarmakers. The masters were forbidden to take any apprentices except their own sons, the carpenters for five years, the caulkers for ten. Thereafter apprentice ship carpenters were to serve eight years, ordinary caulkers eight, *calafati da figgier* ten.[30] For these crafts the prohibition was renewed for five years in 1568, but the number of oarmakers had already been so reduced at that time that they were again encouraged to take apprentices, and even offered an increase in the amount they would be paid for them.[31] When the War of Cyprus made the value of all these craftsmen much appreciated, and, together with the plague of 1575-1577, greatly reduced their numbers,[32] all restrictions on apprentices were relaxed.[33]

Only belatedly, after their number had become a burden, did the government try to limit the multiplication of these craftsmen whose increase was generally fostered. Attempts had been made earlier to find additional employment for them. It was customary for caulkers and carpenters to take service on shipboard. They might find employment at sea not only in their craft but also at other posts. One of the posts which was very profitable even if it did not involve great knowledge or responsibility, was that of bowman on the merchant galleys. Such bowmen not only received good pay but could add to their gains by transporting a few wares among their belongings, and consequently the post was much sought after, and the right to be chosen one of these bowmen was frequently granted by the Senate to needy worthies. Ordinarily these bowmen were chosen by members of the College deputed to go to the archery parks of the city and select the best men, but there was great difficulty in preventing the members of the College from disposing of these positions

[30] Senato Mar, reg. 35, ff. 46-47, 120.

[31] Arsenale, busta 11, ff. 47, 49.

[32] Table I. Priuli in his *Relazione*—A. S. V., Secreta, Relazioni Collegio, busta 57— suggests that the immediate drop 1570-1577 may have been even greater. If the maximum number of six had served on each of the 111 galleys and *galeazze* of Venice at Lepanto, the losses from that fight alone would have been very considerable.

[33] Arsenale, busta 11, ff. 49, 73-76, 88; Marciana *Mariegola*, f. 40; Forsellini, pp. 74-78.

as personal patronage. The profitableness of such positions was also shown by repeated regulations to prevent those granted them from selling to others the right to go in their place.[34]

It was desirable that caulkers and carpenters should take such positions on the galleys because they were reputed the handiest men to have available in any difficulty. To make work for them and relieve the Arsenal of their support, the Senate ordered in 1487 that thereafter three ship carpenters and two caulkers be chosen as bowmen on each merchant galley,[35] and ten years later raised the number to six carpenters and four caulkers.[36] In 1510, when the merchant galleys sailed less frequently, each war galley carried two caulkers and six carpenters among the bowmen.[37] Masters were encouraged to take these posts by the assurance that their ratings on the pay roll of the Arsenal would not suffer because of their absence with the fleet at times when the College of the Arsenal met.[38]

Once accustomed to service with the war fleet many masters passed most of their lives in such employ and rose to posts of authority, although perhaps they did so no more frequently in the sixteenth century than in the fifteenth century.[39] Indeed, one might infer from the need of offering them inducements to go on long voyages that, like many Venetians of the time, they were losing their taste for the sea. But in the latter century the military marine was far larger compared with the merchant marine than it had been earlier, and the importance of the masters as a reserve corps of naval officers increased with the growth of the war fleet. In June, 1568 service in the war fleet was made practically

[34] Senato Mar, reg. 14, f. 153; Molmenti, I, 170-3.
[35] Senato Mar, reg. 12, f. 116.
[36] Arsenale, busta 6, f. 42.
[37] Senato Mar, reg. 17, f. 82.
[38] *Ibid.,* reg. 36, f. 69; reg. 21, f. 127.
[39] Many of the carpenters petitioning the Senate for more than 24 *soldi* a day recount their service at sea on state ships. See Senato Mar, reg. 36, f. 39, file 28, April 29, 1563, for one who had served as *ballestrier, compagno, marangon* and *paron; ibid.,* reg. 37, f. 158, file 34, June 25, 1566, for one who had served six years as *compagno,* three years as *paron,* and two years as *comito.*

obligatory for them. The Lords and Commissioners of the Arsenal were ordered to intimate to the masters that if they were sought by naval commanders and either refused or demanded extra pay, their wage at the Arsenal would be cut in half. Only those who were doing work under contract, or had other tasks which the Lords and Commissioners might decide were of great importance, were to be exempt from service.[40] In the spring of 1570 when the fleet was arming for the Turkish war, so many of the masters were asked by the commanders to serve on ships that it was necessary to limit each galley commander to six masters, and to raise many apprentices to the mastership to make up the deficiency.[41]

As the masters employed in the Arsenal became more and more distinct from other craftsmen, they came to be known less by their craft names than by the general term *arsenalotti*. Beside service on the fleet they had other traditional political duties and privileges. When there was a rumor of conspiracy they were drawn up as a guard in the Piazza, just as they were also called out in case of a dangerous fire. They had the privilege of acting as torch bearers at the funeral of the Doge, and of carrying the newly elected Doge around the Piazza on their shoulders.[42] They stood guard over the Ducal Palace during the vacancy at the death of a Doge.[43] Whenever the Great Council met, fifty of their chiefs, fully armed and led by the Admiral of the Arsenal, reported to the *Procuratori* and under their orders policed the entrance to the palace.[44] Only the *arsenalotti* were accepted as laborers

[40] Arsenale, busta 11, f. 48.

[41] *Ibid.*, busta 11, ff. 72-76.

[42] Museo Civico, Arch. Gradenigo, busta 193, part 2, f. 59.

[43] Arsenale, busta 136, f. 19. At the time of the decree cited, 1556, this function of the *arsenalotti* was considered customary, but it was complained that the Admiral was taking young boys to stand guard with him, hereafter he was to take masters who had held naval offices as follows: " armiragli et homeni de conseglio de galee grosse, armiragli et homeni de conseglio de galee sotile, patroni de nave, comiti et paroni de galee grosse, comiti de galee sotil, penesi de galee grosse ", and if these did not suffice, " nochieri de nave et paroni de galee sottile ". The best exposition of the positions of these different officers on board ship is to be found in Manfroni, " Cenni sugli ordinamenti ", p. 450. The list is given at length to show the high offices at sea which might be held by the masters.

[44] Arsenale, busta 11, ff. 63-4.

in the mint.[45] Thus they were the trusted guardians of the vital points in the city—the palace, the mint, and the Arsenal itself.

The task of the Lords of the Arsenal in managing these workers was not, therefore, a mere " labor problem ". It was also a political problem. A worker might be whipped and his pay reduced for merely shouting out to the Lords of the Arsenal during a military review of the masters,[46] or a worker might receive an advance of pay not for his technical skill but for his military service and suffering.[47] Dismissal from employment, the threat of which is the basis for modern factory discipline, was resorted to by the rulers of the Arsenal only in extreme cases when the stocks and the whipping post were deemed inadequate. The masters were made to feel that the Arsenal was their home, and were treated in a fashion which was certainly paternalistic although sometimes so harsh that one might hesitate to call it paternal.[48] The aid extended to the unfortunate was made to appear more like the provisions of a kind master for faithful servants than any formal accident insurance.[49]

The case of a ship carpenter who was killed fighting the fire in the Fondaco dei Tedeschi illustrates the care of the Lords of the Arsenal in providing for the families of workers and nourishing the masters devoted to the Signoria. The ship carpenter in question must have been a very young master since his pay was only 8 *soldi* a day. At his death his wife was with child and without means of support. The Lords provided that his pay of 8 *soldi* should be paid to the widow. If

[45] Casoni, " Forze ", pp. 149-151.

[46] A vivid account of such treatment is given in the successful petition of Paolo Bernardin for reinstatement, Senato Mar, reg. 37, f. 135, file 34, March 9, 1566.

[47] Senato Mar, reg. 29, f. 2; files, Sept. 1, 1546; Senato Mar, reg. 23, f. 84. Another application of the same principle is found in 1513, Arsenale, busta 6, f. 69. Fifty ship carpenters had been sent to Padua. Those who had not wished to go at the wage offered had their wages in the Arsenal lowered. Those who went had theirs raised.

[48] Examples of interference into the family affairs of the craftsmen; Arsenale, busta 6, f. 39; busta 133, f. 131.

[49] See the following examples: Arsenale, busta 10, f. 29; busta 136, f. 14; busta 7, ff. 28, 61; Senato Mar, reg. 20, f. 184.

the child proved a boy, he was to work in the Arsenal and receive the 8 *soldi,* if a girl he who took her to wife would receive the 8 *soldi.*[50] Thus the family was provided for and the Lords of the Arsenal were assured that the money would not go outside of the select group of *arsenalotti* whom it was their purpose to support.

A strike by this group would have been a dangerous thing if they had had any real spirit of revolt. Even a passing outburst over a particular grievance had to be managed in politic fashion. Such an outburst occurred in 1569 as the result of a decision that they should not be paid for Saturday afternoons since all that afternoon was spent in paying them. The next Saturday, when the bell of the Arsenal sounded at noon for them to go out, and they understood they were not to be paid for that afternoon, there was a great uproar. Some three hundred seized axes and mallets and surged across to the Piazza. They went to the Chiefs of the Council of Ten and demanded in abusive and threatening language that the full day's pay be restored to them. A Chief of the Ten told them they seemed to wish that he hang six or eight of them up by the neck. They replied that they would go where they would be listened to, and burst in upon the College. There the Doge quieted them and sent them away with fair words. When the mob had scattered, the Ten arrested a few of the leaders but let them out again in six months. The next Saturday the Lords and Commissioners called the masters to the office one by one, and by cajoling some and threatening others restored discipline.[51]

[50] Arsenale, busta 6, f. 59.
[51] Bibl. Querini-Stampalia, MSS. cl. IV, cod. 16, *Storia veneziana di Agostino Agostini,* f. 279; Museo Civico, Arch. Gradenigo, busta 193. For the decision which started the trouble see Arsenale, busta 11, f. 55.

CHAPTER XI

INDUSTRIAL DISCIPLINE IN THE ARSENAL

To the shipbuilding craftsmen the magistracy of the Arsenal was not only their employer but their government; the turreted enclosure was not a mere workshop, they called it their home. The managers of the Arsenal did not regard the craftsmen as factory hands but as a valuable arm of the state which it was their duty to strengthen. But the government was not therefore entirely indifferent to inattention to work on the part of the masters. Though most of these had to be employed anyhow, it was obviously objectionable to pay more workers than actually came to the Arsenal, or to allow a full wage to craftsmen who merely paid a perfunctory call at the Arsenal in order to be entered on the pay roll for that day. The first problem of industrial discipline to be recognized was the need of regulating precisely when the masters came to work and when they left, of carefully recording what masters were employed, and of preventing any masters who were supposed to be at work from slipping out of the Arsenal during working hours. Such regulations were necessary to make out the pay roll. In these particulars the need of accurate bookkeeping first touched the lives of the masters.

The hours of the masters were regulated by the ringing of the Arsenal's bell. The bell ringer was required to begin ringing every morning at sunrise when the largest of the bells of the tower of San Marco sounded, that bell which was called the *marangona* because it called the shipwrights to work.[1] For a full half hour the Arsenal's bell sounded and again at noon for a half hour, and anyone who failed to present himself before the bell had ceased to ring was struck off the pay roll of that day. In 1414 it was stipulated by the Senate that the

[1] Arsenale, busta 566, *Quaderno,* f. 22 (1443); Bibl. Nat., Paris, Fonds Français, 5600, f. 118. On the *marangona* see "Nomi antichi delle campane della torre di San Marco" in *Arch. ven., n. s.,* vol. XXXII, pt. I (1886), p. 378, and Boerio, *Dizionario.*

Lord of the Arsenal whose turn it was to be the cashier must check the masters entering and leaving and see that they came on time,[2] but by the opening of the sixteenth century there were special officers, paymasters, whose sole duty it was to keep accurately the lists of what masters and apprentices were to be credited for each day's work. These officers both checked the list of masters as they came in and struck off the list those who went out during working hours. They also acted in conjunction with the Lords of the Arsenal and the various foremen in striking off the pay roll of the day or week masters who did not attend to their tasks.[3] How this worked is illustrated by an incident in 1519. A certain Piero was boss over a group of caulkers but they did not attend to their work and one of them, Sebastiano, went off to sleep. Piero reported to the paymaster of the caulkers, and when Sebastiano came back to work that afternoon the paymaster told him to go away for he had been taken off the pay roll.[4]

But the tendency to use the paymasters as inspectors within the Arsenal to see that the masters were at work was checked by the necessity of having them at the doors at all times so as to strike off the names of masters who slipped out of the Arsenal during working hours. In 1534 the Lords and Commissioners ordered that everyone who went out before the bell sounded the end of the day should be struck off the pay roll for the whole week, and that the chiefs in the Arsenal must report to the paymasters any of their workmen who thus deserted. But the Lords obviously expected to have difficulty persuading the chiefs to enforce the rule or even admit they knew of its existence.[5] Accordingly in 1536 they ordered the paymasters to stay constantly at the doors,[6] but by 1557 at least

[2] Arsenale, busta 5, under date of July 15, 1414.

[3] First mention in 1501—Arsenale, busta 133, f. 5—when a carpenter was rewarded for his good service in cutting wood and bringing it to the Arsenal by the promise of the first post of *appontador* which became vacant. On their duties see Arsenale, busta 133, ff. 17, 24, 48; busta 135, f. 40; Senato Mar, reg. 23, f. 47; reg. 28, f. 128; reg. 32, f. 192.

[4] Arsenale, busta 133, f. 58.

[5] *Ibid.,* busta 133, f. 146.

[6] *Ibid.,* busta 135, ff. 20-1.

one of them had been assigned to go around the Arsenal and see that none of the masters left their work.[7] In 1568 two additional paymasters were elected to tend to the apprentices, one to stand at the door and one to go about inside the Arsenal four times a day and see if they were working with their masters. If they were not he was to call them, and if they failed to answer he was then to strike them off the roll of the day.[8] Apparently it was no concern of the paymaster how hard the men worked so long as they were at their tasks. In 1566 one ambitious master carpenter reported to the Lords and Commissioners that many masters got out of the Arsenal by one ruse or another, and that many who were noted on the pay roll as working by the day, once they were inside, went and worked by the job. He suggested that he be appointed to go about and check all the masters and see how they were working so that his lists could be compared with those of the paymasters. The Lords and Commissioners gave him the job he wished but did not encourage his unsolicited zeal by any raise in pay.[9]

Although the office of paymaster was considered a high position and brought to the holder the use of one of the houses of the state and a raise in pay, so that the hope of attaining it was counted an inducement to the masters to do good work for the Signoria when sent out to cut lumber,[10] yet it was a dangerous position for a man to hold. Masters who had had their pay taken away were in no gentle mood. He who held the post of paymaster, according to the testimony of one who

[7] Senato Mar, files, December 31, 1557, reg. 33, f. 173. An *appontador* was petitioning for a raise of pay and described his task thus: ". . . dapoi subito si hano appontato le maistrance si mattina come depoi manzar e vano in Arsenal, io andassi di continuo attorno di quello et guardando per ogni opera che quelli non mancassino del debito suo in esserli all' opera fino le hore debite all' uscir, et habbiandosi pontati et non trovandoli su l'opera, li disponto, et si nell' uscir che nullo de loro non ardiscono di partirsi dall' opera sua, et vedendoli io li disponto et li tien li denari quali tornano in V. Sta." He was still at these duties in 1570. Arsenale, busta 136, f. 94. In 1572 when his successor was elected, he was referred to as " apontador di dentro ". *Ibid.,* busta 136, f. 104.

[8] Arsenale, busta 136, ff. 86-7.

[9] *Ibid.,* busta 136, f. 76.

[10] Senato Mar, reg. 32, f. 192.

occupied that position, was a much hated man, and he went in danger of his life.[11] On the twenty-third of February, 1568, a carpenter lay in wait for Giacomo de Damian, a paymaster, by the bridge which he had to pass on the way to the Arsenal, and struck him such a blow on the left temple that it was likely to prove fatal. The Lords and Commissioners claimed jurisdiction and the Senate gave them power to proclaim a ban against the culprit and offer 500 lire reward for his capture alive or dead.[12]

Before the appointment of the paymasters the weekly pay roll had been drawn up by one of the bookkeepers and the Foremen; after 1500 all three types of officials were concerned in it. The workers were paid on Saturday afternoons, and except for a short relapse about 1490, the Lord of the Arsenal who was " cashier " personally gave out the money to the workers one by one.[13] That is, he gave out what money there was to be had. Sometimes the masters had to wait a long time for their pay. In December, 1424 the masters were owed four months' pay before the Senate took note of the fact that, as they then put it, the workers had nothing else save that which they were paid from day to day and needed the money to keep their families alive. Provision was then made for paying them, but the next year in August the Signoria was still 4200 ducats in debt to the masters.[14] When there was little money the workers occasionally grew mutinous. As the Lords of the Arsenal recounted the story of Antonio di Giovanni, on such an occasion in 1501 he induced all his art to forget all reverence and fear of justice so that when Tommaso Duodo, Lord of the Arsenal, was paying the workers in his office, they collected there shouting and cursing, complaining of the little money they had received and demanding more. Duodo told them not to fly into a fury because he had given them their share of the little money he had, and next week they should

[11] *Ibid.*, files, December 31, 1557.
[12] Arsenale, busta 11, f. 46. It is significant that the paymasters were elected from those specifically applying for the post. Arsenale, busta 135, f. 44.
[13] Arsenale, busta 5, under date July 24, 1414; busta 6, ff. 44-5, 70.
[14] Senato Misti, reg. 55, ff. 74, 157, 124.

have more. But the masters grew more blasphemous than ever and Antonio waxed so malignantly bold as to throw his money at the noble Lord. Duodo took the money and told him that if he did not wish it he could go with God, as the expression went, the money would be given to others. Whereupon Antonio swore worse than ever and left. Duodo reported the scandalous behavior of Antonio to his colleagues and, in view of the danger of such a lack of obedience and reverence where so many of the masters were creditors, Antonio was forever forbidden to work in the Arsenal.[15] On another occasion all the masters came to the College complaining that for thirteen weeks they had not been paid but were sent away by words and fair promises.[16]

It was considered a regular part of the pay of the masters that they should be supplied with wine while they worked, and wine was passed around the Arsenal five or six times a day. Hence the need of a wine steward who would be as sparing as possible in its distribution, and who would buy only good wine lest, as happened in 1528, it spoil and incapacitate the masters.[17] The attraction of these free drinks drew many to the Arsenal and the consequent heavy consumption of wine was one reason why the doors had to be closely watched.[18]

A careful supervision of who entered and left the Arsenal was also essential to curb thieving. Not only must those who had no business there be kept out, but even those who were legitimately employed had to be carefully examined at the exit to see that they did not take away property of the state. The Lords of the Arsenal were given authority to pay informers and grant them immunity, and to give rewards to the

[15] Arsenale, busta 133, f. 4.
[16] Sanuto, *Diarii*, XII, 562; Arsenale, busta 6, ff. 61-2.
[17] Bibl. Nat., Paris, Fonds Français, 5600, f. 118; Arsenale, busta 133, ff. 94, 108-9; busta 136, f. 50; Senato Mar, reg. 29, f. 55.
[18] In 1438 it was ordered that one of the Lords of the Arsenal must stand at the doors and note anyone entering who did not belong. Senato Misti, reg. 60, f. 97. In the sixteenth century this was the duty of the doorkeepers. Naturally they would not know what masters might be employed that particular week, and the paymasters had to be relied upon to tell which craftsmen had a right to enter. Arsenale, busta 136, f. 50.

doorkeepers who caught thieves.[19] On one occasion the door-keepers discovered a cable thirty-four paces long hidden in one of the barges leaving the Arsenal.[20] But the greatest diffi-culties were not in preventing such large single attempts at stealing, but to prevent constant pilfering by the masters of nails and wood.

This problem was the result of distributing much state property among a great number of workers who had no direct interest in its preservation, and who were not adequately supervised during their work by anyone who did have a direct interest. The difficulty was already serious by the fifteenth century. The inspection of all workers by the doorkeepers was relied upon to prevent most thievery, but small nails were so easily taken out that efforts were made to find the offenders through the ironmasters who bought the nails, and the Lords of the Arsenal had a right to mark iron pieces and have the shops of the ironmasters searched. A discovered thief was whipped around the Arsenal with the nails hung around his neck, or put in the stock several days, or banished from work in the Arsenal.[21]

The difficulty of preventing the waste and stealing of wood was yet greater, for it was complicated by the difficult prob-lem of disposing of the shavings which naturally accumu-lated in the Arsenal in great heaps. In the first part of the fifteenth century it had been customary for foremen to use some of these shavings for their fires,[22] and it was probably the ancient custom of the ship carpenters that they should simi-larly take of the shavings left in the shipyard to supply their fires. When they worked in small groups on one ship amid the lumber which their foreman had selected for that par-ticular ship under the eye of a foreman whose reputation among the private builders was at stake, the system may

---

[19] Arsenale, busta 6, f. 67; busta 133, f. 126.

[20] *Ibid.*, busta 135, f. 15.

[21] Arsenale, busta 566, *Quaderno*, f. 19; Senato Misti, reg. 57, f. 205; Senato Terra, reg. 3, f. 192. For cases of conviction for stealing see Arsenale, busta 133, ff. 5, 23, 24, 28, 34, 98.

[22] Senato Misti, reg. 60, f. 92.

have worked well enough. But in the Arsenal there was a great deal of good lumber and waste wood all piled together hit or miss on the various docks and in the various basins; there were so many workers that the foremen could not keep their eyes on them all; and both foremen and masters felt less personal responsibility. Under such conditions the collection of the shavings by the masters was a cause of grave abuses. Not only did the masters gather up good pieces of wood to take home with them; they even cut up the wood at their disposal to make pieces they could carry out and find a use for, they bound together huge bundles of wood sometimes using the cord of the Arsenal in binding it, and concealing ironwork of the Arsenal inside of it. Thus the practice led to waste of their time, wasteful cutting of the wood, and fine chances for stealing.

Consequently in the second half of the fifteenth century, if not before, the Lords of the Arsenal forbade the masters to carry out shavings. But that prohibition was not consistently adhered to nor was it enforced. Repeatedly the masters were enjoined to carry their coats on their shoulders when leaving the Arsenal that they might not be able to conceal any state property.[23] The problem of disposing of the shavings without the loss of other wood could not be solved until an efficient arrangement of the lumber had been devised and that was very slow in coming.

Aside from the regulation of the comings and goings of the masters, special difficulties of industrial discipline arose only in cases where satisfactory results were not obtained by having work done under contract or at piece-rates. The standard of quality was set for each group of artisans by the craft foreman. It was his business to distinguish good work from bad and to give the masters credit only for what was well done. Most of these foremen could perform their supervision of production satisfactorily so long as they kept their accounts strictly and judged honestly by the traditional standards of

[23] Arsenale, busta 1, papers headed " stelle ", busta 8, ff. 81-82; busta 9, ff. 3-8; busta 133, f. 38.

the craft. Only in the two largest departments, those of the caulkers and carpenters, was this simple system, akin to purchase, an inadequate solution for the problems of speeding up the masters and obtaining sound workmanship.

The Foreman Caulker was in charge of too many workers to be able to keep his own eyes on all of them. Moreover, the quality of the workmanship could not be judged at a glance; after it was done the only real test came too late, when the ship was at sea. He could not keep his masters hard at work by giving them work by the job as was done in most departments. The guild prohibition of piecework was reiterated with regard to the Arsenal by special decrees of the Senate.[24] To be sure, violations might have been winked at occasionally if only the work performed under contract had been well done. But usually it was not. So great, however, was the pressure towards assigning work in that fashion when galleys were needed in a hurry that the Foremen invented a way of giving work by the job while making it appear that the masters were working by the day. A certain task was mutually agreed by Foreman and masters to be worth so many hours of work and was given to the masters on that basis. Then whenever the work was done the masters were entered on the pay roll as having worked the agreed number of hours even if they had done the job in half that time. But that subterfuge also was found out and strictly forbidden by the Senate in 1531 when the galleys of Flanders had been almost wrecked because they had been caulked under that plan.[25]

But even if all the work was done by the day it was still difficult to make the masters do reliable work, and defects in their craftsmanship were likely to produce disasters for which the Foreman would be blamed. In 1501 and 1510 Foremen of the caulkers were dismissed because the galleys were not

---

[24] Senato Mar, reg. 2, f. 50. In 1487 a motion was made in the Senate to give the caulking of seven merchant galleys *sopra di sè* because otherwise they could not be got ready in time and the galleys would not go in time for the *muda*. The motion was defeated, 81 to 68—Senato Terra, reg. 10, f. 54. That contrasts with the readiness of the Senate to sanction work by carpenters *sopra di sè*.

[25] Senato Mar, reg. 22, f. 62.

water-tight.[26] The Foreman Caulker discharged in 1501 claimed that the poor work of the craftsmen was no fault of his but was the result of hiring the caulkers by the alphabet. Even though the Lords of the Arsenal would not accept that as an excuse, yet they seemed to recognize that the Foreman was not alone at fault. They held the gastaldo of the guild equally responsible, and in 1502 the College deposed the gastaldo and empowered the Lords to choose his successor.[27]

The system of hiring different caulkers each week so that every master of the craft might have some employment had obvious disadvantages which caused it to be abandoned again and again. But whenever the Foreman was left free to choose his workers he was accused of playing favorites, and the guild took the position that employment by the alphabet was the means of nurturing those craftsmen who were in greatest demand when a large fleet had to be put to sea quickly. So employment by the alphabet was permanently adopted in 1513, but at the same time an attempt was made to strengthen the authority of the Foreman. He was given the power, with the consent of the Lords of the Arsenal, to reduce the pay of those not good masters, and even to banish them temporarily or permanently from working in the Arsenal. It was hoped that these provisions would cause the masters to be dutiful and reverent to their superiors. But in the face of a feeling of craft solidarity, this power of the Foreman was quite a different thing from the authority to choose masters at his pleasure.[28]

The pride of the craftsman in his craft was obviously not sufficiently strong in the case of the caulkers to obviate the need of constant supervision, nor would one foreman suffice when there were two to three hundred caulkers working about the Arsenal. Assistant foremen were necessary, and in 1501 it was decided to appoint two—one for the masters who

[26] Arsenale, busta 133, ff. 2-3, 35.
[27] Ibid., busta 6, f. 52.
[28] Ibid., busta 6, f. 66.

fastened the planks and timbers, and one for those who filled the seams with oakum or pitch.[29] Besides these permanent supervisors, temporary gang bosses were appointed when needed. In 1513 the Lords of the Arsenal were permitted to choose as many of these as there were galleys to be caulked but no more, and to employ these gang bosses until their job was done regardless of the rotation system.[30] In 1525 four of them were deprived of a week's pay because they had not made the masters work.[31] Such appointments and punishments offered an opportunity to fix responsibility on a chief who was at the head of a group sufficiently small for the bosses really to supervise what the workers did. But to produce the best results, it was desirable that the gang bosses be permanent employees who could look for higher jobs in reward for their services. Thus when Andrea da Modon did good service commanding caulkers of the Arsenal—*squera-rioli* and caulkers who had been called in from the other lagoon cities in the emergency—he was given a permanent position as assistant foreman.[32] In 1546 the Lords of the Arsenal appointed two caulkers to be permanently employed as gang bosses.[33] But permanent employment ran contrary to the settled policy of the Senate of having the master caulkers employed in rotation, and in 1549 all such appointments were declared illegal. Thereafter the Lords of the Arsenal could appoint permanent supervisors only in the number which the College might authorize.[34] In appearance that seemed a victory for the guild contention for equality and no favoritism; in effect it was a tacit recognition that permanent supervisors were a necessity. In 1551 the College authorized the appointment of three gang bosses besides the assistant foremen, the four supervisors of supplies, and the two overseers of the caulkers assigned to work for the Ad-

[29] *Ibid.*, busta 133, f. 3.
[30] Arsenale, busta 6, f. 66.
[31] *Ibid.*, busta 133, f. 78. Another instance: *Ibid.*, busta 133, f. 27.
[32] *Ibid.*, busta 133, ff. 120-1.
[33] *Ibid.*, busta 135, ff. 98-99.
[34] Senato Mar, reg. 30, f. 68.

miral in place of unskilled laborers.[35] The needs of large scale enterprise had finally gained recognition despite the opposition of the guild.

A regular corps of assistant foremen or gang bosses subject to the Foreman was not developed any earlier for the ship carpenters than for the caulkers although in their case there was no guild system of employment in rotation to form a basis for objection. During most of the period under survey the shipwrights' department was called on to meet two different problems: the regular construction of several light galleys and three or four great galleys to be completed every other year; and the emergency building of light galleys needed to increase the war fleet or fill up suddenly created deficiencies in the reserve.

The first of these activities apparently produced no special disciplinary problems, partly because the favors shown by the Senate to the expert galley builders, rivals of the Foremen, had long had the effect of dividing the shipbuilding department. At the time of Baxon and of Nicolò and Giorgio Palopano there were really two departments, one for the light galleys and one for the great galleys. Lest the Foreman, Bernardo, be able to hamper Nicolò in any way, he was given workers of his own selection who were paid according to records of their hours kept by the chief accountant.[36] Giorgio enjoyed yet more independence, for the masters assisting him were not subject to any orders of the Foreman and his wood was kept separate from the rest for his exclusive use. Whenever a boatload of lumber arrived at the Arsenal the Lords assigned him his share.[37] When in 1440 the Lords of the Arsenal were instructed to assign to him three sawyers and fourteen ship carpenters, a separate fund yielding 40 ducats a week was established which was to be used only for paying them.[38] At the end of that century Francesco Rosso similarly was assigned certain masters to work under his direction on the ten light galleys and two

[35] Arsenale, busta 10, f. 5.
[36] Senato Misti, reg. 57, f. 201.
[37] Ibid., reg. 60, f. 92.
[38] Ibid., reg. 60, f. 202.

great galleys which he was to be continually occupied in building.[39] Apparently the regular production of galley hulls in the Arsenal was considered adequately taken care of during the fifteenth century by the supervision of two famous shipwrights each of whom directed the work on from four to twelve galleys at a time, but employed only a moderate number of workers, in view of the number of ships he was building, and so took a long time to bring the hulls to completion.

But on occasions when it appeared that the great galleys demanded for a particular voyage would not be ready in time to permit the trading fleet to leave on schedule, the completion of the galleys was assured by letting contracts to masters who would agree to finish the job before a stipulated date.

To meet sudden demands for light galleys in large numbers, production was usually accelerated by this system of putting the building up at auction and giving it to the master shipwrights who offered to complete the work at the lowest price within the given time. A master who took such a contract did the work in the docks of the Arsenal with materials supplied him.[40] The conditions under which the work was to be completed were specified in a contract made in the presence of the Lords of the Arsenal and registered by the bookkeepers.[41] Sometimes the contractor built according to his own designs, sometimes according to those of the Foreman.[42] The master to whom the job had been let was no

---

[39] Senato Mar, reg. 14, f. 101; Arsenale, busta 6, f. 43.

[40] In January 1442, in order to have galleys ready at the usual time for the voyages, the Senate decreed: "Quod manifactura tamen duarum galearum grossarum dandarum nigrarum in aqua debeat incantari minus petenti, cum hoc quod a nostro comuni detur lignamen et feramenta cetera que omnia necessaria ad fabricanda et complementum earum. Et cum hoc etiam quod patroni et prothomagistri Arsenatus supervidentes et intelligentes diligenter huiusmodi fabricam provideant quod laborerium fiat illis galeis sic erit conveniens et necessarius ad fabricam predictam. Senato Mar, reg. 1, f. 75. The resolution for auctioning the completion of Bernardo's unfinished galleys read in part: "E perche al prexente se trova bonissimi maistri che vuol tuor a complir quelle de marangon a tute suo spexe de maistranza. . . ." Ibid., reg. 1, f. 101.

[41] At least after 1513. Just before that date much work was given out informally by the Foreman. Arsenale, busta 133, f. 42.

[42] Concerning the above cited order of January 1442 the question arose: "Fiat

doubt more active in keeping his men at work than the Foreman was, for the Foreman was paid by the year and lost only in reputation if the work was delayed, while the contractor who failed to finish in the stipulated time was penalized by the retention of part of his pay.[43] Moreover, even if he did complete his task in the allotted time, he would lose money if he had found it necessary to hire more masters than he had counted on when making his bid. The only hope of profit for the contracting carpenter was to work himself and his assistants or associates fast enough to finish the job on time with the services of only a few masters. When galleys were needed in a hurry speedy building was counted an achievement. In a successful petition for a raise of pay in 1560, Matteo di Piero boasted that he as foreman with three other shipwrights had made a galley frame in the record time of four months.[44]

Naturally such a method of assigning the work appealed greatly to the Lords of the Arsenal whenever they were required to prepare a great many galleys in a very short time. The Senate was inclined to be against it in theory on the ground that galleys so made were not carefully built, but so great were the savings in time and money that they frequently approved it. The attitude of the craftsmen varied. It gave them opportunities to show special abilities and win larger earnings, but also a chance to lose by underbidding. It so speeded up production that there was less work for the masters as a whole. Among laws passed in 1402 and 1422 for increasing the number of ship carpenters were temporary and conditional prohibitions of work by the job.[45] On the

dubium si dicti magistri qui acceperunt fabricam predictam supra se debent laborare illas ex suo ingenio sicut in deliberatione et incantu per Sapientes ordinum facto continetur, vel ex ingenio et ordine aliorum prothomagistrorum Arsene ". It was decided that the galleys be made by the contracting shipwrights " ex suo ingenio e suis sextis et suis laboribus ". Senato Mar, reg. 1, f. 77.

[43] Arsenale, busta 133, f. 100 (1529), a record of the deduction of 10 ducats from the pay of each of two masters because they had not finished in the time promised the tasks undertaken, namely, " fornir arsili de marangon ".

[44] Senato Mar, reg. 35, f. 46, and files Sept. 29, 1560.

[45] Arsenale, busta 5, July 20, 1402; Senato Misti, reg. 54, f. 6.

other hand, the masters were accused in 1591 of deliberately loitering at their work in order that it should be necessary to ask them to contract for its completion, and of then arranging their bidding so that all would make good profits.[46] At that time the masters were sure of employment anyhow, and their numbers had been so reduced that there was plenty of work for them and no keen competition among them.

But the extent to which the system of contracts was used did not depend on the attitude of the craftsmen so much as upon the need of the Signoria for galleys. Whenever speed was essential galleys were so assigned. Even if the practice was of doubtful legality, it was accepted as a necessary evil. The law of 1422 which forbade letting contracts for galleys also laid down rules to be followed at times when the law was violated.[47] Of course the Senate which forbade work by the job could by the same power permit it at certain times and did so. Moreover, since the Lords of the Arsenal were repeatedly reproved for violating the law in giving work to the caulkers by the job, it is to be suspected that they also violated the law in giving work to the carpenters by the job. But they were not reproved for these latter violations of the letter of the law.[48] In 1517 the Lords of the Arsenal showed how they could give effect to their own violations of the law. They wished to have fifty galleys ready quickly. This end could be compassed by forcing all the masters in the land to come to the Arsenal, but that would be an enormous expense. So the Lords determined to give contracts for finishing them. But since that was against the law the masters refused to make bids and some of them went so far as to say that if they took the work they would not be paid, thus showing a most lamentable lack of confidence in their superior officers. The Lords put three of the leaders in irons.

---

[46] *Relazione di Giovanni di Priuli,* A. S. V., Secreta, Relazioni Collegio, busta 57.

[47] Each contractor must employ at least 12 masters. The purpose was to increase the work for the carpenters. Senato Misti, reg. 54, f. 6.

[48] Besides exceptions already cited to the law of 1422, see Senato Misti, reg. 60, f. 227 (1440). In 1445 a motion to forbid giving work *sopra de sè* to shipwrights was defeated, 77 to 32. Senato Mar, reg. 2, f. 65.

The effect was excellent. The masters began to bid and the work was all given out.[49] Although regarded as an extraordinary measure by contemporaries, yet letting contracts was the method of building galleys regularly employed whenever a large number were needed in a short space of time.

The terms of the earlier contracts provided that the shipwright should do all the carpentering, or even that he should prepare the galley entirely, " black in the water," which implies that he contracted for the labor of masters of other crafts. But between 1529 and 1534 the Senate formulated a new policy which definitely put a stop to all forms of caulking by the job, and which recognized the distinction between the carpentering of the hull or "live work," and the building of the cabins and superstructures, the "dead work." In the rush to prepare the war fleet in the spring of 1532, all the *squerarioli* and even the house carpenters were called to work in the Arsenal, and many of them were given work by the job making partitions below deck and making and fastening deck furnishings.[50] Since the results of that experience were satisfactory, the Lords of the Arsenal were allowed to let contracts thereafter for the dead work at their discretion; contracts for live work were to be let only on the express orders of the Senate.[51] And the contracts given thereafter for the live work called only for the construction of the frame of the galley.

These distinctions were retained during the rest of the century. Separate treatment was given the two stages of production necessary before the galley was ready to be put aside to await the final outfitting and assemblage of rigging, arms, and oars. The laying of the keel, the setting up of stem, sternpost, and ribs, and the tying of the whole together

---

[49] Sanuto, *Diarii*, XXV, 169.

[50] Senato Mar, reg. 22, ff. 62, 95.

[51] Senato Mar, reg. 23, f. 21: " . . . sia comessa alli proveditori et patroni al arsenal che debino dar a lavorar sopra di sè, come a loro meglio parerà, tutte seraglie et pizuoli delle galie sottil, et etiam tutti li lavori sopra coverta, cioè imbanchar et altri simel lavori, non possendo per cosa alcuna far lavorar si de marangon come de calafado in li corpi e vivi delle galie ". There are frequent references to shipwrights finishing galleys " ala vella " which I take to mean building the dead work.

with the clamps were treated as a single operation which the shipwrights could contract to perform.[52] The second stage of production, covering the frame and building upon it and within it, required the labor of both caulkers and carpenters. Since the fastening of exposed timbers and planks by the caulkers had to be done with great pains to make the ship water-tight, they were paid by the day. Less care being necessary in the carpentering of the cabins and superstructures, that work was given out by the job by the Lords of the Arsenal.

Though it was considered desirable to have all the live work done with the greater care which could be expected from day labor, yet such was the need of speed that every large order for galley frames was accompanied with instructions to let contracts for the work.[53] More elaborate provisions were made, however, for seeing that the contractors did their work well. At first the Foreman, later the Foreman and Appraisers, had been charged with supervision of the work of the contractors.[54] But in the 1530's Leonardo Bressan was too old to oversee the work of thirty or fifty gangs and attend to his other duties as well. Therefore three assistant foremen were chosen and paid 3 ducats a month extra.[55] They did their task so well that they were reappointed the next year, 1535, and again in 1537 when contracts were let for more galley frames.[56] Thereafter, however, we hear no more of the three assistant foremen for overseeing work done by the job, but instead in 1565, when contracts for thirty galley hulls had been let, the Admiral, the Foremen of the carpenters and the caulkers, and the three Appraisers were

[52] Generally the expression used to indicate this stage was " a fili amorsadi ". In 1529 the Lords were ordered to give out work thus: " sopra de si iuxta hordine de la casa a li proti corpi di gallia sotil n° xx cum expresse ordine et patto che le facino incorbade et messe a filli morsadi ", Arsenale, busta 7, f. 85. Cf. above chap. V, note 11.

[53] Above chap. VIII, notes 73-75.

[54] Petitions, in Senato Mar, files, from masters having built under contract are accompanied by reports of the Foreman and Appraisers.

[55] Senato Mar, reg. 23, f. 85; Arsenale, busta 8, f. 42.

[56] Ibid., reg. 24, f. 25; Arsenale, busta 8, f. 76.

charged with strict inspection of the work. They were all six to go around the Arsenal together once a week and see if the work which had been done that week by those working on contracts had been well done with good wood. If they found the work not well done, they were to have it done over by the contracting master at his own expense.[57]

Despite efforts to eliminate it, the system of letting contracts was extensively used during the War of Cyprus and was still a problem at the end of the century. But by that time the workers had been organized under a permanent corps of construction chiefs or bosses so that there was hope at least that the old system of contracts might be dispensed with.

There are only scanty records for the fifteenth century of the assignment of docks to masters or of masters building on their own designs. Perhaps, even then, some masters of proved superior capacity, although subject to the Foreman, were customarily in authority over the ordinary masters. Yet the need of regular supervisors intermediate between the Foreman and the ordinary masters was first keenly felt during the great activity of the Arsenal at the time of the old age of Leonardo Bressan. The appointment of the three assistant foremen in 1534-1538 to supervise the work given by the job was a step forward. Moreover, it is to be noted that all three of the men chosen had already occupied superior positions. One of them was Vettor Fausto. Another was Francesco de Theodoro da Corfu, called Zoto. In 1522 he had been assigned one of the light galleys to be made according to his design. In 1528 he was chief of two docks in the Arsenal and was making one of the *barze* as well, and in consequence obtained a raise in pay to 40 *soldi* a day—considered by the oldest boss carpenters to be the pay usually given masters with such duties.[58] In 1529 the Captain General of the Sea wished Zoto to accompany him on the fleet. The Lords of the Arsenal, on the other hand, insisted that because of Zoto's

[57] Arsenale, busta 136, f. 67, 78.
[58] *Ibid.*, busta 133, ff. 68, 107; Senato Mar, reg. 21, f. 73.

abilities and the old age of Leonardo, it was essential to have Zoto in the Arsenal.[59] The third assistant chosen in 1534 was Vicenzo Vituri, son of the Foreman whom Leonardo Bressan had replaced. As successor to his father he had been chief over some docks and had also obtained the wage of 40 *soldi*.[60] Moreover, these were not the only masters who in the 'twenties made galleys of their own design, for among those to whom galleys were assigned to be built according to their own ideas in 1522 were Gerolamo and Cristoforo Rosso, the sons of Francesco, Francesco Bressan, son of the Foreman, and Francesco Spuazza.[61] By the middle of the sixteenth century such leading masters had become a distinct group separately named in lists of the personnel of the Arsenal as gang bosses or construction chiefs. Those who had attained that position were many of them sons of famous galley builders. Others had done good work for the Signoria in building galleys under contract or in cutting wood. Some had won favor by the excellence of the galleys they had made of their own design when the Lords and Commissioners of the Arsenal had favored them by assigning them a dock in which to try their skill. Some—Rosso, Spuazza, Bordola, and Zaparin—were also famous because of the round ships they had built in private shipyards. Piero Zaparin built three large merchantmen between 1545 and 1556.[62] There was not the least objection to these construction chiefs leaving the Arsenal whenever they wished to work for higher wages outside.

One master whose advancement depended entirely on his work in the Arsenal was Giovanni Antonio de Francesco, called Cavarzere. In 1536-1538 and 1551-1552 he took contracts to build ten galleys one of which was of his own design and the rest of the design of Bressan. Upon the testimony of

[59] Sanuto, *Diarii*, L, 552.

[60] Arsenale, busta 7, ff. 28, 60.

[61] *Ibid.*, busta 133, f. 68. On Gerolamo Rosso see also Arsenale, busta 7, f. 24; Senato Mar, reg. 25, f. 156.

[62] Senato Mar, reg. 28, f. 93; reg. 29, f. 120; and files, Sept. 26, 1556; June 29, 1548, Dec. 21, 1553.

the Foreman and of the Appraisers that the galley made of his design was well made and that the others had done good service his pay was raised to the 40 *soldi* a day usually received by construction chiefs. By 1568 he had made three more galleys of his design including a great galley and a four-oared galley, had built a *bregantine* and a *fregata,* and he had completed under contract the dead work on twenty-four light galleys and eleven great galleys including two which he was then finishing according to the model of the noble Gian Andrea Badoer. On the last two great galleys he was going to lose, he stated, about 200 ducats, and did not know how he was going to pay his debt.[63]

But the mere existence of a group of able construction bosses would do little to increase the efficiency of the work unless the masters were organized into gangs under them so that the higher officials could know how many workmen were under each construction chief and how much work they could expect from him. No such organization of the workers took place, however, till 1569. The haphazard system previously in use is described by the preamble to the new regulation. ". . . The masters of our Arsenal work in great confusion. When they have entered the Arsenal part go wandering around without doing any work, and part work in whatever dock pleases them so that the chiefs do not have certain workers assigned them, nor do the workers know who are their chiefs. And that is because most of the masters are not assigned to chiefs, and if the construction chiefs are blamed

[63] Senato Mar, reg. 30, f. 5; reg. 32, f. 104; and files, September 29, 1548; September 29, 1553; January 24, 1568.

Another construction chief was Alvise de Giovanni di Castello, called Scatola. He built good galleys of his own design and in 1564 had an idea of how to arrange light galleys so that they would both carry more men and be faster under oar and sail, and was given a galley to try his arrangement. He made the bridge of the Rialto as it stood in 1548, doing it in such a way that it could be opened in a quarter of an hour and at a cost of only a ducat. He got the ship of Barozzi, which had been built at Santa Lucia, out into deep water by raising it up in the water two and a half feet. Senato Mar, files, December 31, 1548, and Arsenale, busta 11, f. 22.

Another construction chief was Giovanni de Francesco Piccolo. In 1567 he discovered a way to make a galley with larger frames so that the galley was stronger and yet cost less to make. Senato Mar, files, December 20, 1567.

for having done little work, they say they had few workers."
Of course such a situation is only to be explained by the right
of the ship carpenters to work in the Arsenal when they could
not find jobs elsewhere. Since pay in the Arsenal was considerably less than what they might receive outside, many of
the masters may have regarded their employment in the Arsenal more as a sort of dole from the state than as an occasion
for hard work.

To remedy the situation it was ordered that fourteen of
the construction chiefs who had made galleys of their own
design be chosen, and that under them be placed all the carpenters listed on the paymasters' roll under the first seventeen letters of the alphabet, exception being made of those
assigned to specialized tasks. The masters were to be divided
alphabetically into fourteen parts and assigned to the fourteen chiefs and none was to be changed from one chief to
another without the vote of four out of five of the Lords and
Commissioners. The construction chiefs were given authority to dock the pay of those disobedient to them.

The paymasters at the doors were to have on separate pieces
of paper lists of the names of the carpenters assigned each
construction chief. After the lists had been checked at the
doors as the men entered, the appropriate list was to be taken
to the construction chief concerned for his guidance and returned at noon by him to the paymaster at the door. That
would provide for keeping track of the masters. In order to
check up on the construction chiefs the Appraisers were
bound to estimate under oath the number of days which
would be required by the construction chiefs to finish the
tasks assigned to them, which estimate was to be written in
a book and kept secret. Once a week the Lords and Commissioners were to go around together and inspect the work.
If then, after the time which the Appraisers estimated would
be required for the work had passed, the work was still unfinished, the Lords and Commissioners were to consult the
experts and according to their advice allow a short time for
finishing it. If it then still remained undone they were bound

under oath to deduct from the pay of the delinquent construction chief 10 *soldi* a day, and to take his docks from him and assign them to another.[64] At last the management proposed to require the masters to render an accounting for the time they spent in the Arsenal.

Even though this organization could hardly have been installed before it was temporarily abandoned during the War of Cyprus when for the sake of speed the contract system was again used,[65] its main features survived. At the end of the century the amount of work expected of the construction chiefs was not fixed by the Appraisers, however, but by each chief's own estimate each week of what he could get done that week. When they failed to finish as much work as they promised, they gave as excuses the long time the masters took getting to work after they had entered the Arsenal, and the failure of many who came the first day of the week, and on whom they had counted, to come the rest of the week.[66] Obviously there were enormous difficulties in the way of any effective organization of the workers as long as the master shipwrights were free to come to the Arsenal to work whenever they wished and to leave whenever they found employment at higher pay elsewhere.

The tendency to substitute for contracts and piecework well supervised day labor affected not only the main body of the caulkers and carpenters but also the sawyers and the shipwrights deputed to make furnishings for the cabins and decks. The sawyers worked for the carpenters in the Arsenal as in private shipyards. In the sixteenth century they were not scattered among the docks where the ships were being built, but were grouped together—at first in two docks next to the canal connecting the New Arsenal and the Newest Arsenal, later under a huge shed built in the lumberyard.[67] The supervision of their work was divided among the Fore-

---

[64] Arsenale, busta 11, f. 56.
[65] *Ibid.,* busta 11, ff. 88, 90.
[66] *Ibid.,* busta 533, memorandum of Taduri.
[67] Arsenale, busta 11, f. 47.

man, the Appraisers, the construction chiefs for whom they sawed, and a carpenter deputed especially to supervise them. Since most of them were paid by the piece, or more precisely by the cut, this dispersion of responsibility made it easy for them to overcharge. The Appraisers who made out their pay roll had to rely upon information given them by the construction chiefs who had no personal interest in preventing the sawyers from padding their accounts. If the sawyers worked by the day their attendance could be checked by the paymasters at the doors. Accordingly the number employed at a fixed wage was increased as far as possible by limiting strictly the tasks which could be given by the piece or cut.[68] Concentration of responsibility was delayed by a disinclination to give extra pay and authority to the ship carpenter appointed supervisor of the saws,[69] but a zealous carpenter assigned this post sought and obtained a raise in his own wage in 1558 on the ground that he had prevented the sawyers from overcharging and had saved much lumber through skillful selection of suitable logs for sawing.[70]

The special supervisor appointed over the forty-odd aged shipwrights who were occupied in cabinet work, such as making sea chests, also petitioned successfully to the Senate for an increase in pay. In 1566 he too claimed that he saved money for the state in his management of the wood and iron consumed in his department, and that before he took charge the work had been done by the job at great expense.[71] The sort of piece-rate system in vogue in this department was exemplified in a contract made in 1596 by which two carpenters undertook to make in the Arsenal fifty thwarts for light galleys according to specifications given them by the Foreman from lumber he would supply them. They were not to employ any masters who were on the pay roll of the Arsenal. The sawing of the wood was to be done at the expense of the

---

[68] *Ibid.*, busta 133, f. 146; Senato Mar, reg. 23, ff. 38, 172.
[69] Arsenale, busta 133, ff. 54 (1517) and 133.
[70] Senato Mar, reg. 34, f. 47 and files Oct. 22, 1558.
[71] Senato Mar, reg. 37, f. 189 and files, Sept. 16, 1566.

Arsenal, but the contractors were to pay all other costs not only of masters but also of porters to bring them the wood and carry their finished products to the proper warehouse. Their pay, 6 *soldi* for each bench made and delivered, was to be given them each week according to the report of the Appraisers.[72]

The Signoria had built the strong walls of the Arsenal and brought the masters there primarily to insure the safe-keeping of the ships and materials of war which they made, not—at least initially—with the idea of subjecting the masters to an especially rigid discipline, or of standardizing and regulating the quality of their work. Many craftsmen employed in the Arsenal practiced their craft in the shop or dock provided for them just as they might have done in their shop or in a rented shipyard outside the Arsenal, and so long as the number from any craft employed was not very large, and the craft spirit strong, few or no labor problems were created. The master craftsman used the materials furnished him by the Arsenal, but in many crafts there was nothing new in the customer supplying the artisan with the raw material on which he was to work. Whether the ironworker or the oar-maker who received his wood or iron from the Arsenal and was paid so much a piece for the finished product did the work in a shop of his own outside the Arsenal or in a shop supplied him in the Arsenal did not greatly change his position. The master shipwright who contracted to build a galley in the docks of the Arsenal with the materials there ready was in much the same position as the ship carpenter who contracted with private builders to do the carpentering of a ship in docks which they furnished with the wood purchased by them.

In the main the technique of production escaped regulation by the governing councils and remained in the hands of the individual craftsmen. There were exceptions, cases where standardization appeared necessary. In the fourteenth century all bows were ordered made so that the arrows would fit

[72] *Ibid.*, reg. 56, f. 73.

any of them.[73] Similarly in 1516 it was decided that all stern-posts of light galleys be built on the same design so that each rudder would not have to be especially fitted to its sternpost, but a single type of rudder would do for all the galleys. The Lords of the Arsenal excused this act of standardization on the plea that the design of the sternpost did not in any way improve or detract from the excellence of the galley, and left the design of the standard to the craftsmen.[74] There was great uniformity in the rigging and deck furnishings—that was essential to the rapid outfitting of the hundred galley reserve—but as late as 1580 the galley commanders were accused of having the dead work remade according to their fancy, and a standard arrangement for all galleys was ordered.[75] The Senate fixed the carrying capacities or the primary measures of the merchant galleys, but foremen shipwrights repeatedly built these ships larger than stipulated. If, as Felix Fabri asserted, all Venetian galleys were as alike as two swallows' nests, it was largely craft tradition which made them so.

The distinction between the foremen who designed ships and the ordinary masters who helped them build was naturally carried over into the Arsenal, and the foremen of great reputation, not the Lords and Commissioners, were responsible for the most important tendency towards standardization. It was more usual in the fifteenth century than in the sixteenth for galleys built under contract to be made according to the design of the contracting master. At the later date one or two designs, usually that of Francesco Bressan, provided specifications according to which almost all the light galleys were built. But it is noteworthy that the plan approved in 1569 for organizing all this building under fourteen construction chiefs stipulated that these foremen should all be masters who had made galleys of their own design.

[73] Arsenale, busta 5, chaps. 67, 68, 81, 87, of the first series.
[74] Ibid., busta 133, f. 49.
[75] Ibid., busta 12, f. 48.

It was when the ship carpenters and caulkers had come to total a thousand workers who could not be discharged save for the gravest offenses, and whose daily pay could not be cut except in clear cases of desertion of their duties, that special disciplinary officials, paymasters and gang bosses, were employed to keep them at work. The foremen shipwrights were somewhat longer left to their own devices as experts, but in the middle of the sixteenth century there appeared a tendency to regiment them also. The activity of the Arsenal at that time attained so large a scale that it gave rise to purely directive and administrative offices whose holders developed more of the point of view of a factory management than did the nobles who composed the governing board. After the war of 1570-1573 and the plague of 1575-1577 had sharply reduced the number of masters, and so the problems of management, the offices which had been created for administration, direction, and discipline were retained. So, at the very end of the century, two members of this directive or administrative class, Baldessera Drachio Quintio, a naval man, and Bartolomeo Taduri, a bookkeeper, addressed memorandums to the governing nobility which expressed the ideas of efficiency which might be expected of factory managers in capitalistic industry.

Baldessera Drachio had been an " admiral " on the galley fleets, and his manner of writing suggests that he aspired to a similar position, the nearest approach to managing director, in the Arsenal. He drew up a plan which began with proposals for conserving the raw material and ended with a plea that one capable superintendent be given full powers to reform the Arsenal. He proposed to increase the efficiency in cutting wood and to have it sorted at once according to the uses for which it was fit. Expense in transport could be saved by noting Dalmatian oak available but leaving it where it was until it was needed to repair galleys on that coast. Eight guardians should be appointed over a special part of the Arsenal in which the sawed wood was to be stacked in orderly fashion among the completed galleys.

Drachio disapproved of giving masters a chance to try making galleys of their own design. It resulted in wasteful building and imperfect galleys. All galleys should be built according to the one design selected by the Foreman. Drachio, himself, suggested in another memorandum an ideal design.[76]

He proposed to divide all the master ship carpenters, aside from the mast-makers, into four groups: sixty masters would build new light galleys under the direction of five construction chiefs or gang bosses; another sixty would be under a foreman of the great galleys; an indeterminate number would work under five other bosses repairing galleys returned from voyage; masters over sixty would be deputed to make benches, foot-braces, and the like. The masters would be continually employed in one particular type of work so that they might become expert in that part of the craft, for example, in great galleys or in light galleys. Those working on new galleys would not be allowed to leave to take service at sea. The work of each of these four departments would be done in a separate part of the Arsenal which would make it possible to keep count of the men, time, and money spent on each galley.[77]

Bartolomeo Taduri, chief accountant of the Arsenal, elaborated part of this scheme of organization with a more precise and exacting spirit and with more complete disregard of traditional craft distinctions. In a memorandum presented to the College in 1594 he suggested that the masters be spurred to work by an appeal to the spirit of emulation or competition found in every man. Six masters were to be chosen as construction chiefs. Each was to choose thirty carpenters with their apprentices, six caulkers " da figgier," four sawyers, and six stevedores. Another boss with twenty stevedores was to supply them with necessary materials. Each of the construction chiefs was to be required to finish two light galleys every six months. Then the galleys were to be examined by

---

[76] The *Visione di Drachio* in Arsenale, busta 1.
[77] The *Ricordi intorno la casa dell' Arsenale, ibid.*, busta 533.

the Admiral and Foremen, and the chief-builders praised would receive a ten ducat bonus, those whose galleys were found faulty would be reduced to mere masters. He proposed that the construction chiefs should choose their workers like team captains, first one boss picking a carpenter, then the next taking his first choice, and so on till their gangs were complete. All the masters so chosen would receive an extra day's pay every week for the six months.[78]

Taduri had many other ideas for improving the work in the Arsenal. He thought the masters should be required to stay in the factory at noon, as they often did in winter, and be given only one hour for dinner instead of two. They would lose less time going and coming and putting away and taking out their tools. He asserted that the state would be benefited by employing fewer old and able masters and more of the " journeymen " and young masters, because the older masters received more pay and they hated to take orders from other masters. The young were more amenable. He proposed an elaborate scheme for ranking the masters and advancing them from one rank to another only as vacancies occurred. Taduri figured the exact cost of his scheme for " regulated masters ".[79]

But the treatment of the masters was not a problem to be viewed only through the eyes of an accountant. Giovanni di Priuli, the former Secretary of the Marine who reported to the Signoria on the condition of the Arsenal in 1591, lamented the decline of the *arsenalotti* from the high level attained before the War of Cyprus. Too many had been killed, too few apprentices were taken, and almost all were too poorly paid. The shipwrights were not a quarter of the number that they had been. Only six or eight were expert in the mast-makers' craft, two or three—and those old men—really capable workers on the great galleys. The masters were not of the old-time quality but a sorry lot of rascals. Yet at the outset of his

---

[78] Arsenale, busta 533, " scrittura " of 1594.

[79] *Ibid.*, busta 533, " scritture " of 1593 and 1594. The regulated masters would be 160 *fante*, 160 *garzoni*, 60 *maistri* (*gioveni*), 60 *maistri ordenarii*, 60 *maistri privilegiati*, 6 *capi d'opera ordenarii*, 2 *capi d'opera priviligiati*.

report Priuli called them the " the soul of the Arsenal ", comparing the relation of the masters and the buildings to that of the spirit and the body.[80] And the *arsenalotti* were more than mere manual laborers, they were the palace guard on state occasions and the reserve from which were recruited petty officers for the war fleet. Such a corps of employees might be roused by patriotism to great activity during a crisis when they were preparing a fleet with which many of them expected to sail, or might soldier on the job unmercifully in quiet times. In either case they were maintained as an indispensible part of the naval strength of the state.

[80] Secreta, Relazioni Collegio, busta 57.

CHAPTER XII

THE TIMBER SUPPLIES

Sea power has received so many panegyrics by historians from Thucydides to Admiral Mahan that it has occasionally appeared a disembodied force. Their masterful expositions of the varied ways in which sea power may be used so captivate the imagination as to obscure the consideration that the ships on which the command of the sea depended were themselves products of the land. Like any maritime power Venice was dependent upon access to the terrestrial products from which the ships were made.[1] The prosperity of the private shipyards of the city waned as the timber supplies available for their use diminished. Only the efficient exploitation of the natural resources of the mainland possessions acquired in those Italian wars for which the policy of the Republic has been so frequently criticized enabled the Venetian Arsenal to supply the war fleets which did battle with the Infidel. As the Turkish danger grew, larger fleets had to be kept at sea, more reserve galleys prepared, more timbers piled in readiness; and thus the shock of Christian and Turkish galleys in the waters of the Ionian Sea was echoed by the axes of the woodsmen in the mountains of Friuli and Cadore.[2]

The Venetian ships were built of oak, larch, and fir. The regions around Venice produced varieties of all these trees esteemed excellent for ship timbers.[3] Oak was the most used. Almost all the hull was built of it: curved oak logs for the ribs and for the stem and sternposts; straight oak beams for

---

[1] Cf. Robert G. Albion, *Forests and Sea Power, The Timber Problem of the Royal Navy, 1652-1862* (Cambridge, 1926).

[2] The discussion of the Venetian supply of naval stores is here limited to timber. On hemp see Lane, " The Rope Factory and Hemp Trade ". Pitch was not a serious problem judging by a statement in 1546 that it cost less than formerly. Senato Mar, files, Dec. 28, 1546. On the domestic supply of metals see R. Cessi and A. Alberti, *La politica mineraria della Repubblica Veneta* (Rome, Ministero dell'Economia Nazionale, 1927).

[3] John Fincham, *Outlines of Shipbuilding* (London, 1852), pt. III, pp. 15-27; John Evelyn, *Sylvia; A Discourse on Forest Trees* (York, 1776), pp. 93, 297.

the keel, ceiling, top clamps, and deck beams; and long thick oak boards for the outside planking. For the inside clamps and some of the interior bracing and tying timbers, long larch beams were used. For internal planking, cabins, and superstructures either larch or fir was satisfactory. The greatest importance of fir trees, however, was their value as masts and spars. Elm was desired for capstans and mastheads, and walnut for rudders. But fir, larch, and oak were the essentials: fir for masts, spars, and planking; larch for long strong beams for the interior; and oak for most of the frame and planking.[4]

The fir and larch came from the Rhaetian and Carnic Alps. Examples are not lacking of the cutting of masts for Venetian ships in the Apennines, as in Modena, but the main supply came from the Alpine ranges to the north. By the early thirteenth century the Venetians had tapped the supplies of Cadore and the upper Adige.[5] In the late sixteenth century they were still depending mainly upon that same region. Although there was some concern over a possible scarcity of the long larch beams, in the main the supply of both larch and fir was not only adequate for the needs of Venice but furnished an excess for export. Venice had been a center for the export of wood since the tenth century. The profitable business done in supplying this commodity to the Mohammedans had been the subject of many papal prohibitions during the crusading

[4] Senato Mar, reg. 21, ff. 20, 32; reg. 23, ff. 38, 172; reg. 33, f. 36; reg. 34, f. 100; reg. 37, f. 125. The following list of lumber needed for a great galley is given in the *Fabrica di galere*. A list in Arsenale, busta 1, names more timbers of the same kinds of woods. Cf. Jal, *Arch.*, II, mem. 5.
Oak wood: 380 curved pieces for the ribs, stem, and sternpost—logs 8½-10 feet long and 4-5 feet in circumference. (Venetian feet.)
  150 straight timbers for keel, ceiling, topclamp, deck beams, etc.—logs 24-29 ft. long, 4 ft. circumference.
  280 planks for outside planking—¼ ft. thick (?) sawed from logs 24 feet long, 4-5 ft. circumference.
Larch wood: 35 beams for gangway (*corsia*), outrigger-frame, and inside clamps— logs 40 ft. long, foot and palm in circumference.
Larch or fir wood: 18 beams for deck timbers.
Fir wood: 50 shorter pieces for deck fixings.
  300 planks for interior and deck.
[5] Schaube, pp. 693, 710; *I capitolari,* vol. II, pt. I, pp. 3-7, the " Capitulare seccatorum " of 1262 mentions larch and fir from the Val Sugana and Bassano.

period.[6] In the fourteenth century the elder Marino Sanuto advised the Pope that at Venice one could find the best larch and fir in the world.[7] Two centuries later larch beams and planks were still coming from the Trentino by the way of the Adige to be exported beyond Venice. At the same time the Venetian Arsenal shipped to Corfu and Crete the larch and fir needed there either for building fortresses or for outfitting ships. During the war with the Ottomans in 1570 the communes of Cadore offered the state—beside their lives—six hundred forty-foot larch logs cut from the woods of the communes and transported to the Arsenal at Venice at their expense. Even if the number of large fir trees in the Venetian domain suitable for masts might give the Arsenal some concern for its war-time supply, an adequate number were normally available in the adjacent Hapsburg territories.[8]

The sources of oak timbers were more varied and yet more quickly depleted. The earliest supply may well have come from the forests which once surrounded Mestre and extended along the edge of the lagoons.[9] Further inland both the Po Valley and the plains between the Eastern Alps and the head of the Adriatic had in ancient times been thickly studded with oak groves.[10] Their extent had been reduced as the land became more thickly settled. In the fifteenth century the Venetian shipyards were largely supplied by logs which came down the rivers from the oak forests in the Trevisana and Friuli. Istria, across the Gulf of Venice, was also an important source of supply especially for the curved logs of which great numbers were needed to construct the ribs of the galleys. But at the end of the fifteenth century the supplies available in these regions were diminishing in an alarming fashion.

---

[6] Schaube, *loc. cit.*

[7] *Op. cit.*, lib. II, pt. IV, cap. XIII.

[8] *Bilanci generali,* vol. I, tomo I, pp. 196-7; Senato Mar, reg. 29, f. 41; Arsenale, busta 11, f. 80.

[9] Adolfo di Berenger, *Saggio storico della legislazione veneta forestale dal secoli vii al xix* (Venice, 1862), p. 25; Christoforo Tentori, *Della legislazione veneziana sulla preservazione della laguna dissertazione storico-filosofico-critica* (Venice, 1792), pp. 20-34.

[10] *The Histories of Polybius* (tr. by E. S. Shuckburgh, London, 1889), I, 112.

Among the first signs of this progressive deforestation was the movement of the barge-building industry inward from Venice. This was well under way by the second quarter of the fifteenth century. At about the same time the devastation of those woods which were near the rivers led to an increase in the extent to which logs were sawed and shaped at the place of cutting. Laws for the protection of the city craftsmen which had forbidden such working up of the logs in the woods were relaxed in view of the high cost of transporting the unworked logs since they now had to be carried so far overland.[11] The importance of the transport problem was emphasized in the report of Marco Corner who was sent through the Trevisana and Friuli in 1441 with a general commission to better the supply both of firewood and construction timbers. He reported finding large forests containing many good trees for ship timbers and considered the immediate difficulty, especially the scarcity of firewood, to be due to the innavigability of many of the streams and canals leading into the woods.[12] The high cost of fuel, at the time the chief concern, was not, however, purely a question of transport, but was also the result of the reduction of former woodlands to cultivation or pasture.[13] The general deforestation was recognized as a danger to the lagoons since it increased the amount of silt brought down by the rivers. To prevent this filling up of the lagoons, the Council of Ten ordered the replanting of all cut-over woods at the edges of streams or salt water.[14]

A definite policy designed specifically to conserve and increase the oak groves was first formulated between 1470 and 1492.[15] This policy concerned the woods of the Signoria, of

---

[11] Senato Misti, reg. 54, f. 5; reg. 59, ff. 19, 153.

[12] Bibl. Naz., Venice, MSS. Ital., cl. IV, cod. 590.

[13] Senato Terra, reg. 1, f. 83; Berenger, pp. 12-16.

[14] Arsenale, busta 8, ff. 9-10.

[15] Arsenale, busta 6, ff. 16-30; Senato Terra, reg. 8, f. 39; reg. 10, ff. 115, 137, 172. Apparently unexecuted orders for a cadaster of the state forests had been issued in 1461. It was desired as a means of preventing the alienation of these woods which were felt to be all the more important since private woods were being continually cut down and reduced to cultivation " a gran danno dei legnami de lavoro e da fuoco ". Senato Terra, reg. 4, f. 177.

the subject communes, and of private persons. The principle at first proposed was that no oak should be cut anywhere without license from the Arsenal. This implied the important step, at least in theory, of recognizing that these forests were not to be treated as mere means of raising revenue but as public resources to be conserved, and that their management should be taken out of the hands of the fiscal officials of the local governments and assigned to the naval administration. But for a time this transfer remained largely a matter of theory. The inhabitants of the mainland protested against the necessity of applying to the Arsenal whenever an oak log was needed, and consequently the Senate permitted officials resident in the subject cities to grant licenses to cut the oaks needed for mills, houses, bridges, etc., a ruinous exception to the authority of the Arsenal which retained control only over cuttings made professedly for ship timbers. And for the enforcement of even this authority the Arsenal possessed no adequate corps of inspectors or guardians in the woods.

In other respects the program was much more advanced than the provisions for its execution. A census of all the oaks was to be taken village by village. All the communes east of the Mincio were to devote one-tenth of their common lands to oak and to dig a ditch around this oak grove to protect the seedlings from live stock. Special sowings were to be made near the lagoons. Whenever cuttings were made a record thereof was to be kept and a proper number of seedlings left. But the enforcement of all these regulations depended upon the Podestas and Rectors or their subordinates in the villages. To be sure, the appointment of two inspectors was authorized, one for the Trevisana and one for Friuli. But they were not even expected to cover their territory more than once a year. On their yearly visits they were to oversee thinning, planting, and enclosing the woods. In view of the large territory they had to cover it is plain they were likely to act as foresters rather than guardians.

These good resolutions utterly failed of immediate effect in conserving or replenishing the timber supply, and lamentation over the destruction of the oak woods continued during the sixteenth century. In its conservation policy the state came in conflict with two other interested groups, the villagers near the forests and the private shipbuilders or timber merchants. The conflict with the local users appears at first glance a conflict between efficiency and waste. One can easily sympathize with the indignation in the breasts of Lords of the Arsenal at the thought that noble oaks, which they considered sacred to the sea, should be consumed by charcoal burners and barrel-makers. But the villagers were accustomed to consider the woods their own. Moreover, oaks which once fell under the eyes of the officials of the Arsenal became a burden to all the neighborhood. They could not be removed at the first profit-able occasion but must await special license. If the trees were desired by the Arsenal for its own use, then indeed they be-came a curse. When the Arsenal cut lumber, the villagers were obliged to undertake the labor of transport to the nearest waterway, giving their own unpaid labor with that of their wagons and their animals. Land once devoted to oaks was obliged to remain so, continually unprofitable and periodically oppressive to the peasantry. Small wonder that as the Arsenal grew more eager to secure and preserve oak groves the vil-lagers grew more anxious to destroy them![16]

But the agents of the Arsenal were not the only envoys coming to the forests from the timber-hungry sea. Lumber merchants and merchant shipbuilders came also, not to con-serve but to consume. Since they paid for the services of the peasants they were much more welcome to the neighborhood. Many of these lumber dealers must have been men of guile and influence. Even after 1520, when the Arsenal had finally been given the sole right to grant licenses to cut oak for any purpose, even after the Council of Ten had taken all oak woods under its special protection, the destruction went on in defiance or evasion of the laws, and the offenders possessed

[16] Berenger, pp. 19, 30-31, 80-81; A. S. V., Arsenale, busta 6, ff. 72-74; busta 10, ff. 37, 53-54; Senato Mar, reg. 10, f. 78; Secreta, Relazioni Collegio, busta 58, *Relazione di Alvise Bembo* (1588).

such influence that even if condemned they often secured the remission of the penalties imposed upon them.[17]

Nevertheless the conservation of forests under the direction of the Arsenal slowly achieved a definite though limited effectiveness. The first complete cadaster of the oaks was compiled in 1568 and thereafter until 1660 the periodic surveys showed a constant increase.[18] But the Arsenal was naturally mainly concerned with its own supply. While private builders might depend on timbers from foreign lands the Arsenal could not rely upon any region not under Venetian dominion lest in time of war when the wood was most needed their supply be cut off. Nor could a shortage be met as the need arose. When ships were demanded the Lords of the Arsenal had to look for trees that had been saplings at the time of their grandfathers.

Accordingly, the forest administration developed by the Arsenal concerned itself less with general development of oak groves in such fashion as might ultimately prove beneficial to private shipbuilding than with reserving certain woods and trees for its own use. This was done by the banning of the desired woods—a solemn ceremony of proclamation in the name of the Doge with the sounding of trumpets on three successive holidays. The limits of the reserved woods were then fixed and marked by a ditch which in some cases was more than a boundary line for it was designed to keep out cattle and unlicensed wagoneers. Individual trees could be placed under the ban beyond the jurisdiction of the local authorities by marking them with the seal of the Arsenal—one seal for those reserved for shipbuilding, two seals for those forbidden to private builders and destined exclusively for the Arsenal. Banned woods might be extensive forest areas, small wood lots, or isolated trees. Periodically one of the Lords of the Arsenal was sent around to ban new woods and inspect the old. The first cadaster, that of 1568, was made during such a

[17] Berenger, pp. 18 ff., Senato Mar, reg. 19, f. 120; Arsenale, busta 8, ff. 73-75; busta 9, ff. 10, 93; busta 10, f. 38; busta 11, ff. 14, 28; busta 135, ff. 135-136.
[18] Berenger, pp. 26, 36-38, 124-126.

tour by Nicolò Surian aided by a secretary and page, six ship carpenters, and several laborers. Such a comprehensive survey was essential both to make the trips of inspection effective in detecting the cutting of forbidden trees and to permit an estimate of the adequacy of both the immediate and future supply. In view of the urgent need of conserving future supplies, in the sixteenth century even the Lords of the Arsenal were forbidden to cut any trees in the main forest reserves without specific license from the Council of Ten for the number of trees required. Thus, on the eve of the War of Cyprus, the Arsenal, to insure its supply of raw materials, had added to its many other activities the management of its own forests through its own agents subject to the supreme authority of the Council of Ten.[19]

The most important of these forests was at first that of Montona in the interior of Istria across the head of the Adriatic from Venice.[20] In this province forests had long been public domain. The Venetians had inherited the imperial forestal rights and used them to reserve the woods for the use of the Arsenal. The Val di Montona furnished curved oak logs for the galley frames, elm for capstans and mastheads, and ash for spear-shafts. During the first decades of the sixteenth century the woodcutters from the Arsenal found adequate supplies in this forest while reporting none were available elsewhere. But here too the enemies of the forest were at work. The local official responsible failed to prevent illegal cutting and pasturage. After 1557 a ship carpenter from the Arsenal was chosen " captain " of the forest to live there and devote all his time to riding about keeping out marauders. But the task was too much for either the honesty or energy of one man, and in 1565 he was given nine guardians to help and check him. For the harvesting of the timber crop the forest had been divided into eighteen parts to be cut over in succession. Of the nine guardians each was assigned two of these divisions and

---

[19] Berenger, *loc. cit.*, and pp. 41-42; Arsenale, busta 7, f. 45.
[20] Berenger, pp. 75-77, says it covered 1738 *ettare;* Sanuto, *Diarii,* XXIV, 652— under date 1517—says it was 18 to 20 miles (Venetian) long.

every two months they were moved to other parts. Besides the timber thieves and live stock, other enemies of the forest were the milldams built along the streams within the woods. They caused the death of many trees by impeding the drainage of the valleys. The Arsenal also had to watch against the danger that the state officials who were sent out to Istria to clear out worthless trees for firewood accidently or purposely cut some of their sacred ship timbers. To prevent it they sent one of their ship carpenters to oversee each cutting. Amidst the record of all these difficulties, however, can be seen the growth of an enlightened conception of forest management, a realization that a forest should not be exploited like a mine but that timber was a crop to be cultivated under a definite plan.[21]

North and west from Istria, in Friuli, there were a great number of banned woods in the valley of the Livenza between the foothills of the Alps and the Sea, from Conegliano and Sacile to Caorle and Portogruaro. It was in this region that small oak groves and isolated trees banned by the Arsenal were most numerous. Here the much desired curved timbers were prepared artificially by envoys of the Arsenal who bent and fastened young trees so that they would grow to the desired shape.[22]

In the Trevisana there were also many scattered groves, but one forest overshadowed all others in importance, that of Montello, the isolated group of foothills northwest of Treviso. Legally it had been reserved for the Arsenal since 1471, but practically it was not efficiently patrolled until much later. The difficulties were much the same as those encountered at Montona but more pronounced, for the earlier policy had left the administration of these woods to the

[21] Bernardo Benussi, *Istria nei suoi millenii di storia* (Trieste, 1924), pp. 273, 365; Berenger, *loc. cit.*, and pp. 26-29; Senato Mar, reg. 32, f. 119; reg. 36, ff. 140-145; reg. 37, f. 157; Arsenale, busta 9, ff. 46, 81-82, 87-88; busta 10, ff. 29, 43; busta 11, ff. 13, 23, 38, 42. Sanuto, *Diarii,* V, 174, suggests the cutting for firewood occurred every ten years.

[22] Arsenale, busta 6, ff. 72-74; busta 8, f. 39; busta 136, ff. 47-48; Secreta, Relazioni Collegio, busta 58, *relazioni* of 1528 and 1586.

communes of the neighborhood which accordingly became accustomed to using them for their own needs. But after 1527 the guardianship was taken from the communes and given to a "capitano di Montello" selected, after 1527, from among the ship carpenters of Venice. The limits of the forest were marked by ditches, or hedges, or stone pillars four feet high. Merely entering the woods with cutting instruments was made punishable by fine and severe whipping. A monastery which distributed alms was located within the woods. Five hundred people came in ostensibly to get alms but really—so said an inspecting Lord of the Arsenal—to collect bundles of wood. He made the monks go outside the confines to give alms. All charcoal furnaces were destroyed for five miles around. In time, Montello became the most famous of the oak reserves of the Arsenal, sown and harvested according to a systematic plan.[23]

In 1538 another oak reserve was acquired at Asolo about fifteen miles northwest of Montello. Theoretically it amounted to one hundred thousand trees. The initiative towards its creation came from the inhabitants of the Podesterate who agreed to grow that amount of wood perpetually for the use of the Arsenal in return for freedom in disposing of the rest of their trees. The conservation policy requiring that certain lands remain forever oak groves had been the occasion for such vexatious extortion by the officials that the owners of the woods sought to rid themselves of the restrictions. The offer was accepted, and in return for guarding the one hundred thousand trees the landowners of the district were given freedom to cut and sell all their other oaks at their pleasure. But first a Lord of the Arsenal was sent to oversee the usual details of the establishment of such a preserve—marking confines, ditching, thinning, trimming, and sealing particular trees. Thereafter the guardianship was left to the local officials subject to occasional visits from

[23] Berenger, pp. 41-2, 66; Evelyn, *Sylvia,* p. 597; Sanuto, *Diarii,* III, 1098; Arsenale, busta 1, unnumbered papers; busta 6, ff. 4, 6, 32, 72-73; busta 8, f. 56; busta 9, ff. 29, 45, 76, 79; busta 10, f. 48.

the captain of Montello and triennial inspections by a Lord of the Arsenal.[24]

Near Padua there was but one important oak forest, that of Carpeneda. The inspecting Lord of the Arsenal reported in 1588 that that had suffered but little damage, while, on the contrary, in the private woods of the district all the oaks were being cut and seedlings killed because of the fear of the owners that their possession of oak trees would be made a burden to them. Every one cut in the private woods on the assumption that if he had the consent of the owner he had also the license from the Arsenal. The inspector recommended that the state purchase what remained, thus confessing the complete bankruptcy of the earlier policy of compelling the conservation of all woods, public and private.[25] The only efficiently protected woods were those treated as state property and watched over by the forest administration of the Arsenal.

Once the Arsenal was launched on the policy of taking into its own hands the management of the forests whence it drew its timbers, it extended its activity beyond oak woods to include those of beech, fir, and larch. Beech came to be regarded as essential for oars, and since two hundred oars hardly sufficed for one voyage, large beech forests were almost as necessary to the Arsenal as oak woods.[26] In the fiftenth century the beams from which the oars were made had been bought already split at Segna, or Zengg, in Croatia, and brought to Venice in barges.[27] But in 1548 a supply of beech under Venetian control was secured when the Lords of the Arsenal and the Foreman of the Oarmakers reported to the Council of Ten that a wood called Alpago lying be-

[24] Berenger, p. 39; Arsenale, busta 8, ff. 74-5; busta 11, f. 37.

[25] Secreta, Relazioni Collegio, busta 58; Arsenale, busta 11, f. 16. Complaints of deforestation in 1502—Sanuto, *Diarii*, IV, 459.

[26] Report of 1581 and other papers in Arsenale, buste 1 and 2; Henri Louis Duhamel du Monceau, *Du transport, de la conservation, et de la force des bois,* . . . *faisant la conclusion du traité complet des bois et des forêts* (Paris, 1767), p. 369, gives the reason why beech was preferred.

[27] " Fabrica di galere ", f. 87, whether these " stelle " were beech is not stated. From Segna also came fir for lances.

tween Vittorio, Belluno, and Aviano would yield sufficient
ɔar wood if properly preserved. Following the precedent of
Montello the Council of Ten withdrew the forest from the
various officers who had had jurisdiction over it, and appointed a captain to protect it from the charcoal burners.
This forest was over eighty miles in circumference and its
chief enemy was the livestock pastured therein during the
summer months. Not until 1576 were sheep entirely excluded and the cattle limited to five hundred head. Despite
the dangers of excessive pasturage and heavy cuttings—from
ten to twenty thousand oars were cut at a time—Alpago was in
the seventeenth century considered one of the finest and best
governed woods in Italy yielding fir and larch as well as
beech.[28]

The fir masts and the long larch beams came mainly from
the mountain sides higher up the Alps. Much was bought
from the communes of Cadore at the head waters of the
Piave. A fifteenth century expert held that while larch might
be had from many places Ampezzo and Auronzo furnished
the best. The logs from Ampezzo were the finest, but those
from Auronzo were larger and easier to get out.[29] To secure
its supply of masts the Arsenal had banned a number of
small woods in this same general region, but as these were
inadequate to meet the need, a forest in Claut on the river
Cellina, a remote tributary of the Livenza was also banned.
This led to a conflict with private lumbermen the story of
which is highly illuminative of the opposition which was
being aroused by the forest policy of the Arsenal.

Active exploitation of the forest of Claut by the Arsenal
began in 1588 when the Foreman of the Mast-makers, Giovanni di Antonio Piccolo, was sent to cut masts and larch
wood. The main difficulty he encountered was in transporting the logs out from the forest. For that purpose a road had
to be built, and the villagers of Claut, they and their draft

---

[28] Arsenale, busta 2, misc. papers; busta 9, ff. 82-3; busta 10, f. 46; Berenger,
pp. 10, 69-120. In 1572, 1900 cattle and 11,000 sheep were pastured within the woods
in summer.

[29] *Fabrica di galere*, ff. 84-5.

animals, were called out to work on the road. Not unnaturally they felt oppressed by the unusual burden and petitioned for recompense, representing that such a very poor village of woodsmen in the remotest mountains of Friuli had already been ruined by the reservation of the woods and could not bear this additional burden. The Lords and Commissioners of the Arsenal hearkened to their plea and decided that some compensation be granted them. The masts and spars were successfully brought out. Indeed, according to the expense account of Giovanni di Antonio Piccolo, they came to the Arsenal cheaper than if they had been bought abroad.[30]

But these proceedings did not please certain lumber merchants, the Lazzari, who had previously rented the woods from the villagers. In the 'sixties and 'seventies they had cut many masts of which they had then, naturally enough, boasted the excellence. Some of these had been sold to the Arsenal and some brought to their lumberyard to sell to private shipowners. They, too, had devoted capital, seven hundred ducats according to their account, to the development of the forest. They had protested against the state taking it over and soon found a way which promised to place the woods again in their hands.

In 1591 Cristoforo Venier, one of the Lords of the Arsenal, was sent by the Senate to inspect the woods. He reported that there were very few good masts there, and that transport was so difficult that even these, when taken from the woods and brought to Venice, would cost more than buying masts abroad. Accordingly, the Lazzari sought the release of the woods from reservation basing their case on Venier's report and on that of a foreman mast-maker who said that the masts had not given good service. But the Lazzari had presumed overmuch on the shortness of official memory. It was recalled that they themselves had proclaimed the sufficiency of masts from these same woods sold by them to the Arsenal. Giovanni di Antonio Piccolo persisted in his report of the value of the forest. Investigation revealed the

[30] Arsenale, busta 1, *passim,* esp. the report of 1581; busta 10, f. 66.

fact that Venier did not himself go into the woods. Instead he had sent assistants, and had given them as guides two men of Claut who were much suspected both because the father of one of them was known to be hand in glove with the Lazzari, and because they were men of the village likely to be opposed to the interference of the Arsenal on account of the forced labor required of the peasants. In view of these evidences that fraud had been used, the Arsenal was able to keep the woods.[31]

The position of the lumber merchants and the villagers in this competition for masts is illustrative of the factors which brought the two parts of the oak conservation policy of the state into conflict. The general deforestation and shortage of oak timbers which became apparent in the later part of the fifteenth century prompted a policy which both commanded the growth of oak trees and reserved all those grown for shipbuilding, private or public. But the contemporary alarm for the future supplies of the Arsenal served to defeat the more general program of conservation. Earlier the Arsenal had, except for its reserve in Istria, secured its timber mainly by buying in the open market where it competed on an equal basis with private shipbuilders.[32] Now the Arsenal undertook to find and manage its own forests under the authority given it to ban desired woods. But once a forest or tree was banned for the Arsenal that forest or tree became a burden upon the community. Fear of this calamity was a positive incentive to further deforestation. The fear grew as the Arsenal showed more vigor in extending its reserves. These reserves were successfully established, but the program of general conservation in aid of private shipbuilding suffered. What the Arsenal failed to protect was dissipated; what the Arsenal did protect, at least the best of such trees, it desired for its own use. The builders of small craft might

---

[31] Arsenale, busta 1, *passim*.

[32] Examples of such contracts, on which the Arsenal must have been mainly dependent before it secured woods of its own, Arsenale, busta 133, ff. 6, 45. The Arsenal also bought from foreign powers when occasion offered. For example, in 1542 they sent a shipwright to Ferrara to negotiate with the duke for some oak. *Ibid.*, busta 9, f. 33.

still find the wood they needed at the traditional source of supply, but the builders of large merchantmen were driven to look beyond the Venetian dominion for most of their oak timbers.

There is positive evidence that they were doing so by the mid-sixteenth century. In 1546 a proposal to charge for licenses to cut oak was backed by the assertion that it would not greatly affect the builders of large ships for they did not cut on Venetian territory one-third of the oak logs they used. In 1559 the Lords of the Arsenal, in order to make easier the conservation of their own supply, arranged with private shipbuilders that the latter furnish themselves from foreign lands. The Senate provided that thereafter all those receiving state loans to build ships must not cut any oak within the Venetian dominions and in compensation for this new restriction raised the amount of the loans. Other evidences of the dependence on oak timbers brought from abroad may be found in the readiness of the Venetians to buy foreign ships if they could obtain for them Venetian registry, and in the examples of building or buying hulls of ships which were brought to Venice for completion and rigging. Of similar significance are the many instances in which Venetians built at Curzola in Dalmatia, but exported from Venice their fir and larch wood, iron, pitch, and cordage.[33]

Unable to rely upon their accustomed source of supply in the hinterland of Venice, the private shipbuilders could, in the sixteenth century, find no abundant supply elsewhere near at hand. In the second half of the fifteenth century the scarcity of oak timbers seems to have been peculiar to Venice. At least the Ragusans had a more plentiful supply and their competition was severely felt.[34] At the end of the sixteenth century there seems to have been a general shortage of oak throughout the Mediterranean countries. To be sure Monte San Angelo in northern Apulia was still famous as the source of the timbers used in the celebrated Ragusan

[33] Lane, " Venetian Shipping ", pp. 233-234.
[34] Senato Mar, reg. 12, f. 21.

ships,[35] and at a much later date oak logs were obtained from Emilia, Pesaro, and Ancona.[36] But in the fifteenth century there had been extensive deforestation on the Apennines of Emilia.[37]

The inadequacy of the supplies to be had on any of the nearby coasts is suggested by the distant origin of the ships bought by the Venetians after the ban against purchasing foreign ships had been removed late in the sixteenth century. Out of twenty-five such ships whose origin is definitely named between 1590 and 1616 eleven were from Holland, seven from Patmos, four from the Black Sea, and one each from Constantinople, the Basque country, and the Straits of Gibraltar.[38] It was in those years that Dutch ships, constructed of Baltic timbers, were capturing the carrying trade not only of both the Indies but even of the Mediterranean.

For reasons of topography, climate, and history the lumber resources of the Mediterranean region were more quickly exhausted than those of the Baltic. Particularly was this true of woods which might economically be exploited for ship timbers. The cost of hauling big logs overland for considerable distances was prohibitive before the days of the railroad. Exploitable forests had to be near waterways. In the north, heavy snowfalls made easy the sliding of logs into the rivers. A light snow meant high timber prices.[39] The Mediterranean was largely hemmed in by young mountains unpierced by navigable rivers while even the slopes of the Carpathians contributed to the timber resources of the Baltic. In contrast to the heavy precipitation of Northwest Europe, the rainfall of the typical Mediterranean climate was too slight to nourish tall oaks or firs except in elevations above two

[35] Crescentio, pp. 3-5; Pantera, p. 67.

[36] Weil, pp. 104-105; N. Battaglini, *Le costruzioni navali nell' estuario veneto* (Venice, 1870), pp. 18-20.

[37] Guiseppe Prato, " Il problema del combustibile nel periodo pre-rivoluzionario, come fattore della distribuzione topografica delle industrie", *Memorie delle R. Accademia delle Scienze di Torino*, ser. 2, vol. LXIII (1913), classe di scienze morali, stor., e fil., p. 3. Cf. on Friulian forests, *ibid.*, p. 15.

[38] Lane, " Venetian Shipping ", pp. 235-236.

[39] Albion, p. 145.

thousand feet. The Po Valley and the Venetian Plain were in these respects more likely ground for lumbering than most of the regions bordering the Mediterranean. Their climate was more moist and the mountain barrier further from the coast. When the forests of this region were no longer available the Venetian shipbuilders had to turn to areas whose natural resources were less, regions which had long been exploited and even in some measure deforested.[40] While their merchant marine was suffering from the consequent timber shortage, the shippers found their ports visited by cheap northern ships. The Dutch were building more efficiently and drawing their supplies from the plentiful Baltic forests. The Venetian merchant marine came increasingly to consist of foreign built ships, and the native shipwrights earned their livelihood in the Arsenal, the sole remaining support of the maritime reputation of the Republic.

[40] Ellen Churchill Semple, *The Geography of the Mediterranean Region; its Relation to Ancient History* (New York, 1931), chap. xi.

TABLES

TABLE A

PRIMARY PROPORTION OF SHIPS OF VENICE, ENGLAND, SPAIN, AND HOLLAND, AT VARIOUS DATES.

Maximum width of ship = 1.

Measures which are compared with the width	Proportions of Ships											
	Venetian					English		Spanish			Dutch	
	Cog, c. 1410	Merchantman, c. 1550	Galleon, c. 1550	Light galley, c. 1550	Great galley, c. 1550	Merchantman, 1582	Warship, 1633	Merchantman, 1587	West Indiaman, 1613	West Indiaman, 1679	East Indiaman, 1697	Warship, 1695
Length of keel.	2.5	2.2	2.7	..	4.9	2.3	2.9	2.1	2.7	2.9	..	..
Length on top (keel + rakes)	3.6	3.1	3.6	8.1	6.0	..	..	3.2	3.4	3.6	4.0	3.8
Depth (from maximum width)	.49	.5	.45	.34	.39	.5	.38	.65?	.5	.48	.43	.37

The Venetian cog of 1410 is the " nave quadra " or " coccha " in the *Fabrica di galere*, f. 37; the other Venetian ships are from the *Instructione*. The English ships are the " Ascension " (1582)—M. Oppenheim, " The Royal and Merchant Navy under Elizabeth," *The English Historical Review*, VI (1891), 492—and the " Leopard " (1633)—*Idem*, " The Royal Navy under Charles I," *E. H. R.*, IX (1894), 99. The Spanish ships are those given for the years mentioned by Gervasio de Artiñano y de Galdácano, *La arquitectura naval española* (*en madera*), *bosquejo de sus condiciones y rasgos de su evolución* (Madrid, 1920), pp. 128-9; 287-90, 307. The Dutch East Indiaman is the first of the three of which the measures are given by J. C. de Jonge, *Geschiedenis van het nederlandsche zeewesen* (3rd ed., Zwolle, 1869), III, 756. The Dutch warship is the " Admiral Generaal ". *Ibid.*, III, 730.

TABLE B

PROPORTIONS AND MEASURES OF VENETIAN LONG SHIPS.

Type and Date	Proportions: Beam = 1			Measures in Venetian feet				
				Width				
	Length on deck	Depth	Width tholepin to tholepin	Floor	Beam of hull	Tholepin to tholepin	Depth	Length on deck
Great Galleys:								
1. For the voyage of Cyprus, 1318..	7.6	.47		9	15⁵⁄₁₆		7²⁄₁₆	116¼
2. For the voyage of Flanders, 1320	7.2	.44		9½	16¹⁄₁₆		7²⁄₁₆	116
3. Described by Sanuto the Elder, c. 1324	7.5	.46		9½	15½		7³⁄₁₆	117
4. For the voyage to Romania, c. 1410	7.15	.44		9¹⁴⁄₁₆	16½		7⅓	118
5. For the voyage to Flanders, c. 1410	6.8	.45		10	17½		7¹⁴⁄₁₆	118½
6. Described by Timbotta, c. 1445..	8.2 ?	.47		10	17		8	139 ?
7. Standard just before 1520......								137½
8. Legal standard 1520-1549.......	5.9	.4			22½		9	132½
9. Legal standard by laws of 1549 and 1557..................	6.0	.39			23		9	137½
10. Described by Theodoro, c. 1550.	6.1	.39	1.3	11½	22¾	29	9	138
11. War *Galeazza* of seventeenth century....................	6.9		1.7		21	37		145
12. For voyage to Spalato, c. 1620...	5.4	.3			23		7	125
Light Galleys:								
13. Described by Sanudo the Elder..	8.1	.45		9½	14½		6½	116
14. "Galley of the guard," c. 1410.	8.9	.41		7	12½		5⅛	111½
15. Described by Timbotta, c. 1450..	8.4	.39		8	14		5½	117½
16. Considered standard, c. 1550....	8.1	.34			14¾		5	120
17. Described by Theodoro, c. 1550.	8.4	.34			14½		5	122
18. Described by Drachio, c. 1593...	8.3	.33	1.5	7½	15	22	5	125
Oared Galleons:								
19. Described by Theodoro, c. 1550 (a)	5.	.33			18		6	90
20. " " " " (b)	4.8	.31			21		6½	100
21. " " " " (c)	5.4	.33			27		9	145

Entries 1 and 2 are from Jal, *Arch. nav.*, I, 271; Marin, V, 211; Entries 3 and 13 from Sanuto the Elder; cap. xi, p. 65; Entries 4, 5, and 14 from the *Fabrica di galere,* ff. 73, 75, 77; Entries 6 and 15 from Anderson, "It. Nav. Arch.", pp. 143, 144; Entries 7, 8, 9, and 16 from Senato Mar, reg. 19, f. 126; reg. 30, f. 37; Arsenale, busta 1, busta 10, f. 46; Entries 10, 17, 19, 20, and 21 from the *Instructione*; Entry 11 from Coronelli, *Navi e Barche* (no date) section "Barche di Venezia"; Entry 12 from A. S. V., Cinque Savii, ser. i, busta 145, f. 64; Entry 18 from the *Visione*.

TABLE C

MEASURES OF VENETIAN ROUND SHIPS.

Measure of the Ships in Venetian feet. (Ven. foot = 1.1 Eng. feet.)

Designation of the Ships	Length: Keel	Length: 1st deck	Length: 2nd deck	Rake: Fore	Rake: Aft	Width: Floor	Width: 1st deck	Width: 2nd deck or max.	Width: Tolda	Depth amidships: 1st deck	Depth amidships: 2nd deck	Depth amidships: Tolda	Height at ends: Stem	Height at ends: Stern post	Capacity in botte
1. *Fabrica di galere*, 1420.															
Nave Quadra *f.* 37	65		95	**22⅔**	5	9¾		26½		7½	5½				
Nave Quadra *f.* 88	65		**95**	30½*	5½			27		8½ to 9					500
Nave Latina *f.* 33	60		80			9		24		9½					
2. Timbotta MS. a, 1450	85					11		**34**		12			45½	35	1000
Timbotta MS. b	72½					10		28		11			36	21	700
Timbotta MS. c	70					10		28					36	21	700
Timbotta MS. d	72½					9		25		11			34	25	500
Timbotta MS. e	63					10		25		10			35	19	
Timbotta MS. f	62½					7		22½		7½			25	15½	300
Timbotta MS. g	60					8½		20½		8½			27	19	250
Timbotta MS. h	60							**18½**					25	18½	200
3. State ship, 1422	92														1200 *or* more
4. "Nave" built for bounty, 1515	70							24		8	5¼				500
5. Theodoro's Nave, 1550	50			15	6½	7	20	23		6½	5	6	20	18	
Theodoro's Galleon, 1550	100			24½	11	11	33	37½	34½	11	6	7	3	30	
6. Burlioni's Nave, 1591	55			20	12	6	23	27		7	6½	5			832
7. Steffano's Nave, 1597	52						21	24½		6½	6	6			600
8. Casotti's Nave, 1599	52½						20	25		6	8	5½			700
9. Steffano's Nave, 1608		66	71				21	25		6	5¾				495

* It is given as the same as its length and as 6½ feet. But the length given is 6½ paces. 6½ ft. must be a mistake.

1. Bibl. Naz., Florence, Coll. Magliabecchiana, cl. XIX, cod. 7.
2. Anderson, "Ital. Nav. Arch.", p. 150.
3. A. S. V. Notatorio, reg. 7, f. 184.
4. Senato Mar, reg. 18, f. 71.
5. *Instructione.*
6. Senato Mar, files, July 13, 1591; capacities in botte: "soto prima coverta, 273; infra coverte, 324; soto la tolda, 236.
7. *Ibid.*, Feb. 11, 1597.
8. Cinque Savii, third series, busta 97.
9. *Loc. cit.*; capacities given in botte: under first deck, 210; under second deck, 285.

TABLE D

NUMBER AND CAPACITY OF LARGE ROUND SHIPS ON LISTS DURING
DIFFERENT PERIODS, 1405–1465.

CLASSES	Dates	Number and Capacity				
		Number of ships	Capacity			
			D. W. Tons		Botte	
			Total	Average	Total	Average
All	1405–17	25	9,165	367	15,275	611
Classes	1425–33	32	13,377	418	22,295	697
	1449–50	21	10,153	484	16,922	806
	1456–65	24	12,957	540	21,596	900
1000 botte or over	1405–17	0	0	0	0	0
600 d. w. tons or over	1425–33	1	600	600	1,000	1,000
	1449–50	6	3,957	659	6,595	1,099
	1456–65	9	6,420	713	10,700	1,190
800–999 botte	1405–17	1	510	510	850	850
480–599 d. w. tons	1425–33	4	2,193	548	3,655	914
	1449–50	3	1,689	563	2,815	938
	1456–65	5	2,680	536	4,466	893
400–799 botte	1405–17	24	8,654	361	14,424	601
240–479 d. w. tons	1425–33	27	10,584	392	17,640	653
	1449–50	12	4,507	376	7,512	626
	1456–65	10	3,858	386	6,430	643

The table shows the appearance of the 1000 botte ship about 1430, and the increase in the number of ships of that size thereafter till 1465. The table is a tabulation of the ships mentioned in the Arch. di Stato, Venice, Notatorio di Collegio, numbers 5 through 10, new numbering. There are recorded the numbers and sizes of the ships applying to serve the state as war vessels, and of those applying to go on the Syrian voyage under state control. It is likely, therefore, that the largest cogs of Venice appear on these lists. The ships applying for the Syrian voyage are more frequently recorded in the first three decades of the century than in the later period, which explains why fewer of the middle sized cogs are recorded for the later dates. Ships from 400 to 799 botte predominated on the Syrian voyage. In 1456 and 1457 only two of the eight ships applying for that voyage were over 799 botte.

Only one rating is given for the ships listed 1405–1417 and for the reasons explained in Appendix 1, I have considered them fairly accurate, and have made no corrections.

Two or three different ratings are frequently given of the ships listed 1425–1433, but only in a few cases do the ratings of the same ship vary as much as ten per cent. In the cases where more than one rating is given for the same ship, a rough average between them has been used in compiling the table.

Ratings varying ten per cent. or less one from the other are given for 4 of the ships listed 1449-1450. Rough averages between the two ratings have been used.

During the period 1456-1465 widely differing ratings are sometimes recorded for the same ship. At that time the ships had been underestimated by the *Consoli dei Mercanti* so that the ratings claimed by the owners when the ship was to be rented by the Signoria were far higher than the official ratings. A ship rated as 900 botte, for example, was said to have carried 1200 botte. New official ratings were consequently ordered. In these cases, I have tried to strike a rough balance between the two extremes and used figures which allow for a very considerable underestimate by the *Consoli dei Mercanti,* but which also allow for some exaggeration by the owner when renting to the Signoria.

There is no such question of double rating for the largest ship mentioned on these lists. That ship is the " Christoforo Soligo " of 1440 botte mentioned in 1465.

TABLE E

NUMBER AND CAPACITY OF THE ROUND SHIPS OF DIFFERENT SIZES ON THE LISTS OF 1499.

(Not all Venetian built, some estimated, see appendix III.)

Classes	Number and Capacity of Ships			
	Number	Per cent. of total	Capacity d. w. tons	botte
All classes..........................	107	100	25,848	43,080
Over 1500 botte or 900 d. w. tons. All state built or owned..........	4	20 —	5,100	8,500
1000–1500 botte 600–900 d. w. tons................	2	6 —	1,500	2,500
800–999 botte 480–599 d. w. tons................	2	4 —	960	1,600
400–799 botte 240–479 d. w. tons................	26	33 —	8,520	14,200
120–399 botte 72–239 d. w. tons................	73	37 +	9,768	16,280

TABLE F

NUMBER AND CAPACITY OF LARGE ROUND SHIPS, 1558-1559.

CLASSES	Average				1558				1559			
	Number	Per cent. of total	d.w. tons	botte	Number	Per cent. of total	d.w. tons	botte	Number	Per cent. of total	d.w. tons	botte
All Classes..........	37	100	17,550	29,250	38	100	18,000	30,000	36	100	17,100	28,500
1000-1500 botte 600-900 d.w. tons......	11	38 —	6,600	11,000	11	37 —	6,600	11,000	11	39 —	6,600	11,000
800-999 botte 480-599 d.w. tons......	14.5	44 —	7,650	12,750	15	44	7,920	13,200	14	43 +	7,380	12,300
600-799 botte 360-479 d.w. tons......	1.5	3 +	600	1,000	2	4 +	780	1,300	1	2 +	420	700
400-599 botte 240-359 d.w. tons......	10	15 +	2,700	4,500	10	15	2,700	4,500	10	16 —	2,700	4,500

Museo Civico Correr, Venice, Arch. Donà della Rosa, busta 217, MS. entitled "Navi grosse de Venetia, loro viaggi e loro patroni". The first section records the voyages, and has been summarized in Lane, "Venetian Shipping", Table A. This table is based on the second section, an alphabetical list of the ships with their sizes given in round numbers. The MS. also contains a chronological list of the ships launched from December 8, 1557, to June 2, 1560, inclusive, and alphabetical lists of the *patroni* and *scrivani*.

In compiling this table I have omitted all ships wrecked or torn down during the given year, and all not launched till a later year. This method of analysis has had the consequence that the largest ship on the list, the "Morosini e Tiepolo" of 1500 botte is not recorded at all on the table for it was launched in 1558 and wrecked that same year on the voyage to the English Channel. Six ships of which the voyages are recorded are not included because, their size being a matter of guess work, to include them would prejudice the question of the number of ships in the different classes. Allowing for these corrections we reach the conclusion that the total size of the fleet of merchant ships of 400 botte—240 tons—or more was about 30,000 botte—18,000 tons—in some 40 ships.

TABLE G

GREAT GALLEYS MADE IN THE ARSENAL BY DIFFERENT MASTERS.
1496–1505.

	NUMBER BUILT BY DIFFERENT MASTERS		
Date when first sent to sea.	Leonardo Bressan	Marco Francesco Rosso	Builder not named
1496	1	1	0
1497	1	0	0
1498	4	1	1
1499	0	0	0
1500	5	1	0
1501	0	0	0
1502	1	0	0
1503	0	0	0
1504	1	2	0
1505	2	1	0

This table is based on a list in the *Diarii* of Sanuto, X, 891-895. It is without a title and is dated August 1, 1510. Each of the great galleys is listed under a date. Then there is recorded its voyage and the name of the " Captain." Comparison of these names with the lists of the " Captains " of the Flemish galleys given by Rawdon Brown, *Calender of State Papers, Venetian,* vol. I, p. cxxxiv, shows that they are the names of the " Captains " in charge of the first voyage of the galleys, and that the date under which the galleys are listed are the dates of the first voyages. Similarly recorded are the dates and " Captains " of the last voyages made by the galleys. These names and dates may be checked by looking up the names of the " Captains " in the index to the *Diarii* of Sanuto.

That this list is not a list of the galleys in the Arsenal in 1510 is shown by the mention of a galley lost at sea. It must be taken to be a list of the new galleys delivered by the Arsenal to commanders from 1496 to 1510, the builders of the galleys, and their first and last voyages. Accordingly it implies that no new great galleys were sent out from the Arsenal between 1505 and 1510, but that is not unlikely in view of the interruption of many galley voyages at that time.

TABLE H

NUMBER OF GREAT AND LIGHT GALLEYS, BUILT AND BUILDING, IN THE ARSENAL, 1504–1602.

(Only the general trend is significant since, for a particular date, the totals and the number of galleys built may give a false impression because of the number at sea.)

Date	Totals			Built		Building			
							Light Galleys		
	Great Galleys	Light Galleys	Galee Bastarde or Bastardelle, etc.	Great Galleys	Light Galleys	Great Galleys	First stage see text Chap. VIII	Second stage see text Chap. VIII	Third stage ready to pitch and launch
1504	32	83	5	12	28	20	13	42	—
1518	9	56	21	0	—	9	—	—	—
1544	12	131	12	4	—	8	—	—	—
1559	6	120	10	3	27	3	3	60	30
1583	18	117	0	11	—	7	—	—	—
1590	18	118	0	11	—	7	—	—	—
1602	8	135	0	6	—	2	—	—	43

The figures are taken from the following sources:

1504, Sanuto, *Diarii*, V, 926.
1518, *Ibid.*, XXV, 538.
1544, A. S. V., Arsenale, busta 1.
1559, Museo Civico, Arch. Gradenigo, busta 193.
1583, Bibl. Naz. Marciana, MSS. It. cl. VII, cod. 1745.
1590, Museo Civico, Arch. Gradenigo, busta 170.
1602, *Relazione del Proveditore sopra le Cento Galee* (ed. Ettore Sorger, Venice, 1868), p. 14.

In the column *Galee Bastarde* are entered those called "da 4 remi" and, in 1544 and 1559, that "da 5 remi", the quinquereme of Fausto, as well as those called "bastarde" and "bastardelle." No galleys with these names appear on the lists of 1582, 1590, and 1602 because by that time galleys were rowed several men to an oar instead of several oars to a bench.

Dashes have been used in cases where the sources do not list the light galleys in such a manner as to permit tabulation of their condition.

TABLE I

NUMBER OF SHIP CRAFTSMEN EMPLOYED IN VENICE AND IN THE ARSENAL IN VARIOUS YEARS, 1503–1591.

	NUMBER OF CRAFTSMEN							
DATE	Ship carpenters				Caulkers		Oarmakers	
	On craft roll	Employed in Arsenal, private shipyards, and at sea.	On Arsenal Roll	Employed in Arsenal	On the Roll	Employed in Arsenal	On the Roll	Employed in Arsenal
1503	866[a]	613[a]		361[a]				
1531				221[b]				
1536			581[d]		415[c]		40[c]	
1538			693[d]		652[c]		36[c]	
1553				600[f]	556[g]	250[f]		60[f]
1554			1016[d]				146[d]	
1559			1024[d]	600[e]		300[e]	146[c]	60[c]
1560			1200[h]		1000[h]			
1591			431[k]	200[k]	786[k]	450[k]	161[k]	100[k]

(a) Sanuto, *Diarii*, V, 928-930.
(b) Senato Mar, reg. 22, f. 76. Number employed a particular week, and considered extra small.
(c) Museo Civico, Arch. Gradenigo, busta 193, booklet entitled " Arsenal."
(d) *Ibid.* These figures are the totals given at the bottoms of the columns summarized in Table J. A mistake in addition appears in 1554, but the total has been used as given, for it seems probable that the mistake comes from the omission from the itemized list of the numbers receiving 10 *s.*
(e) *Ibid.* These figures are general estimates, apparently the number of workers counted on by the Lords of the Arsenal in figuring expenses.
(f) Museo Civico, Arch. Morosini, busta 302. General estimates as described above.
(g) *Ibid,* f. 8. Figures given in detail as follows:
" Calafai da magio con fante......................... 245.
Calafai da magio senza fante......................... 146.
Calafai da fiza senza fante........................... 60.
Calafai da fiza con fante............................. 105."
(h) General statement in Senato Mar, reg. 35, f. 46-7.
(k) A. S. V., Secreta, Relazioni Collegio, busta 57, *Relazione di Giovanni Priuli.*

TABLE J

RATES OF WAGES OF SHIP CARPENTERS AT THE ARSENAL, 1536–1560, BOTH THOSE ON THE ROLL OF THE ARSENAL AND THOSE EMPLOYED THERE.

Rate of Wage	Ship carpenters on the roll of the Arsenal.											Ship carpenters employed in the Arsenal	
	1536		1538		1554		1559		1560				1553	
	No.	*Per cent. of total	No.	*Per cent. of total	No.	*Per cent. of total	No.	Per cent. of total	No.	Per cent. of total		No.	Per cent. of total
Totals	581	100	693	100	971	100	1024	100	1200	100		626	100
6s.–17s.	215	37 +	278	40 +	240	27 +	301	29 +	564	47		157	25 +
18s.–23s.	185	32 —	166	24 —	264	25 —	197	19 +				139	22 +
24s.	181	31 +	249	36 —	467	48 +	504	49 +	600	50		312	50 —
30s.–52s.			unknown				22	2 +	36	3		18	3 —

* Excluding those receiving 30s.–52s.

The figures for 1536, 1538, 1554, and 1559 are taken from the booklet entitled "Arsenal" in Museo Civico, Arch. Gradenigo, busta 193. It is clearly stated that the figures for 1559 include pulley-makers and mast-makers. Whether they are also included in the other three years is not clear, but the presumption is that they are.

The figures for 1560 are from the preamble to a law by the Senate for the purpose of reducing the numbers of the masters. Senato Mar. reg. 35, f. 46.

The figures for 1553 are from Museo Civico, Arch. Morosini, busta 302.

Except for 1560, the totals given have been obtained by addition. For 1536 and 1538 they are the same as those given in the MS., for 1554 the total in the MS. is 1016 as explained in note d to Table I, for 1559 no total is given, for 1553 the total in the MS. is 630. They have been grouped above to bring out clearly the effects of the policy of the College of the Arsenal.

In the MSS., for 1536, 1538, 1554, 1559, 1553, the number of masters is given separately for each rate,—6s., 7s., etc.

For some years the number of masters having apprentices is given, as follows:

Date	Number
1536	272
1538	307
1554	503

APPENDICES

APPENDIX I

WEIGHTS, MEASURES AND MONEYS.[1]

LENGTH.

Unit: 1 piede = .347735 meters = 1.1 English feet. (Martini).
1 deda = 1/16 piede
1 passo = 5 piedi

WEIGHT.

The Venetians used four different pounds for weighing, the heavy pound, the light pound, the pound for weighing gold, silver, and pearls, and the pound for weighing gold or silver thread. Only the heavy pound and the light pound need be explained here.

A list of goods weighed with the heavy pound and of goods weighed with the light pound is given by Paxi.

1 Lira or Libbra grossa = 476.99872 g. (Martini) = 1.05 Eng. lb.
= 1.06 Eng. lb. (Postlethwayt).
= 480 g. (Schaube)
= 1.04 English lb. (Brown) (Paxi)
= 1.05 English lb., value here used.
1 Lira or Libbra sottile = 301.230 g. (Martini) = .66 Eng. lb.
= .635 lira grossa (Paxi) = .66 Eng. lb.
= .657 Eng. lb. (Postlethwayt)
= 302.4 g. (Schaube)
= .66 Eng. lb., value used here.

CAPACITY, DRY.

1 Staio or Ster = 83.3172 liters (Martini) = 2.3 Imp. bushels.
82.75 liters (Schaube) = 2.3 Imp. bushels.
1 Moggio = 4 Staia or stara

CAPACITY, WET.

Unit: 1 Mastelli = 75.1170 l. (Martini)
1 Bigoncia = 2 Mastelli
1 Anfora = 8 Mastelli
1 Botta = 10 Mastelli
1 Burchio = 600 Mastelli
1 Secchie = 1/7 Mastelli
1 Barila = 6/7 Mastelli

[1] The chief authorities consulted on weights and measures were Bartholomeo de Paxi, *Tariffa de pexi e mesure* (Venice, 1503) no paging; Lewes Roberts, *The Merchants' Mappe of Commerce* (London, 1638); Malachy Postlethwayt, *The Universal Dictionary of Trade and Commerce; translated from the French of the celebrated M. Savary with large additions and improvements* (2nd. ed. London, 1757); Angelo Martini, *Manuale di Metrologia* (Turin, 1883); Rawdon Brown, ed., *Calender of State Papers and Manuscripts relating to English Affairs, Existing in the Archives and Collections of Venice and in other Libraries of Northern Italy* (London, 1864 ff.), vol. I, introduction; and Schaube's *Handelsgeschichte*.

245

WHEAT MEASURES CHECKED.

1 Staio or Ster $=$ 132 lire grosse [2] $=$ 138.6 Eng. lb.

$\qquad\qquad$ $=$ 2.3 Imp. bushels $=$ 144.9 Eng. lb. (English standard).

SHIP MEASURES.

Among the great variety of tons offered by modern usage, only two can profitably be employed in coverting the old Venetian measures into modern terms. First, there is the long ton of 2240 lb. The tonnage of a ship figured in tons of that measure indicate the amount of weight it is able to carry without overloading, i. e., the dead weight tonnage. Second, there is the freight ton usually equal to 40 cubic feet but varying according to the cargo. The tonnage of a ship figured in tons of that measure would indicate the cubic capacity. The ton now most used in giving the tonnage of ships, the net registered tonnage, is an artificial modern creation which allows for factors not involved in the days of the sailing ship such as space for engines and coal.

The ton of 2240 lb. and the ton of 40 cubic feet are approximations one of the other; 2240 lb. of water occupies 35.9 cubic feet, and 2240 lb. of wheat about 45 cubic feet.

The sizes of Venetian ships of the fifteenth and sixteenth centuries are most frequently estimated in terms of botte. The botta was a measure of capacity, a wine measure from Crete. Yet the value of the botta is also stated as equal a certain number of pounds. It is repeatedly equated with 10 stara,[3] while the staio in turn, though a measure of capacity, is frequently referred to as equal a certain number of pounds. Thus we start with the following results:

$$1 \text{ staio} = 2.3 \text{ Imp. bushels} = 2.9 \text{ cu. ft.} = .0725 \text{ freight tons.}$$
$$= 132 \text{ lire grosse} \quad = 138.6 \text{ lb. Eng.} = .061 \text{ long tons.}$$
$$1 \text{ botta} = 10 \text{ stara} = .725 \text{ freight tons.}$$
$$= .61 \text{ long tons.}$$

The size of a botta may also be computed from its approximate measures. The rule for measuring given below shows that it must have been $3\frac{1}{4}$ Ven. ft. long. In the *Fabrica di galere*, f. 37, we are told that since the height of the first deck is $7\frac{1}{2}$ Ven. ft., 3 botte may be put there one above the other; and that since the second deck is $5\frac{1}{2}$ feet above the first, 2 botte may be put there one above the other. It is to be presumed that the casks were piled after the manner shown in Albertis, p. 52, the upper ones being placed above the meeting point of those below. If "a" be taken to represent the radius of a botta, then in the first case

$$(7.5 - 2a)^2 = 16a^2 - 4a^2 \quad \text{and} \quad a = 1.37 \text{ Venetian feet,}$$

and in the second case

$$(5.5 - 2a)^2 = 4a^2 - a^2 \quad \text{and} \quad a = 1.47 \text{ Venetian feet.}$$

Assuming then for purposes of computation that the botta was a perfect cylinder, which of course it was not, then:

the cubic capacity of a botta $= 1.37^2 \times \pi \times 1.1^3 \times 3.25$

$\qquad\qquad\qquad\qquad = 25.51$ cu. ft. Eng. $= .63$ freight tons

or $\qquad\qquad$ 1 botta $= 1.47^2 \times \pi \times 1.1^3 \times 3.25$

$\qquad\qquad\qquad\qquad = 29.32$ cu. ft. Eng. $= .73$ freight tons.

---

[2] Paxi gives in lire grosse not only the equivalent of a ster or staro of wheat, but also that of a ster or staro of oats, ship biscuit, nuts, raisins, etc. Roberts, p. 72, R. Brown, I, cxli, and Sanuto, *Diarii* I, 886 give merely one ster as equal to 132 lire grosse.

[3] Senato Mar, reg. 18, f. 138; in the ship lists of 1499 in Sanuto, see Appendix III; and *Bilanci generali*, I., 1, 631. In all these cases where 1 botta is equated with 10 stara botte are being used as ship measures.

The use of the botta as a ship measure seems to have resulted from the importance of the Cretan wine trade, and the botta loaded in Crete were equal to 48 mastelli.[4] But I have been unable to find the equivalent of the Cretan mastelli. Martini gives the botta as a Venetian wine measure, although it is not mentioned by Paxi. If it be assumed that the botta given by Martini is the same as that used by the ships, the measure having perhaps finally become so familiar as to be used not only on ships but also on land as a regular Venetian measure, that gives the following:

1 botta = 751.170 liters = 26.55 cu. ft. Eng. = .66 freight tons.

An English statute of 1483 said butts of malmsey used to be seven score gallons or six score six gallons, but that rascally foreigners now had butts that held only five score eight gallons. Thereafter none were to be imported which contained less than 126 gallons.[5]

1 botta = 126 gallons = 20.2 cu. ft. = .505 freight tons.
= 140 gallons = 22.4 cu. ft. = .56 freight tons.

Professor Luzzato, on the basis of measures given by Mr. Anderson — above, Table C — figured that the botta would be .7 to .75 tonnelata, although that seemed surprisingly high to him.[6] Corazzini gives it as equal to 28 cubic feet, although what kind of feet is not stated.[7] Fulin quotes a text of 1519 which gives it as equal to one-half a tonelle of Portugal.[8] A sixteenth century French document gives it as 1500 lira,[9] presumably lira grossa, which would make it equal to .703 long tons.

Ancient ratings of ships were not minutely accurate. I have found two rules of Venetian origin for obtaining the capacity of the ship in botte, one very crude and not official, the other more sophisticated and, at least for a while, official. The former is in the *Fabrica di galere*.[10] The rule is to multiply the beam in feet by the depth in feet, multiply the result by the keel in paces, and divide by six, i. e. reducing all measures to feet. $\dfrac{K. \times B. \times D.}{30}$ = equals capacity in botte. The other rule is given in the Statutes of the *Consoli dei Mercanti*, copied from the book in which the estimates of ships were kept by that magistracy. It appears twice, the first time in Venetian,[11] the second in Latin.[12] The first entry would appear to date from the first part of the fourteenth century, and the second from the first part of the fifteenth.[13] Apparently two types of instruments were used in estimating a ship, one a measuring cord on which paces were marked off and which was used to take the length of the ship. But these were not ordinary Venetian paces. Instead a special pace of 3¼ Venetian feet was used for this particular purpose. The other instrument was simply the hoop of a barrel. With these hoops was determined the number of botte which

---

[4] Sanuto, *Diarii*, II, 479.

[5] *Statutes at Large from the First Year of King Richard III to the Thirty-first Year of King Henry VIII* (ed. Danby Pichering, Cambridge, 1763), IV, 19.

[6] " Costruzioni navali ", p. 390, note.

[7] *Vocabulario nautico italiano* (Turin, 1900-1907), I, 355.

[8] *Diarii e diaristi veneziani* (Venice, 1881), p. vii, note 2.

[9] Bibl. Nat., Paris, MSS, F. F. 5600, f. 120.

[10] The two texts of the rule are given by Albertis, p. 218.

[11] Chapter 164. At the top is written, " Ex libro estimationum Navium in fine ". There are two copies of the *Capitolare dei Consoli dei Mercanti*. That in the Arch. di Stato, Arch. dei Consoli dei Mercanti, busta 1, is apparently of the early 16th century, and that in the Museo Civico Correr, Rep. Commissioni, 331 of the late 16th.

[12] Chapter 328. At the top is written, " Ex libro ordinum officio consulatus ad cartam 192 ". The two rules describe exactly the same method.

[13] They are not dated but such is the inference from the dates of the chapters among which they are placed.

could be put under the decks one beside the other and one above the other. Such a calculation was made in three places, in the center, at an eighth of the way aft from the prow and at an eighth of the way forward from the stern. The number of hoops contained in the center was multiplied by half the length of the ship in paces; the number of hoops that could be placed at the stations at poop and prow were added together and multiplied by one quarter of the length. The results added together gave the size of the ship in botte and there was no need for the then difficult process of division. The Latin text:

" Modus extimandorum navigiorum talis est. Accipiatur primo trazola cuius primum caput trahatur a rumbo prove usque ad impostruam puppis et id quod ipsius trazola evolutam fuerit mensuretur cum passu buttarum, que mensura debet servare memorie. Et postea debet inveniri medietas ipsius navis perplicatam mensuram ditte trezolae et postea accipere circulos et videre quot circulos capiat ipsa medietas positos per latitudine ipsius navis, a corbis usque ad chopertam, et numerum ipsorum circulorum servare memorie et postea debet invenire octava pars longitudinis eiusdem navis perplicatam trazolam preditum a latere puppis et provae et facere in dictis locis idem quod factum extitit in medietate, et postea acciepiatur medietas dicta Jongitudinis et multiplicetur cum numero circulorum qui ceciderunt in medio dicte navis et quod ex ipsa multiplicatione exierit teneantur memorie. Et postea accipiatur quarta pars dicte longitudinis et multiplicetur cum numero circulorum quos cepit prova et puppis in octavis partibus ipsius longitudinis ipsius navis et id quod exient ex ipsa multiplicatione annotetur sub eo quod exivit ex prima multiplicatione et summentur insimul et id erit portata navis extimatae ut in exemplo infrascripto:

Longitudo 20. 10
In medio circuli............................ 17. 17
                 170
Ad puppin circuli.......................... 15. } 29
Ad prova circuli........................... 14. } 5
                 145
                 170

Et hec extimatio est ad buttas et integris...................... 315

Extimatio ad milliaria et in ruptis sequitur ad hoc signum et Capitulo. Passus quo mensurantur naves debent esse longitudinis pedum trium et unius quarti, ad mensuram pedum passus quo mensurantur tabule et alia ligna per carpeniarios."

As the close of the quoted passage shows, the ships were estimated not only in botte to determine their cubic capacity, but also in milliaria to find how much weight they could carry without sinking too low in the water.

1 milliarium = 1000 lire grosse (Martini) = 1050 lb. Eng. = .47 d. w. tons.

Ships were also estimated in other measures of capacity. A writer at the end of the sixteenth century said they should be officially estimated not only in the three measures already discussed but also in moggi of salt, miara of oil, carra of wood.[14] On one occasion I have found their size given in anfore. The anfora works out thus:

1 anfora = 600.936 liters (Martini) = 21.21 cu. ft. Eng. = .53 freight tons.

Although there was in the fifteenth century an official rule as to how ships were to be estimated, it does not appear that there was ever developed an official rating

---

[14] Treatise of Drachio on the Admiral, Bibl. Naz. Venice, Marciana, MSS. It. cl. IV, cod. 177.

different from the generally recognized capacity of the ship.[15] To be sure there was considerable fraud practiced and complained of by the state, but if the frauds were found out reestimation of the ships was ordered.[16] Also there were cases in which only the capacity under the first deck was counted. But all the sizes of ships in botte given in the text were, I believe, meant to represent somebody's best guess at what the ship could actually carry.

The figures for the first half of the fifteenth century taken from the "Notatorio di Collegio" are from an official source. The ships were to be hired by the state, or were to be sent on a merchant voyage in which a portion of the total freight collected by all the ships in the convoy would be distributed among them according to their size. Consequently when such voyages were common, it was not in the interest of the shipowner to have his ship rated too low, and there were others with an interest in not having it rated too high. Only about the middle of the century do the figures run into difficulties. Then since state regulated voyages were less common, many shipowners succeeded in having their ships registered at far below their true size, but when it was a question of sending them in convoy, they claimed the ships were larger than recorded and offered them only if they were reestimated. Then both sizes were given. On the lists on which the largest of the merchant ships of that time were mentioned there is given their official ratings and frequently the number of botte they had actually carried on their voyages from Crete to the English Channel.

Most of the figures for about 1500 and 1550, being in round numbers, are apparently the commonly known sizes of the ships. When a ship was of extraordinary size rumor was inclined to exaggerate, as may be judged by the different sizes given for the same ship in such cases, but there was no reason to do so when the ships were of ordinary size and the errors in judgment should balance each other. In Sanuto's diary the size and cargoes of ships casually mentioned are sometimes given and they agree.[17]

In general the only corrections which have been applied to figures of size have been to lower somewhat the wild rumors concerning the size of the largest ships, and raise a little the sizes recorded on the official records. Those corrections have been applied only when indicated. There is of course a margin of error in all the figures. There is not therefore any great value in averaging out to several places a factor for conversion from botte to tons. But it is pretty clear that 1 botta = *circa* .6 dead weight tons.

SPICE MEASURES.

Spices were measured by the light pound at Venice, their price usually given in centi or cargi.

> 1 centi = 100 lire sottile = 66 lb. Eng.
> 1 cargo or carica = 400 lire sottile (Schaube, Paxi) = 264 lb. Eng.

At Alexandria pepper, the king of spices, was quoted at so much per sporta.

---

[15] *Capitolare dei Consoli di Mercanti,* chapter 200 (1362), declared ships were being built so as to be estimated low by the method then used in estimating—presumably that which has been described, and which appears in an earlier chapter of the *Capitolare.* The *Consoli* were ordered not to be bound by convention but to compute all the capacity of the ship. The remarks of Drachio on the duties of the Admiral make it plain that he was not supposed to be bound by convention, but was to make his best guess.

[16] *Capitolare dei Consoli,* chapter 250, and ff. 117-118 of the copy in the Arch. di Stato; Senato Mar, reg. 20. f. 190.

[17] For example in the *Diarii,* XVII, 222, he mentions a nave of 400 botte carrying 4000 stara. See also *ibid.,* I, 373; XIX, 328.

1 sporta = 700 to 720 lire sottile (Paxi) = 462 to 475 lb. Eng.
        = 217.5 kg. (Schaube) = 478.5 lb. Eng.

At Lisbon spices were quoted in the light cantar.

1 cantar = 112 lb. Eng. (Roberts)
        = 168 lire sottile (Sanuto)[18]   = 110.8 lb. Eng.
        = 176 lire sottile (Paxi)   = 116.2 lb. Eng.
        = 150 lire sottile (Ca Masser)[19]   = 99. lb. Eng.
        = 112 lb. Eng. = value here used.

But the figures given by Priuli and Sanuto of the amount of spices brought back by the galleys from the east are given in colli. The collo was obviously a package, a bale, used for shipment but not for sale. Consequently it is not given by Paxi, and its capacity was not rigidly standardized. If it had not approximated some standard, however, it would not have been used at all to show the amount of cargo.

The colli were of at least two kinds, the colli grandi or colli alexandrini, used for the spices from Egypt, and the colli used in loading in Syria.[20] I have found only one equivalent for the colli Alexandrini.

1 collo of Alex. = 10 cantars of Portugal (Sanuto)[21] = 1120 lbs. Eng.

There are two indications which tend to confirm that reference, however. In 1450, it was moved in the Senate that whereas the " collis specierum " at Alexandria used to be about 720 lire or thereabouts but were now being made of 1000 and 1500 lire so that they were hard to move, therefore it should be forbidden to make them larger than a sporta. But that was defeated 58 to 15. The motion passed, on the other hand, provided that, in view of the harm which would come to the Venetian merchants in case any words of the matter came to the ears of the Moors, 1000 ducats fine should be paid by anyone who spoke of the subject to Moors in Alexandria.[22]

The second indication is from the number of colli loaded on a great galley. Both Priuli and Sanuto give the impression that 400 colli is to be counted a full cargo for a galley. Sanuto says specifically once that 1031 colli were the cargo for 2½ galleys,[23] and again that 1100 colli were half the cargo for 5 galleys.[24] The capacity of the galleys has been shown to be from 450 to 500 milliaria. Then:

440 to 400 colli = 500 to 450 milliaria
If 400 colli = 500 milliaria, 1 collo = 1312.5 lbs. Eng.
If 440 colli = 450 milliaria, 1 collo = 1073.9 lbs. Eng.

Neither the resolution in the Senate about fifty years earlier in date, nor the figuring from the capacity of the galleys, yield a result sufficient to stand by themselves, but taken together they are sufficient to bring substantial support to the statement of Sanuto that 1 collo = 1120 lb. Eng.

---

[18] *Diarii*, V, 133.
[19] " Relazione sopra il commercio dei Portoghesi nell' India, 1477-1506," *Arch. stor. ital. appendice*, II, 25.
[20] Fulin, p. 247. There Priuli speaks of " colli grandi, zoè colli alexandrini, cussi nominati tra marchadanti ". Then when speaking of the galleys of Beyrut he says they had a good cargo " . . . zoè . . . piper over pevere colli piccoli a quello viagio consueto advenire numero mille et seicento per mancho, et 600 colli de zenzeri, et garofale colli, zoè sache, 400 et piu. . . . "
[21] *Diarii*, XVII, 191.
[22] Senato Mar, reg. 4, ff. 6-7.
[23] *Diarii*, IV, 49, 260.
[24] *Diarii*. IV, 281; V, 78.

The colli used in loading the galleys of Beyrut were much smaller. That appears from the larger number sometimes brought by a single galley. Dues were charged in Venice in the following proportion: 2 ducats per collo of Alexandria, ½ ducat per collo of Beyrut, 2 ducats per collo "serici", or of Syria.[25] It is not impossible that the galleys of Beyrut loaded some colli four times as big as others.

Paxi and Priuli use sachi and colli interchangeably to describe the bales loaded by the galleys in Syria.[26] From an indication in Sanuto it appears that 1 sacho = 400 lire sottile.[27] A decree of the Senate of 1428 gives the sacho of cotton of Damascus and Hamah as 400 lire, and that of Latakia as 700 lire.[28] It seems safe to say, therefore, that the bales loaded by the galleys of Beyrut, indiscriminately called colli or sachi, weighed at least 400 lire sottile, or 264 lb. English, but some of them may have been considerably larger.

MONEYS.

Prices and wages have invariably been given in the text in the same moneys of account in which they were given in the sources. No attempts have been made to transform the sums into modern equivalents because there would be more delusion than meaning in such conversions. The figures are significant for comparison among themselves. On the pay roll of the Arsenal, for example, 8 *soldi di piccoli* a day was the lowest wage paid to men, 20 *soldi* to 24 *soldi* the pay of skilled labor, 48 *soldi* that of the expert shipwrights.

The gold DUCAT coin or ZECCHINO, containing 3.5 grams of gold, equal to about $2.25 U. S. A. dollars of the gold content of 1932, was one Venetian coin that escaped the debasement that afflicted almost all mediaeval coinage. Debasement was so common that accounts were kept in ideal monetary units called moneys of account, even if these units had no counterparts in the coins in circulation.[29] Three such moneys of account were used in fourteenth century Venice. In each of them the largest unit was the *lira,* which was divided into 20 *soldi* and 240 *denari,* so that in the language of the moneys of account there were three kinds of *lire,* three kinds of *soldi,* and three kinds of *denari.* About 1400 each of these three systems of ideal money had its representative in the coinage in common use. The value, in metallic content, of all the denominations of any one money of account was determined by the gold or silver content of the coin upon which that particular system of account was based. The three systems of money of account were:

1) The *lira di grossi a oro* = 20 *soldi di grossi a oro* of 12 *denari di grossi a oro* of 32 *piccoli di grossi a oro.* Its metallic representative was the gold DUCAT coin.

1 gold DUCAT coin = 2 *soldi di grossi a oro.*
The ducat was also used as a money of account giving this alternate and more common way of figuring with the *lira di grossi:* 1 *lira di grossi* = 10 *ducati* of 24 *denari di grossi a oro* commonly called *grossi a oro.*

2) The *lira a grossi* = 20 *soldi a grossi* of 12 *denari a grossi.* Its metallic representative was the silver GROSSI coin.

1 silver GROSSI coin = 26 *denari a grossi.*

---

[25] Senato Mar, reg. 12, f. 136.

[26] The alternate use by Priuli in the quotation in note 20 above. Paxi refers to sachi being sent to Beyrut to be loaded on the galleys.

[27] *Diarii,* XVII, 191.

[28] Senato Misti, reg. 56, f. 109. Licia has been identified as Laodicea ad mare or Latakia, Aman as Hamah. Both these places are mentioned by Paxi as famous for their cotton. Siamio is to be identified as Damascus. See Wilhelm von Heyd, *Histoire du commerce du levant au moyen age* (Leipzig, 1886), II, 153-156.

[29] On moneys of account see Allan Evans, "Some Coinage Systems of the Fourteenth Century," in *Journal of Economic and Business History,* III (1931), 481-496.

3) The *lira di piccoli* = 20 *soldi di piccoli* of 12 *denari di piccoli*. Its metallic representative was the silver SOLDINO coin.

1 silver SOLDINO coin = 1 *soldo di piccoli*.

The relation of the moneys of one system of account to the moneys of another system of account ordinarily changed as the relative value of the coins upon which they were based varied from time to time in the fineness and weight of the precious metal they contained. About 1423 the Venetian GROSSI coin contained 1.6 grams of silver, the SOLDINO coin .4 grams of silver so that 1 GROSSI was reckoned as 4 *soldi* of the *lira di piccoli* at a time when 1 gold DUCAT coin equalled 104 *soldi di piccoli*.[30] The GROSSI thereafter depreciated and were withdrawn from circulation in 1472. They were called in at 2½ *soldi di piccoli* at great expense to the state.[31]

That left two systems of moneys of account: the *lira di grossi* on a gold basis for represented by the gold DUCAT coin, and the *lira di piccoli* on a silver basis for represented by the silver SOLDINO coin or by newly coined silver LIRE or TRONI coins equal to 1 *lira di piccoli*. Before 1472 the *lira di piccoli* had depreciated in terms of the *lira di grossi* either because of the falling ratio of silver to gold or because of the progressive diminution of the silver content of the SOLDINO coin. In 1282 the DUCAT was valued at 2 *lire* 14 *soldi* of the *lire di piccoli*, in 1376 at 3 *lire* 14 *soldi* of the *lire di piccoli*.[32] In 1472 the *lira di piccoli* had been so much further debased that 1 DUCAT was valued at 124 *soldi* of the *lira di piccoli*.

This last relationship, 1 ducat = 124 *soldi di piccoli*, was made the basis for creating a ducat of account which became distinct from the DUCAT as a gold coin. From 1472 to 1509 the ducat as a money of account was equal to the DUCAT as a gold coin whether figured as equal to 2 *soldi di grossi a oro* or as equal to 124 *soldi di piccoli*; but, surprisingly enough, the two parted company, and the ducat was used after 1509 as a money of account dependent for its metallic value upon the silver coins which represented the *lira* and *soldo di piccoli*, even though this ducat of account was called the *ducato a oro, ducato di valuta, ducato corrente*. The ducat as a money of account equal to 24 *grossi a oro* was also not the equivalent of gold DUCAT coin, but of 124 *soldi di piccoli*. To specify the DUCAT coin it was necessary to say *ducato d'oro in oro novo di zeccha*, or at least *ducato d'oro in oro*.[33] Before 1555 the accounts of the Arsenal were figured in *lire di piccoli*, thereafter in ducats and *lire di piccoli* on the basis: 1 ducat = 124 *soldi*.[34] To give metallic representation to this common usage silver DUCAT coins were issued in 1562. Silver DUCATS, HALF-DUCATS, and QUARTER-DUCATS were minted bearing the figures 124, 62, and 31 to indicate their value in *soldi di piccoli*. The legal price of the gold DUCAT coins rose as the silver coinage was debased: in 1545, 1 gold DUCAT coin equalled 7 *lire* 17 *soldi* of the *lire di piccoli*; in 1570, 1 gold DUCAT coin equalled 8 *lire* 12 *soldi* of the *lire di piccoli*.[35]

Whenever *lire* and *soldi* have been used in the text above, *lire di piccoli* are meant. References to ducats before 1500 are to the gold DUCAT coin or its equivalent as a money of account equal to 24 *grossi a oro*. References to ducats thereafter are to ducats of account equal to 124 *soldi* of the *lira di piccoli*.

---

[30] Nicolò Papadopoli Aldobrandini, *Le monete di Venezia* (Venice, 1893-1907), I, 257.

[31] *Ibid.*, II, 3.

[32] *Ibid.*, I, 131; Roberto Cessi, " Problemi monetari e bancari veneziani del secolo xiv ", in *Archivio veneto-tridentino*, IX (1926), p. 298.

[33] Papadopoli, II, 3, 91, 100, 177, 212-213.

[34] Arsenale, busta 10, ff. 26-27.

[35] Papodopoli, II, 214, 270, 310-311.

APPENDIX II

DOGE MOCENIGO'S ORATION AND THE VENETIAN FLEET, 1420-1450.

The substantial reliability of the "deathbed oration" of the Doge Mocenigo has been accepted not because of the character of the manuscripts in which it is found, but because of the extent to which the statements made there have been confirmed. Most of the manuscripts at the Marciana in which the speech is to be found are party pamphlets containing other less reliable tracts opposing an adventuresome Italian policy and advocating vigorous maritime action.[1] But Professor Gino Luzzato has shown that there is a very considerable amount of independent evidence to support the financial figures given by Mocenigo.[2] The statement that Venice had 300 *navi*, is confirmed by the statement in the preamble of a law of the Senate that that was the common number from 1420-1450.[3] The preamble refers to the records of the *Consoli dei Mercanti* as the source of the information. The figure of 8,000 as the number of sailors employed on these ships, allowing an average of 26 or 27 men per ship, is not improbable.[4] That there were 3,000 small craft employing 17,000 men, or 5 or 6 each, cannot be confirmed, but presents no impossibilities if it be assumed that the whole of the Dogado is included. Such an assumption is necessary to explain also the 3,000 ship carpenters and the 3,000 caulkers, because a preamble to a law of the Senate states that the number from 1460 to 1463 was 750[5] and much later, in 1560, when the Arsenal was employing a far larger number than at the time of Mocenigo, the existence of 1,200 carpenters was considered excessive.[6] But the figures for 1500 surely, and that for 1460 presumably, do not include those craftsmen who merely made or repaired small boats and never worked on the seagoing ships nor do they include those living in the small towns around the lagoons outside of Venice. Unless Mocenigo's figures be taken to include these, it is out of proportion, and it seems large even then.

The number of galleys sailing each year is given as 45. At the time of Mocenigo the state merchant galleys sailed each season as follows: to Romania and the Tana, 3; to Alexandria, 3; to Beyrut, 4; to Flanders and England, 4; to Aigues Mortes, 2.[7] Since the voyage to England took a year, one year's fleet may have sailed before that of a previous year had returned so that this figure might be counted twice, perhaps. Two or three private galleys went each year to Jaffa with pilgrims.[8] Of other private

---

[1] Bibl. Naz., Venice, MSS. Ital. cl. VII, cod. 793—Sanuto's copy—; cod. 794—the copy at the front of the *Cronaca Dolfina*, source of the printing by Kretschmayr, *Geschichte von Venedig* (Gotha, vol. I, 1905; vol. II, 1920), II, p. 617—; cod. 1563; cl. XI, cod. 6.

[2] "Sull' attendibilità di alcune statistiche economiche medievali", *Giornale degli econonisti*, anno XLIV, n° 3 (March, 1929), p. 126; *I prestiti della Repubblica di Venezia* (*Doc. Finan.* ser. iii, vol. I, pt. I), p. ccxiii.

[3] Senato, Mar, reg. 15, f. 145.

[4] According to *Gli statuti marittimi veneziani*, Statuti di R. Zeno, chapter 20, a sailor was required for each 10 milliaria, which would mean that the average size of these vessels was 260-270 milliaria. But by the fifteenth century, the number of men required averaged less than one for each 10 botte. See the A. S. V., *Capitolare dei Consoli dei Mercanti*, chapters 200, 247, 250, 251.

[5] Senato, Mar, reg. 9, f. 19.

[6] *Ibid.*, reg. 35, ff. 46-7.

[7] These figures are based on the numbers given in the auction contracts of the galleys in the registers of the Senate, series Misti for the years 1420-1423 inclusive.

[8] Senato, Misti, reg. 49, f. 165; reg. 58, ff. 48, 110.

galleys I have found no mention. As for war galleys the Senate in the first decade of the century usually voted each year that 10 galleys be sent to protect the gulf, but the actual provision was made later.[9] In time of war the number planned would be larger. In 1424 when a powerful fleet was desired it was voted to arm 25 galleys.[10] These indications from contemporary sources suggest that Mocenigo's figure may be exaggerated but is not out of proportion.

The 45 galleys are reported as employing 11,000 seamen which would mean 244 or 245 to a galley, certainly a large figure, but again not out of proportion for the required crew of a great galley as fixed by law in 1412 was 212 all told from the commander to the cook.[11] Frequently they were required to take ten or twenty extra bowmen,[12] and yet more frequently, it is to be suspected, the commanders failed to employ all the crew that the law required. A list of the crew of a war galley of later date, 1510, shows more bowmen and less oarsmen with a total of 206.[18]

This examination of the data given by Mocenigo concerning ships and sailors in one case provides exact confirmation and in the others shows that there is nothing unreasonable in his figures. I have accepted them therefore as substantially correct.

To use the data effectively it is necessary to determine what sized ships were included in the designation *nave,* what were the smallest vessels included among the 300.

First, there is to guide us the limits given by Mocenigo to his smaller class, the *navilii.* He says they range from 10 to 200 anfore. The implication is obvious that only those over 200 anfore are included among the *navi.* Figuring with the anfore as 21 cubic feet as indicated above, 200 anfore would be 106 freight tons.

Second, the implications of the *Statuti marittimi* of Venice, over 100 years earlier in date, are that *navi* were not less than 200 milliaria. That is the smallest ship for which there is given the permitted loading in cantars, the number of sailors required, etc. In the statutes concerning the tarettes, on the other hand, such provisions are phrased to apply also to vessels of 200 milliaria or less. Moreover, for a long time, certainly until the institution of new harbor dues in 1407, only ships of 200 milliaria or more were estimated by the *Consoli dei Mercanti.*[14] Now, 200 milliaria equal 212,000 English pounds or 94 tons. Thus these two independent sources, one of which deals in terms of weight, and the other in terms of capacity, give us very nearly the same conclusion. The 300 *navi* were ships of c. 100 tons, or c. 166 botte, or larger.

The only detailed ship lists of the time of Mocenigo which I have found are in the " Notatorio di Collegio". They suggest some ways of going beyond his figures and estimating how many big ships there were among the three hundred existent from his time until 1450. The lists given there are of cogs offered by their owners for the service of the state for a particular voyage, usually that of Syria, to be regulated by the state. After the cogs had been so registered they were voted on by the Senate and a certain, predetermined number which received the largest number of votes were chosen for the voyage or to be armed. Thus, although only two or three were to be chosen, five or six might apply. The cogs so recorded represent only a part of the merchant fleet, but the lists give directly a minimum figure for the number of big ships of that time.

---

[9] *Ibid.,* reg. 47, ff. 24, 90.

[10] *Ibid.,* reg. 55, f. 90.

[11] *Ibid.,* reg. 49, ff. 114-5.

[12] For examples, *ibid.,* reg. 47, ff. 30, 60.

[13] Senato, Mar, reg. 17, f. 89.

[14] *Capitolari dei Consoli dei Mercanti,* chapters 200, 247, 353, and Senato Misti, reg. 47, f. 152.

From the beginning of 1449 to the end of April 1450 there are on these lists 21 different ships of over 400 botte whose masters wish to arm them for the service of the state or to send them to Syria.[15] Their total capacity is 16,922 botte. There is no reason to think that during those sixteen months all the cogs of Venice should have been offered for military service or the Syrian voyage. Therefore a guess based on this figure would give a total of at least 20,000 botte for the cogs of 400 botte or over.

Entries are also very numerous between 1425 and 1433 inclusive.[16] During those nine years 32 different cogs of 400 botte or over are mentioned. Their total carrying capacity amounts to 22,295 botte. The period covered is roughly the same length as the life of a ship. Of the 32 cogs, however, two are mentioned in 1417,[17] and so may be presumed to have gone out of use by 1431, one is recorded as new in 1433, and one is also mentioned in 1443.[18] At least four ships must therefore be omitted in guessing at the size of the merchant fleet in 1431. On the other hand, at least 16 ships must be included as at least that many are mentioned in the one year 1431.

A more satisfactory way of estimating the number of cogs of 400 botte or over about 1450 is to work backward from 1558-1559 by comparing the number of ships engaged in the most important voyages. The number and size of the ships trading to Syria in the first half of the fifteenth century can be fairly well determined from the decrees of the Senate regulating that trade together with the lists of the ships going as recorded in the "Notatorio di Collegio." This trade was organized into two voyages a year by regulations which permitted Venetian ships to load cotton in Syria only at fixed periods called *mude* or *muduae,* one of which came in the spring and the other in the fall.[19] The galleys went only in the fall and are not here considered. Sometimes the fear of pirates or quarrels with the Soldan of Syria and Egypt caused the Senate to forbid the departure of any cogs except certain selected ones which sailed in convoy under a commander chosen by the state. At such times the "Notatorio" preserves the list of the cogs which went. When the trade was left open for all cogs there are no such records except for one *mude,* that of the spring of 1418 when it was first resolved to send all the cogs in one fleet but later permitted that they sail unrestricted. On that occasion 10 cogs with carrying capacity of 6177 botte registered as intending to sail for Syria or Acre, although some of them intended to seek part of their cargo at way stations.[20] From 1426 to 1433, when these records are most numerous, there are records of eight out of the possible sixteen voyages, as follows:

1) 1426 Spring 7 cogs—5132 botte.[21]
2)   Fall   4 cogs mentioned—2947 botte, others implied.[22]
3) 1427 Spring 3 cogs—2715 botte.[23]

[15] Notatorio di Collegio, reg. 10 (modern numbering), ff. 85, 94, 95, 96, 104, 108-9.
[16] *Ibid.,* reg. 8. The term cog is here applied generally to the large round ships to distinguish them from the smaller types. On the lists the ships are usually called *cocche,* sometimes *navi.*
[17] *Ibid.,* reg. 7, f. 75.
[18] *Ibid.,* reg. 9, f. 59.
[19] A. S. V., Archivio dei Ufficiali al Cattaver, busta I, capitolare I, ff. 65-72 or chapters 136-145. That these laws were still in force in the fifteenth century is shown by decrees prolonging the *mude* because ships had been delayed.
[20] Senato Misti, reg. 52, ff. 66-7. Notatorio, reg. 7, the numbering of the Notatorio is double and confusing. The lists are to be found at about the date indicated by the decree of the Senate.
[21] Senato Misti, reg. 55, ff. 181, 185, 191, 184.
[22] *Ibid.,* reg. 56, ff. 16, 17, 25, 56.
[23] *Ibid.,* reg. 56, ff. 71, 75.

4)   Fall   7 cogs—5613 botte.[24]
5) 1428 Spring 7 cogs—5045 botte and others.[25]
6) 1431 Spring 6 cogs—3851 botte. Also went to Alexandria.[26]
7)   Fall   6 cogs—4098 botte.[27]
8) 1433 Fall   6 cogs—4658 botte.[28]

During the first gap in this record, references make it sure that there was no stoppage of trade.[29] During 1432, on the other hand, the war with Genoa prevented sailings for Syria.[30] It was voted in June of that year that six cogs of over 450 botte be sent under a special admiral to Crete, but the space left in the "Notatorio" to register the ships applying is left blank so that there is doubt whether they went.[31]

At the end of our period, for the fall voyage of 1449, 6 cogs totaling 4966 botte were chosen.[32]

Averaging the eight years of most frequent records gives 5.75 cogs equalling 4257 botte each *muda*. In view of the figures for 1418 and 1449 it would seem conservative to estimate the normal number of clearances from Venice for Syria as 12 cogs and 9000 botte per year.

For the other voyages made in the first half of the fifteenth century it is necessary to rely on casual references.

Trade to English Channel:

1446 3 cogs ordered to go in convoy.[33]
1448 proposed to send 5 cogs.
1449 4 cogs were in Channel ports in June.[34]
1449 2 cogs proposed for the voyage. They may not have gone because of war.[35]

It is repeatedly stated that the Channel voyage employed the largest of the ships. Two of those mentioned above may be identified as ships elsewhere recorded as over 1100 botte. At this time there were in the Venetian merchant marine at least six ships of 1000 botte or over.[36] Among the ships applying to serve the state as warships in 1462, one is recorded as estimated at 825 botte but as having carried 1050 botte to Flanders, one as 900 botte but as having carried 1300 botte to Flanders, and a third as officially estimated as 1000 botte but as having carried out 1156 botte and on the return voyage 1300 botte.[37] In view of these facts it would not seem exaggerated to estimate that some three cogs a year capable of carrying 3000 botte cleared from Venice for the Channel ports.

Trade to Romania, Constantinople and the Tana:

1446 4 cogs or more.[88]

---

[24] *Ibid.*, reg. 56, ff. 104, 114.
[25] *Ibid.*, reg. 56, ff. 152-6.
[26] *Ibid.*, reg. 58, ff. 19, 22, 26, 45.
[27] *Ibid.*, reg. 58, ff. 53, 60, 62, 63, 72.
[28] *Ibid.*, reg. 58, f. 190.
[29] Senato Misti, reg. 57, ff. 139, 184, 186, 218-9.
[30] *Ibid.*, reg. 58, ff. 31, 97, 202.
[31] *Ibid.*, reg. 58, ff. 125, 139; Not. reg. 9.
[32] Notatorio, reg. 10, f. 96, July 16, 1449.
[33] Senato Mar, reg. 2, f. 156. The one which can be identified on the lists in the Notatorio is 1155 botte.
[34] *Ibid.*, reg. 3, f. 43, 48-9, 70, 121. The two which can be identified are 1100 botte, and 732 botte.
[35] *Ibid.*, reg. 3, f. 135.
[36] Table D, above.
[37] Notatorio, reg. 12, f. 98.
[88] Senato Mar, reg. 2, f. 134.

1448 3 cogs, returning, captured.[39]
1448 (later in year) 4 cogs at least are expecting to go.[40]

At the very beginning of the century the ships going to Constantinople and the Black Sea went under state regulation and were as follows:

1398 2 cogs, 1400 botte.
1400 3 cogs, 2200 botte.
1401 3 cogs, 1800 botte.
1402 3 cogs, 2100 botte.[41]

Apparently one voyage a year was made, leaving in the spring or late winter.

In the 'twenties and 'thirties three galleys were sent every year besides the cogs. In 1431 and 1432 the voyages of the cogs to the Black Sea were stopped because of the war with Genoa. Consequently two additional galleys were sent as if they were the absolute minimum required to remove heavy wares accumulated at the Tana.[42]

Although these scattered items are not much to go on, yet such as they are they indicate that three or four cogs able to carry around 2200 botte left Venice each year for Constantinople and the Black Sea.

These figures compare with those for 1558-1559 as follows:

	About 1448		About 1558 [48]	
	ships	botte	ships	botte
Clearings for Syria and/or Cyprus	12	9000	13	11950
English Channel	3	3000	3	3050
Constantinople	3-4	2200	3-4	2800

This comparison of the three trades for which there is most evidence in the earlier period, though the figures given be only probabilities, reveals that the voyages to these points occupied about as many ships at the earlier date as at the later.

The next step is to consider the probabilities regarding the other voyages made about 1558.

Ships clearing for voyages in search of grain are the second most important item on the lists of 1557-1560 accounting for about 23% of the total tonnage cleared. Part of the grain supply of Venice had been imported from an early date, and in the early fifteenth century Venetian ships brought in grain from Egypt, various ports of Greece, and Sicily, and in times of plenty were left free by the state to carry from Sicily to the eastern Mediterranean, and from ports in the east to the region west of Sicily.[44] In 1502 one reason alleged by the shipbuilders for the small number of ships was the fact that freedom to carry grain between ports of the western Mediterranean had been taken from them.[45] I have no figures, however, as to how many large ships were employed. The number needed to supply the needs of Venice herself will be considered much less at the earlier date if Beloch's figure [46] of 80,000 for the population in 1422 be accepted for comparison with the figure of 158,069 in 1552. The source of Beloch's figure is a statement that the amount of wheat provided each year by the grain magistrates was about 350,000 stara. Yet I know no reason to think

[39] *Ibid.*, reg. 3, f. 48.
[40] *Ibid.*, reg. 3, ff. 53, 58.
[41] Notatorio di Collegio, reg. 5, ff. 19, 43, 54, 77.
[42] Senato Misti, reg. 58, ff. 31, 58, 116-9.
[48] Lane, " Venetian Shipping ", Table A.
[44] Senato Misti, reg. 47, ff. 69, 154; reg. 52, f. 3, and in reg. 53, under date August 9, 1420—f. 151 of the copy; Senato Mar, reg. 4, f. 19.
[45] Senato Mar, reg. 15, ff. 145-6.
[46] " La Popolazione di Venezia nei secoli XVI-XVII ", p. 46.

that all the grain supply of the city was provided by the grain magistrates. The source states the population as 190,000. Out of the 346,000 stara, 170,000 came from Dalmatia, Albania, and Greece, 146,000 from the west side of the Adriatic, and only 30,000 from Padua and Treviso.[47] Although no mention is here made of Sicily, grain certainly came at times from there to Venice.[48] These figures show that the equivalent of 31,600 botte was imported each year by water, but we are entirely in the dark still as to how many cogs of 400 botte or over were engaged in this trade. The reasonable assumption would seem to be that some were so employed even if the number was not as large in the fifteenth century as in the sixteenth.

Trade to Catalonia is mentioned in 1446 and 1448. Only in the latter case is the number of ships, three, given. The ships may be identified from other lists and their total capacity calculated as 1,700 botte.[49]

Cogs clearing for Alexandria about 1448 are not referred to in the records I have examined, but there is evidence that oil, nuts, and fruit were being carried there.[50]

The voyage to Jaffa with pilgrims was not, in the fifteenth century, made by cogs, but by two privately owned galleys devoted to that purpose especially.[51]

As for the other, mostly shorter voyages which about 1558 formed about 15% of the total capacity cleared, there is no reason to think that such voyages were not also made in the early fifteenth century, but it may be questioned whether they were not at that time made mostly by smaller ships.

On the other hand, in the fifteenth century there were frequently two of the largest of the privately built cogs serving the state even in times of peace as war vessels for the extermination of pirates.[52] In 1558 such was no longer the practice.

However, if we assume that at this time when the maritime enterprise of the Venetians was most famed, their cogs were doing any part of the carrying trade for other nations either in the east or west Mediterranean, then there are other ships to be considered in our comparison.

Granted again that I am here dealing not with certainties, but only with probabilities, I consider that the comparisons presented above lead to the conclusion that the number of ships of 400 botte or over in the Venetian merchant marine in the earlier period was very nearly as many as in the later, but the average size was less. The fleet in 1558-1559 contained about 40 ships.[53] Assume, then, that there were 35 ships of this same class in the fleet in 1449. Then there remain 14 ships besides those which happened to be mentioned on the ship lists 1449-April, 1450. Estimating the 14 as 600 botte each—or slightly less than the average of 12 ships mentioned which were between 400 and 799 botte [54]—and adding the 14 to our list, gives as an estimate of the total capacity of ships of this class in 1449-1450, 25,322 botte—c. 15,193 tons—as compared with about 30,000 botte—c. 18,000 tons—for the years 1558-1559.

On the whole the comparisons possible between the amount of trade at the two dates about a century apart reveal a remarkable stabilization of the volume of goods moved on those well established long distance voyages of which Venetian cogs or caracks were the chief carriers.

---

[47] Paolo Morosini, *Historia della città e republica di Venetia* (Venice, 1637), p. 403.
[48] See references in note 44, above.
[49] Senato Mar, reg. 2, f. 117; reg. 3, f. 43.
[50] Heyd, II, 441, 427-430.
[51] Senato Misti, reg. 49, ff. 15-6, 30, 85, 94, 96.
[52] Notatorio di Collegio, reg. 10, ff. 15, 16, 30, 85, 94, 96, 118-9; Senato Mar, reg. 2, f. 110.
[53] Table F, above.
[54] Table D, above.

APPENDIX III

THE SHIP LISTS OF 1499

About half-way between 1420-1450 and 1557-1560, during a period which general statements declare to be one of depression, there are three indications of a specific nature concerning the number of ships of 400 botte or over.

The first is a statement which occurs in the diary of Marino Sanuto.[1] He noted down in December, 1498, that Benedetto Giustinian, *Savio a Terra Ferma,* remarked that at that time there were in the country, namely of Venetians, only 12 ships of 500 botte while at the time of Mocenigo there had been 350. Since the figure given for the time of Mocenigo is inexact, and since it is only a casual report of what seems to be a careless statement, it is obvious that not much reliance may be placed on it.

Of more value is the statement in one of the resolutions of the Senate of 1502 [2] that "there can hardly be found 16 [ships] which by our laws and ordinances can bring salt, which are of 400 botte and more, the bulk of which are ready to be torn down; and of less [than 400 botte] there are very few including the caravels of Dalmatia, and *marani,* of which there could not be less."

The third source is the most valuable. In the diary of Marino Sanuto are two ship lists for 1499. Sanuto was at the time one of the *Savii agli Ordeni* so that it is a reasonable assumption that the lists were taken from official sources. The first list follows letters dated August 21, from the Captain General of the Sea then off Zante ready for battle with the Turk.[3] The second is a list of ships at Venice, August 14, 1499,[4] probably made as a preliminary to arming caravels to police the gulf.[5] It seems probable that all Venetian ships of 400 botte or over are included on these lists except possibly two or three which reached Cyprus between August and September,[6] for the mobilization of the merchant fleet, either into the war fleet or into safe harbors, had begun in the spring. It was in April that the state began negotiating for the ships to be armed in Venice.[7] The six ships detained at Cyprus are mentioned in a letter dated April 22;[8] the detention of ships at Crete had begun by June,[9] and at Modon by April 25.[10]

---

[1] *Diarii,* II, 225.

[2] Senato Mar, reg. 15, f. 145.

[3] In the edition of Sanuto's diary this list is in volume II, columns 1241-1249. In the original manuscript of the Marciana, cl. VII, cod. 230 this list is on ff. 481-483. The summary here given contains two corrections of the list as printed.

a) The caravel Nic° di Algreto is mentioned in the MS. among those taken in Venice, manned in Dalmatia and sent to the fleet. It is omitted in the published diary.

b) The list of ships detained at Crete are in the MS. totaled up to 18 although there are only 17 names. Then, a line below the addition, is listed " Item nave di sier Piero Ruzeir ", with the capacity not given. In printing " Item nave di sier Piero Ruzeir " and " 18 " are wrongly printed on the same line so as to give the impression that 18 is the capacity of the ship. But in Vol. III, col. 810 the *nave* Ruziera di Candia is given as 1000 botte. I have so listed it.

[4] In the printing, Vol. II, 1080-1081. In the MS. f. 418.

[5] Sanuto, *Diarii,* II, 917, 928.

[6] Senato Mar, reg. 14, f. 196. In September eight to ten merchantmen detained at Cyprus were permitted to continue their voyages.

[7] Sanuto, *Diarii,* II, 629.

[8] *Ibid.,* II, 784.

[9] *Ibid.,* II, 919.

[10] It is so indicated on the ship list.

Accordingly it seems probable that all Venetian ships trading to Sicily or the Levant would have been detained during spring and summer either by the war fleet in the Ionian Sea or by the authorities at one of the ports. On the other hand, any ships which had left for western voyages before April and had not returned to the Ionian Sea by August would not be included. But the only long voyage westward in connection with which Venetian ships are mentioned at this time is the wine trade from Crete to the English Channel, which, on an average, only occupied about one ship a year. The ship which left Venice early in 1498 for that voyage was recalled when war threatened and is on the list,[11] and a ship leaving in 1499 would have been at Crete during the summer loading and presumably would have been detained there. It looks as though the attorney who prosecuted Grimani, the defeated Admiral, was correct in saying that Venice had cleared the sea of her ships in anticipation of the coming fight.[12] Nevertheless we can not assume that all the Venetian caravels customarily employed within the Adriatic had been concentrated in Venice or in the fleet and would appear on the list. The lists give a fairly accurate enumeration, however, of all ships of 400 botte or over, and includes a certain number, especially among the smaller types, which can not properly be considered Venetian but should rather be counted as Cretan or Dalmatian.

The items on the lists, with my own supplementary estimates and interpretations are as follows:

1) 48 light galleys.
2) 17 great galleys manned for the usual trading voyages. Only those to Aigues Mortes and Constantinople are missing.
3) 3 " navi di comune ", one of 2500 botte, two of 2000 botte.
4) 1 nave, the " Rosetta " or " Pandora ", of 2000 botte which had been sold by the state in Sept. 1497. App. VII.
5) 1 " belingier " of 400 botte, a type of oared galleon. I have included in it the table of round ships.
6) 1 nave armed at Venice of 300 botte.
7) 1 nave armed at Venice of 800 botte.
8) 8 navi armed at Venice of 500 to 700 botte inclusive: total 4900 botte.
9) 1 nave of 1500 botte recalled from Sicily, had been to Iviza to load salt when recalled for fleet that spring. Sanuto, *Diarii*, II, 814, 1201.
10) 2 navi of 600 botte each, pilgrim ship, and ship which had been carrying wood to Sicily, detained in fleet.
11) 1 nave of 600 botte, *patron* from Lesina, detained at Modon.
12) 2 navi, of 250 botte and 300 botte detained at Modon.
13) I nave returning from Constantinople — *ibid.*, II, 710 — estimated as 500 botte, retained at Modon.
14) 2 navi retained at Modon, estimated at 300 botte each. Estimates made according to other ships in the group.
15) 1 nave of 700 botte, *patron* and owner from Lesina, sent from Corfu to the fleet.
16) 1 nave of 400 botte detained.
17) 1 nave of 300 botte detained.
18) One ship of 800 botte retained by error in Cyprus. The ship appears also on the list of ships retained in Cyprus.
19) 4 navi detained, estimated, on the basis of the other ships in the group, 2 at 500 botte, 2 at 300 botte.
20) 6 Spanish and Biscayan barze.

---

[11] The " Pandora ", Sanuto, *Diarii*, I, 780, 923; Malipiero, p. 646.
[12] Sanuto, *Diarii*, III, 172.

21) 16 caravels, taken in Venice, armed in Dalmatia with 35 to 50 men each, estimated, on the basis of the average size of other caravels mentioned, as 200 botte each, total 3200 botte.

22) 6 caravels detained in fleet, sizes similarly estimated, total 1200 botte.

23) 2 navi and one navilio detained in the fleet, estimated that one of 500 botte, 2 of 300 botte.

24) 2 caravels detained at Modon, estimated at 200 botte each.

24) 19 gripi, some "armati a modo di fuste", not included on the table of round ships for they were very likely less than 100 tons.

25) 5 fuste armed in Corfu. Fuste were long ships smaller than galleys.

26) 1 nave detained at Cyprus of 800 botte.

27) 1 nave detained at Cyprus of 300 botte.

28) 3 navi detained at Cyprus of 500 botte to 600 botte inclusive, total 1700 botte.

29) 1 nave detained at Cyprus, estimated at 500 botte.

30) 1 galley and 7 fuste left to guard the gulf.

31) 1 nave of 400 botte belonging to a Cretan and detained at Crete.

32) 10 navi detained in Crete of 130 botte to 300 botte, total 1930 botte.

33) 6 caravels detained in Crete of 60 to 250 botte, total 910 botte. The one of 60 botte is not entered in the table.

34) 1 nave detained at Crete, the "Ruzier". In Sanuto, *Diarii*, III, 810, the nave "Ruziera di Candia" is given as 1000 botte.

35) 1 nave of 600 botte at Venice.

36) 2 navi of 400 botte at Venice, total 800 botte.

37) 6 navi of 250 botte to 330 botte at Venice. Total 1780 botte. One had sought in vain that month for permission to go to Crete to load wine. *Ibid.*, II, 1120.

38) 12 caravels of 1500 to 3000 stera, i. e., 150 botte to 300 botte, at Venice, total 2500 botte.

39) 1 belingier of the Signoria of 250 botte at Venice.

40) 1 schierazo of 2000 stera at Venice. Entered on table.

41) 1 gripo of 120 botte at Venice.

42) 1 nave in bad condition, estimated at 300 botte to conform with the small size of most of the ships left at Venice.

43) 1 maran of 300 botte at Venice.

All the round ships except the Spanish and Biscayan have been entered on Table E. The long ships have not. Their sizes are doubtful, but only the great galleys had a cargo capacity as large as 240 tons.

To obtain a figure for comparison with those for 1448 or for 1558-1559 the state built ships and the Cretan and Dalmatian ships — items 3, 4, 11, 15, 31, 34 — should be deducted from the totals given in the table. Those deductions leave a total of 26 ships of 9,660 tons capacity, of which 5 ships of 1,500 tons capacity have been put in that class only because so estimated. The ship lists thus suggest a somewhat larger fleet than that indicated by the law of 1502. The three year interval between 1499 and 1502 was a period of hard times and discouraging naval activities when a decline in the size of the merchant fleet might be expected. Yet it is probable that the shipping interests exaggerated their distress in 1502 in order to push through favorable legislation. Probably the fairest general conclusion is that private shipbuilding fell off between 1460 and 1488 so that the fleet of privately built large ships was but half of what it had been. Then there was a revival in the 'nineties which carried the fleet up to about two-thirds its former size. Then again there were a few years of very hard times until in 1502 began the first really satisfactory revival. Meanwhile large ships built by the state had served to keep the total carrying capacity of the fleet very near to the amount necessary to handle the customary trade of Venice.

APPENDIX IV

FREIGHT RATES.

Merchandise of the Muda of Syria.

On the regulated voyages of the round ships of the *muda* of Syria, mentioned in Appendix II, the freight rates Syria to Venice fixed by the state to be charged by all the ships accepted for the voyage were:

COTTON (per milliarium subtile)—7 ducats in spring of 1426; 6 ducats in fall of 1426; 5 ducats in fall of 1427; 6 ducats in spring of 1428, fall of 1430, and and spring of 1431; 10 ducats in fall of 1431; 6 ducats in fall, 1433.
    Conclusion: 6 ducats was median.
ALUM or ASHES (*Cenere*) (per milliarium grossum)—2½ ducats in spring of 1426; 2 ducats in fall of 1426, fall of 1427; spring of 1428; fall of 1430; spring of 1431; 3 ducats in fall of 1431; 2 ducats in fall of 1433.
    Conclusion: 2 ducats was median.

The high rates in 1431 were due to the extra number of bowmen carried. Scattered earlier figures: on the same basis: [1]

COTTON—12 ducats in fall 1405; 7 ducats in spring 1406; 6 ducats in fall 1417.
ALUM or ASHES—3 ducats in fall 1405, 2½ ducats in spring 1406; and in fall 1417.

The decree of the Senate of 1502 lamented the low freight rates obtained by the shippers and fixed a long list of freight rates.[2] The ships were forbidden to take goods for less. While these rates appear to have been minimum freights they also appear to have been higher than those customarily obtained by the shipowners just before 1502. Among these freights were:

COTTON from Syria and Cyprus (el mier)—duc. 4.
COTTON THREAD (el mier)—ducats 5.
ALUM or ASHES (*Cenere*) (el mier)—1 ducat, 12 grossi.

Wine.

1473. Crete to "West", Genoese have cut the rate to 3 ducats to the ruin of the Venetians.[3]
1488. Crete to England, foreigners have cut to 4 ducats, Venetians need to charge 7 ducats.[4]
1505. Crete to Southampton, motion defeated to limit the amount the Venetians could charge to 5 ducats, having 2 ducat per botta bounty from the government.[5]

---

[1] Senato Misti, reg. 47, f. 7 (1405); reg. 47, f. 25 (1406); reg. 52, f. 22 (1417).
[2] Senato Mar, reg. 15, ff. 145-146.
[3] *Ibid.*, reg. 9, f. 162.
[4] *Ibid.*, reg. 12, f. 157.
[5] Senato, Secreta, reg. 40, f. 133.

APPENDIX V

THE AGE OF SHIPS.

GALLEYS IN GENERAL.

In 1423 the galley sold to the Duke of the Archipelago in 1413 was declared to be too old. Arsenale, busta 5, ff. 5, 85.

A decree of the Senate of 1560 contained the assertion that whereas galleys used to last a long time and those then presented to other princes lasted 18 to 20 years, the galleys recently made in the Arsenal were unseaworthy in 3 or 4 years. Senator Mar, reg. 35, f. 2.

About 1593, Drachio, in his memorandum on the Arsenal, said galleys only lasted 8 or 9 years. Arsenale, busta 533.

GREAT GALLEYS OF TRADE.

In 1454 the merchant galleys sent out were said to be 13 years old so that they could not be used any more. Senato Mar, reg. 5, f. 62.

In 1462 the decision to build new galleys was deferred until an examination could be made of the galley made in 1452 to see if it was fit for the Levant voyages that year. *Ibid.*, reg. 7, f. 58.

The lists of galleys used in preparing Tables H and I imply that 13 years was the age limit for these ships.

ROUND SHIPS.

Two state ships were finished in the summer of 1425. Senato Misti, reg. 55, f. 134. One of them was wrecked in 1432. *Ibid.*, reg. 56, f. 246. In March, 1432, it was considered advisable to begin two more, but work on one was abandoned. *Ibid.*, reg. 58, f. 103, 171. In February, 1437, it was resolved to arm the two state ships, but one of them was reported to be no longer seaworthy. Senato Misti, reg. 59, f. 190. Apparently one of the ships built in 1432 had given service for 14 years.

The state ship, "Pandora", was sold at auction when 8 years old and was burnt in battle two years later. Sanuto, *Diarii*, I, 780; III, 2.

The "Marcella", which the state had bought, was dismantled when 8 years old because no longer seaworthy and too costly to refit. *Ibid.*, V, 122.

A state *barza* was declared no longer seaworthy when 10 years old. Senato Mar, reg. 16, f. 107.

The galleon built by Matteo Bressan, launched in the fall of 1530, was declared unseaworthy in the winter of 1547. *Ibid.*, reg. 22, f. 37; reg. 29, f. 125.

Judging from the ship lists used for Table D some merchantmen served 11 or 12 years. Thus the ship of 950 botte called the "Giovanni Contareno" appears on lists of 1430, 1431, 1437, 1439, 1440. The "Blasius Alberegno" appears as a new ship in 1426 and is mentioned in 1431, 1433, 1437. A new ship is usually so called, but some of the identifications are open to doubt.

The purport of all these indications is to support the traditional figure for the life expectancy of the ships, 10 years.

APPENDIX VI

THE COST OF SHIPS.

In the Museo Civico Correr, Venice, Archivio Donà della Rosa, busts 155, there is the following exposition of the cost of a light galley:

" Fu posto già molti anni esser il costo di una gallea con tutti i
  suoi fornimenti espedita alla vella della casa dell'Arsenale—

	Ducati	Anno 1600
Quanto al proto di marangoni per i legnami e fatture de marangoni, sieghe, et fachini...........................	1300	d. 1735
Quanto al proto di callafadi et fauri per le ferramente stopa, pegola, et callafadi.................................	1200	1600
Quanto al proto di albori per li albori, antene, et 2 timone con le ferramente.....................................	110	146
Quanto al proto di remeri per li remi, cavalleto et repetti....	196	261
Quanto al proto delle taglie per li calcesi, taglie raggi, tampagni, et marsioni...................................	36	48
Quanto all'Armiraglio per le velle, sartiami, armizi, et rampeggoni da sarze.....................................	1200	1600
Quanto al masser per le artellerie, monitioni, arme, et rispetti.	2000	2666
Essendo acresciuti le precii de tutte le cose et il sold alle maestranze si aggioinge uno terze se ben de alcune cose eccieda	2014	
Suma	8056	[8056]"

Comparing these figures with those in Forsellini's table, p. 116, gives the following results concerning the relative increases in the costs of the hull and of the munitions:

	Cost in ducats for light galley at various dates			Increase
	ca. 1580	1600	1643	*ca.* 1580–1643
Munitions and arms......	2000	2666	4287	114%
The hull (wood, iron, tow, pitch, labor)...........	2806	3742	8800	214%

A comparison of the data on the pay of the masters about 1640—Forsellini, p. 87—and the figures given above in Chapter X and Table J shows that the labor cost for the hull had not risen more than 100%, if that much. Forsellini's table shows that most of the cost of materials was for lumber. Therefore the greater increase in the cost of the hull must have been mainly due to the fact that the cost of lumber rose faster than the cost of munitions, faster than the general rise of the price level. This gives an additional indication of the growing scarcity of ship timbers.

In a petition for a loan to help him build a merchantman, Piero Solto stated that the cost of building used to be 15,000 to 16,000 ducats but that it now cost 35,000 to 36,000 ducats, and submitted the following itemized list of the cost of a 800 botte (480 ton) merchant ship under the date December 28, 1586—A. S. V., Misc. codici, 665.

	Ducats
Oak wood...	3500
Pine or fir wood..	1000
Ironwork, 50 miera at 52 the mier...........................	2600
Carpenters	2000

Caulkers	1000
Fachini for the needs of the work	500
Wine for the masters	500
Hemp for the rigging, 50 miera at 100 the mier	5000
Artillery, 40 miera at 140 the mier	5600
Masts and spars	1400
Sails for the ship, 8 miera at 100 the mier of canvas, and the work, with other fixings	1000
6 large anchors and other ironwork, 25 miera at 70 the mier, plus the work	1750
Pulleys and such work, gun carriages and fixings	500
Tar to tar the cables and fixings of the ship, 18 mier	900
Gunpowder and shot	500
Men by the day to clean up the ship and carriers for extras	500
Ship supplies	200
Pay and provisions for feeding the men	2500
Barks for towing the ship to Malamocco and tow ropes	300
Tow and pitch for making the ship and to have on hand	1000
	32,250

This may be compared with the itemized list of the expense of building a galleon found in a document concerning the Arsenal dating from about 1560—Museo Civico Correr, Venice, Arch. Gradenigo, busta 193. The size of the galleon is not there stated but probably that launched in 1559 and said to be 1200 botte is the ship upon which the figures are based:

	Ducats
Wood and labor of carpenters, sawyers, and *fachini*	5830
Masts and spars	509
Tow, pitch, iron, and work of caulkers	3112
Ropes, mooring, sails	6165
Artillery	14,842
Munitions for the guns	2364
[Total	32,822]

APPENDIX VII

ROUND SHIPS BUILT BY THE GOVERNMENT.

Cog, authorized as 1200 botte in 1422 to be built in place selected by College, finished about 1425. Foreman shipwright Micheletto di Piero. Senato Misti, reg. 54, f. 63; reg. 55, ff. 125, 134; Notatorio di Collegio, Dec. 8 and 11, 1422.

Cog, authorized as 1200 botte in 1422 to be built in place selected by College. Foreman shipwright Francesco de Negroponte. *Loc. cit.*

Maran, authorized in 1425 to be built in place where one of the above cogs had been finished, from the wood left over, by letting contract for the work. Senato Misti, reg. 55, f. 125.

Nave, authorized as 1500 botte in 1432, built outside Arsenal. Foreman shipwright Marcus Blondo. *Ibid.*, reg. 58, ff. 103, 171; reg. 59, f. 106.

Nave, authorized as 1500 botte in 1432, built outside Arsenal, work deferred in 1433, but apparently finished in 1435. *Loc. cit.*

Nave, authorized as 2000 to 2500 botte in 1451, wood ready in 1453, finished about 1457. Foreman shipwright Zaninus. Senato Mar, reg. 4, ff. 88, 162; Senato Terra, reg. 4, f. 104; Notatorio, no. 10, f. 148.

Nave, similar to the above. Foreman shipwright Bradimente. *Loc. cit.* At least one of these ships was built at San Trinità, *Memoria istoriche del Coronelli*, MS., f. 7.

Nave, authorized as 1000 to 1200 botte in 1475, finished in 1476. Senato Terra, reg. 7, ff. 98-99, 157, 177, 192.

Nave, similar to the above. *Loc. cit.*

Nave, authorized as 1000 to 1200 botte in 1475, in *squero* in 1481—Senato Mar, reg. 11, f. 103. Same as the 4000 botte ship which Malipiero, pp. 622-623, says was piloted out of Chioggia harbor in 1486 and burnt the next year?

Nave, authorized as 1000 to 1200 botte in 1475. Same as the ship described in 1488 as begun many years before but no good for rotted in its *squero* at Sant' Antonio? Senato Mar, reg. 12, f. 153.

Nave, authorized as 1200 botte in 1487. Senato Mar, reg. 12, f. 123. Same as the " Rosetta " or " Pandora " said to be 8 years old when sold in 1497—Sanuto, *Diarii*, I, 780—and appearing on ship list of 1499 as 2000 botte?

Barza, authorized as " nave " of 1200 botte in 1487. Senato Mar, *loc. cit.* Identified with the barza which Leonardo Bressan built at Pupilia, launched in 1492—*ibid.*, reg. 13, f. 90—and appearing on ship lists of 1499 as 2000 botte or 2500 botte.

Nave or barza, authorized in 1491—*ibid.*, reg. 13, f. 50—on lists of 1499 as 2000 botte or 2500 botte.

Barza, authorized in 1492, built at Poveglia, launched 1497. Foreman shipwright Leonardo Bressan. *Ibid.*, reg. 13, f. 90; Sanuto, *Diarii*, I, 502, 607, 714, 769-773.

Barza, authorized in 1498, 2000 botte to 3000 botte, built in *squeri* at Sant' Antonio, launched June, 1501. Foreman shipwright Leonardo Bressan. Senato Mar, reg. 14, f. 141; reg. 15, f. 48; Sanuto, *Diarii*, I, 849-850; III, 122, 140; IV, 51; Mapiliero, p. 645.

Barza or nave piccola, authorized in 1498 as 500 to 700 botte, being built at Sant' Antonio in 1500. Senato Mar, reg. 14, f. 196, Sanuto, *Diarii*, III, 122.

2 barzoti being built in the Arsenal in 1508—Senato Mar, reg. 17, f. 24. One the same as the "barza" of 400 botte sold in 1518? *Ibid.*, reg. 19, f. 77.

Barza or barzoto grande, authorized as 800 botte in 1526—Senato Mar, reg. 20, f. 192, made in the Arsenal, launched in 1530, said to be 1200 botte, necessary to break Arsenal walls to get it out—Senato Mar, reg. 21, f. 171; Sanuto, *Diarii*, LII, 151, 484; LIII, 164. Foreman shipwright Leonardo Bressan. Senato Mar, reg. 21, f. 160.

Nave or barza, authorized as 800 botte and so described, built and launched like the above. *Loc. cit.,* Sanuto, *Diarii*, LIII, 91. Foreman shipwright Francesco de Todaro (Theodoro) da Corfu called Francesco Zoto. *Ibid.*, XL, 803. Senato Mar, reg. 21, f. 73.

Galleon, authorized as 800 botte, but probably larger, built and launched like the two above. Foreman shipwright Matteo Bressan, Arsenale, busta 7, ff. 54, 84.

Galleon, authorized in 1554, built in "squero di Sant' Antonio", launched in 1559. Foreman shipwright Giovanni Maria Spuazza. Senato Mar, reg. 32, ff. 26, 110, 179; reg. 34, f. 64; Arsenale, busta 135, f. 141-147.

Galleon, authorized in 1547 and begun soon thereafter by Vettor Fausto, but left unfinished at his death, finished just before 1570 by Giovanni Maria Zulle. Senato Mar, reg. 29, f. 125; Arsenale, busta 136, f. 94. Pantera, pp. 40-43, says it was of 12,000 salme, about 2000 tons.

This tabulation supports the conclusion that round ships of the state were generally built outside the Arsenal. Casoni, "Forze", p. 122, implies that large round ships were generally built within the Arsenal, and particularly that the *barza* finished in 1497 was built there. He cites Sabellico without giving an exact reference. If, as seems likely, the passage in Sabellico to which he refers is that in "De situ urbe" (*Opera*, Venice, 1502), liber secundus, p. 88, the passage is at least vague and seems to refer to a ship being built in the "squeri" near the church of Sant'Antonio. Some indication of the location of the "squeri di Sant'Antonio", frequently mentioned in the tabulation, is given by the reference in Senato Mar, reg. 22, f. 82, to a ship "rebaltata nel canal grande per mezo li squeri di Sant'Antonio".

An early sixteenth century French manuscript—Bibl. Nat., Paris, F. F. 5600, f. 118— adds to its description of the Arsenal the statement that galleys and not "nefs" (round ships) had been discussed because no *nefs* were made in the Arsenal and that for two reasons. First the entrance to the Arsenal was not sufficiently deep to permit the passage of large round ships. (Hence the breaking of the wall in 1530 to launch ships directly into the lagoon.) Secondly, the Signoria of Venice made at most no more than two or three *nefs* at a time, and those very large. Instead the Signoria loaned to merchants building large *nefs* and used these ships in time of war.

BIBLIOGRAPHICAL NOTE

This study is based primarily upon a perusal of fifteenth and sixteenth century manuscripts in the public depositories of Venice. In order to present the results it was found necessary to trace developments of earlier centuries, principally the fourteenth, even though the surviving records of the earlier period had not been examined with equal thoroughness.

The greatest mass of material was found in the R. Archivio di Stato di Venezia (cited as A. S. V.) commonly called the Frari. The most complete description thereof, *Statistica degli archivii della regione veneta* by Bartolomeo Cecchetti (Venice, 1880-1881, 3 vols.) is supplemented by manuscript inventories kept in the archive. The registers recording legislation and administrative regulation, initially those of the Senate and secondarily those of subsidiary magistracies such as that of the Arsenal, were the main type of source there available. Consequently this study has been unable to escape entirely from the disadvantages which result from reliance upon that kind of source material. But scattered documents of a different character assisted the critical use of the laws and decrees. For the Arsenal, were available: petitions and reports from employees of the Arsenal used in preparing the decrees of the Senate and preserved in its files; the reports of various *Provveditori* and *Savii,* and of administrators like Taduri and Drachio; lists of employees and expenses, actual or estimated, preserved in family collections of administrative papers and now deposited with the Museo Civico Correr; various entries in chroniclers or diarists, especially Marino Sanuto. For the private shipbuilding the chief reliance was on the indirect evidence of laws, petitions, guild statutes, and a few notarial documents. For the ships themselves, the gleanings from travelers, chroniclers, painters, writers of technical manuscripts on ship construction, and modern authors served to push the legal source material quite into the background.

All works cited have been entered in the index, and the complete reference is given at the first mention in the footnotes.

INDEX

Accaton, 19, 20, 22.

Accounts, of ship building partnership, 117; of the Arsenal, 153-156, 195, 214, 252, *see also* Pay roll; of state building of round ships, 118, 119 and n.

Acre, 255.

Adige River, 218, 219.

"Admiral" of fleet, 151 n., 165, 170, 213.

Admiral of the Arsenal, duties, 151, 156, 160, 165, 167-171, 175, 204, 215, 249 n.; funeral of, 175; salary of, 161, 171.

Adriatic, guard of, 145, 259, *see also* Police Fleet. *See also under* Trade, Voyages.

Ægean, war in, 138.

Africa, *see* Voyages along.

Agostini, Agostino, *Storia veneziana di* (MS.), 188 n.

Agostini, Giovanni degli, *see* Giovanni degli Agostini.

Aigues Mortes, *see* Great galleys of.

Albania, 258.

Alberti, A., and Cessi, R., *La politica mineraria*, 217 n.

Albertis, E. A. d', *Le costruzioni navali e l'arte della navigazione*, 1 n., 47 n., 51 n., 52 n., 53 n., 246, 247 n.

Albion, R. G., *Forests and Sea Power*, 217 n., 232 n.

Alexandria, 249, 250, *see also* Great galleys of, Voyages to.

Allegri, Marco, ed., 7 n.

Alpago, forest of, 227-228.

Alps, forests of the, 218, 228.

Alum, 46, 262.

Alviano, Bartolomeo d', 64.

Alvise de Giovanni di Castello, called Scatola, 122, 158 n., 207 n.

America, discovery of, 41.

Ampezzo, timbers from, 228.

Anchors, in the Arsenal, 141, 144, 160, 168, 169; on ships, 12, 17, 18, 36, 38.

Ancona, oak from, 232.

Anderson, R. C., 70 n., 90 n.

———, "Italian Naval Architecture about 1445", 8 n., 23, 44 n., 45, 89 n., 93 n., 94 n., 95 n., 236 n., 237 n., 247.

———, "Jal's Memoire no. 7", 36 n.

Anderson, Romola and R. C., *The Sailing-ship*, 1 n., 8 n., 35 n., 37 n., 41 n., 42 n., 47 n., 48 n., 141 n.

Anfora, equivalent of, 248.

Annali genovesi di Caffaro, 5 n.

Anthiaume, A., *Le navire; sa propulsion en France*, 1 n., 42 n.

———, *Le navire; sa construction en France*, 1 n., 8 n., 37 n., 38 n., 41 n.

Apennines, forests of, 218, 232.

Appontador, 190 n., *see also* Paymasters.

Appraisers of the Arsenal, 62, 157, 162, 165, 204 n., 208, 209-211.

Apprentices, age of, 82-83; examination of, *see* Mastership; in Arsenal, 161-163, 166, 179-181, 183-184, 191; limitation of, 82, 183-184; number of, 82, 112, 126, 161 n., 162-163, 215, 243 n., 244 n.; registration of, 81-82, 180; term of, 83; wages of, *see* Wages.

Apulia, timbers from, 125 n., 231.

Aragon, 134.

Archers, *see* Bowmen.

Archery parks, 184.

Archimedes, 70.

Archipelago, Duke of the, 263.

Aristotle, 64.

Armament of ships, 24, *see also* Arms, Artillery, Bowmen.

Armiraglio, 151 n., 157 n., *see also* Admiral.

Arms, carried on great galleys, 19, 24, 25; cost of, 264-265; in Arsenal, 129, 141, 143, 144, 152 n., 159, 160, 172-175, 203. *See also* Bows.

Arms steward of Arsenal, 156, 157, 163, 167 and n., 170.

Arquebus, 10.

Arsenal, appropriations for, 137 and n., 139 and n., 154, 155-156; assistant foremen, *see* Construction chiefs, Gang bosses; bell, 163, 188, 189; captain in, 163; clock, 163; craft foremen in, 164, 167, 168, 169, 170, 172, 195, 213; departmental organization, 57, 159-164, 167, 196, 199, 214; dismissal of workers, 167, 176, 178, 187, 193, 194, 197, 213; docks in, 129, 139, 140, 142, 144, 158,

174, 195, 200, 205, 209, 211; door-keepers of, 153, 157, 163, 193 n., 194; employees in, list, 161-163, see also Caulkers, Mast-makers, etc.; employees in, number of, 136, 146, 152, 161-163, 182, 213, 215; executive of, 153, 161, 164-165, 213; expenses of, 139 n., 146, 151-152, 155 and n., 156 n.; explosions in, 61, 174; fire protection, 153; guarding of, 153, 158; importance, 101-104, 110, 131-132; inventory, 130, 160, 168, 169; loaning by, 150, 169; lumberyard, 158-159, 173, 209; military discipline in, 187; not for private property, 150; officers of, 161-164, see also Admiral of, Arms steward of, Bookkeepers of, etc.; outside employees, 136, 150, 163 n.; parts of, 158 n., 173; purchases by, 148, 151, 155, 157, 196, 230 and n.; round ships built in, 101, 118, 267; shipments from, 148, 151, 152, 156-157; size of, 129, 130, 140, 146; stealing in, 158, 193-195; supervisors of materials in, 165 and n., 198; warehouses in, 129, 142, 145, 152 n., 156, 160, 161, 168, 170 n., 171, 172, 173-175, 211; watch-men of, 153 and n., 163. See also Accounts, Conservation, Labor, Produc-tion, Reserve Fleet, Timbers, War fleets.
Arsenalotti, ceremonial functions of, 74, 186; distinguished from squerarioli, 84; laborers in the mint, 186-187. See also Arsenal, employees of, Craftsmen.
Arsenals, auxiliary, 152 and n.
Arsili, 132 n., 201 n.
Arti, 72, 73.
Artillery, cost of, 264-265; in Arsenal, 150, 160, 173, 174; on ships, 13, 27, 31, 33, 45, 51, 60, 66.
Artimon, 22.
Artiñano y de Galdácano, Gervasio de, La arquitectura naval española, 235 n.
Artisans, see Craftsmen.
Ashburner, W., Νόμος 'Ροδίων Ναυτικός. The Rhodian Sea Law, 46 n.
Ash wood, 224.
Asolo, forest at, 226.
Atlantic, see Shipbuilding: Regional tradi-tions of.
Auronzo, timbers from, 228.
Aviano, forest near, 228.
Awning, use on galleys, 23, 67.

Badoer, Gian Andrea, 31, 207.
Ballast, 21.
Balistas, 172.
Baltic, forests, 232-233; ships, see Ship-building: Regional traditions of, northern.
Banzonus, 35 n.
Barbary, see Great galleys of.
Barge-building, 85, 106, 111, 112, 220.
Barozzi, Nicolò, ed., 7 n.
Basque, see Biscayan.
Bassano, timbers from, 218 n.
Bassanus, see Baxon, Theodoro.
Battaglini, N., Le costruzioni navali, 232 n.
Battles, naval, 4-5, 27, 31, 33, 49, 140.
Barza, 50, 51, 60, 63, 64, 102, 205, 260, 263, 266-267.
Barzoto, 267.
Bayonne, sailors from, 12, 37.
Baxon, Theodoro, 8 n., 56-57, 136 n., 199.
Beech wood, 227 and n.
Belgrano, Tommaso Luigi, ed., 5 n.
Belingier, 260, 261.
Belluno, forest near, 228.
Benches, see Thwarts.
Beloch, J., "La popolazione di Venezia," 182 n., 257 and n.
Bembo, Alvise, report of, 222 n.
Bembo, Pietro, Cardinal, 67 and n.
Bensa, E., Francesco di Marco da Prato, 26 n.
Benussi, Bernardo, Istria nei suoi millenii di storia, 225 n.
Berchet, Guglielmo, ed., 7 n.
Berenger, Adolfo di, Saggio storico della legislazione veneta forestale, 219 n., 220 n., 222 n., 223 n., 224 n., 225 n., 226 n., 227 n., 228 n.
Bernardo di Bernardo, 55 n., 57-58, 97 n., 199, 200 n.
Besta, E., see Il Senato.
Beyrut, see Great galleys of.
Bilanci generali, 155 n., 219 n., 246 n.
Bilge water, 21.
Bill of lading, 157 n.
Biondo, Alvise, 170.
Biremes, 9 n., 17, 65 n.
Biscayan ships and seamen, 37, 42, 49, 64, 104, 232, 260.
Black Sea, ships from, 110, 232. See also Voyages to.
Board of Manufactures (Provveditori di Comune), 81, 85.

Board of Trade (*Cinque Savii alla Mercanzia*), 106, 127, 151.
Boerio, Guiseppe, *Dizionario,* 93 n., 189 n.
Bombarda, 19.
Bombardana, 19.
Bonnets, 37.
Bookkeepers of the Arsenal, 154, 163, 192, 200, 213.
Bordola, Antonio, 123 n., 158 n., 206.
Botta, equivalent of, 246-249.
Bounties, *see* Subsidies.
Bowline, 37.
Bowmakers, 167 and n.
Bowmen, 10, 17, 19, 24, 26, 39 and n., 184-185, 262.
Bows, 10, 17, 19, 167 n., 211-212.
Bowsprit, 44.
Boycott, 79.
Bregantini, 13, 68, 142, 207.
Bressan, Francesco, 56 n., 67 n., 70 and n., 71, 122, 206, 212, 266, 267.
Bressan, Giovanni, 59.
Bressan, Leonardo, 50, 51, 56 n., 60, 61, 62, 63, 64, 65, 97 n., 204, 205, 206, 241.
Bressan, Matteo, 51, 62, 63 and n., 64, 65, 69, 263, 267.
Breydenbach, Bernhard von, *Peregrinatio in Terram Sanctam,* 18.
Brown, Horatio F., *Studies in the History of Venice,* 147 n.
Brown, Rawdon, *Calender of State Papers, Venetian,* 241 n., 245 and n., 246 n.
Brunetti, Mario, *Contributo alla storia delle relazioni veneto-genovesi,* 132 n.
Bucentoro, 53 n., 176.
Bucius, 35 n.
Business organization, 115-120, *see also* Accounts.
Buss, 4, 35-37, 38, 39, 40, 45, 52.
Buzo, 35 n.
Byrne, E. H., *Genoese Shipping,* 35 n., 40 n., 53 n., 123 n.

Cabins, 25, 203, 218.
Cables, 17, 38, 141, 150, 157, 160, 169, *see also* Cordage.
Cabotage trade, *see under* Trade.
Cadiz, 27, 61, 134.
Cadore, 217, 218, 219, 228.
Caffaro, *see Annali genovesi.*
Calender of State Papers, Venetian, see Brown, Rawdon.

Ca' Masser, Leonardo da, "Relazione", 250 and n.
Cambrai, League of, 16.
Campagna, 139, 158 n., 174.
Canal, Gerolamo de, 67.
Canal boats, 53, 102, *see also* Bargebuilding.
Canale, Martino da, *see* Da Canale, Martino.
Canvas, *see* Sailcloth.
Caorle, 225.
Capi d'opera, 164, *see also* Gang bosses.
Capital, advanced by state, 110 and n., 124-129; from craftsmen, 125; from merchants, 124, 127; recruited by shares, 116; required in shipbuilding, 114; produces division of labor, 100.
Capitalism, contrasted with communal shipbuilding, 101 and n.; contrasted with craftwork, 100; extent of, 124; possibilities of, 115.
Capitano, see Captains General of the Sea, Fleet commanders.
Capitolare dei Consoli dei Mercanti (MS.), 39 n., 247, 248, 249, 253, 254.
Capitolare dei squerarioli (MS.), 75 n., 76 n., 77 n., 85 n., 86 n., 113 n.
Capitolarium nauticum pro navis (MS.), 36.
Capo di sesto, 92 n.
Capstans, 99, 218.
Captains General of the Sea, 132, 138, 147, 170, 205, 259.
Captains of ships, *see* Galley commanders, *Patroni.*
Carack, 41-42, 44, 45, 52, 102.
Carati, 116.
Caravans, *see* Convoys.
Caravel, 48, 50, 52-53, 259, 260, 261.
Careening, 169.
Cargoes, of great galleys, 14, 15, 25-27, 134, 136, 250-251; of round ships, 5, 6, 46, 47, 48, 52 and n., 53 and n., 103, 104, 106, 255, 257-258, 260, 262. *See also* Grain, Salt, etc.
Carpaccio, Vittore, painting by, 41.
Carpathian forests, 232.
Carpeneda, forests of, 227.
Carrack, *see* Carack.
Casola, Pietro, *see* Newett, M. Margaret.
Casoni, G., "Forze militare", 7 n., 13 n., 53 n., 54 n., 63 n., 65 n., 70 n., 129 n.,

130 n., 139 n., 140 n., 172 n., 187 n., 267.

——, *Dei navigli poliremi*, 65 n.

——, *Guida per l'arsenale di Venezia* 69 n.

Catalans, 64.

Catalonia, 258.

Caulkers, *da fizer (figgier)*, 98 and n., 126, 162, 184, 214, 243 n.; *da maggio*, 98 and n., 126, 162, 184, 243 n.; employed at sea, 49, 184-186; employed in Arsenal, 81 n., 162, 176, 177, 181-182, 197-199, 243; employed in rotation, 81, 181-182, 197; employed for unskilled labor, 161-162, 171, 198-199; number of, 162, 182, 184 and n., 243, 253. *See also* Foremen, Guilds, Labor.

Cecchetti, B., *Mariegole dei calafai*, 74 n., 75 n., 76 n., 98 n.

——, notes of, 134 n.

——, *Statistica degli archivii*, 268.

Cellina River, 228.

Cenedese, 122.

Cessi, Roberto, ed., 129 n., 130 n.

——, " Le relazioni commerciali tra Venezia e le Fiandre nel secolo xiv ", 16 n., 52 n., 134 n.

——, " Problemi monetari e bancari veneziani del secolo xiv ", 252 n.

—— and Alberti, A., *La politica mineraria*, 217 n.

Charcoal burners, 222, 226, 228.

Charles VIII, King of France, 60.

Charnock, John, *A History of Marine Architecture*, 51 n.

Chavo di sesto, 92 n.

Chests carried on galleys, 20, 210.

Chinazza, Daniele, *Cronaca della guerra di Chiozia*, 132 n., 133 n.

Chioggia, war of, 132-133.

Chioggia harbor, 266.

Chorba della onza, 93 n.

Chodera chorba, 92 n.

Chochina, 20, 22.

Chronica supposta Barbara (MS.), 7 n.

Cinque Savii alla Mercanzia, see Board of Trade.

Clamps, 8, 92, 97, 218, *see also* Fili.

Clark, G. N., *The Seventeenth Century*, 141 n.

Claut, forest of, 228-230.

Coadjutori, 163 n.

Cocha, 43, 53 n., 255 n., *see also* Cog.

Codice per la veneta mercantile marina, 116 n., 123 n.

Cog, 37-40, 43-44, 52, 102, 103, 130, 131, 235, 238, 255, 266.

Cogitori, 163 n.

Collective bargaining, 81.

College (*Collegio*), 63, 65, 66, 85, 119, 137, 147, 148, 149, 152, 155, 158, 164, 176, 178, 184, 188, 193, 197, 198, 214.

College of the Arsenal, 178-180, 182, 183, 185.

Colleggetto, 179 n.

Collegio da Milizia da Mar, 149.

Collo, equivalent of, 250-251.

Commissioners of the Arsenal (*Provveditori all' Arsenale*), creation of, 148, 149 and n.; functions of, 147-152, 155, 164 and n., 167, 169, 178, 192, 208; terms of, 152 and n.

Commissioner of Artillery (*Provveditore sopra le Artiglierie*), 150, 156.

Commissioners of the fleet (*Provveditori d'Armata*), 147, 157.

Competing centers of shipbuilding, 104, 107, 110, 231-233.

Conegliano, 225.

Conservation, 220-230.

Consoli dei Mercanti, 151, 238, 247, 254.

Constantinople, ships from, 232; Turkish conquest of, 138. *See also* Trade with, Voyages to.

Construction chiefs of the Arsenal, 122, 162, 166, 190, 204-210, 214-215.

Contador, 163 n.

Contarini family, 19.

Contarini, Francesco, report of, 159 n.

Contract, work under by foremen shipwrights, 113 n., 115, 121, 123 and n., 124-127, 200-205; by *squerarioli*, 85, 113 and n.; forbidden caulkers, 80, 85, 120, 196, 203; guild regulation of, 79, 113 n., 120; in the Arsenal, 122, 169-170, 172, 186, 195, 196, 200-205, 206-207, 209-211, 212; on big ships, 113-114, 121; on *maran*, 266. *See also* Piecework.

Convicts, 6 n.

Convito all'arti, 74.

Convoys, 4, 7, 14, 29, 40, 46, 130, 131, 249, 255.

Cooking galley, 18, 19, 22, 25.

Corazzini, F., *Vocabulario nautico italiano*, 247.

Corbett, J. S., *Drake and the Tudor Navy*, 27 n.

Cordage, 17, 21, 25, 172, 231; cost of, 264, 265; manufacture of, 150, 169; storage of, 141, 144, 159, 160, 175.

Corfu, 53 n., 219.

Cornelius, Flamininus, ed., 132 n.

Corner, Marco, report of, 220.

Coronelli, M. V., *Navi e barche*, 32 n., 236 n.

Corsairs, *see* Pirates.

Corsia, 20 n., 97, *see also* Gangway.

Corunna, 27.

Cotton, 46, 48, 251 and n., 255, 262.

Council, Ducal, 130 n., 147, 176, 179 n.

Council, Great, 129, 137, 146-147, 166.

Council of Ten, 62, 142 and n., 147-149, 152, 153, 220, 222, 224, 227; Chiefs of, 85, 188.

Craft divisions, between house carpenters and ship carpenters, 99 n.; between ship carpenters and caulkers, 98 and n., 142 n.; between *squararioli* and caulkers, 85-86; between *squararioli* and other ship carpenters, 85, 178.

Craftsmen, groups employed in shipbuilding, 88, 98-99; laws for protection of, 109, 177; obligations to state of, 73, 84, 176. *See also* Caulkers, Mast-makers, Shipwrights, etc.

Craft tradition, disregard of, 214. *See also* Arsenal, craft foremen; Craft divisions; Shipwrights.

Craftwork, *see* Retail handicraft.

Cremona, 62.

Crescentio, B., *Nautica mediterranea*, 13 n., 51 n., 92 n., 94, 95 n., 97 n., 125 n., 232 n.

Cretan ships, 47 n., 51 n., 260, 261.

Crete, 57, 138, 219, 259, 260; galleys armed in, 132, 219. *See also* Trade with, Voyages to.

Crew, of armed caravels, 261; of *barza*, 60; of buss, 39; of cog, 39, 253 and n.; of great galley, 14, 17, 24, 28, 141, 254; of light galley, 10, 254.

Crews, payment of, 7, 117; enrollment of, 147, 150; signs of decadence in, 145. *See also* Bowmen, Oarsmen, Officers, Sailors.

Crimea, 103, 257.

Cronaca Dolfina, 253 n.

Crow's-nest, 20, 42, 52, 53 n.

Crusades, 1, 29, 32, 36, 37, 218.

Cuirass-makers, 163, 167, 174.

Cuore veneta legale (MS.), 152 n.

Curzola, shipbuilding at, 117, 118, 120, 231.

Customs, 29, 136.

Cyprus, War of, 32, 69, 144, 184, 186, 205, 209, 213, 215, 224. *See* Great galleys of, Trade with, Voyages to.

Da Canale, Martino, *Cronaca veneta*, 4 n., 5 n., 7 n.

Dalmatia, 26, 104, 213, 231, 258; ships armed in, 132, 261.

Dalmatian ships, 53, 260, 261.

Damascus, 251.

Dandolo, Andrea, *Chronicon*, 5 n., 7 n., 40 n.

Dantzig, 42 and n.

Daru, Michele, 5.

Dead work, 8, 98-99, 203, 207, 212.

Deck beams, 9, 97, 218 n.

Decks, 3-4, 237, 246.

Deforestation, 219-220, 222-223, 230, 232, 233.

Degl' istorici delle cose veneziane, 27 n., 33 n.

Deliberazioni del Maggior Consiglio di Venezia, 129 n., 130 n.

Demand for ships, shifts in, 108; size of, 108, 114.

De Monacis, Laurentii, *see* Monacis, Laurentii de.

Dimensions, *see under* Great galleys, Light galleys, Round ships.

Direct-line layout, 172.

Documenti Finanziarii, 130 n., 253 n.

Dogado, 77 n., 177, 253.

Dogaressa, 74.

Doge, 4, 66, 67, 72, 147, 148, 176, 188, 223.

Drachio Quintio, Baldessera, 67 n., 70 n., 159 n., 169 n., 213-214, 236, 248 n., 249 n., 263, *see also Visione di Drachio*.

Dragomani, Francesco Gherardi, ed., 37 n.

Drake, Sir Francis, 27.

Ducal palace, 7, 166, 186.

Ducat, value of, 251-252.

Duhamel du Monceau, H. L., *Du transport, de la conservation, et de la force des bois*, 227 n.

Duhamel du Monceau, H. L., *De l'exploitation des bois*, 88 n.
Duodo, Tommaso, 192-193.
Dutch ships, 35 n., 44, 110, 128, 232, 233, 235.

Education of shipwrights, 55.
Egypt, Soldan of, 255.
Egypt, *see* Trade with.
Elm wood, 218, 224.
Emilia, 232.
Employers, *see* Arsenal, Foremen, Shipowners.
Employment in rotation, *see* Caulkers, Veterans.
England, navy of, 141. *See also* Trade with.
English Channel, *see* Voyages to.
English ships, 47, 48, 235.
Entrepreneurs, *see* Foremen, Shipowners.
Epidromus, 19.
Epistolae clarorum virorum, 65 n.
Estimating of ships, 151, 246-249.
Evans, A., " Some Coinage Systems of the Fourteenth Century ", 251 n.
————, *Francesco Balducci Pegolotti, La Practica della Mercatura* (MS.), 29 n.
Evelyn, John, *Sylvia; A Discourse on Forest Trees*, 217 n., 226 n.
Explorations, oceanic, 35, 41, 45, 48, 52.

Fabri, Felix, 17, 18, 22, 212; *see also Fratris Felix Fabri; The Book of.*
Fabrica di galere (MS.), 8 n., 9 n., 10 n., 12, 20, 22 n., 38, 44 n., 53 n., 57 n., 89 n., 90, 92 n., 98 n., 135 n., 218 n., 227 n., 228 n., 235 n., 236 n., 237, 246, 247.
Fachini, 99, 154 n., 172 n., *see also* Stevedores.
Factory managers, ideas of, 213-215.
Fairs at Venice, 46, 136.
Famagosta, 127.
Fausto, Vettor, 32, 63 n., 64-71, 99, 205, 242, 267.
————, *Victoris Fausti Veneti, orationes quinque*, 65 n., 70 n.
————, *Aristotelis mechanica*, 65 n.
Ferrara, oak from, 230 n.
Fiandra, Francesco da, *see* Francesco da Fiandra.
Fili, 92 n., 93 n., 204 n.
Finance, *see* Capital.

Fincati, L., *Le triremi*, 9 n., 10 n., 11, 65 n., 89 n.
————, " Ordini e segnali della flotta veneziana da Messer Giacomo Dolfin ", 23 n.
Fincham, John, *Outlines of Shipbuilding*, 217 n.
Finisterre, Cape, 61.
Firewood, 220, 225.
Fir wood, cost of, 264; sources of, 218-219, 228-231, 232; uses of, 217-218. *See also* Timbers.
Fishing, 52, 103.
Flanders, *see* Great galleys of, Voyages to English Channel.
Fleet commanders, 14, 31, 61, 132, 138, 147, 151, 241; *see also* Captains General of the Sea.
Fleets, *see* Great galleys, Merchant Marine, Police fleet, Reserve fleet, War fleets.
Fondaco dei Tedeschi, 187.
Fonti per la storia d'Italia, 5 n., 73 n.
Forecastle, 4, 13, 36, 37, 44, 52, 53 and n.
Foreign ships, *see* Ships, purchased abroad; Biscayan ships, Genoese ships, etc.
Foreman Caulker of the Arsenal, apprentices of, 164; difficulties of, 196-197; duties of, 165-166, 170, 204, 215; election of, 164; salary of, 161, 162, 171.
Foreman Mast-maker of the Arsenal, 63, 162, 164 and n., 165, 166 and n., 170, 171, 228.
Foreman Oarmaker of the Arsenal, 163, 164 and n., 166, 170, 171, 227.
Foreman Shipwright of the Arsenal, apprentices of, 82, 164 n., 180 n.; duties of, 165-166, 170, 179, 192, 204 and n., 209-210, 215; election of, 164; rivals of, 56-65, 70; list, 55 n.-56 n.; salary of, 161, 162, 171.
Foremen caulkers, as employers, 81, 121, 171; economic position of, 120-121; selected by shipowners, 81 and n., 119.
Foremen shipwrights, apprentices of, 112; contractors, *see* Contract, work under; entrepreneurs, 115, 124-128; heads of shipyards, 123, 124-126; not heads of shipyards, 122, 124, 126; of state round ships, 266-267; technical directors, 54-55, 88, 89, 115, 118, 119, 212.

Forests, banning of, 223, 225, 228, 230; cadaster of, 220 n., *see under* Oak; enemies of, 224, 225, 228; guardians of, 221, 224, 228; inspections of, 221, 223, 226, 227, 229; of Signoria, 220 and n.; of communes, 219, 221-222, 225-226, 228; private, 220 n., 226, 227. *See also* Deforestation, Timbers.

Forsellini, M., " L'organizazione economica dell'arsenale di Venezia ", 135 n., 142 n., 163 n., 165 n., 181 n., 184 n., 264.

Foscarini, Marco, Doge, 7 n.

Framework, breaks in, 97; design of, 89-96; of round ship, 44; number of ribs in, 8 and n., 56; rapid building of, 143-144, 201; slow building of, 97; timbers needed for, 218 and n. *See also* Dead work, Stages of Construction.

France, 54 n., 64, 141.

Francesco da Fiandra, 32, 170 and n.

Francesco de Janutiis de Negroponte, 121 and n., 266.

Francesco de Theodoro da Corfu, called Zoto, 205-206, 267.

Fraterne, 115 n.

Fratris Felicis Fabri evagatorium in Terrae Sanctae, 6 n., 17 n.

Fregate, 13, 207.

Freight rates, on great galleys, 14 and n., 25 and n., 28, 29 n., 136; on round ships, 45-46, 109-110, 249, 262.

Frescobaldi, Leonardo di Nicolò, *see Viaggio di*.

Friuli, 119, 217, 219, 220, 221, 225, 229, 232 n.

Fulin, R., *Diarii e diaristi veneziani*, 247, 250 n.

———, ed., 7 n., 24 n.

" Full-rigged ship ", 27-28, 34, 40-42.

Fuste, 13, 53 n., 69 n., 142, 261.

Galea bastarda, 58, 66, 68, 142, 242.

Galea bastardella, 58, 242.

Galea grossa, 70 n.

Galeazza, 70 and n., 71, 145, 236.

Galeotta, 13.

Galera-tarete, 52 n.

Galilei, Galileo, 71.

Galleon, 50-51, 63 and n., 64, 69 and n., 102, 119, 235, 237, 263, 267; commercial, 51 n., 127; oared, 50, 133, 236, 260.

Galley commanders, 18, 25, 62, 171, 212. *See also Patroni*, of Great galleys.

Galley of a Captain General, 91.

Galleys, built outside Arsenal, 130; built in Arsenal, *see* Arsenal, importance, Production; double-decked, 32 and n.; four-oared, 32, 68, 207, 242 n.; of the guard, 10, 132, 136; stages of construction of, 93 n., 143. *See also* Framework, Great galleys, Light galleys, Oarage, War fleets.

Galley slaves, 6 n., 17 and n., 20, 70 n.

Gallicciolli, Giambattista, 7 n.

Galvani, Giovanni, ed., 4 n.

Gang bosses in Arsenal, 161-166, 171 and n., 172, 190, 197-199, 213, 214-215.

Gangway, 9, 10, 20 and n., 97, 218 n.

Gar, Tommaso, ed., 25 n.

Gastaldo, 73, 75, 76, 78, 79, 81, 83, 86, 121, 176, 177, 179, 197.

Genoa, *see* Wars with.

Genoese shipbuilding, 123 n.

Genoese ships, 4-5, 35 n., 40 n., 43, 104, 135 n., 262.

Germany, 64.

Giacomo de Damian, 192.

Gibraltar, Straits of, 39 n., 232.

Giomo, G., ed., 131 n.

———, " Le rubriche dei Libri Misti del Senato perduti ", 7 n., 14 n., 15 n., 131 n.

Giorgio the Greek, *see* Palopano, Giorgio.

Giovanni degli Agostini, Frate, *Notizie istorico-critiche intorno la vita e le opere degli scrittori viniziani*, 64 n., 65 n., 67 n., 70 n.

Giovanni di Antonio Piccolo, 228-229.

Giovanni di Maria di Zanetto, called Zulle, 56 n., 71, 267.

Giustinian, Benedetto, 259.

Giustizia Vecchia, see Justices.

Gli statuti marittimi veneziani, 35 n., 37 n., 39 n., 253 n., 254.

Goldschmidt, L., *Handbuch des Handelsrechts, I, Universalgeschichte des Handelsrechts*, 116 n.

Gondolas, 53, 85, 111.

Government aid, *see* Subsidies.

Government regulation, of pilgrim galleys, 30; of merchant galleys, 14 and n., 29 and n., 130-131, 133-134, 136-137; of voyages of round ships, 14, 29 n., 31, 46 and n., 249, 254-255. *See also*

Conservation, Crews, Freight rates, Guilds, Overloading.

Grain, 47, 48, 52 n., 53, 103, 104, 106, 107, 108, 128 n., 246, 257-258.

Granada, 134.

Grand Canal, 67, 136, 267.

Grappling irons, 168, 169.

Gras, N. S. B., *Industrial Evolution,* 112 n.

Great galleys, age of, 263; *al trafego,* 134, 136; boats of, 19; capacity of, 15 and n., 16 n., 25-26, 59, 134, 212, 250; cargoes of, *see* Cargoes; commercial advantages of, 14, 25-27; commercial disuse of, 26-29, 141, 241; crew of, *see* Crew; descriptions of by pilgrims, 17-22; dimensions of, 16, 20, 27, 235, 236; first builder of, 54; importance of, 26, 101, 103; introduction of, 7, 13-14, 40, 130-131; military uses of, 24-25, 31-34, 132-133, 138, 140-141, 142, 260, *see also Galeazza;* number of, 103, 133, 134 and n., 137-138, 142, 241, 242, 253, 260; oars of, *see* Oarage; of Aigues Mortes, 134 and n., 137 n., 165, 253, 260; of Alexandria, 15, 16 n., 26 and n., 29 n., 134 and n., 136, 137 and n., 250, 253; of Barbary, 49, 134, 136; of Beyrut, 26, 29 n., 30, 134 and n., 136, 137 and n., 250-251, 253; of Cyprus, 133, 236; of Flanders, 8 n., 15, 16 and n., 25 and n., 28 n., 29 n., 58, 59, 61, 90, 133, 134 and n., 135, 136, 137 and n., 196, 236, 241, 253; of Romania, 8 n., 15, 16 n., 59, 133, 134 and n., 135 n., 136, 137 and n., 236, 253, 257, 260; of Trebizond, 15; privately built, 131, 134, *see also* Pilgrim galleys; revenues from, 137 and n.; renters of, 14, 136-137, 141; rig of, 18-20, 22, 23, 38, 136; sailing qualities of, 16, 22-24, 28, 61; stores of, 18, 19, 25, 30; use by pilgrims, *see* Pilgrim galleys; voyages of, *see al trafego,* of Aigues Mortes, of Alexandria, etc. *See also* Government regulation, Production.

Greece, *see* Trade with.

Greek literature and science, 64, 67, 68 n., 70, 99.

Greek shipwrights, 56-59.

Greek ships, 9.

Geographical discoveries, 35, 41, 45, 48, 52.

Grillo, Simone, 4, 5.

Grimani, Antonio, 260.

Gripo, 53 and n., 261.

Grossi, value of, 251-252.

Guilds, disputes between, 73, 85-86, 99 n., 121; dues of, 73, 75, 78, 81 n.; genesis of, 72; meetings and banquets of, 74; political position of, 72; property of, 73, 76 and n.; officers of, 72, 73, 78; regulation of employment by, 79-81, 120-121, 181, 198, 199; religious activities of, 75-76; statutes of, 74, 77 n., 83. *See also* Apprentices, Gastaldo, Journeymen, Mastership, Sawyers, Social Insurance, *Squerarioli.*

Gun carriages, 163 and n., 173, 265.

Gun-founders, 163, 167 and n.

Gun foundry, 156, 173.

Gunpowder, 62, 159, 173, 174, 264, 265; use of, *see* Artillery.

Hagedorn, B., *Die Entwicklung der wichtigsten Schiffstypen,* 1 n., 8 n., 40 n., 41 n., 42 n.

Hamah, 251.

Haring, C. H., *Trade and Navigation between Spain and the Indies,* 48 n.

Hatchways, 18, 20.

Hazlitt, W. C., *The Venetian Republic,* 130 n., 131 n.

Hemp, 150 and n., 155 n., 169, 217 n., 264, 265.

Hemp Officials (*Ufficiali al Canapa*), 150.

Henry III, King of France, 144.

Heyck, E., *Genua und seine Marine,* 53 n.

Heyd, Wilhelm von, *Histoire du commerce du Levant,* 251 n., 258 n.

Holland, navy of, 141; ships of, *see* Dutch ships.

Holy Land, *see* Voyages to.

Hours of labor, 79, 121, 189, 215.

House carpenters, 99 and n., 177, 178, 203.

Humanists, 65, 67.

I capitolari delle arti veneziane, 73 n., 74 n., 76 n., 79 n., 80 n., 82 n., 86 n., 112 n., 113 n., 120 n., 121 n., 176 n., 177 n., 218 n.

Il Senato veneziano, 147 n.

Imperiale, Cesare, ed., 5 n.

Indiamen, 47, 48, 235.

Industrial organization developed in Arsenal, 146, 153, 211-216; forms of used by Arsenal, 151-152, 168; forms of determined by product, 100-101, 110-111; guild influence on, 87, 120-121. *See also* Capital, Foremen, Labor, Shipowners.

Instructione sul modo di fabricare galere (MS.), 3, 8 n., 50 n., 89 n., 91, 95 n., 235 n., 236 n., 237 n.

Insurance, maritime, 25, 26 and n.; social, *see* Social Insurance.

Ionian Sea, 103, 260.

I prestiti della Repubblica di Venezia, 130 n., 253 n.

Iron, more plentiful elsewhere, 107; export of, 118, 231.

Ironsmiths, 160, 162, 163, 168, 173, 194, 211.

Ironwork, 165, 168, 169, 174, 194, 195, 264, 265.

Istria, 53 n., 219, 224-225, 230.

Italy, 64, 228; *see also* Wars, Italian; Shipbuilding, Mediterranean.

Iviza, 109, 260.

Jaffa, 31, 253, 258.

Jahrbuch für Gesetzgebung, Verwaltung und Volkswirtschaft, 154 n.

Jal, A., *Archéologie navale,* 1 n., 12 n., 16 n., 32 n., 35 n., 36 n., 37 n., 40 n., 53 n., 65 n., 89 n., 218 n., 236 n.

———, *Glossaire,* 5 n., 9 n., 25, 50 n.

Jonge, J. C. de, *Geschiedenis van het nederlandsche zeewesen,* 235 n.

Journeymen, 82, 215.

Jurien de la Gravière, *La guerre de Chypre,* 13 n., 31 n.

———, *La marine des anciens,* 6 n.

Justices (*Giustizia Vecchia*), 72, 73, 74, 80 n., 81, 82.

Keel, laying of, 88-89.

Keelson, 97.

Kretschmayr, H., *Geschichte von Venedig,* 253 n.

Krishna, Bal, *Commercial Relations between India and England,* 48 n.

Labor, cost, 264-265; days of in year, 135 and n.; discipline of, 189-191, 195-199, 207-211, 213-216; disputes, 80-81,
188, 192, 202; division of, 166, 214, *see also* Craft divisions; forced, 176-177, 228-230; gangs, size of, 118, 126, 135-136, 202 n., 214-215; time expended on galleys, 135 and n., 201. *See also* Contract, work under, Foremen, Guilds, Hours, Wages.

Laborers, unskilled (*manuali*), 161-162, 169, 170, 171, *see also* Stevedores.

Lagoons, silting up of, 220, 221.

Lajasso, 134.

Lance-makers, 163, 166, 174.

Lane, F. C., "The Rope Factory and the Hemp Trade", 150 n., 217 n.

———, "Venetian Naval Architecture", 89 n.

———, "Venetian Shipping", 47 n., 104 n., 105 n., 109 n., 110 n., 231 n., 232 n., 240 n., 257 n.

———, *Venetian Ships and Shipbuilders* (MS.), 152 n.

Larch wood, sources of, 218-219, 228; uses of, 217-218. *See also* Timbers.

Latakia, 251.

Lateen rig, 23, 37-38, 51 n., 52, 53 n., *see also* Sails.

Latin language, 55, 64.

Launching, 114, 141, 142, 143, 144 n., 158, 160, 169, 171, 240, 267.

Lazzari, lumber merchants, 229-230.

Lazzarini, V., "La battaglia di Porto Longo", 132 n.

Lepanto, battle of, 31, 33, 184 n.

Lesser Armenia, 133, 134.

Lettere di Collegio, 1308-1310, 131 n.

Letts, Malcolm, ed., 172 n.

Levanters, 47.

Levantine colonies, 132.

Levant trade, *see* Trade.

Levi, C. A., *Le navi da guerre costruite nell' arsenale di Venezia,* 34 n.

———, *Navi veneti,* 36, 43 and n.

Lido, 66.

Light galleys, 9-13; commanders of, *see* Galley commanders; crew of, 10, 254; dimensions of, 3, 8, 9, 12-13, 56, 235, 236; innovations in construction of, 63 n., 68, 207 n.; speed compared to quinquereme, 66, 67 and n. *See also* Oarage; Production, volume of, speed of; War fleets.

Lighthouses, 150.

Lira, value of, 251-252.

Lisbon, 61, 134, 250.

Livenza River, 225, 228.

Live work, 8, 9, 98, 203, 204.

Long ships, see Ships, types of; Galleys.

Lords of the Arsenal (*Patroni all'Arsenale*), election of, 129; functions of, 83, 119 and n., 129-130, 147-152, 154-157, 164, 165, 167, 169, 178, 180, 190, 192, 193 n., 197, 199, 200, 202, 203, 204, 208, 223, 227; houses of, 62, 129; pages of, 154, 163 and n.; term of office of, 152 and n.

Louis IX, King of France, 36, 40.

Luzzato, G., " Per la storia delle costruzioni navali a Venezia ", 104 n., 108 n., 109 n., 110 n., 124 n., 247.

——, " Sull attendibilità di alcune statistiche economiche medievali ", 253 n.

Lumber, see Timbers, Wood.

Lumber merchants, 99, 222-223, 228-230.

Lumberyards, private, 88, 99, 229; state, see under Arsenal.

Luminaria, 75 and n., 77 n.

Magistrato sopra le Acque, 122.

Mahan, A. T., Admiral, 217.

Malipiero, Domenico, *Annali veneti dell' anno 1457 al 1500,* 25 n., 27 n., 47 n., 49 n., 50 n., 132 n., 138 n., 139 n., 141 n., 260 n., 266.

Malmsey, 247.

Manfroni, C., " Cenni sugli ordinamenti delle marine italiane nel medio evo ", 7 n., 186 n.

——, " La crisi della marina militare di Venezia dopo la guerra di Chioggia ", 133 n., 134 n.

——, *Storia della marina italiana dalla caduta di Costantinopoli alla battaglia di Lepanto,* 13 n., 27 n., 33 n., 47 n., 70 n., 130 n., 132 n., 138 n., 141 n., 145 n.

——, *Storia della marina italiana dalle invasioni barbariche al trattato di Ninfeo,* 7 n.

——, *Storia della marina italiana dal trattato di Ninfeo alla caduta di Costantinopoli,* 5 n., 14 n., 130 n.

——, *Scritti . . . in onore di, see Scritti.*

Maran, 52 n., 53 n., 259, 261, 266.

Marangona, 189.

Marciana *Mariegole, see Mariegole dei calafai* (MS.).

Marciliana, 52 n., 53 n., 123 n.

Mare clausum, 46 and n.

Mariegole dei calafai (MS.), 75 n., 76 n., 77 n., 79 n., 80 n., 81 n., 82 n., 83 n., 86 n., 121 n., 176 n., 177 n., 181 n., 184 n.

Marin, C. A., *Storia civile e politica dal commercio di Veneziani,* 14 n., 134 n., 236 n.

Marines, see Bowmen.

Market organization, 46.

Martini, A., *Manuale di Metrologia,* 245 and n., 247, 248.

Maserio, Gerolamo, 64.

Masser, of Arsenal, 157, see also Arms steward; of guild, 73, 78.

Mastership, admittance to, 83-84, 179-180, 183-184, 186.

Mast-makers, 99, 162 and n., 166, 173, 176, 177, 214, 215, 244.

Masts, cost of, 264-265; of buss, 36; of carack, 41-42; of cog, 37, 43, 44 n.; of great galley, 18, 19, 22, 23; of light galley, 10; of sixteenth century round ships, 44-45; of tarette, 37 n.; stepping up of, 114, 171; stored in Arsenal, 141, 144, 159, 160, 173, 174; supply of, see Fir wood.

Mathematics, study of, 55, 65 n., 70; use of in designing ship, 92-93, 96.

Measures, of capacity, 245-249; of length, 245; of weight, 245, 246, 248, 249-251.

Measures of ships, how determined, 89-90. See also Great galleys, Light galleys, Round ships, dimensions of.

Mechanics, science of, 64, 70, 71, 99.

Mediterranean, forests, 232-233; ships, see Shipbuilding, Regional traditions of; trade, 27, 232, 257, see also Trade; warfare, 6, 28, 31, 34, 38.

Meduna, 122.

Meigs, J. F., *The Story of the Seamen,* 1 n., 31 n., 39 n., 42 n.

Merchant galleys, see Great galleys.

Merchant marine, size and composition of, 53 n., 101-107, 238-240, 253-261; supervision of, 151. See also Government regulation, Great galleys, Round ships.

Merchantmen, see Round ships, Great, galleys.

Merchants, Moorish, see Moors; of lumber, 99, 222-223, 228-230; shippers,

26; passengers, 25, 29. *See also* Ship-owners.
Mesavala, 19, *see also* Mizzen.
Mestre, forests around, 219.
Meza-luna, 94-96.
Mezana, 10 n., *see also* Mizzen.
Midship frame, design of, 91.
Milliarium, equivalent of, 248.
Mincio River, 221.
Miscellanea di storia veneta, 131 n., 132 n., 147 n.
Mizzen, 19, 28, 42 and n., 43-44, 45.
Mocenigo, Tommaso, Doge, 102 and n., 103, 104, 105, 106, 123, 253, 254, 259.
Models of ships, 51, 63, 69, 96.
Modena, timbers from, 218.
Modon, 259, 260, 261.
Mohammedans, export of wood to, 218; pirates, 29 n. *See also* Moors.
Molmenti, P., *La storia di Venezia nella vita privata,* 53 n., 73 n., 74 n., 185 n.
Monacis, Laurentii de, *Cronicon de rebus venetis,* 132 n.
Moneys, equivalents of, 251-252.
Monopolies of trade, *see* Government regulation.
Montello, forest of, 122, 225-226, 228.
Monte Sant' Angelo, forest of, 125 n., 231.
Monticolo, Giovanni, ed., 73 n., 113 n., 120 n.
Montona, forest of, 224-225.
Moors, 29, 134, 250.
Morea, war in, 138.
Morosini, Paolo, *Historia della città e republica di Venetia,* 258 n.
Mortars, 172.
Motta, 122.
Muda, 196 n., 255-256, 262.
Murano, 122.
Muratori, L. A., ed., 5 n., 132 n., 133 n.
Muskets, 163.

Nadal, Demetrio, 54.
Nails, 112, 160, 165, 168, 169, 194.
Nance, R. M., " Some Old-time Ship Pictures ", 29 n.
Nani Mocenigo, M., *L'arsenale di Venezia,* 34 n., 48 n., 173 n.
Naples, *see* Neapolitan shipbuilding.
Naval administration, 146-151, 221.
Naval stores, 129, 151, 217 n., *see also* Cordage, Pitch, etc.

Nave, 35 n., 53 n., 255 n., 260-261, 266-267.
Nave-tarete, 52 n., 53 n.
Navy, *see* War fleets.
Neapolitan shipbuilding, 94.
Negroponte, siege of, 138.
Nelson, Horatio, Viscount, 35.
New Arsenal, 130, 131, 132, 139, 140, 173, 174-175, 209.
Newest Arsenal, 140, 141, 158 and n., 172, 173, 174, 209.
Newett, M. Margaret, *Canon Pietro Casola's Pilgrimage to Jerusalem,* 6 n., 18, 19 n., 23 n., 26 n., 30 n., 31 n.
Nicolò the Greek, *see* Palopano, Nicolò.
Nobles, 18, 30, 57, 65, 68, 72, 120 n., 127, 128, 129, 147, 152, *see also* Fleet commanders, Lords of the Arsenal, Shipowners, etc.
Nolhac, Pier de and Solerti, Angelo, *Il viaggio in Italia di Enrico III,* 144 n.
" Nomi antichi delle campane della torre di San Marco ", 189 n.
Normans, 64.

Oak, Arsenal's reserves of, 223, 224-227, 231; cadaster of, 221, 223-224; cost of, 264; cutting by *squerarioli,* 113; Dalmatian, 213; kept under water, 159; licenses to cut, 221, 222, 224, 231; procured abroad, 120, 223, 231; shortage of, 230-232; sources of, 219, 231-232; uses of, 217-218. *See also* Timbers.
Oakum, *see* Tow.
Oarage, 3, 9-11, 13, 16 and n., 18, 23, 24, 31 and n., 32, 33, 65, 66, 69, 71, 159 n.
Oarmakers, 161 n., 163, 166, 173, 175, 176, 177, 182, 183, 184, 211, 243.
Oars, cost of, 264; cutting of, 228; size of, 10; stored in Arsenal, 142, 143, 144, 159 and n., 160, 172, 173, 175, 203; use of, *see* Oarage.
Oarship, *see* Ships, Galleys, Oarage.
Oarsmen, arrangement of, 9-11, 17; nearly frozen, 67; number of, 24; recruitment of, 6-7, 17, 84-85; wares of, 26.
Oar wood, 227 and n.
Officers, petty, 20, 145, 185-186, 216.
Officiales Rationum Veterum, 119 n.
Oil, 48, 53, 103, 106.
Old Arsenal, 129, 139, 158 n., 159, 172, 173, 175.

Oppenheim, M., *A History of the Administration of the Royal Navy*, 42 n.
———, " The Royal and Merchant Navy under Elizabeth ", 235 n.
———, " The Royal Navy under Charles I ", 235 n.
Ordnance, *see* Artillery.
Otranto, 16.
Outriggers, 3, 8-13, 16, 20, 33, 50, 99, 218 n.
Overloading, of great galleys, 20, 25 n., 26 n.; of round ships, 151.

Padua, 122, 187, 227, 258.
Pageants, 74.
Palopano, Giorgio, 56 and n., 58-59, 97 n., 136, 199.
Palopano, Nicolò, 56, 57-58, 199.
Pantera, Pantero, *L'armate navale*, 33 n., 45 n., 51 n., 53 n., 232 n., 267.
Panzonus, 5 n.
Papadopoli Aldobrandini, N., *Le monete di Venezia*, 252 n.
Papafigo, 20, 22.
Parcenevoli, 115 n.
Parte prese nell'Eccellentiss. Conseglio di Pregadi, 46 n., 52 n.
Partisone, 95 n., 96.
Partnership, 115-119.
Paruta, P., *Della guerra di Cipro*, 33 n., 145 n.
———, *Dell'historia venetiana*, 27 n., 29 n., 143 n.
Passengers, *see* Merchants, Pilgrim galleys.
Patmos, ships from, 110, 232.
Patroni, as ship captains, 99, 117, 240, 260; as shipowners, 115, 121 n.; of great galleys, 16, 18, 19, 25, 136-137, 141.
Patroni all' Arsenale, 129 n., *see also* Lords of the Arsenal.
Patron saints, 75, 81.
Paxi, Bartholomeo de, *Tariffa de pexi e mesure*, 245 and n., 246 n., 247, 249, 250, 251 and n.
Paymasters of the Arsenal, 163, 164-165, 180, 190-192, 193 n., 208, 210, 213.
Pay roll of the Arsenal, 154, 166, 185, 189-191, 196, 199, 210, 251.
Pensions, *see* Veterans.
Pesaro, oak from, 232.
" Peter of La Rochelle ", 42 and n.
Phoenicians, 2.

Piazza San Marco, 7, 62, 73, 74, 77, 78, 81, 188.
Piave River, 228.
Pichering, Danby, ed., 247 n.
Picheroni della Mirandola, Alessandro, 65 n.
Piecework, by sawyers, 80; in the Arsenal, 151, 162, 166, 168, 195, 209-211. *See also* Contract, work under.
Pilgrim galleys, 17-22, 29-31, 103, 132 n., 253, 258.
Pirates, 25, 29 n., 37, 48, 49, 52, 65, 105, 108, 131, 132, 255, 258.
Pisani, Vettor, 132.
Pitch, 21, 98, 112, 119, 142, 143, 159, 160 and n., 165 and n., 174, 217 n., 231, 264, 265.
Pitch-makers, 162, 165 n.
Pizolo, pizuol, 19, 25.
Plague of 1575-1577, 184, 213.
Planking, 8 and n., 42 n., 44, 98, 143, 204, 218 and n.
Podestà, F., *Il porto di Genova*, 43 n.
Podestas, 221.
Pola, 61 and n.; battle of, 132.
Police fleet, 103, 132, 134.
Polidori, Filippo Luigi, ed., 4 n.
Polybius, The Histories of, 219 n.
Poop, *see* Stern, Stern castle.
Pope, 32, 145, 218-219.
Population, 182, 257-258.
Po River, 123 n.
Port, repairs on, 150 n.
Portogruaro, 225.
Portuguese ships, 52, 104.
Posticcia, 93 n.
Postlethwayt, M., *The Universal Dictionary of Trade and Commerce*, 245 and n.
Po Valley, forests of, 219, 233.
Poveglia, shipyards of, 266.
Powder-maker, 163, 167.
Prato, G., " Il problema del combustibile ", 232 n.
Predelli, Riccardo, ed., 35 n.
Pre Todaro, *see* Theodoro de Nicolò, Pre.
Prevesa, battle of, 27.
Prices, rise in, 183, 264.
Priuli, Gerolamo, *I diarii*, 26 n., 47 n., 250.
Priuli, Giovanni di, report of, 160 n., 164 n., 173 n., 184 n., 202 n., 215-216, 243 n.
Private shipyards, *see* Shipyards.

Production, direct line, 172-173; large scale, 101 n., 129, 176, 199, 213; of great galleys, 60, 61, 134-137, 177, 199-200, 241; organization of, see Industrial organization; speed of, 114 and n., 144 and n., 199-201; stages of in Arsenal, 160, 170, 203, 242, see also Galleys, stages of construction; volume of, 106-108, 134-136, 143, 144 and n., 241, 242.

Protection, of craftsmen, 77 n., 109, 220; of shipowners, 109.

Proti, 54, 112, 117, 164, see also Foremen.

Provençals, 64.

Provveditore sopra le Artiglierie, 150, 156.

Provveditori all' Arsenale, see Commissioners of the Arsenal.

Provveditori all' Armar, 147.

Provveditori d'Armata, see Commissioners of the fleet.

Provveditori de le cose da mar, 149 n.

Provveditori di Comune, see Board of Manufactures.

Pulley-makers, branch of ship carpenters, 99; in Arsenal, 160 n., 161 n., 162, 167-168, 174, 176, 177, 244.

Pupa alla Faustina, 70 n.

Pupa alla ponentina, 70 n.

Pupilia, shipyard of, 266.

Quadriremes, 65 n.

Quarantia, Chief of, 179.

Qudiera chorba, 92 n.

Quinquereme, 9, 64-68, 71, 242.

Quintavalle, shipyards of, 120 n., 122.

Ragusa, 5, 231.

Ramusio, Paolo, 65 n., 67, 70 n.

Rectors, 221.

Reef-points, 37.

Refitting, 120 n., 169, 171, 214, 263.

Regional traditions, see under Shipbuilding.

Registry, Venetian, grants of, 110, 231.

Relazione del Proveditore sopra le Cento Galee, 242 n.

Rerum italicarum scriptores, 1st ed., 5 n., 132 n., 133 n.; 2nd ed., 26 n.

Reserve fleet, 130, 133, 141-143, 146, 155, 159, 174-175, 199, 242.

Retail handicraft, 100, 101, 112.

Rhodes, 57.

Rialto, 62; bridge of, 207.

Rio dell' Arsenale, 172, 173.

Rig, see Lateen rig, Masts, Sails, Square rig.

Rigging, in Arsenal, 142, 143, 160, 173-175, 203.

R. I. S., see Rerum italicarum scriptores.

Roberts, Lewes, The Merchants' Mappe of Commerce, 245 n., 246 n., 250.

" Roccaforte ", 4-6, 7, 35 and n., 36, 39, 40, 44, 49.

Roman ships, 1, 9, 68.

Romania, see Great Galleys of.

Rope-spinner, 169.

Ropewalk, see Tana.

" Roqueforte ", see " Roccaforte ".

Rosso, Bernardin Sebastiano, 124-126.

Rosso, Cristoforo, 158 n., 206.

Rosso, Gerolamo, 206 and n.

Rosso, Francesco di Antonio, 122, 123 n., 206.

Rosso, Marco Francesco, 61-62, 199, 206, 241.

Round ships, cargoes of, see Cargoes; compared to galleys, 24, 35; commercial uses of, 4-6, 28, 29 n., 47, 52; dimensions of, 3, 36, 44, 50, 235, 237; individual, named, 28 n., 38, 42, 47 n., 49, 122, 235, 238, 240, 260 and n., 261, 263, 266, see also " Roccaforte "; military uses of, 4-6, 27, 28, 33, 34, 39, 130, 131, 238, 254, 256, 258, see also state built; number of, see Merchant marine, size; rig of, see Masts, Sails; sizes of, 39-40 and n., 47 and n., 48, 53, 60, 102-103, 105-106, 238-240, 249; state built, 40, 47, 50, 51, 60, 63, 105, 114 n., 118-119, 121 n., 260, 261, 263, 266-267; time spent in building, 108; use by pilgrims, 31, 260; voyages of, see Voyages; where built, 101, 267, see also Shipyards, private.

Rowing, see Oarage.

Rudder hinges, 168.

Rudders, 18, 19, 99, 212, 218; in Arsenal, 159, 160, 173; types of, 12, 36, 37, 70 n.

Russian slave, 121.

Sabellico, Marco Antonio, " De situ urbe ", 267.

Sacerdoti, Adolfo, ed., 35 n.

Sacile, 225.

Sagittea, 5 n.

Sagredo, Augustino, ed., 25 n.

Sailcloth, 168, 174, 264.

Sail-making, 162, 168.

Sailors, on buss and cog, 39; on great galley, 20, 26; on light galley, 10. See also Seamen.

Sails, cost of, 264-265; of buss, 36-37, 39; of carack, 28, 40-42, 43; of cog, 37-38, 43; of galleon, 51; of great galley, 17-20, 22, 23, 25; of light galley, 10, 12; of sixteenth century round ships, 44; of tarette, 37 n; stored in Arsenal, 141, 144, 159, 160, 168, 175. See also Lateen rig, Square rig.

Saint Vincent, Cape, 61.

Saloni, squeri di, 120 n.

Salt, 48, 52 n., 104, 107, 109-110, 248, 259, 260.

Sandi, Vettor, Principi di storia civile della Repubblica di Venezia, 150 n.

San Fosca, 75.

San Francesco della Vigna, church of, 63 n.

San Giovanni e Paolo, church of, 62.

San Marco, 74, 75.

San Marco: church of, 175; square of, see Piazza San Marco; tower of, 136, 189.

Sansovino, Francesco, Venetia, città nobilissima et singolare, 31 n., 74 n., 134 n.

San Stefano, monastery of, 75.

Santa Lucia, shipyards at, 207 n.

Santa Maria della Celestia, monastery of, 158.

Sant' Antonio, shipyards of, 119, 122, 123 n., 266-267.

Santo Spirito, shipyards of, 120 n.

San Trinità, shipyards at, 266.

Sanuto, Marino (the elder), Liber Secretorum Fidelium Crucis, 9 n., 32 n., 52 n., 97 n., 219, 236 n.

Sanuto, Marino (the younger), 60, 61, 66, 69, 253 n.

————, Edificazioni (MS.), 168 n.

————, I diarii, 7 n., 15 n., 16 n., 24 n., 26 n., 28 n., 29 n., 32 n., 47 n., 51 n., 53 n., 60 n., 61 n., 63 n., 65 n., 66 n., 67 n., 68 n., 93 n., 107 n., 114 n., 116 n., 131 n., 136 n., 138 n., 140 n., 141 n., 148 n., 161 n., 163 n., 167 n., 169 n., 171 n., 193 n., 206 n., 224 n., 225 n., 226 n., 227 n., 241 n., 242 n., 243 n., 246 n., 247 n., 249 n., 250, 251, 259 and n., 260 and n., 261, 263, 266, 267.

Sanuto, Marino (the younger), La spedizione di Carlo VIII in Italia, 24 n., 25 n.

————, Vitae ducum Venetorum, 133 n., 134 n.

Saseno, battle of, 4-5, 7, 14, 40.

Savii agli Ordeni, see Secretaries of the Marine.

Savii di Terra Ferma, 148, 179 n.

Savii Grandi, 147, 179.

Savina, Gerolamo, chronicle of, 32 n., 69 n.

Sawing, 88 and n., 220.

Sawyers, guild of, 73, 76, 77-79, 80; in Arsenal, 157, 162, 169, 183 and n., 199, 209-210, 214; obligations to state of, 176-177; wages of, 80. See also Labor.

Scandolar, 25, see also Cooking galley.

Scatola, see Alvise de Giovanni di Castello.

Schaube, Adolf, Handelsgeschichte der romanischen Völker, 46 n., 116 n., 218 n., 219 n., 245 and n., 249, 250.

Schiraci, schierazo, 53 n., 261.

Schulte, A., Geschichte der grossen Ravensburger Handelsgesellschaft, 25 n.

Scritti storici in onore di Camillo Manfroni, 104 n.

Scrivan, 25, 240.

Scuola, 72, 73, 81 n.

Seamen, number of, 253-254. See also Crews.

Seasoning timbers, 97, 159.

Sea power, 217.

Secretaries of the Marine (Savii agli Ordeni), 147, 148, 157, 164, 179 n., 215, 259.

Segna, wood from, 227 and n.

Segre, Arturo, ed., 26 n.

Semple, E. C., The Geography of the Mediterranean Region, 233 n.

Senate, 24, 29, 30, 56, 57, 58, 59, 63, 65, 68, 113, 131, 137, 139, 141, 143, 144 and n., 147-149, 152, 155, 158, 164, 176, 178, 180, 181, 183, 184, 185, 192, 196 n., 202, 203, 212, 221, 231, 254, 255, 259, 263.

Shares, 116 and n, 118.

Shavings, 194-195.

Shield-makers, 167.

Shipbuilders, see Shipowners, Shipwrights.

Shipbuilding:

Communal, compared to private, 100-104, see also Arsenal.

Private, decline of, 80, 104, 105, 106,

110, 127, 178, 217, 230-231, 259, 261; volume of, 106-108, 261.

Regional traditions of, Atlantic, 1, 40, 48; Greek tradition, 56, 59; Mediterranean, 1, 2, 12, 35, 37, 38, 40-41, 42, 43, 47; Northern, 1, 8, 12, 37, 38, 40, 42.

Technique of, 88-97, 211; guild influence on, 87. *See also* Craft divisions, Framework, Planking, Stern, design of, etc., Shipwrights.

See Competing centers of, Industrial organization.

Ship carpenters, *see* Shipwrights.

Ship of the line, first built in the Arsenal, 34, 48; first differentiated from merchantman, 141.

Shipowners, aided by Arsenal, 150; as entrepreneur builders, 114-115, 119-120, 127, 128 n.; individual, named, 116-118, 119, 120 n., 122, 123, 128 n., 237; relations with craftsmen, 80-81, 99. *See also* Shares.

Ships, age of, 108, 263; cost of, 114, 264-265; purchased abroad, 106, 109, 110, 231-233; size of, 15-16, 39-40, 47-48, 53, 102-103, 105-106, 238-240; types of, 2-6, 50, 51-53, 101. *See also* Galleys, Round ships.

Ship timbers, *see* Timbers.

Shipwrights:

Craft tradition of, content of, 89-96, 99; empirical character of, 54, 69-71, 90; family character of, 55, 60; Fausto's influence on, 69-71, 99; influence of French theoretical studies on, 54 n.; mechanics in, 99; standardizing influence of, 212.

Divisions of, 54-55, 84-85, 99, 124, 178.

Employment of, at sea, 55, 184-186, 214; in Arsenal, 162, 176-182, 208, 209, 243; in private shipyards, 55, 84-85, 104 and n., 177, 178 n., 243; to cut woods, 122, 190 n., 191, 206; to guard forests, 122, 224, 225, 226.

Individual, named, 32, 54-71, 119-128, 158 n., 205-207, 266-267.

Number of, 162, 182, 184 and n., 243, 244, 253.

See also Foremen, Guilds, Labor, *Squerarioli.*

Shipyards, private, activity of, *see* Ship-

building; ownership and location, 120 and n., 122, 123 and n., 266-267.

Shuckburgh, E. S., ed., 219 n.

Siamio, 251 n.

Sicily, 4, 52, 128 n., 134, 257, 258, 260.

Siepie, 91.

Sieveking, H., " Aus Venetianischen Handlungsbüchern ", 154 n.

Silks, 14, 26, 136.

Silting, *see* Lagoons.

Slaves, 6 and n., 121.

Social insurance, by guilds, 76; disability, 76, 78, 79, 187-188; dowries, 76 n.; old age, *see* Veterans; unemployment, 178.

Soldo, value of, 251-252.

Solerti, Angelo, and Nolhac, Pier de, *Il viaggio in Italia di Enrico III,* 144 n.

Solto, Piero, 127, 264.

Sombart, W., *Der moderne Kapitalismus,* 48 n., 101 n.

———, *Krieg und Kapitalismus,* 135 n.

Sopra sè, 113 n., 200 n., 201 n., *see also* Contract, work under.

Sorger, Ettore, ed., 242 n.

Southampton, 16, 27, 61, 134, 262.

Spain, 64; *see also* Voyages to.

Spalato, 26, 236.

Spanish ships, 50, 104, 235, 260.

Spars, 141, 144, 159, 160.

Spices, 14, 26, 29, 134, 136, 249-251.

Spuazza, Giovanni Maria, 119, 122, 123 n., 206, 267.

Spuazza, Francesco, 206.

Square rig, contrasted with lateen, 37-38, 52; use in Mediterranean of, 37.

Square sails, on galleys, 20, 38. *See also* Sails.

Squerarioli, activity of, 106, 112-114, 124; apprentices of, 82, 112; distinguished from *arsenalotti,* 84; employed in Arsenal, 178, 198, 203; employment of veterans by, 77; separate guild of, 84-85.

Stages of Construction, of galleys, *see under* Galleys; of round ships, 92 n.

Staio, equivalent of, 246.

Standardization, 211-212, 214.

State built ships, *see* Great galleys, Round ships, War fleets.

Statutes at Large, 247 n.

Statuti marittimi, see Gli statuti.

Stefani, Federico, ed., 7 n.

Stella, Giorgio, *Annales genuenses,* 132 n., 133 n.
Stem, design of, 91.
Ster, see Staio.
Stern, design of, 70 n., 91, 212.
Stern castle, 4, 8, 9, 18, 19 and n., 36, 37, 44, 52, 53 and n.
Stevedores (*fachini*), 62, 88, 99, 126, 135, 154 n., 161, 163, 171-172, 211, 214, 264.
Stewart, Aubrey, ed., 17 n., 23 n.
Straccha, Benevento, *De navibus,* 116 n.
Strikes, *see* Labor disputes.
Subsidies, 105, 107-110, 114 n., 124-129, 231, 262.
Suchem, Leopold von, *Description of the Holy Land and of the Way Thither,* 30 n.
Sugana, 218 n.
Surian, Nicolò, 10 n., 13 n., 70 n., 97 n., 224.
Sword-makers, 163, 167.
Syria, *see* Trade of, Voyages to.

Tacking, 12, 37, 39, 42.
Taduri, Bartolomeo, memorandum of, 135 n., 209 n., 213, 214-215.
Tafur, Pero, *Travels and Adventures,* 172 n., 175.
" Tail-frames ", 92-95.
Tana (Azov), 134 n., 256-257.
Tana (ropewalk), 62, 169 and n., 173, 174, 175.
Tar, 19 n., 143, 265.
Tarette, 4-6, 35 n., 37 and n., 40, 52 n., 53 n.
Tarn, W. W., " The Oarage of Greek Warships ", 9 n.
Technique, *see under* Shipbuilding.
Tentori, C., *Saggio sulla storia . . . della Republica di Venezia,* 90 n., 131 n., 147 n., 148 n.
———, *Della legislazione veneziana sulla preservazione della laguna,* 219 n.
Terzarolo, 22.
The Book of the Wanderings of Brother Felix Fabri, 17 n., 23 n.
Theodoro de Nicolò, Pre, 89 n., 236, 237, *see also Instructione.*
Thucydides, 217.
Thwarts, arrangement of, 9-11, 19, 20 n., 32, 99; in Arsenal, 141, 159, 160, 210, 214; number of, 9, 17.

Timber merchants, *see* Lumber merchants.
Timbers, arrangement of in Arsenal, 157-159, 165, 194-195, 199, 213; Arsenal's supply of, 150, 224-231; cost of, 232, 264-265; curved, 97, 217, 218 and n., 219, 225; cutting of by Arsenal, 155 n., 190 n., 191, 206, 213, 222, 224, 228; export of, 118, 120, 157, 218-219, 231; loaned by Arsenal, 150, 157; more plentiful elsewhere, 107; procured abroad, 122, 124, 125 n., 126, 229, 230 n.; scarcity of, 124, 220, 230-233, 264; selection of, 55, 88, 99, 118, 119, 166, 210; transport of, 220, 222, 228, 229, 232. *See also* Fir wood, Larch wood, Oak, Seasoning.
Timbotta, Giorgio, 23, 89 n., 92 n., 93 n., 236, 237.
Timon, bavonescho, 12; *alla ponentina,* 70 n.
Tolda, 237 and n.
Tonnage equivalents, 246-249.
Tools, 54, 87, 97, 188, 215.
Topsail, on great galleys, 22, 23 n.; on round ship, 28, 42.
Tourist trade, *see* Pilgrim galleys.
Tow, 98, 112, 119, 142, 143, 160, 165, 173, 265.
Trade, Adriatic, 53 and n., 103, 105, 258; cabotage, 52, 102, 105; of western Mediterranean, 14, 29 n., 104, 109, 134, 257, 200; volume of, 48, 258; with Constantinople, 128 n., 256-257, *see also* Great galleys of Romania; with Crete, 38, 46, 47, 53, 104, 105, 246, 247, 249, 260, 262; with Cyprus, 52 n., 109, 257, 262; with Egypt, 249, 257, 258, *see also* Great galleys *al trafego,* of Alexandria; with England, 29 n., 38, 46, 47 and n., 104, 262, *see also* Great Galleys of Flanders; with Greece, 29 n., 53, 257, 258; with Syria, 46, 251, 255-256, 262, *see also* Great galleys of Beyrut.
Trebizond, *see* Great Galleys of.
Trentino, 219.
Trepie, 91.
Trevisana, 219, 220, 221, 225.
Treviso, 258.
Trinketum, 22, 23 n.
Triremes, 9-11, 17, 65 n., 66, *see also* Light galleys.

Tumble home, 44.
Tunis, 14, 36, 49, 134.
Turks, Ottoman, 59, 138; galleys of, 13.
    See also under War fleets, Wars.

Ufficiali al Canapa, 150.
Ufficiali del Frumento, 154 n.
Unemployment, 81, 178, 181.

Venezia e le sue lagune, 7 n.
Venier, Cristoforo, 229-230.
Veterans, 76-77, 83.
Viaggio di Leonardo di Niccolò Fresco-
    baldi, 30 n., 40 n.
Victoris Fausti, see Fausto, Vettor.
Viking ships, 1, 8.
Villani, Giovanni, *Cronica,* 37 n., 38 n.
Visione di Drachio (MS.), 3, 55 n., 67 n.,
    70 n., 89 n., 90 n., 92 n., 93 n., 95 n.,
    214, 236 n.
Vittorio Veneto, forest near, 228.
Vituri, Nicolò, 56 n.
Vituri, Vicenzo, 158 n., 206.
Vogel, W., *Geschichte der Seeschiffahrt,*
    8 n., 42 n.
Voyages, Adriatic, 27, 53 and n., 111;
    along northern Africa, 29 n., 49, 134;
    times of, 45-46, 136, 255; to Alexandria,
    46 and n., 258, *see also* Great galleys of
    Alexandria; to Constantinople and the
    Black Sea, 7, 46 n., 53 and n., 103,
    256-257, *see also* Great galleys of
    Romania; to Crete, 52, 53, 67, 256, 260;
    to Cyprus, 46, 47, 52 n., 133, 134, 257,
    259 and n., 261; to English Channel,
    38, 103, 240, 249, 253, 256, 257, 260,
    262, *see also* Great galleys of Flanders;
    to the Holy Land, 17, 29, 31, 103, 253,
    255, 258; to Spain, 29 n., 134, 258;
    to Syria, 4, 7, 39, 45-46, 48, 103, 128 n.,
    238, 254-256, *see also* Great galleys of
    Beyrut. *See also* Trade: cabotage; of
    western Mediterranean.

Wages, in the Arsenal, 152, 161-163, 177-
    180, 182, 186, 187, 188, 192-193, 197,
    208, 215; modern equivalents of, 251;
    of apprentices, 82, 162, 177, 180; of

caulkers, 80-81, 98, 121, 162, 182-183,
    197; of oarmakers, 163; of construction
    chiefs, 162, 209, 244; of shipwrights,
    114, 162, 177-179, 180, 183, 187 n.,
    244; of stevedores, 161; of unskilled
    labor, 161-162; in kind, 193, 194.
Walnut wood, 218.
War fleets:
    Venetian, composition, 4-7, 13, 27-28,
        31, 33-34, *see also* Round ships,
        Great galleys, military uses of; out-
        fitting of, 129, 144-145, 160, 170 and
        n., 171-172; size of, 103, 130, 132-
        133, 138-140, 142, 145, 254, 260.
    Ottoman, 27, 31, 105, 138-141, 143,
        145, 147.
Wars, Italian, 50, 133, 138, 140, 217; with
    Genoa, 4, 14, 35, 130, 132, 133, 138,
    256, 257; with Ottoman Turks, 34, 104,
    138-139, 140-141, 142, 151, 181, 217,
    259, *see also* Cyprus, War of.
Warships, *see* War fleets, composition of.
Weights, *see* Measures.
Weil, A., *The Navy of Venice,* 7 n., 14 n.,
    232 n.
Wine, as cargo, 38, 46, 47, 48, 53, 104,
    105, 106, 246, 247, 260, 261, 262;
    given out to workers, 62, 163, 174,
    193, 265.
Women, employed in Arsenal, 162, 168;
    in guilds, 75.
Wood, as cargo, 53 and n., 103, 125, 248,
    260, *see also* Timbers.
Wrecks, 24 and n., 25 n., 28 n., 108, 240,
    263.

Yard, 22, 36, 37, 39, 43, 44 n.
" Yoke ", 97.

Zanetti, G., *Origine di alcune Arti,* 43.
Zante, 52 n., 53 n., 259.
Zaparin, Giacomo, 126-127.
Zaparin, Piero, 122, 123 n., 158 n., 206.
Zengg, *see* Segna.
Zeno, Nicolò, 133.
Zonchio, battle of, 27.
Zoto, *see* Francesco de Theodoro da Corfu.
Zulle, *see* Giovanni Maria di Zanetto.